KINTYRE

The Hidden Past

With best wishes
to Ellen Kerr
from your daughter Eric's
neighbour, Angus Martin
Campbeltown, 8 December 1984

In memory of my dear parents

Angus Martin
and
Amelia McKenzie

Yet in my heart I'll cherish still
  A memory fresh an' green,
The kindly hearts o' other days
  And a' the joys I've seen.
In fancy's bower wi' vanished bliss
  On time I'll be avenged,
Where a' remains unchanged to me,
  Where a' remains unchanged.

(from *The faces a' hae changed,* by Daniel MacMillan,
born in Dalintober, 1846)

KINTYRE
The Hidden Past

Angus Martin

JOHN DONALD PUBLISHERS LTD
EDINBURGH

ISBN 0 85976 119 3

Exclusive distribution in the United States of
America and Canada by Humanities Press Inc.,
Atlantic Highlands, NJ 07716, USA.

Phototypeset by Wright Printers Ltd., Dundee
Printed in Great Britain by Bell & Bain Ltd., Glasgow

Preface

This work is an attempt to explore areas of the cultural and social history of Kintyre which have hitherto been 'hidden' (or, at least, hard to get at). I have avoided the well-trodden paths which lead inevitably to THE HANGING OF KING JAMES IV'S GOVERNOR, THE MASSACRE AT DUNAVERTY, and a string of other played-out historical dramas.

Personal and place-names are almost invariably spelled as I found them in the records. 'Ballochantee' I have preferred to the now standard 'Bellochantuy'. I make that my only protest against the linguistic eccentricities of the Ordnance Survey.

I have been very fortunate in the quality of the assistance given to me throughout the researching and writing of this book, and I must acknowledge it adequately. No one could be more conscious than I myself of the many imperfections of this work. I trust only that preventable errors have been prevented – for the rest, I resign myself to fallibility and concede personal responsibility.

Campbeltown, January 1984

Acknowledgements

I owe an incalculable and unrepayable debt of gratitude to Mr Murdo MacDonald, archivist of Argyll and Bute District Council, Inveraray, for his patient and thorough involvement in all stages of the work. Without his guidance and support, much of the material in this book would have escaped my notice.

To Dr. Colm Ó Baoill, Department of Celtic, University of Aberdeen, I extend sincere thanks for his rigorous criticism of Chapters 1, 2, 4, and 5, and of Appendices I and II. His contribution to this work, rendered at unreasonably short notice, consists in the final reckoning not so much in what is in the book as in what is out of it.

I thank John Tuckwell of John Donald Publishers Ltd. for having taken on another book of mine, and for having mercilessly dragged me through an early attack of romantic fever, the ineradicable traces of which may – for the curious – be found in Chapter 8.

I have to record my sincere appreciation of the Scottish Arts Council bursary awarded to me in 1981, without which this undertaking would have been financially perilous.

Mr Archibald Hogarth, former proprietor of the *Campbeltown Courier* newspaper, kindly allowed me to consult, at home, the files of that paper, and thereby eased what would otherwise have proved an interminable labour.

Ms Rene MacDonald attended selflessly to my welfare and gave me immeasurable moral support. Her son, John, was my constant companion on innumerable hiking and camping trips throughout Kintyre. Each has my gratitude.

Professor Derick S. Thomson, Department of Celtic, University of Glasgow, assisted invaluably by his criticisms of Chapters 1, 2, and 3; his colleague, Mr Kenneth D. MacDonald, advised on Appendix III and various other parts of the work; the Rev. William Matheson, Edinburgh, read and commented on two drafts of Appendix II, and a part of Chapter 2; Mr Steaphan MacEachainn, Aberdeen, criticised Chapter 3; the late George Campbell Hay, Edinburgh, read Chapter 3 and Appendix III, and kindly permitted extensive quotation from his published verse; Dr. Alan Bruford, School of Scottish Studies, Edinburgh, criticised Chapter 4; Mr Ted Ramsey, Glasgow, read Chapter 7; Mr Edward P. Lafferty, Campbeltown, Chapters 8 and 10; Dr. J. A. Gibson, Kilbarchan, Chapter 9; Professor R. A. Rankin, Glasgow, Chapter 3; Alasdair and Agnes Stewart, Chapter 8 – I thank them all for their indispensable criticism and advice.

Collectively, I thank sincerely the staffs of Campbeltown Public Library; the Mitchell Library, Glasgow; the National Library, Edinburgh; the

Scottish Record Office; General Register Office for Scotland; the Registrar's Office, Lochgilphead; the Fishery Office, Campbeltown.

Space simply does not permit me to mention here all those who, to varying degrees, contributed to this work. Most of them are named in text, references, or notes. Of those who assisted, but who are not mentioned in the body of the work, I have to acknowledge: Mr J. K. Bates, formerly of the Scottish Record Office; Dr. Alexander Fenton, National Museum of Antiquities of Scotland; the late Eric R. Cregeen, School of Scottish Studies; Mr Robert Smith, Auchindrain Museum, Inveraray; Mr Robert Reid, Achnacarnan, Tarbert; Mr Terence Nelson, Ballymena, Antrim; Ms Alison Todd, librarian, Campbeltown Public Library; Mr A. I. B. Stewart, Campbeltown; Dr. Eric Bignall, Clachan, Kintyre; and Nils M. Holmer for permission to quote from his *The Gaelic of Kintyre*.

Contents

	page
Preface	v
Acknowledgements	vii
Abbreviations used in chapter notes and references	xi
Chapter 1. Aspects of Culture and Language	1
Chapter 2. The Gaelic Decline	26
Chapter 3. George Campbell Hay: Bard of Kintyre	48
Chapter 4. John Campbell: Tradition-Bearer	72
Chapter 5. The Irish in Kintyre	82
Chapter 6. Destitution, Disease, and Death	110
Chapter 7. The Resurrection Men	134
Chapter 8. The Western Shore	141
Chapter 9. Wild Goats	156
Chapter 10. The Coasters	175
Abbreviations used in appendices	198
Appendix I. Irish Immigrant Fishing Families in Campbeltown	199
Appendix II. Surname Changes in Kintyre	208
Appendix III. Gaelic-derived Words in the Dialect of Campbeltown	216
Appendix IV. The Thatchers of Glenrea	221
Index	222

ABBREVIATIONS OF WRITTEN SOURCES

AD	Records of the Lord Advocate's Department, Scottish Record Office (West Register House), Edinburgh.
AHJ	Author's Hiking Journal, I-IV (1980-83).
AP	Argyll Papers, Inveraray Castle.
C	Census, followed by year and parish, unless explicit in text, and by district division number (*d*) and page number (*p*). These records, which are held in New Register House, Edinburgh, are not in published form, but are the actual returns on which were based the greatly condensed published statistics.
Cam (Par)	Campbeltown (Parish).
CC	*Campbeltown Courier* weekly newspaper, 1873-
Kilcal Par	Kilcalmonell Parish.
K & K Par	Killean and Kilchenzie Parish.
NSA	New (Second) Statistical Account.
ORB	Old Register of Births for the Parish of Campbeltown, I (1794-1819), II (1820-1855).
ORBL	Old Register of Births List, being an unsigned and undated ms. of 'names mentioned in copy of this register (ORB I, above) believed to be changed and now known by the surnames stated in the following list'.
OSA	Old (First) Statistical Account.
PB	Parochial Board, records held in Argyll and Bute District Council archive (ref. CO 6).
RB	Register of Births, in Registrar's Office, Lochgilphead.
RD	Register of Deaths, *ib.*
RM	Register of Marriages, *ib.*
RP	Register of Poor, followed by parish, unless explicit in text. Held in Argyll and Bute District Archive (ref. CO 6).
Sad Par	Saddell Parish.
Skip Par	Skipness Parish.
SLK	Survey of the Lands of the Lordship of Kintyre, recording names of tenants and others, with numbers of horses and cattle, c. 1630 and c. 1653. AP Bundle 746.
So Par	Southend Parish.
Tar	Tarbert.
TC Cam	Town Council of Campbeltown (minute-books only referred to), in Argyll and Bute District archive (ref. DC/1).
TKM	*The Kintyre Magazine,* published by Kintyre Antiquarian and Natural History Society.
WHT	Work Horse Tax, 1797-8, being a tax (of 2s) on all working horses. Scottish Record Office, refs. E326 10/1 and 10/7, being identical records except in the variability of personal and place-name spellings.

List of tape-recorded informants (excepting those in appendices): *Calum Bannatyne, Campbeltown (b. Rosehill, 1900); *Archibald D. Cameron, Southend, b. 1894; John Campbell, Campbeltown, b. 1904; *George Campbell Hay, Edinburgh, b. 1915; Duncan Jackson, Campbeltown (b. Islay, 1912); Edward P. Lafferty, Campbeltown, b. 1934; Annie (Galbraith) McAllister, Saddell, b. 1905; William McArthur, Flush, Campbeltown, b. 1916; Caroline (Martin) McCallum, Campbeltown, b. 1904; *Donald MacDonald, Gigha, b. 1891; Alexander MacDougall, Clachan (b. near Kilmartin, 1895); *Hugh MacFarlane, Tarbert, b. 1884; Duncan MacKeith, Saddell (b. Sunadale, 1887); *Graham MacKinlay, Saddell, b. 1895; Duncan MacLachlan, Campbeltown, b. 1908; *James McMillan, Machrihanish, b. 1918; Donald Sinclair, Ronachan (b. Machrihanish, 1934); John Smith, Campbeltown, b. 1936; Neil 'P.O.' Thomson, Muasdale, b. 1900.

N.B. Informants who, at the completion of this work, are dead, have been indicated by an asterisk.

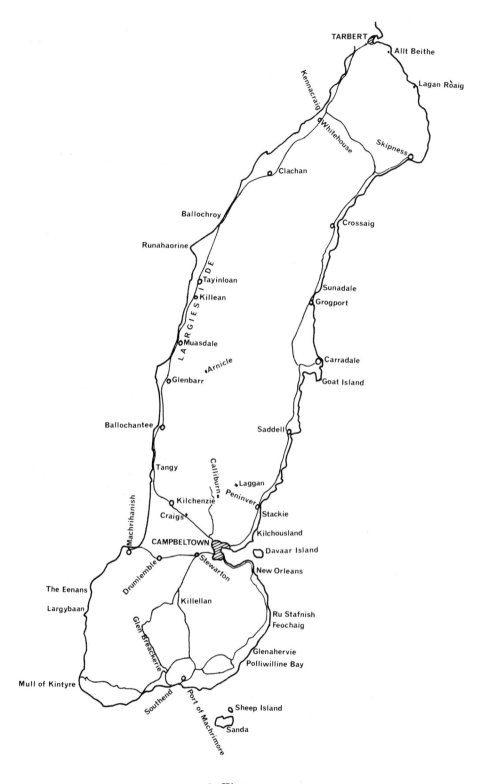

1. Kintyre

CHAPTER 1

Aspects of Culture and Language

The culture of Kintyre, within the period with which this chapter deals, involves two linguistic forces. When cultures clash, the battle-ground on which is settled the issue of supremacy is that of language. That the Scots language, introduced to Kintyre in the seventeenth century by Lowland plantation stock, was inimical to the native Gaelic is indisputable. Yet, the effect on Gaelic of that conflict has been grossly misunderstood and misrepresented. The late Alasdair Carmichael could maintain, in 1974, that 'there is no native Gaelic in Kintyre today'.[1] There was native Gaelic in Kintyre then, and still is (1984). I know six natives of Kintyre for whom Gaelic was their first language, and if none may be classed as an habitual and practised speaker of the language, then that is scarcely surprising considering the scarcity of Gaelic speakers, native or otherwise, in Kintyre.

If Gaelic may be considered as surviving marginally – nominally, even – in Kintyre, what of Scots? That is an altogether more difficult question. Scots, the historical language of the Lowlands, derives from the English of northern England.[2] Its divergent regional characteristics are of such complexity as to lie beyond the modest scope of this account, but of its status as a language distinct from English no doubt need be admitted.

At the opening of the seventeeth century, the language spoken in Kintyre was Gaelic, which was introduced – probably in advance of the settlement in Scotland of Fergus Mór mac Eirc, c. 500 A.D.[3] – by immigrant Dál Riada from that part of Ulster which corresponds more or less with northern Antrim. If that migratory colonisation came out of the west, then the next major colonisation was to be launched out of the east, and in that cardinal opposition may perhaps be seen a fitting significance.

The Lowland colonisation of Kintyre was carried out with relatively little risk. That plantation was essentially a political action, and may in its objectives – if not its consequences – be compared with the contemporaneous and ultimately disastrous settlement of English and Lowland Scots on forfeited lands in Ulster.

As early as 1597, Kintyre had been marked down as one of three rebellious areas of the Gaelic west requiring particular attention. What, in that year, the Scottish government proposed was the establishment of a burgh and burgh town in Kintyre, as also in Lewis and Lochaber.[4] The concept, basically, was this – if civilisation could not be inculcated by punitive means, then it should be grafted on to the violent and resisting Gaelic body politic. Nothing of the plan materialised until ten years later, when the Crown lands of Kintyre passed finally from the hereditary control of Clan Donald into the hands of Archibald Campbell, Earl of Argyll.[5] He quickly set about the foundation of a burgh in Kintyre, and that burgh was at Campbeltown, or *Ceann Loch* ('Loch Head') as it then was, and continues to be in Gaelic speech. Major colonisation by Lowland lairds and their followers began in 1650.[6] The history of that plantation is, in its particulars, a complex one, which Andrew McKerral examined soundly in his definitive *Kintyre in the Seventeenth Century*. It is enough, for the purpose of this chapter, to declare that in that year Lowlanders – principally from Ayrshire and Renfrewshire – arrived in Kintyre in significant numbers, and with the intention of staying.

Just how unbridgeable was the cultural divide across which the natives of Kintyre and the Lowland settlers confronted one another? The issue has its roots in old and long-buried strata of social history; the stock is tough and unyielding and the branches thorny; its mature fruits hang in clusters of paradox and inconsistency, and if one will unearth these deep old roots the method will not be a direct one.

In Peter MacIntosh's little *History of Kintyre*, first published in 1857, may be glimpsed a few flashes of the receding brilliance of that old Gaelic society. That old Peter had pride enough in the Gaelic oral tradition which was his inheritance to put some part of it into writing is fortunate indeed, because the attrition of the Gaelic language in Kintyre – albeit a slow and as yet unfinished process – effectively cast into oblivion a great body of traditional tales. He neither questions nor asserts the historicity of his tales. He relates them as stories which were worth the hearing and, so, worth his retelling, and if none of them may be verified now – as, no doubt, even then – they shine as mirrors shine.

A few features are plain enough. There is the social intercourse between Kintyre and the north of Ireland, which could even then – these stories of MacIntosh's belong, in the main, to the eighteenth century, or so he reckons – be sustained by bonds of kinship and a common culture. There is the hospitality of the people, an attribute which has perhaps been overstressed in the evaluation of 'Highland' character. The provision of food and shelter to travellers was obligatory, more or less, which is not, however, to imply that what was given would necessarily have been given grudgingly. One may conjecture, however, that on occasion – for instance, after a bad harvest – the stranger's portion might have been reckoned better left with the people from whom it had been exacted. From a manuscript of the late seventeenth century, documenting 'Highland rites and customs':

> They are generally very hospitable. Strangers may travail amongst them gratis. When a Stranger comes they direct him to an house which is design'd on purpose for that use, and they send him his Victuals plentifully. Snuff is useful amongst them to make acquaintance.

If the Stranger be an Acquaintance or person of Account, they send or go themselvs to attend him. When the number of Strangers is great, then the people contribute for provision to them which is called *Coinaeh* (*Coinmheadh*).i. common.[7]

Gentlemen are very charitable to their poor: some will have 20 or moe every meal in the house.[8]

The denial of food and drink to a traveller would have been a rare occurrence. The breaching of that code of hospitality brought an uncanny revenge on the women of Allt Beithe township on the coast south of Tarbert. The day was in July, 'a blazing hot summer's day', and a man came down the hill to a house in which the women only were. He stood at the door and said: 'I've been walking since yesterday morning. I've had nothing to eat and nothing to drink. Give me a drink of milk.' The head woman of the house replied: 'We can't give you anything. Go to the burn and take a drink out of that.' – '*Yes,*' he said, 'is that so?' He stepped into the house and put his hand under his oxter where there was a small leather pouch, and he pulled a hazel twig out of the pouch and began stabbing at the thatch of the ceiling with it. And all the time he was doing that the women could not stop dancing, and he carried on without stopping until they all fell down exhausted. He put the twig back into the little pouch, and he said to them: 'The next time a man comes to this house for a drink of milk, you'll give it to him.' With that, he 'disappeared over to Skipness'. His name was MacFarlane, and he belonged to that family in Tarbert which was distinguished by its reputation for sorcery.[9]

The generosity of the poor people in Kintyre was no doubt real enough, but selfless it was not entirely. MacIntosh himself wrote of those itinerants whose very existence was grounded on charity:

Some of these beggars amused the people with stories and songs and could repeat many of Ossian's poems, many of them having extraordinary memories. The people were very glad when any of them came that way, and made an effort in being successful in getting them to their houses, and the neighbours would assemble at night to hear their stories. Some of them could play on the bagpipes and fiddle.[10]

Itinerants were, in the very nature of their lives, not just repositories of accumulated funds of music, song and story, but were also bearers of news, and the importance of that service cannot be fully realised without an appreciation of the extreme – and seldom relieved – isolation in which a great part of the rural population then existed. Roads were crude and transport primitive; letter-post and newspapers had hardly yet reached them. Travellers were therefore welcome – indeed, coveted – guests. MacIntosh records a tradition that 'a vagrant taking his round' of the communities between Machrihanish and Southend could rely on 'hospitable entertainment' for four months,[11] which seems not in the least implausible.

There is, in these stories, evidence of the popular value invested in knowledge, both of the traditional and the learned kinds; there is delight in spontaneous versification – 'no bard was worth his salt who could not improvise at least a quatrain'[12] – and rapid word-play. That such stories belonged to and circulated in the folk tradition of the time indicates a level of popular cultural appreciation that would be ill satisfied with the thin stuff of today's newspapers and television.

The Tales

The first tale selected concerns a 'superior piper and a poet', William MacMurchy (p. 8), who lived in Largieside. He was visited one day by a poet and scholar[13] who had heard of MacMurchy's reputation and resolved to test his 'powers of poetry'. The unsuspecting MacMurchy received the gentleman 'in a very respectful manner'; if he divined in the visit any uncommon purpose, then MacIntosh scarcely suggests as much. MacMurchy played a few tunes on his pipes, but the visitor's mind was turning over all the while in a frame of critical detachment, until, fixing his attention on some 'scones of bread' toasting at the fire, he rose abruptly and, making for the door, declaimed:

> Pìobaireachd is aran tur,
> 'S miosa leam na guin a' bhàis.
> Fhir a bhodhair mo dhà chluais,
> Na biodh agad duais gu bràth.

> (Piping and dry bread,
> worse to me than pangs of death.
> You man who deafened both my ears,
> may you never get a reward.)

This, one may construe, was a measure in the testing of MacMurchy's 'powers of poetry', and was no foolish insult. If, however, MacMurchy had not had the measure of the man, then that, indeed, would have been the gentleman's parting shot, and a shot which would have brought down MacMurchy's reputation in wreckage about him. But MacMurchy was equal to the occasion, and, dropping the pipe from his mouth, retorted:

> Stad a dhuine, fan ri ciall,
> 'S olc an sgial nach boin ri bun.
> Tha mo bhean a' teachd on chill,[14]
> Is ultach don ìm air a muin.

> (Stop, man, give ear to reason,
> bad is the story that has no foundation.
> My wife is coming from Keill
> with a load of butter on her back.)

This tale, unlike the following, ends happily in the reconciliation of the contestants. MacIntosh: 'The gentleman, finding that he had met his match, returned, and a very friendly conversation took place till MacMurchy's wife came home with the butter. The gentleman partook of the toasted bread and butter, and came away wondering that such a man as MacMurchy could be found in such a sequestered spot.'[15]

MacIntosh's story of the humiliation of 'MacKinven's bard' can be ascribed fairly certainly to the late seventeenth or early eighteenth century. In his preamble he writes: 'The Macneals being a powerful clan were connected to the Macneals of Ireland, and had some lands there. They also kept up a correspondence with Irish gentlemen, who occasionally visited Macneal of Tirfergus . . .'[16] Four sons of Lachlan MacNeill of Tirfergus are known to have settled in the north of Ireland. One of them, Neil 'Buidhe', described 'of Killoquin (in County Antrim) and Machrihanish', died in 1722. From his son Lachlan the MacNeills of Cushendun are descended.[17] From that Neil 'Buidhe' also stem the MacNeills of Ballyucan, Ballycastle, Craigs, Drumaduan, Parkmount (all in County Antrim), and Culbane in County Derry.[18]

These 'Irish gentlemen' who frequented Tirfergus – which lies inland from Machrihanish – would be accompanied by harpers[19] and bards. One of these Irish bards left behind his *cochull* – which was the distinctive hood signifying bardic status – and this cochull was appropriated by a 'ready-witted' weaver in Tirfergus Glen who, being hard pressed to keep a large family of children, decided to try his luck in bardic guise.

He put on the cochull and set off down the glen. He arrived at Strath House and went in. The incumbent bard, seeing the cochull on him, at once gave out a challenge: *Am bàrd thusa?* – 'Are you a poet?' This question the weaver mischievously twisted, and answered: *Cha b' àrd na ìosal mi, a dhuine* – 'Neither high nor low, man.' (*Am bàrd thusa* and *Am b' àrd thusa* – 'Were you tall, or high-ranking' – are homophonic, that is, sound exactly the same.) After a further and more complex exchange, in which the weaver, with his tricky ear for the ambiguities of language, was obviously getting the better of the resident poet, a servant hurried upstairs to inform MacKinven that his bard and a strange bard were 'combating each other at a great rate'. MacKinven summoned the two upstairs and at once threw a gold coin on the table and announced that the first of them to make a verse on the gold would have it. MacKinven's bard was still clearing his throat when the weaver began to declaim:

> *Chuir Mac Ionmhuinn nam bosa mìn,*
> *Or fìor-ghlan air a' bhòrd lom,*
> *Chuir a bhàrd fèin smugaide*
> *Air a' chuid do'n bhonn.*

> (MacKinven of the soft hands
> threw down pure gold on the table,
> and his own bard spat
> upon his share of the coin.)

The weaver picked up the coin, and MacKinven's bard turned about and left Strath House. He was never again seen there. The weaver then entertained MacKinven with songs and stories, of which he had an abundance. MacKinven was so impressed with the weaver's performance that he offered him patronage if he and his family would move to Strath; but the weaver declined the offer, content with the gold no doubt, and perhaps unwilling to further tempt providence.[20]

A couple more of MacIntosh's tales − summarised − will further cement the traditional evidence of a continuing free-flowing intercourse between Ireland and Kintyre. In the first, a distinguished Irishman, who had served as a mercenary in European wars, traverses Kintyre in a tragic state of insanity − exiled under punishment of death − until transported to Knapdale by MacDonald of Largie, by whose treacherous charity he had been ensnared.[21]

In the other, a native of Tirfergus Glen, Torquil MacNeill, returns to Kintyre from a forty-year absence in the north of Ireland, where − having 'a knowledge of reading Gaelic, and English writing and arithmetic, and being gifted with an extraordinary memory . . .' − he had run an 'adventure school'.[22] An aged man, he was adopted by a family of MacMaths in Machrihanish and there remained, 'treated like a father', until his death.[23]

The expansion of the Gaelic dynasty of Dál Riada ultimately created two nations, geographically separate, but culturally and politically unified. That mutual identification brought professional poets from Ireland to Scotland, and vice versa. MacIntosh's tale of the Tirfergus weaver recounts a visit to Kintyre by 'Irish gentlemen' accompanied by bards and harpers. But that tale, whatever its historical value, constitutes, by its dating, a late example both of the survival of bardic practice in an institutional frame and of the continuing association of the two culture groups.

The Mac Mhuirich Bardic Family

Perhaps the most significant of all the Irish poets who reached Scotland belongs to a much earlier period − the early thirteenth century. That was *Muireadhach Albanach,* of the Irish literary family of *Ó Dálaigh* (O'Daly). His departure from Ireland was both dramatic and inauspicious − he axed to death a tax-collector who was antagonising him (an impulse which has scarcely lost its appeal), and, following a fugitive spell in Ireland, chose exile.[24] Muireadhach Albanach's claim to notice rests not only on his literary accomplishment, which merits respect, but also on his founding of a long line of hereditary poets in Scotland, the Mac Mhuirich family.

That family served, for more than five hundred years, as professional poets and historians, first to Clan Donald in Argyll and latterly to Clanranald in Uist. Of its presence in Kintyre there is adequate evidence (and that relating to specific land tenure) which begins in 1502 with a Gillecallum McMurrich in Lepeyn Stra and Lylle (Lailt – of which he had a half part), which lands in 1506 transferred to Gallicallum McCosenach,[25] of the family of hereditary harpers to Clan Donald,[26] now known in Kintyre as MacShannons. From 1505 to 1541 the poet Johannes (John) McMurich held, rent-free, by virtue of his office, the Southend farms of Katadill, Gardeveyne, Caprigane, Braclaid and Gartloskyn[27] (i.e. Cattadale, Gartvain, Keprigan, Brecklate and Gartloskan), a sizeable holding indicating high social status. Sometime between 1541 and 1596 the Mac Mhuirichs lost or abandoned their hereditary holdings in Kintyre.[28]

That Mac Mhuirichs went to Uist from Kintyre in the sixteenth century is suggested in later evidence.[29] Whether a branch, or branches, of the family remained in Kintyre is conjectural, but it does seem a probability. Andrew McKerral, remarking on the disappearance of the bardic line from Kintyre by the end of the sixteenth century, adds: '. . . but individuals of the name, most probably descendants, occur as tacksmen in later rentals.' He equates, without reservation, 'MacVurich' (*Mac Mhuirich*) and 'MacMurchy' (*Mac Mhurchaidh*),[30] as does Dr. W. M. Conley, another native historian.[31] But the possibility has to be considered that more than one family is involved.

By the end of the eighteenth century, three accepted anglicised forms of Mac Mhuirich remained current in Kintyre, viz. MacMurachy, MacMurchy, and the final, clipped form Currie.[32] (The latter two are still current.) These forms appear in the Work Horse Tax returns of 1797-98, and I list them in their entirety, from north to south, approximately: Donald and John Curry in Ranachan; Archibald Curry in Carnmore; Archibald MacMurachy in Runaherin; John Curry in Muasdil; John MacMurachy in Bellochochuchan; Nicol MacMurachy in Gartgrulin; Archibald and Donald Curry in Balwillen; William MacMurchy in Mey; Donald MacMurchy in Ban.[33]

The form 'MacMurachy' in the above list undoubtedly represents the old velar form – -ch- as in 'loch' – which has softened into the more English-sounding 'MacMurchy', -ch- as in 'church'. That old pronunciation has gone entirely, and remains only in the memories of a few old people.[34] There is a statement – in a late eighteenth or early nineteenth century anonymous manuscript compilation of surname changes in the parish of Campbeltown – that 'Murphy' became 'MacMurchy'.[35] Quite what 'Murphy' is meant to represent – ?Irish *Mac Mhurchada* – remains unclear, and the statement itself remains unverified. Certainly, however,

MacMurphy, Murphy, and MacMurchy were interchangeable in nineteenth century Kintyre (p. 213), but that is probably a quite different matter. The subject is altogether too heavy with linguistic and genealogical ambiguity to carry further.

The form Mac Mhuirich survives − if tenuously − in Kintyre only in a minor place-name: MacVoorich's − or MacVoorie's − Rock is on the west shore of Davaar Island,[36] and its location may be seen from Campbeltown when heavy seas break on it. That the mainland farm of Kildalloig − which faces across to the west side of the island, and which probably then, as now, included the island − was held in 1505 and 1506 by one Johannes McMurthe or McMurchie,[37] and in 1541 by one Donaldus McMurchy or McMurchie,[38] merits notice. To enlarge on that evidence by the linking of the place-name with one or other of these known tenants might be over-fanciful, but the possibility remains a tantalising one.

If hereditary vocation may outlast its apparent end, throwing up, in later generations, isolated practitioners from a gifted strain, then Kintyre produced, in the period after the Mac Mhuirich departure, two poets of the name MacMurchy. That a single name group should have yielded two writers − each well known in his time, and remembered beyond it − is perhaps too exceptional to be accounted for by coincidence alone, but speculation, however incisive, cannot replace informed judgement. In the final analysis, there is apparently no evidence to positively connect either man with the Mac Mhuirich bardic line.

Two MacMurchy Poets

William MacMurchy, the earlier of the two, died c. 1778. He has been connected with Largieside, but his actual birthplace is unknown. Peter MacIntosh recorded a couple of tales concerning MacMurchy, one of which is given on p. 4. His interests and accomplishments were varied. He was a piper, and in that capacity served MacDonald of Largie; he wrote and collected Gaelic poetry, and also collected proverbs, which collection was used by Donald Mackintosh in compiling his *Proverbs* of 1785; and there is suggestion of his activity in the notation of pipe music. After MacMurchy's death, his manuscripts passed through a succession of hands until, in 1808, the remains were obtained − through the agency of his nephew, James MacMurchy, a Paisley manufacturer − for the Highland Society of Scotland. That acquisition is now in the National Library of Scotland.[39] A text, translation, and exposition of one of MacMurchy's extant poems appeared in *Scottish Gaelic Studies* in 1966. Its lengthy Gaelic title, translated, reads: 'A song by William MacMurchy, a man of the people of Kintyre, on his enlisting in the Army through need, and becoming aware of

the difference between the soldier's life and that of the farmer.' The first of
nine stanzas runs:

> 'S tìm, tuirseach mo dhusgadh,
> 'S cha bu sugaidh mo shuain domh;
> Mar fhear air ùr theachd a meisg mi,
> Làn de bhreisleach, 's de bhuaireadh;
> Le m'ath-shealladh de m' ghòraich
> Làn de bhròn, a's de uamhann:
> Gu'n do reic mi mo shaorsadh,
> Mo theaghlach, 's mo shuaimhneas.

> Spiritless and sad is my awakening
> And not refreshing was my slumber:
> Like a man newly coming out of a spree I am
> Full of confusion, and of annoyance;
> With looking back on my folly
> Full of grief and of horror
> That I sold my freedom,
> My family, and my peace.[40]

The work of James McMurchy attracted negligible interest beyond
Kintyre. That work was in English – he evidently was not a Gaelic
speaker[41] – and in a thin style of literary Scots. There is little genuine
poetry in McMurchy's verse, which is too narrowly local in subject matter
to be of general interest, and too weak on native idiom and vocabulary to be
of much local interest. The vitality of language and robust native character
which have kept alive in the tradition of Kintyre the song *Flory Loynachan*
are plainly absent from McMurchy's work. That his name, rather than his
verse, survives is perhaps the fairest judgement. He was a poet of the
occasion – just about any occasion – as the titles of his verse indicate: *On
the Departure of Mr Walter Loring Macneal for India; Lines on the Death of
Mr John Colville, yr., of Burnside; Lines on the Opening of the 'Royal Lodge'
of Good Templars at Drumlemble*, and so on. Much of his subject matter,
therefore, was not the most promising of stuff, but when he employed his
talent simply and directly he was occasionally capable of the sure touch. His
nature verse, particularly, has both charm and sincerity.

> The modest primrose sweetly smiled
> Frae many a cosy den,
> As forth I went wi' hurried steps
> To seek the lonely glen.

> When on Cnoc Moy's lofty crest –
> Queen o' the hills is she –
> Before my gaze wi' many a bend
> Lay sweet Glenbreckerie.

> (from *Glenbreckerie*)

> Amid the winter storms ye smile
> As fair as any flower in June,
> The silent songsters look the while,
> But, ah!, they canna gie a tune.
>
> (from *The Snowdrop*)

> 'Twas autumn, and the yellow grain
> From off the fields was gathered fast . . .
>
> (from *Lines on the Funeral
> of Mr McLean, Drumlemble*)

> Noo, Tibby, get your pen an' ink,
> An write a line or twa
> On him who often we do think,
> This nicht is far awa.
>
> (from *John's Birthday*)[42]

He was born in 1835, the son of John McMurchy, coal miner, and Jean Watson.[43] His was one of the Kintyre families which used 'MacMurphy' and its contraction 'Murphy' alternately with MacMurchy, and he himself was both MacMurphy and Murphy at various times (p. 213). His brief schooling ended at nine years of age, when he went to work in Drumlemble colliery. He taught himself to write, and, when a herd boy along Machrihanish Bay, would spell out the characters of his own name in the sands. While employed as a drainer and fencer about Kintyre he began to visit the elderly and the sick wherever he found himself, and so attracted the interest of the evangelist John Colville. McMurchy himself became an evangelist and was 'well known in the countryside from the Mull to Killean'. He was a regular contributor to the *Campbeltown Courier,*[44] which in 1888 published a collection of songs and verse titled *Memories of Kintyre.* James McMurchy died on 16 April, 1909, at Machrihanish, not far from his native Drumlemble, which he celebrated – unevenly, as ever – in *My Heilan Hame.*

> . . . *There often I've wandered when school hours were gane,*
> *To bathe in the linn a great pleasure I ta'en,*
> *Or watched the wee fishes that sported sae free –*
> *They seemed to rejoice and be happy like me.*[45]

The Mac Mharcuis Bardic Family

Another bardic family, whose presence in Kintyre places it in a contemporary relation with the Mac Mhuirichs, was that of the name Mac Mharcuis. Its appearance in Kintyre is undateable, but in 1506 John McMarkisch was tenant in Kyram Mor (Kerranmore) and in that year also acquired Lagane (Laggan) in Glenlussa,[46] which, significantly, is represented in two seventeenth century maps by the names *Balamak Marquis* and *Balamack markish*[47] (*Baile mhic Mharcuis*, 'the farm of Mac Mharcuis'). John, above-mentioned, evidently had Laggan at a reduced rent until 1528, when payment seems to have been entirely waived. These concessions were granted 'by the grace of the lord king' (James IV), in virtue of his office (he was designated *carminista*, 'singer' or 'versifier').[48]

In 1541 Gilnow McMarcus and Gilnow McMarkische, of Keranemore and Laggen respectively, most probably represent a single person, whom Derick S. Thomson has suggested was the Giolla na Naemh MacMharcuis to whom are attributed two stanzas in the *Book of the Dean of Lismore*,[49] a sixteenth century manuscript collection of Gaelic verse.

In 1596, Laggan was held by Donald Makmarkie, and Kerranmore by Donald McVarchis, probably one and the same. Nine years later, in 1605, both farms were declared 'waist' (unoccupied),[50] though c. 1630 the former was once more occupied by a member of the family, Jon McMarcus[51] (who may be that John referred to in the next paragraph). He would appear to have been the last of the name in Laggan.

Scattered references to individuals of the name Mac Mharcuis include an account of the theft, in 1685, of a boll-and-a-half of meal, valued at £10, from Robert Colvill in Crossibeg. The person accused was one 'Neil McMarqueis in Keillibill'[52] (Killypole, now a part of Calliburn). 'Jon mc Marques in Kintyr, ane old man and able in the Irish language', whose metrical versions of the Psalms were included in the initial collection of fifty translations published in 1659 by the Synod of Argyll,[53] almost certainly belonged to the bardic family.

The last of the name known to have practised in the literary tradition of the family was Domhnall Mac Mharcuis. The little of his life that is known, and the sole surviving example of his verse, have been elucidated by Colm Ó Baoill. He is on record in Farr, Sutherland, in 1681,[54] and reappears in Lochaber, as a catechist in the employ of the Synod of Argyll, from 1697 to c. 1701. Appended to that sole poem – a rather trivial and ingratiating address, in the old Gaelic script, to his employers, the Synod – is a note, also in the old hand, in which Mac Mharcuis describes himself *'gan lagan'*. This, Ó Baoill suggests, represents *'dhe 'n Lagan'* ('of Laggan').[55] There is, however, no evidence that he ever lived in Laggan, but the reference does indisputably demonstrate his kinship with the bardic family.

A Mac Mharcuis poet, Ainnrias (Henry), of whose work only one example has survived, is on record in 1601 and 1602 in County Antrim, and Ó Baoill conjectures a relationship with the bardic line in Kintyre.[56] The name itself in Ireland is rarely found outwith County Antrim,[57] and the case for ascribing to it a Scottish origin is a reasonable one, though, by the kind of convolution which, in Chapter 5, will be seen to characterise intermigrationary relations between the north of Ireland and south-west Argyll, the Mac Mharcuis family is reckoned, originally, to have emerged in Ireland, where it was probably connected with the bardic family of Clann Chraith in Antrim and Thomond and with the ecclesiastical family of that name in Donegal.[58] In 1669, two individuals of the name were recorded in the Glens of Antrim – Don McMarkee in Unshanagh in the parish of Ardclinis, and Jo McMarke in Droagh in the parish of Tickmacrevan.[59] The name in County Antrim has been anglicised as Marcus, Marks, and Marquess.[60]

In Kintyre the name was anglicised as Marquis, and with the extinction of the fishing family of that name in Tarbert, within recent times, has disappeared.[61]

Edward Lhuyd in Kintyre

The first linguistic study of Kintyre Gaelic belongs, remarkably, to the year 1700. Its author was the extraordinary Welshman, Edward Lhuyd, described by John Lorne Campbell as 'the first great modern Celtic scholar'.[62] Lhuyd's pioneering achievements encompassed comparative Celtic philology, Scottish Gaelic dialectology, lexicography and place-names, Highland folklore, and the systematic collection of Gaelic manuscripts, fields which thereafter largely lay fallow until the nineteenth century.[63]

Lhuyd first appeared in Kintyre sometime in the autumn of 1699, having been travelling in Ireland since August of that year. He crossed by ferry from Ballycastle to Southend (p. 97), and continued, by the west road of Kintyre, towards his ultimate destination, Iona. J. L. Campbell, the author of the account of that journey – in *Edward Lhuyd in the Scottish Highlands* (1963) – postulates that Lhuyd must have met, at Kilchenzie, the schoolmaster Hugh MacLean 'who knew Gaelic well and could write it'.[64] The theory that MacLean was involved in the tuition of William MacMurchy (p. 8) has been advanced on the basis of the similarity of their Gaelic script.[65] Gaelic manuscripts which belonged to Hugh MacLean are now in the National Library of Scotland and in Trinity College Library, Dublin.[66]

Lhuyd reappeared in Kintyre, en route to Ireland, at the very end of 1699. He had left Glasgow by ship on 21 December, but was 'detain'd about 5 weeks at the Mull of Cantire' by broken weather, a misfortune of which J. L. Campbell remarked: 'The gales that kept Lhuyd storm-stayed at the Mull of Kintyre in January 1700 had done a service to Scottish Gaelic lexicography'.[67] The evidence indicates quite plainly that Lhuyd's translation, into a south Argyll dialect, of John Ray's *Dictionariolum*

Trilingue must have been undertaken during that involuntary stop in Kintyre, although, it must be declared, there are no internal clues as to the identities of Lhuyd's informants, or their specific origins. Hugh MacLean, however, may well have been one.[68] That book, the work of the English naturalist, John Ray (1627-1705), was a vocabulary in English, Latin, and Greek, and formed the basis of Lhuyd's linguistic researches.

These Argyll translations, together with a list compiled from an Inverness-shire informant, constitute the core of *Edward Lhuyd in the Scottish Highlands*. The Argyll dialect represented in these translations has, significantly, 'much in common with Ulster Irish', whereas the Inverness-shire list evinces a greater dependence on Scots loan-words.[69] Lhuyd's phonetic system was based on Welsh orthography, and has been judged 'remarkably accurate for a self-taught pioneer in Gaelic dialect studies'.[70]

He died in 1709, at the age of 49 years, his great work unfinished. Of his entire collection of various manuscripts, notes, and journals, only those Gaelic materials which he gathered up in Ireland and Scotland, together with some Welsh materials, escaped destruction.[71]

Nils M. Holmer

The first comprehensive analysis of the Gaelic dialects of Kintyre was undertaken, more than two centuries later, by Nils M. Holmer for the Norwegian Linguistic Survey. That study spanned the late 1930s and the early 1940s, but even then he was too late to be able to represent completely the dialectal variations. Southend Gaelic then scarcely survived, and is represented in Holmer's subsequent publication, *The Gaelic of Kintyre*, by merely six speakers, three of whom – Jessie, Katie, and George Todd – were of mid-Argyll parentage, though born at Strone.[72] The Southend Gaelic was, not surprisingly, locally held to have been more 'Irish' than the Gaelic spoken in any other part of Kintyre.[73] Holmer declines, in the published work, to commit himself to that thesis, having no doubt weighed the evidence and found it lacking, but in an interview, in April 1938, his more expansive view was that 'the Gaelic spoken around Southend and Machrihanish . . . resemble(s) the Erse spoken in Rathlin Island and the Glens of Antrim'.[74] The citation of a conversational remark, belonging to the early stages of a lengthy study, may be conceived as less than just. It might, however, put into the picture what scholarly caution – however commendable – ultimately left out.

Holmer found three roughly classifiable dialects: 1. Largieside, from Ballochantee to Rhunahaorine; 2. Southern Kintyre, including the east side as far as Carradale; 3. Northern Kintyre. But within these broad divisions peculiarities emerge – the supposed Irish influence on Southend Gaelic, already mentioned; the heterogeneousness of the dialect spoken about Skipness; and the exclusion of the Gaelic of Tarbert, which – owing to its geographical position, at the very top of the peninsula, and to 'the varied provenance of its population' – he considered 'hardly typical of Kintyre'. On Holmer's own admission: 'There exists in each of the different parts of Kintyre a distinct variation in dialect, but on account of the scantiness of good speakers in the south and east it is rather a hard task to define these differences.' The most typical and best represented dialect was spoken in the Largieside, particularly at Tayinloan, he considered.[75] More Gaelic speakers in Largieside are cited by Holmer as informants than the combined numbers of the other districts. The specialist nature of *The Gaelic of Kintyre* renders it too dense to attempt summarisation even of its most general linguistic content.

Recent Linguistic Researches

Research on the dialects of Kintyre Gaelic was resumed in 1951, by a Scottish institute – the Gaelic section of the Linguistic Survey of Scotland, attached to the School of Scottish Studies in the University of Edinburgh. The Survey was founded in 1949-50, to collect and study the dialects of Scots and Gaelic. The priority was to tackle those areas in which Gaelic was most endangered. Carefully selected informants were taken through a questionnaire of some 1200 items, designed to cover the phonology and morphology of any dialect. Samples of the informants' speech were then tape-recorded for later analysis.[76]

Kintyre, by reason of the weakened state of the language there, was dealt with at the outset. One of the first collectors in the field there was Derick S. Thomson, now Professor of Celtic at the University of Glasgow. David Clement began his work in Kintyre in 1973, and since then has visited Robert MacCuaig, Clachan, Neil Rowan and Gilbert MacCallum, Tayinloan, James and Maggie MacKinnon, George and Neil 'P.O.' Thomson, Muasdale, and the brothers Duncan and John MacKeith, Saddell, most of whom are now dead. Clement is now (1983) working with only one Kintyre native, George Thomson, a retired gamekeeper, and a fluent Gaelic speaker.[77]

The basic importance of the Survey has been its recording and analysis of the language in mainland areas in which it is on the verge of extinction. The record of the language, as spoken in Kintyre in the mid-twentieth century, will, when published, testify to a linguistic heritage which endured there some fifteen hundred years.

Kintyre Gaelic also came into the scope of the *Linguistic Atlas and Survey of Irish Dialects,* published in four volumes between 1958 and 1969, under the direction of Professor Heinrich Wagner of Queen's University, Belfast. Wagner had already been twelve years engaged in the project when, in 1961, an assistant, Colm Ó Baoill, was detached to Scotland to complete a limited comparative survey of Scottish Gaelic. The first of five Kintyre informants was the late Neil MacDougall in Carradale (also recorded by Holmer and, in 1951, by the Linguistic Survey of Scotland), but the greater part of the questionnaire was covered by Neil 'P.O.' Thomson in Muasdale. Ó Baoill, during his two-week stay in Kintyre, was guided by Willie Mitchell in Campbeltown, widely recognised as a significant singer and collector in the Scottish folk tradition. The results of Ó Baoill's work in Kintyre were published in an appendix to Volume IV of Wagner's *Atlas*.[78]

Some of that Kintyre material was later utilised in Ó Baoill's *Contributions to a comparative study of Ulster Irish and Scottish Gaelic*, which presented a body of lexically oriented evidence demonstrating identical features in the Gaelic usage of Ireland and parts of Scotland, on the one hand, and Scotland and parts of Ireland on the other. The volume contains a small section of items attested in Ireland, and in Scotland attested only in Kintyre – including (in Kintyre Gaelic) *maide briste* ('fire-tongs') and *pigein* ('piglet') – as well as a good deal of Kintyre words attested elsewhere in Scotland.[79]

My own work (which, however, was neither systematic nor scholarly) for the *Historical Dictionary of Scottish Gaelic*,[80] between 1976 and 1981, fundamentally involved the collection of vocabulary. That work was initiated in Campbeltown, Carradale and – most intensively – Tarbert, in an effort to gather as much of the traditional terminology of fishermen as had survived the technological transformation of the fishing industry in this century. Only one old fisherman merited repeated tape-recording over a period of months. He was Hugh MacFarlane in Tarbert, who died in 1979 at the age of 94 years. Though unable to converse with any degree of fluency in the language, his Gaelic vocabulary – both technical and general – was of exceptional richness. As the geographical range of the work extended – into the rural areas of Kintyre, and beyond Kintyre, to Gigha, Islay, and mid-Argyll, increasingly involving fluent speakers – so too did the subject matter, which finally encompassed agriculture, peat-cutting, domestic environment, natural history, etc. A small part of the content of these extensive recordings (some 60 hours), drawing on residual Gaelic in Campbeltown, is represented in Appendix III.

The Scots Dialect of South Kintyre

In 1934, Latimer MacInnes predicted that the dialect of Scots spoken in south Kintyre would 'soon be the concern of scholars and not the speech of the common people'.[81] Neither of these predictions has been fulfilled. MacInnes himself was the first – and, as yet, only – person to subject the dialect to rigorous analysis, albeit without the scholarly apparatus which would no doubt now accompany such an undertaking. Nor has the dialect ceased to be spoken. Decline it certainly has, in all respects – phonemically, idiomatically, and, especially, in the density of its vocabulary – and will continue to decline; but despite the aural assaults of the English language and its North American variants through radio and television (destructive agencies which MacInnes could scarcely have anticipated), the dialect, in however attenuated a form, looks fit to survive a generation or two beyond the generation now in infancy.

Avoid it or despise it, that dialect is intrinsically a part, and an indispensable part, of what distinguishes the native of south Kintyre from the native of any other place on earth. I shall be dealing here exclusively with the dialect of south Kintyre – i.e., approximately, from Campbeltown west to Machrihanish, and south of that line – both because MacInnes's published work exists as a comparative source, and because as a native of the south, myself, I can write of the dialect, as I speak it, with a degree of confidence – but the same applies to the dialects spoken in Tarbert and Carradale, as elsewhere in Kintyre.

There is nothing of the 'wha's like us' attitude in this. Rather, I address the antithesis. The advance of cultural standardisation can be delayed only by resistance on a broad front, and the point is worth making – however cursorily – that the English language, in England, has its many regional forms, which have no less a claim to retention.

The Gaelic language in Kintyre, as a native feature, will certainly be lost by the end of the century. And yet it need not be entirely lost. Throughout Kintyre, among people who think no more on Gaelic than on the Basque language of north-eastern Spain, its legacy persists. It is present most obviously in place-names, unintelligible as these have become to the generality of those who daily use them. It is present, too, in the speech of the people – in words, in the pronunciation of words, and in the ways words are arranged. I am hardly suggesting that what survives will, in any way, compensate for the loss of a language entire, nor am I suggesting that anything substantial can be reconstructed from the debris. Rather, I suggest that the little that remains of the mass of Gaelic words which was assimilated into the Scots of Kintyre, and the Scots words which have survived, in turn, the eclipse of that language, must be retained. But the exhortations of scholars and writers will not forestall the decline of any language or dialect – MacInnes's publication is proof enough of that. Its appearance, by instalments, in the local newspaper certainly assured it of a maximum public. Yet, it effected no reversal, however partial or temporary, in the decline of that dialect which, word by word and idiom by idiom, MacInnes laid open.

Latimer MacInnes, ironically, was born in England, but his father, Duncan MacInnes – a seaman – was a native of Campbeltown, and returned there while Latimer was still a young boy. With the exception of his dialect study, MacInnes's various publications – which include botanical and ornithological catalogues, a collection of verse, and a compilation of 'essays, impressions, and fantasies' titled *Flotsam and Jetsam* – were privately circulated. It was written of him that 'he wrote for the love of it, not for any pecuniary reward'. He seems to have learned Gaelic, and was a founder-member of the Campbeltown branch of An Comann Gaidhealach, [82] though, paradoxically perhaps, he earlier taught classes 'for the study of elocution'. [83]

His direct involvement in local dialect began in 1926, as one of two collectors appointed to serve the *Scottish National Dictionary*, that enormous project which was completed only in 1976 with the appearance of the tenth and final volume. His collaborator was to have been the Rev. John MacRae, minister of the Relief Church in Southend, but MacRae had no sooner been appointed than he removed to Lochgelly. As MacInnes later complained: 'I was, in consequence, deprived at the very outset of his aid in collecting material, and his advice and counsel in sorting it out, and had to carry on the work single-handed. This was a misfortune in every way, the more so as the dialect of Southend, probably because of its long and intimate connection by sea with the north of Ireland, presents features interesting in themselves, and not found in the dialect of the town.' [84]

The results of MacInnes's solitary labours may be found scattered through the volumes of that dictionary. In 1934, however, at the conclusion of his own commitment, he assembled the material into a paper which he delivered to the Kintyre Antiquarian Society. That paper was later serialised in the *Campbeltown Courier*, and, still later, was issued in booklet form. It appeared under the title *Dialect of South Kintyre*, sub-titled 'An Interesting Study', which, if somewhat surprising as an authorial evaluation, is nonetheless entirely just. The study is interesting, and, more than that, invaluable as a description – both meticulous and responsible throughout – of the condition of the dialect between the wars. His introduction lends itself to extensive quotation:

> Considering how long and intimate has been the association between Gaelic and Lowland Scots in Kintyre, the influence of each language on the other has been astonishingly small. In the case of Gaelic it is indeed almost negligible. English words such as stiff, dull, dinner, breakfast, and the like, are heard in local colloquial Gaelic where perfectly good Gaelic equivalents exist, and in pronunciation I have noticed that the characteristic *ao* sound (almost the same as the *oe* sound in the French word *coeur*) in words like *gaoith* and *gaol* has been thinned into the long *a* in the English word gale. [85]

Once or twice I have heard the Gaelic shibboleth-terminal *th:* sous and norse instead of south and north. But . . . the verbal borrowings on the side of Lowland Scots, have, considering the disparity of the two languages, been extensive, and Gaelic has also considerably affected the idiom. Also in pronunciation one occasionally hears the more explosive *t* and *d* of Gaelic in such words as turnip, turkey, helter, stirlin (starling), dirty, dirl, slidder, pooder.

As a rule, all over the area under observation, the dialect of the younger generation is more anglicised, is nearer standard English, than that of their parents, and still more of their grandparents. Anyone who will take the trouble to compare the speech of old folks in Campbeltown with that of the rising generation, cannot fail to be struck by the encroachments of school English. But that that decay had set in long before school English became a marked influence is shown by going back a further fifty years or so. In the *Argyllshire Herald*, of 3 June, 1882, there appeared a short story entitled 'Shadows of the Far Past: A Dramatic Sketch in the Kintyre Dialect' . . . Probably we shall not be far wrong in assuming that the sketch is illustrative of the dialect at the beginning or in the first quarter of last century. While sketches of this kind cannot be regarded as true pictures of a dialect, inasmuch as selection seizes on picturesque, obsolete, or obsolescent words and drags them in by the head and shoulders, without regard to other and perhaps more characteristic features of the dialect, a few sentences from this sketch will help to show the decay, both in vocabulary and idiom, in the local speech within the space of a century. Many of the words and turns of phrase quoted will be unknown or unfamiliar even to the older generation: 'Whaur ir ye gaun strallopin an haikin aboot the hoose wi a bumple o' loodjacks in your oxter like a leuchter o' pease strae . . . Come awa ben, woman, an tak a bit scowther o' the grieschach . . . Muruah! she hadna a skeelag o' furshot atweesh the four wa's o' her hoose . . . He was a bit wanthrifty naughlat o' a wishless craytor amang the lave o' the grulshie graisk in the lone . . . Ye needna be sae nebby an prood, sailin there like King Auchasuyrus, wi aa your tartles an trooshlach, weenglan aboot your muckle spaagach, sclaffran cluits! Ye're haingt deuschach, so ye ir . . . Ye ogly groosamach, broeskach sclyog, it ye ir . . .'
   The last sentence illustrates a feature of the dialect which thrust itself on my notice in the course of my work, namely, its richness in offensive and derisive words. For these toll has been levied both on Gaelic and Lowland Scots . . . The contempt expressed in such phrases as 'a hochlan scleurach' or 'a claaty skybal' must be heard to be appreciated. On the other hand, as might have been anticipated, the dialect is poor in terms of affection and endearment. Of these, one from the Gaelic, current when I first came to Campbeltown in my early boyhood, seems to have entirely disappeared: the word maytil (Gaelic *m'eudail*, 'my treasure'). The caressing tenderness of the term as addressed to a child by its mother, or a kindly old Highland woman, still lingers in my memory . . .
   I may mention, incidentally, another feature which indicates decay, namely, uncertainty as to the correct pronunciation of certain dialect words. For instance, on a single day I got from five persons five different pronunciations of the word *abune*, viz., abane, abin, abeen, abun, and abuin. This could not occur in a pure dialect.[86]

The time is long past for argument about the value of dialect. It needs not justification, but the exercising of its powers. Such words – be they of Gaelic or of Scots origin – as have survived in the speech of Kintyre survive by virtue of particular attributes. Fundamentally, they survive because they still work, and they will continue to survive for as long as they are allowed to work. An examination of MacInnes's vocabularies will reveal the nature of the eliminatory process and how it has operated on the dialect in the sixty-odd years which have passed since he began his work. Two examples from Gaelic and two from Scots will serve the purpose.

Gaelic: 1. *fraochan* − 'the toe-piece of a boot'; *kaepar-ordaig* − 'bread and butter and a slice of cheese, the butter spread with the thumb'.[87]

Scots: 1. *booyangs* − 'the straps buckled over trousers below the knees'; 2. *swee* − 'the iron bar for hanging a pot over an open fire'.[88]

The redundancy of these words requires no explanation. Social change will not, however, account for the greater part of the dialect vocabulary which has disappeared. Many lost words could still have functioned usefully in the dialect, yet slipped out of currency. Some of these, no doubt, were too cumbersome to be spared − linguistic dinosaurs such as the Gaelic-derived *brothachraich* (a hairy caterpillar, literally 'heather caterpillar'), *gilliegibanach* (the daddy long legs, literally 'the tattered lad'), and *greimachrottach* ('depressed, melancholy').[89] The disappearance of the majority of vernacular words is, however, inexplicable except in terms of a widespread disinclination to keep the dialect going, which has much to do with cultural conditioning and little to do with the dialect itself.

Words on paper have no life except the life a reader puts into them. Words which are unrecognisable − whether because foreign or redundant or simply unknown, though of the reader's own language − remain dead. Words exist through recognition and through the particular − and ultimately personal − associations which they engender. With dialect, the matter enters a difficult impasse. Dialect, because seldom written, may survive only in speech − indeed, the root meaning of 'dialect' is 'to converse'. If the dialects of Kintyre are to survive in any form, however attenuated, then the means of that survival is plain − they must be spoken, and their vocabularies − particularly − consciously and conscientiously imparted to the children of Kintyre.

How many of the words listed by MacInnes do survive? The late Alasdair Carmichael, in his book *Kintyre*, assembled a chapter titled 'Traditional Speech'. The greater part of that chapter consists of direct borrowings from MacInnes's paper, though his debt to MacInnes is nowhere in the book explicitly acknowledged. When, however, Carmichael ventures beyond MacInnes's example, he betrays a sorry unfamiliarity with the subject. The very passage which opens the chapter exposes his ineptitude: 'When, in Valparaiso or Bombay or any port between, a ship's captain is overheard to announce his intention of casting off "the ee noo", it will be known that the speaker is a native of South Kintyre and that the business of casting off is to be put in hand immediately . . .'[90] 'The ee noo' is of Carmichael's own construction, and looks very much like an unwitting fusion of 'the noo' and 'ee noo', which are distinct usages.

A more serious misrepresentation which requires to be challenged, and challenged definitively, is his estimate that of '169 words of recognisable Gaelic origin (collected by MacInnes) . . . forty-five years later only 7 per cent survive . . .'[91] Quite how Carmichael computed that absurd percentage he does not declare, but had he taken the trouble of showing that list to any native of Campbeltown over the age of even 30 years, then he would have found himself with an altogether different figure. I shall dispense with percentages (how does one account for .83 of a word, given that 7 per cent of 169 is 11.83?) and simply list those words which I have used myself since childhood: *bocan, boose, boosach, canejach, ceilidh, colligleen* (for MacInnes's *corriegleen*), *crechan* (for *cracken*), *crann, cruban, cuddin, fallachan, galarplocach, gleshan* (for *glaishan*), *moggans, moorlach, mougrin, neonach, owdan, peuchty, pluke, scrabed, sile, skelf*, and *squite*.[92] Remove 'ceilidh' and 'crann' (cran – a measurement of herring), which are in general English use, and also 'squite' which is not positively identifiable as Gaelic, and 21 words remain (or almost twice the number conjectured by Carmichael). To these may be added some 30 others which I have heard in local speech. Many, to be sure, were isolated occurrences, and others, repeatedly heard, were heard from only one person, but all may fairly be reckoned persistent in the dialect, if certain soon to be lost.

MacInnes's list of 184 'obsolete and obsolescent' words presents quite as much interest. MacInnes immediately concedes the uncertainty of deciding 'when, in a particular dialect, a word is obsolete', and rationalises: 'A word may drop entirely out of common use and yet be preserved, and so in a measure survive, in literature, in a proverbial saying, or in the memory or speech of old people.' Yet, his summary – 'All that need be said for the words in this list is that, while many of them still live in the memory or linger on the lips of old folks, they do not come simply and naturally to the rising generation . . .'[93] – may fairly be disputed. Of these 184 words, 14 have been in my own vocabulary since boyhood, viz: *carseckie* ('an overgarment', now specifically a fisherman's canvas top); *carnaptious* ('crabbed, ill-tempered'); *cuif* ('a fool, a simpleton'); *glessy* ('a glass marble'); *gunker* ('chagrined disappointment'); *jaary* ('an earthenware marble'); *nyaff* ('a disagreeable, useless person'); *oose* ('fluff'); *plunker* ('a large marble'); *renege* ('to deny or refuse'); *scran* ('refuse or broken stuff'); *shnashters* ('a contemptuous term for pastries or dainties', now sweets generally); *snoke* ('to poke round inquiringly, like a dog sniffing'), and *sweert* ('reluctant').[94] Eleven other words remain, by my reckoning, in local speech, while at least twelve more are remembered and emerge occasionally in conversation which evokes the past.

What MacInnes, understandably, did not attempt was an enumeration of dialect words then current and evincing no sign of failure. Some of these words undoubtedly have gone, or could now be classed as 'obsolete or obsolescent', but I shall list none of these here. It will be enough to say that innumerable Scots words – and several words of Gaelic derivation which MacInnes either missed or omitted (see Appendix III) – are 'still to the fore' in the vernacular of south Kintyre.

The attenuation of the dialect has been a lengthy process, as yet uncompleted. It has gone on unobstrusively for generations, in a slow but sure dismantling of the machinery of local speech. What remains is a sadly stripped-down version of an engine of expression which was once efficient and serviceable. The initial assaults on the dialect were unquestionably external, issuing from schoolroom and pulpit. The Scots language, unlike its Gaelic counterpart, lacked its own translation of the Bible, and, so, from the Reformation on, the Protestant faith was ministered through the medium of English, with the result that '. . . the Scots . . . associated English with the solemn, formal and intellectual, and Scots with the homely, sentimental and humorous aspects of life'.[95] The destruction of the Gaelic and Scots languages in Kintyre proceeded simultaneously, more or less. As Scots pressured Gaelic, so English pressured Scots, until these two, finally, became essentially undifferentiated and, as one, pressured Gaelic the more.

That merging of Scots and English has been accomplished largely at the expense of Scots. The result is dialect, which, now in Kintyre, means a form of English which is far from being 'standard', but which nonetheless owes little enough to its Scots – and, later, Gaelic – descent. External assault has been succeeded by internal decay, which looks set to finish the dialect. That decay is basically psychological in its origin, because there is nothing inherently diseased in the dialect. It is wasting away through neglect, but so deep a neglect that reversal of the condition seems absolutely improbable. The primary symptom of that decay is that dialect words and phrases are becoming mere curiosities, amusing to the very people whose cultural inheritance they are.

The problem has to be interpreted in terms of conflict, which is fundamentally one of tradition and anti-tradition. The anti-traditional attitude is, to be sure, essentially an unarticulated one, operating negatively but for no readily adduceable reasons. These reasons are buried in history, and some of them will be uncovered and examined, in a specifically Gaelic relation, in the next chapter.

B

REFERENCES AND NOTES

1. *Kintyre*, Newton Abbot 1974, 160.

2. D. Murison, 'The Scottish Language', in *A Companion to Scottish Culture* (ed. D. Daiches), London 1981, 345.

3. J. Bannerman, *Studies in the History of Dalriada*, Edinburgh 1974, 122-6.

4. A McKerral, *Kintyre in the Seventeenth Century*, Edinburgh 1948, 23.

5. *Ib.*

6. *Ib.*, 99.

7. Probably a misprint for *coinnmheadh*, which is the indexed spelling.

8. J. L. Campbell (ed.), *A Collection of Highland Rites and Customs*, Cambridge 1975, 45.

9. J. C. Hay, recorded 14 May, 1979.

10. P. MacIntosh, *History of Kintyre*, Campbeltown 1930 (3rd edition), 39.

11. *Ib.*

12. J. MacInnes, 'The Oral Tradition in Scottish Gaelic Poetry', *Scottish Studies* Vol. 12, 40.

13. MacIntosh: '. . . a learned gentleman . . . himself a poet . . .', suggesting professional status, or something very like it.

14. *'On chill'* is simply 'from the churchyard', but MacIntosh in his translation gives 'Keill' with a capital – a place-name – in which case the Gaelic should be *'on Chill'*. K. Sanger (*TKM* No. 13, p. 18) accepts that the reference is to an actual place – the farm of Keill, on Gigha – and reasons that 'given Gigha's reputation for dairy products and that anyone returning from Cill on Gigha by ferry would be quite visible from Largieside . . .' This theory seems to strain too much for a validation which may not be there. I have let the inconsistency stand.

15. MacIntosh, *op. cit.*, 31.

16. *Ib.*, 27.

17. R. McDonnell, 'The McNeills of Cushendun and the McNeiles of Ballycastle', *The Glynns* Vol. 1, 21.

18. B. S. Turner, Distributional aspects of family name study illustrated in the Glens of Antrim (unpublished Ph.D. thesis, Queen's University, Belfast, 1974), 129.

19. The County Derry harper, Denis O Hampsey (or Hempson), who died in 1807 and claimed to have been born in 1695, recounted a trip round Scotland which he undertook at about the age of 28. He had a fund of 'facetious stories' about the 'gentlemen' he encountered in his travels. One of these anecdotes – contained in Edward Bunting's *The Ancient Music of Ireland*, Dublin 1840, 74 – is of particular interest, both in its location and in its recollection of patronage: '. . . In passing near the residence of Sir J. Campbell, at Aghanbrach, he learned that this gentleman had spent a great deal, and was living upon so much per week for an allowance. Hempson through delicacy would not call, but some of the domestics were sent after him. On coming into the castle, Sir J. Campbell asked him why he had not called, adding, "Sir, there never was a harper but yourself that passed the door of my father's house." To which Hempson answered, "that he had heard in the neighbourhood his honor was not often at home", with which delicate evasion Sir J. was satisfied. He adds, "that this was the stateliest and highest bred man he ever knew; if he were putting on a new pair of gloves, and one of them dropped on the floor (though ever so clean), he would order the servant to bring another pair."' That fastidious gentleman may be identified as Sir James Campbell of Auchinbreck, in the parish of Glassary, mid-Argyll. He died in 1756, and was succeeded by his grandson, also Sir James. The Campbells of Kildalloig in Kintyre – the first, John, chamberlain of Kintyre, who married Elizabeth, or Elspeth, daughter of Lachlan MacNeill of Lossit, in 1660, and died c. 1706 – were of the same line. *Burke's Peerage*, London 1938 (96th edition), 480-1.

20. MacIntosh, *op. cit.*, 27.

21. *Ib.,* 39.
22. 'Such schools supplemented the more orthodox methods of imparting instruction. They were run by cobblers and cripples and tailors and others whose avocation or want of it enabled them to spend the day indoors.' J. E. Handley, *The Irish in Modern Scotland,* Cork 1947, 194.
23. *Op. cit.,* 40.
24. D. S. Thomson, 'The MacMhuirich Bardic Family', in *Transactions of the Gaelic Society of Inverness,* 1966 (an offprint, re-numbered as a separate publication), 4-5.
25. *Ib.,* 18.
26. The family held substantial rent-free holdings in Southend down to 1540, when the Clan Donald lands in Kintyre were formally annexed to the Crown. A. McKerral, 'The McOshenags of Lephenstrath', *CC, 18 Jan. 1941.*
27. *Thomson, op. cit.,* 19; McKerral, *Kintyre in the Seventeenth Century, op. cit.,* 168.
28. Thomson, *op. cit.,* 22.
29. *Ib.*
30. *Op. cit.,* 11, 168.
31. 'A Poem in the Stewart Collection', *Scottish Gaelic Studies,* Vol. XI, pt. 1, 1966, 26. (Wallace MacCallum Conley was born at Campbeltown in 1887, son of Neil C, distillery clerk, and Jeannie Wallace, and grandson of Dugald C, carter, and Margaret MacCallum. He attended Glasgow University and graduated M.A. in Classics, before turning to medical study, from which he graduated M.B., Ch.B. He was a doctor in West Hartlepool until his retirement in 1954, after which the study of the history and literature of the West Highlands became his chief interest. *RB;* Obit. *CC,* 9 Dec. 1965.)
32. Thomson, *op. cit.,* 22: 'With the final *c* of *Mac* attached to the personal name we get the Islay form *McCurich* and the S. Uist form *McCureich.* It commonly happens in semi-Anglicised districts to the present day that the *Ma-* of Mac is dropped in certain names (cf. such Kintyre colloquial surnames as Cairter < MacArthur, Kinlay < MacKinlay, Clean < Maclean, and Cleod < MacLeod). This process explains the final form of MacMhuirich, which is Currie.'
33. *WHT,* 4-9.
34. 'MacMurrachie' and 'Murrachie' − -*u*- pronounced as in 'Murray' − noted from John Campbell, 22 Dec. 1983.
35. *ORBL.*
36. Oral tradition. I have noticed only one written reference, which gives 'MacVouran's Rock' − *CC,* 1 Nov. 1894.
37. *Exchequor Rolls* XII, 699, 708. He also held the farms of Knokquhyrk and Achaquhone (Auchenhoan).
38. *Ib.* XVII, 630-1. Also Corsyne (Corphin) and nearby Bairfarne.
39. National Library of Scotland, Catalogue of Gaelic MSS − Adv. MSS. 72.2.12, 72.2.15, compiled by R. Black; Sanger, *op. cit.*
40. 'A Poem in the Stewart Collection', *op. cit.,* 27-30.
41. C91 Cam Par/d3/p11. Described as a missionary, aged 52, he was then living at West Machrihanish Cottage with his unmarried daughter Jane, aged 22. The Gaelic column is left blank.
42. *Memories of Kintyre,* Campbeltown 1888, 20, 18, 14, 13.
43. *ORB* II, 8 Oct. His father registered as 'John Murchy'.
44. Obit. *CC,* 24 April, 1909.
45. *Memories of Kintyre, op. cit.,* 45.
46. C. Ó Baoill, 'Domhnall Mac Mharcuis', in *Scottish Gaelic Studies,* Vol. XII, pt. II, 1976, 183.

47. *Ib.*, 183-4. The former name appears on the manuscript map drawn between 1620 and 1640 by Robert Gordon of Straloch, and almost certainly based on a survey by the Rev. Timothy Pont between 1580 and 1600. The latter name appears on the map of Kintyre – also based on Pont's survey – published in 1654 by Willem and Jan Blaeu.

48. *Ib.*, 183.

49. D. S. Thomson, 'Gaelic Learned Orders and Literati in Medieval Scotland', in *Scottish Studies*, Vol. 12, pt. I, 1968, 73.

50. Ó Baoill, *op. cit.*, 184.

51. *SLK.*

52. *An Account of the Depredations committed on The Clan Campbell, and their Followers, During the Years 1685 and 1686*, Edinburgh 1816, 109.

53. *Minutes of the Synod of Argyll*, Vol. II, Edinburgh 1944, 177; Ó Baoill, *op. cit.*, 184.

54. A. Mackay, *The Book of Mackay*, Edinburgh 1906, 441-2.

55. Ó Baoill, *op. cit.*, 191.

56. *Ib.*, 184.

57. P. Woulfe, *Sloinnte Gaedheal is Gall*, Dublin 1923, 390.

58. Thomson, 'Gaelic Learned Orders . . .', *op. cit.*

59. Hearth Money Roll, reproduced by Turner, *op. cit.*, 246, 255.

60. *Ib.*, 269, 317, 394.

61. In 1881 in Tarbert there were three family groups of the name Marquis, but (b) and (c) probably headed by sons of (a) – Dugald (61), fisherman, with wife Mary (56), sons Archibald (23) and Donald (19), both fishermen, and daughter Catherine (17); (b) Dugald (29), fisherman, with wife Margaret (30), and son Donald (2); (c) Alexander (34), fisherman, with wife Margaret (34), and children Mary (8), Hugh (5), Catherine (3), and Dugald (1). All were Gaelic speakers, with the exceptions of the children of (b) and (c) – C/d1, pp.22, 28; d3/p.6. When George Campbell Hay was going out to the herring fishing as a boy on board the skiff *Liberator* (p. 56), one of her crew then was Hughie Marquis (above, as a child of five years), whom Hay remembers primarily by his enigmatic advice to him: 'Him that follows *freits* (superstitious customs), the freits'll follow him.' G. C. Hay, *op. cit.*

62. J. L. Campbell and D. Thomson, *Edward Lhuyd in the Scottish Highlands*, Oxford 1963, xvi.

63. *Ib.*, xxii-xxiii.

64. *Ib.*, xvii.

65. National Library of Scotland, Catalogue of Gaelic MSS, Adv. MS. 72.2.12.

66. Campbell and Thomson, *op. cit.*, 10.

67. *Ib.*, xxi.

68. *Ib.*, 92.

69. *Ib.*, 97.

70. *Ib.*, 98.

71. *Ib.*, xiv.

72. N. M. Holmer, *The Gaelic of Kintyre*, Dublin 1962, 4. The statement is very doubtful. In 1861 the family was in Lergybaan: George Todd, 56, shepherd, with two sons and two daughters. Of Holmer's informants, only one – George Jr – is included in that census, as a boy of 14. His birthplace is recorded as Campbeltown Parish (C So Par/d1/p3). His obituarist specifies 'Allt nan Tairbhe, now part of Stramollach', and states that the family later moved to Largybaan, 'whence he attended Glenbreckrie School, over four miles distant' (*CC*, 31 Dec. 1932). The Todd family was of Dumfriesshire shepherding stock, but a settlement in mid-Argyll – George Sr was born in the Parish of Glassary – effected its Gaelicisation.

73. *Ib.*, 107.

74. 'Scandinavian Expert Studying the Gaelic of Kintyre', *CC*, 9 April, 1938.

75. *Op. cit.*, 1-2.

76. K. D. MacDonald, 'The Gaelic Language', in *The future of the Highlands,* London 1968, 184-5.

77. R. D. Clement, letter to author, 12 Oct. 1983.

78. C. Ó Baoill, letters to author, 12 and 23 Dec. 1983. A stimulating appreciation of Willie Mitchell, by Hamish Henderson, appeared in *Tocher* No. 31, 1-26 (published by the School of Scottish Studies, 27 George Square, Edinburgh EH8 9LD).

79. Belfast 1978 (Institute of Irish Studies, Queen's University). The section 'Ireland and Kintyre', 29-33.

80. That project was begun in 1966 at the University of Glasgow. Its object is to provide for Scottish Gaelic as complete a lexical record of the language as remains possible. See K. D. MacDonald, 'The Historical Dictionary of Scottish Gaelic', in *A Companion to Scottish Culture, op. cit.,* 344-5.

81. *Dialect of South Kintyre,* Campbeltown 1934, 3.

82. Obit., *CC,* 10 Jan. 1948.

83. *CC,* 13 Oct. 1888.

84. *Dialect . . . , op. cit.,* 1.

85. This is old in Gaelic, and not due to English influence. Prof. D. S. Thomson, letter to author, 11 Dec. 1983.

86. *Dialect . . . , op. cit.,* 3-5.

87. *Ib.,* 11.

88. *Ib.,* 13, 15.

89. *Ib.,* 10-11.

90. *Op. cit.,* 160.

91. *Ib.,* 163-4.

92. *Dialect . . . , op. cit.,* 10-13.

93. *Ib.,* 13.

94. *Ib.,* 13-15.

95. Murison, *op. cit.,* 347.

CHAPTER 2

The Gaelic Decline

There is little contemporary record by which relations between the native Gaels and the immigrant Lowlanders can be assessed. The most frequently quoted account of these relations was written in 1843 by the eccentric Rev. Daniel Kelly, a native of Campbeltown, and parish minister in Southend from 1816 to 1833. He described the Lowlanders as 'a sober, hard-working, industrious class of people, who have very rarely amalgamated themselves by intermarriages with the Highlanders'. To an excess of that 'unsocial feeling' and an antipathy to the Gaelic language he largely attributed the separation of the Lowland part of the Southend congregation from the Gaelic part, and the founding, in 1797, of an alternative, Relief church, 'detached only by a strand from that of their Highland brethren'.[1]

The facts are, however, rather more complex. That alternative church was founded in protest against the Rev. Donald Campbell – then parish minister – whose intemperance and negligence had alienated him from his congregation (a circumstance to which Kelly merely alludes in an offhanded manner[2]). That church was built not by a part of the congregation, but by – and for – the congregation entire, and the intention was not to secede from the Church of Scotland, but to call another minister. Congregational unity prevailed until the church was built and ready for service.

A crucial issue then emerged, and it was that issue which, in the end, was to split the congregation. The issue was, in short – should the new church be established as a Gaelic charge, or should a non-Gaelic-speaking minister be called? Ultimately, the Lowlanders carried, by a majority, a resolution that the minister should be English-speaking, and the upshot was that the Gaelic speakers returned *en masse* to the parish church. The impracticability of maintaining co-existent Church of Scotland congregations within a single parish was resolved by the secession of the Lowlanders to the Relief Synod.[3]

In Campbeltown, a similarly divisive issue had not yet been resolved. When, in 1781, the Rev. Dr. John Smith – in his time an author and Gaelic scholar of distinction, and a powerful preacher – was inducted to the Highland, or Gaelic, charge in Campbeltown, his church was ruinous and his congregation resigned to regular worship in the church on Castlehill,[4] built in 1778-80 for the Lowland congregation.[5]

The Lowland Church in Campbeltown had been founded early in the plantation period – in 1654 – to satisfy the settlers' want of a ministry conversant with their own language:

> ... Their happiness was embittered by the want of the Gospel, and their uneasiness under the want of this daily increased. For although the Gospel was preached in the country it was in a language not understood by them.[6]

The native ministers evidently had little sympathy with the settlers, whom they considered intruders and wished to repel. So much so that, according to tradition, the Lowlanders in the earliest, most difficult years of the plantation preferred to return to their native parishes for the annual communion, and to have their marriage and baptismal services performed then.[7]

By the end of the eighteenth century, however, a new strength – both numerical and civil – was with them, and, assuredly, 'the boot was on the other foot'. Smith's efforts to get an independent church built for his congregation – '. . . towards 4000 souls (are) destitute of their legal and established place of worship . . .'[8] – were repeatedly defeated by the determined opposition of the heritors. The reasons for that resistance were several, and included financial reservations – more than £1360 had already been spent in building the capacious Lowland Church – but the linguistic argument is worth quoting:

> When this church was built, the Heritors had in view that it should serve both congregations, in the manner it now does, otherwise the plan and expense would have been greatly circumscribed; besides that, the Gaelic language in this part of the country is dying out, and the whole or the greater part of the Highlanders now understand and attend the English service.[9]

The prejudicial weight of that argument may be counterbalanced by Smith's own estimation, in 1794, that 'nearly two-thirds of the people are Highlanders (i.e. natives or settled Gaelic speakers) and belong to the Highland charge'.[10] There are no means of computing accurately the Gaelic-speaking presence in the community at that time, but unquestionably it was of sufficient strength to justify an exclusive place of worship. That charge – of an insufficiency of monoglot Gaelic speakers to justify provisions for Gaelic speakers as a whole – will be encountered again (p. 38). It will be enough, in the meantime, to record the failure of the heritors' opposition. Smith finally appealed to the General Assembly of the Church of Scotland and won his case.[11] A new Highland church was built between the years 1803 and 1806[12] and is used to this day.

Cultural Intimidation

An analysis of the factors contributing to the steady displacement of Gaelic by English cannot fail to take account of the potent psychological forces at work. These were institutional in origin, operating through the whole repressive system by which government of people is conducted. Once projected, these forces gathered momentum, rather as a land-slip high up may run on, given right conditions, and sweep all before it in an unstoppable avalanche. The erosion of Gaelic began at the top and, in Kintyre at any rate, has reached bottom.

To put the matter in terms of cultural intimidation – subtle in many ways, no doubt, but nonetheless effective – would not be over-statement. An integrated people with a mature and rich culture simply does not voluntarily wrench itself out of the security of its racial mould and seek to contort itself into an alien one. The contortion act has, of course, failed, at least in the deeper levels of the national psyche. Though the stage, on which that bizarre tragedy was enacted, has receded into a shimmer of history, the descendants of these consenting actors are left with an uneasy sense of unfulfilment and of a betrayal committed (mistakenly) on their account. That heritage, which was so easily thrown away, has acquired, by its very loss, a value which increases the more irrecoverable it appears to be.

Gaelic is in fashion and Gaelic is safe, safe enough for babies even. But how has this remarkable transformation come about? The beast is emasculated and lies subdued somewhere in its lair in the far west. It may now be ministered care and comfort, for it will never rise again. Politicians, educationalists, and the other props of a mighty English civilisation are free now to creep out and declare themselves committed to the noble rescue of the ailing culture. In North America, a comparable reassessment has, in popular consciousness, elevated the indigenous culture from a low, barbarous level to a marvellous 'national' heritage. 'The Indian is safely in his reservation – let us celebrate the Indian!'

But cynicism is a hard and bitter fruit, and sterile to the core. It blossoms but once and leaves a stink behind it. Gaelic culture was not without its distinguished champions, even in the extremities of its travail, and in quietly committed ways many 'ordinary' people held fast to what was their heritage, yet did not withhold it from children and grandchildren. All honour to them – what exactly were they up against?

Gaelic and the Educational System

The first school in Campbeltown – and undoubtedly in Kintyre – was a burgh school, founded by 1622. From then on, English must have been taught in the burgh. After 1686, the burgh school became known as 'the Grammar School of Campbeltown',[13] but it was also, significantly, referred to in the seventeenth century as 'the English School', as not a few entries in the minute-books of Campbeltown Town Council attest.[14]

The cultural assaults began in infancy. Until the close of the nineteenth century, for many children living outwith south Kintyre, Gaelic was their first and only language at the time of entry into school. But Gaelic was not, even in predominantly Gaelic-speaking areas, an officially recognised teaching medium. More than that, an active hostility to the language permeated the whole educational complex from top to bottom. The unreasonableness, if not absurdity, of attempting to teach young children in a language incomprehensible to them – a foreign language, no less – is plain, and the confusion and distress of such children may be imagined. This anomaly did not, of course, suddenly materialise with the introduction of compulsory, state education. The precedent had been long established.

Old Peter MacIntosh understood the mental and emotional harm done to Gaelic-speaking children by enforced instruction in the English language. As a Gaelic speaker himself, who received a limited education in his youth, and as a teacher of many years' experience in the 'side schools' in and around Campbeltown, he was well qualified to judge the system from both ends. And judge he did, uncompromisingly: 'In (their) earliest days, having been sent to school to learn to read English, and tortured with tasks and tawse, without understanding the meaning of what they learn or read, they contract a strong dislike to that language.'[15]

If the following simple account, taken down in the late 1930s from Sarah MacPhail, Acha'n Bhealaidh, Clachan, may be trusted – and there is little reason to question its authenticity, however outrageous its implications – children were encouraged, in the cause of rooting out Gaelic, to inform upon their classmates:

> Bha seo deich as ceithir fichead bliadhna air ais. 'Na bha mo mhàthair anns a sgoil, cha robh de chridhe aig a' chlann bhith air an cluinntinn cainnt na Gàidhlig 'na bhiodh iad a cluich, na (= 'or') gheibheadh iad an gabhail orra. Bha iad ri innseadh air a chéile nuair a bhiodh (iad) air an cluinntinn a' cainnt Gàidhlig. Bha caile anns a' sgoil air a cluinntinn ag uinnsneachadh na Gàidhlig, agus dh'innis ban-chompanach do'n mhaighstir sgoil, agus fhuair i gabhail oirre.[16]
>
> This was ninety years ago. When my mother was in school, the children didn't dare let themselves be heard speaking Gaelic when they were playing, or they would be punished. They were to report each other if they were heard speaking Gaelic. A girl in the school was heard speaking Gaelic, and another girl told the schoolmaster, and she was punished.[17]

In the surviving log-books of the rural schools may be glimpsed the attitudes and the problems of teachers working in the Gaelic-speaking areas of Kintyre towards the end of the nineteenth century. Some of these teachers were Gaelic speakers, but others were not, and their troubles were undoubtedly the more testing. Indeed, if authority and power and punitive privileges had not all been invested in them, then they would have been, as much as their pupils, entitled to sympathy.

The schoolmaster appointed to Ballochantee had no Gaelic; his pupils had little else. That he was thereby seriously handicapped he realised early, yet he did not acknowledge that the deficiency might lie with him, albeit through the agency by which his appointment was permitted. Rather, for him, the deficiency was with the children in his charge. On 24 June, 1882 he noted: 'The fact that Gaelic is their vernacular demonstrates that we have serious difficulties to grapple with.' Subsequent entries register his increasing disillusion – 5 July, 1882: 'As the Gaelic language is their vernacular, some time must necessarily elapse ere great results can be expected.' 23 December: 'No real progress can possibly be made by children to whom English is, for years, a foreign language.' On 27 October, 1883 he set down a remarkable theory, by which he relieved himself of any responsibility for the evident failure of his undertaking: 'The intelligence of Gaelic-speaking children is not developed at an early age, nor is it possible for them to make decided progress in English.'

His bitterness found expression in thin nostalgic effusions which evoke the virtues of urban society. He considers himself condemned to 'the back woods' and for consolation reflects that he 'may be accomplishing very useful work, though he cannot score the complete passes which are possible in a refined and highly educated burgh town' (15 November, 1883). 'How miserable should we be in this obscure corner did we not know what life means among the upper "Ten Thousand"' (25 July, 1882).[18] Such was the mind of the master who came to Ballochantee to equip for their society the sons and daughters of fishermen and farmers.

His name was Dugald Thomson, which, superficially, would suggest a Glenbarr or Muasdale origin. In fact, he was a native of north Bute, and so, one would suspect, not far removed from Gaelic influence; but he was without that language.[19] He had not, however, been without the opportunities of learning Gaelic, having taught at the General Assembly School in Bowmore, Islay for an unknown period which ended in 1869 when he transferred to Drumlemble General Assembly School.[20] There, as at Ballochantee, he indulged his utterly futile prejudice: 'No easy matter to interest the scholars in their work. I do wish Gaelic were an unknown language, at least to boys and girls, whose progress, I find, it greatly retards.'[21] The schools' inspector, visiting Drumlemble some months after Thomson's departure, was moved to remark that 'the new teacher has much to do to raise the character of the School'.[22] Dugald Thomson left Ballochantee sometime in 1885/6, and settled in Glasgow.[23] Whether he achieved his ambition of teaching in an academic environment commensurable with his great abilities remains – fortunately, perhaps – unknown.

The schoolmaster at Rhunahaorine, farther north, was evidently without such conceits, and appears to have coped rather better. His infrequent complaints about the handicap of his youngest pupils' monoglotism were confined to one subject of the curriculum – arithmetic. A couple of these entries will suffice. On 27 July, 1874: 'Considerable difficulty is experienced with the youngest Arithmetic class, arising from the fact that to the children English is a foreign language.'[24] On 26 March, 1875: 'The youngest Arithmetic class is making some progress, but great difficulty is found in making the children understand the property of numbers. This, to a great extent, arises from their ignorance of English.'[25]

There is some evidence that not all school boards were hostile to Gaelic. A newspaper notice of August 1888, advertising for a male certificated teacher for Whitehouse school, in north Kintyre, specified that applicants 'must be qualified to teach Gaelic'.[26] That is not, of course, quite the same as teaching *in* Gaelic, but demonstrates, nonetheless, an unusual compliance with, one must suppose, public feeling. That same school board, Kilcalmonell and Kilberry, was instructing, less than a year later, in April 1889, the teacher at nearby Clachan that he 'must give lessons in Gaelic at least three times a week'. That injunction was the direct result of complaints by ratepayers that Gaelic was not being taught in that school.[27]

The primary teaching of Gaelic became, in 1906, the subject of an intense, protracted debate in the London *Times,* and J. R. Moreton MacDonald, laird of Largie, entered the thick of it. His social origin and educational experience – Eton and Oxford – might have predisposed him against the Gaelic movement, but a career as an historian[28] effectively reinforced his awareness of the history and the culture of his own people. His letter of 21 July – in which he attacks an earlier correspondent, Charles Stewart – delivers a series of persuasive thrusts:

> Put shortly, [Stewart's indictment] is simply this:– We cannot afford in these strenuous days to waste any particle of the children's time on any subject that does not directly help them to earn a living. It is an old, and I should have thought a worn-out, argument. One has only to remind oneself that, if Mr Stewart's theory were to be carried to its logical conclusion, not only 'our poor Gaelic' would go to the wall, but with it would have to disappear such subjects as history, literature in all its branches, and religious knowledge; for no one of these can be said to contribute directly to that procuring of employment which is the sole object of Mr Stewart's curriculum. But the case for a liberal education hardly needs rearguing at this late date; only it is interesting to find a man of Mr Stewart's position and attainments calling it in question.
>
> Mr Stewart either does not realise or else he wilfully refuses to give due value to the fact that the children to whom we would teach the Gaelic are already Gaelic speakers. To refuse to cultivate an acquirement the roots of which have already struck deep would be as foolish as to stifle a taste for music, or (*pace* Mr Stewart) an aptitude for mathematics. The rudimentary knowledge pre-exists, and it is the function of the teacher to avail himself of it. And it must not be forgotten that the time necessary to introduce pupils to the beauties and refinements of a language with which in its colloquial aspect they are already familiar bears no comparison with the time required for the teaching of a new language. To ignore pre-existing knowledge such as this is an obvious injustice to Gaelic-speaking children.
>
> But these are not the main arguments of those who, like myself, favour the teaching of the Gaelic to Gaelic children. We look forward with apprehension to the time when the whole Empire shall have been levelled to a single standard of Cockney dulness, when local feeling, costume, customs, and speech shall have perished, and all that we have in exchange for our soul is that commercial efficiency for which Mr Stewart believes that we are willing to sell it.[29]

There are no native Gaelic-speaking children now in Kintyre, and there have not been for decades. Gaelic is not taught at any school, primary or secondary, and if, in the future, the language were to be introduced to the curricula of schools, then it would be as a foreign language, in effect – just as English was, a century and more ago. The change in official educational policy towards Gaelic – exemplified in the pronouncement of the Scottish Education Department, in 1965, that 'it would be absurd that children who come to school speaking only Gaelic should have their early lessons in reading and number in English . . .'[30] – came half-a-century too late to serve the interests of the language in Kintyre.

The impingement of anglicising forces on the life of an adult Gaelic-speaking population was less direct and certainly less effective. Rather, that latent hostility was more likely to deter Gaelic-speaking parents from transmitting the language to their children than to discourage its use between themselves and among neighbours and friends. In many households, Gaelic served as a kind of private language, by which parents could discuss, in complete confidence, the intimate and the sensitive in their lives. This was certainly true of my own family, paternal and maternal, and that denial levied its toll of resentment in later generations. My maternal grandmother's only Gaelic phrase, from a childhood spent with a mother and grandmother who were both Gaelic speakers, was *Dùin an dorus,* 'Close the door' – the command which signalled the children's expulsion from the kitchen when the Gaelic-speaking country relations arrived and the whole tenor of the household was turned about for their reception.

As I have elsewhere[31] remarked, 'The association of the English language with educational and social advancement encouraged, to a great extent, an hostility to Gaelic in that section of the community which had successfully "gone over" to the professionally more useful of the two languages.' That notorious pronouncement of the Rev. John MacArthur, minister of Kilcalmonell and Kilberry – 'The Gaelic is the vernacular language of the parishioners, but the English is displacing it, and the sooner it overmasters it the better . . .'[32] – is worth quoting, and requoting, as an example of the intensity of the recoil from Gaelic which characterised many a disaffected Gael. When John MacMaster Campbell (p. 36), as a pupil-teacher in his native Inverness-shire, began to learn the language, he was warned by his educational superiors that he was jeopardising his chances of promotion, for Gaelic was 'a barbarous patois unworthy of the study of any man who aspired to culture'.[33]

For most Gaelic speakers emerging from the coils of the educational system, such English as they had acquired would be of little general use to them. They were assimilated into communities which were Gaelic by pre-disposition and in which the English language was seldom heard. This was perhaps most true of Largieside, even into the present century. Neil Thomson, who was born in Muasdale in 1904, replying to the question: 'Was Gaelic the main spoken language in your youth?' – 'I think I can safely say that it was. I can remember as a boy goin round to any of the farms and there'd be very few (where) I wouldn't be addressed in Gaelic, very few. There may have been some incomers, but round about here the farmers were mostly all old natives. It died away very quick, ye know.' – Angus Martin: 'Have you any explanations of that?' – Neil Thomson: 'We call it progress.'[34]

The Gaelicisation of Lowland Stock

The cultural cross-over from Gaelic to English (or Scots) has, perhaps, been over-stressed at the expense of the counter movement. Latimer MacInnes was prepared to concede that 'bi-lingualism' – i.e., Scots speakers adopting Gaelic – had been 'occasionally present', but insisted that 'it is clear that there was no intention or desire on the part of these Lowlanders to be absorbed in the native Gaelic-speaking population, probably because they regarded themselves as superior stock'.[35] This is both a generalisation and a distortion. Certainly, there is, for south Kintyre, no evidence of any general or sustained shift from Scots to Gaelic, but the first Gaelic census, in 1881, arrived too late, and was altogether too unreliable, to demonstrate the nature of the cultural interaction of the preceding two centuries. Rather, it demonstrates the obvious *fait accompli* – Gaelic in recession. Quite obviously, had there been such a shift to Gaelic within the Scots-speaking community in south Kintyre, the Gaelic decline there would not have been so far advanced by that year. The conclusion has to be that the very concentration of Lowland families in that area swung the balance critically. The proportion of Lowlanders which did adopt Gaelic remains, therefore, conjectural, but it may be supposed greater than has hitherto been accepted. As late as 1881, a few Lowland-named families of Campbeltown origin were recorded as Gaelic-speaking – namely, Houston, Mitchell, and Watson (indeed, the Gaelic precentor then was one Archibald Watson, a 'draff' (grain) storekeeper born in Campbeltown c. 1840).[36]

Outwith south Kintyre, a counter trend prevailed. In Largieside, Tarbert, and Carradale, Lowlanders entering the Gaelic sphere were encompassed entirely by it and became as Gaelic as their native neighbours. The process of conversion was no doubt a rapid one, as, indeed, it had to be to overcome initial alienation in overwhelmingly Gaelic communities. In Largieside, an inward movement of Lowland farming stock was under way by the late eighteenth century, and in 1797-8 the following Lowland tenants (supplemented, no doubt, by unknown followers) were established: Rob

Wallace in Kilmory; Archd. Fleeming, Achapharick; Gilbert Ramsay, Tornalein; Alexander Armour and John Watson, Bellochochuchan; John and William Colven (Colville), Barlea; and John Watson, Amaud.[37] Among Gaelic speakers recorded in the census of 1881 appear the following families, all born in Killean and Kilchenzie Parish: Armour, Blackstock, Colville, Mitchell, and Wallace.[38]

In Tarbert, the early nineteenth century settlement of Ayrshire fishermen produced a first generation of Gaelic speakers, so that in 1881 the families Bruce, Hay, and Law appear as Gaelic-speaking. Additionally, Easton (of Barrhead origin), Jackson (of Paisley and Glasgow origin), Hill, Mitchell, and Fleming.[39]

In the Carradale district, the following assortment: Allan, Blackstock, Bruce, Mitchell, Muir, and Wallace.[40]

Gaelic Monoglotism, and Bilingualism

Monoglot Gaelic-speaking persisted in Kintyre until beyond the mid-nineteenth century. The Swedish linguist Nils M. Holmer encountered, while researching his survey of the Gaelic of Kintyre (p. 13), old people in the Largieside who could 'tell about persons they knew in their own childhood who did not understand English'.[41]

The position in 1891, from the evidence – which may be accepted as roughly indicative – of the published census statistics of that year (the first to separate monoglot Gaelic speakers from bilingual speakers) was:

Parish	Population	Gaelic only	Gaelic and English
Campbeltown	10,260	11	1,448
Tarbert (village)	1,775	13	794
Killean/Kilchenzie	1,293	17	808
Southend	844	1	115
Saddell	757	6	390
Kilcalmonell	502	11	369
Skipness	395	–	298

Bilingualism is assuredly a complex facility, which the simple classifications of conventional surveys – the successive national censuses from 1881 onwards, included – cannot possibly encompass. Competence in one, let alone two languages, will vary so radically from one individual to another that any evaluation must, without the most meticulous of analyses, fail to reach other than the broadest of conclusions. Even so, it is worth examining the evidence of linguistic aptitude in Gaelic and English, both, in an entirely arbitrary – indeed, fortuitous – population sample from north Largieside in the year 1855.

That evidence consists of marginal and textual annotations on the precognitions – i.e., the statements of unsworn witnesses – taken preparatory to a charge of assault against one Duncan MacConachy. The assault – MacConachy bit Hector MacLean – occurred at the farm of Taychroman on 11 September, 1855, during post-harvest ('caelach'[42]) celebrations. In all, nine witnesses, and Duncan MacConachy himself, were interviewed. Of these ten persons, the linguistic capacity of only one – Mary Bell – was unnoted.

1. Donald MacMillan, aged 54, farmer at Taychroman in joint tenancy with his unmarried brother Archibald – 'I understand English when I hear it spoken, but I cannot express myself in the English language.'

2. John MacMillan, 18, son of Duncan MacMillan, farmer at Clachaig – 'Witness speaks English imperfectly.'

3. Mary Bell, 17, servant to Donald MacMillan – .

4. Jean MacGill, 28, wife of Donald MacMillan – 'I understand English a little, but cannot speak it.'

5. Margaret MacKay, 20, servant to Donald MacMillan – 'Speaks English.'

6. James MacDonald, 52, labourer at Taychroman – 'Speaks English imperfectly.'

7. Donald MacDonald, 17, servant to Donald MacKinven, farmer at Tayinloan – 'Examined in Gaelic.'

8. Hector MacLean, 55, servant to Donald MacMillan – 'Speaks English.'

9. James Anderson, 15, herd to Donald MacMillan – 'Speaks English.'

10. Duncan MacConachy, 21, son of Archibald MacConachy, cottar at Achafarick – 'Examined and interrogated in the Gaelic language through the medium of Hector MacNeill, police officer in Campbeltown, sworn interpreter.'[43]

Of these nine individuals (Mary Bell discounted), three – 5, 8 and 9 – had sufficient English to undergo examination in that language, but all three – with the possible exception, on the appearance of his name alone, of James Anderson – were more than likely also Gaelic speakers. Turning to the evidence of monoglot Gaelic-speaking, merely two of the remaining six witnesses may be considered definitely to have been entirely without spoken English – Donald MacMillan 1, and his wife Jean 4, who stated plainly that they could not express themselves in English. The qualification 'examined in Gaelic' – 7 and 10 – may denote total inability to speak English; conversely, it may equate, more or less, with 'speaks English imperfectly' – 2 and 6 – which is exactly the middle ground – having the one language, but not quite enough of the other for fluent use – which confounds the neat distinctions of statisticians.

Such evidence may serve to prove almost anything; analysed rigorously, it may be seen to prove nothing. It is a sample only, and, albeit that its very arbitrariness removes all elements of calculation, it cannot be considered truly representative. Another sample from that same area and of that same period might − were such a sample extant − yield a result of one hundred per cent monoglot Gaelic-speaking. It might, on the contrary, do nothing of the kind. All factors considered − place and period and the absolute preponderance of Gaelic-speaking in the Largieside throughout the nineteenth century − the conclusion may not be unreasonable that those witnesses whose examination was in Gaelic lacked a sufficiency of English to render the business feasible in that language. (An examination of the incidence of Gaelic-speaking at Taychroman in the censuses of 1881 and 1891 might have proved interesting, but by 1881 the MacMillan family was no longer there. The tenancy had been taken over by a family Greenlees from Kilchenzie parish, and there was no Gaelic among them.[44])

The preceding statistical juggling may not be without interest. The basic material, however, illustrates something else. The judicial system in Kintyre − as elsewhere in the Gaelic-speaking area − was fundamentally English-oriented. When the procurator fiscal's scribe recorded 'speaks English' against the names of witnesses in the course of such preliminary investigations as those detailed above, then one may be sure that he did so with relief. Statements were written down entirely in English − that is, in many cases, in translation − and no allowance was made for the language preferences of individuals. Admittedly, a translator would usually be present, but the whole alien conduct of the business was likely to have intimidated and unnerved Gaelic-speaking witnesses beyond the common expectation.

In courts of law, the Gaelic speaker's sense of alienation and inadequacy was the more intense. Even with a knowledge of English, the insufficiency − real or imaginary − of his English put him at a disadvantage at once, unless he were fortunate enough to have the assistance of a court official familiar with his own language. John MacMaster Campbell, sheriff at Campbeltown from 1910 until his death in 1939,[45] was fond of intervening to help out Gaelic-speaking witnesses, as in a civil case from Gigha in 1910, when he 'exercised his Gaelic by putting several questions to a witness in that language, when English seemed to have exhausted its capabilities of making him understand what the lawyers were driving at'.[46]

The uncertainty of a Tarbert carter as to the competence of his English lightened the proceedings of a court case heard in 1888, but the man's persistent pleading to be heard in Gaelic suggests a degree of agitation belied by the superficiality of its treatment, both by the court and by the newspaper in which the case was reported:

Archibald Bell, carter, Tarbert, who was the second witness called for the prosecution, said, in good English, that he would prefer to give his evidence in Gaelic.
Lord Craighill (to witness) – Oh, but I don't prefer that. (Laughter.)
Witness – But I can't speak English well.
Lord Craighill – You are speaking as good English as I am.
Witness – But there are words in English I can't understand.
Lord Craighill – Oh, we'll get along. We'll try.
Witness (to the Advocate-Depute) – Will you speak plain, then? (Laughter.)
The Advocate-Depute – I'll do my best. (Laughter.)[47]

Whenever Gaelic speakers – with or without a complementary knowledge of English – came into contact with officialdom, their native language would, more often than not, be exposed as, if not a positive handicap to them, then at least no positive asset. This recurrent anomaly in the criteria of appointment of officials, whereby a non-Gaelic speaker could be judged fit to transact business with a Gaelic-speaking population, was seldom publicly challenged, but one instance of such a challenge merits examination.

In 1848, Peter Hunter was elected inspector of poor by the Parochial Board of Campbeltown, the authority empowered to dispense money and goods to the poor of the parish. His appointment was at once contested by the minister of the Highland charge in Campbeltown, and himself a member of the Parochial Board, the Rev. George MacLean. MacLean, a native of Dingwall, was minister in Campbeltown from 1844 until 1852, when he emigrated to Australia and left the ministry for a teaching career.[48] His objections were on points of constitutional irregularity, and all but one of these points may, for present purposes, be ignored.

That one relevant objection was that Hunter was unfit and unqualified for the job, '. . . he being ignorant of the Gaelic language, and incapable of translating to the Parochial Board the facts or details of the cases of those paupers who cannot state their claim to Parochial Relief in the English language'. MacLean argued that the job required bilingualism, there being 'from three to four thousand souls of the population whose vernacular tongue is Gaelic', of which number 'many . . . really cannot state their own case in English or understand it when it is stated to them in that language'. He set out a case – not a particularly convincing one, it must be admitted – for Campbeltown as 'the metropolis of the West Highlands . . .' and 'subject to continual influx of a Celtic population from the adjacent districts . . .'[49] (which, however, is indisputable, as the registers of poor – to cite but one, most relevant, source – substantiate).

The Board refused to rescind the appointment, and informed its central authority – the Board of Supervision, in Edinburgh – of that decision, enclosing a copy of MacLean's letter. That Board accepted MacLean's case, and reasoned that 'in a parish in which it is found necessary to provide religious instruction to the people in the Gaelic language, it is necessary that the Inspector should be capable of communicating with the paupers and applicants for relief in that language'. Hunter was, in effect, being asked to resign, without which resignation, he was informed ominously, the Board of Supervision would 'adopt ulterior measures'.[50] He refused to give way, and a petition was prepared, by a committee of the Parochial Board of Campbeltown, and submitted to its superior authority. That petition is of singular value as a document of the times:

> That the attention of your memorialists has been directed to the opinion expressed in a letter recently addressed by your Secretary to the Inspector of Poor in this Parish – 'that in a parish in which religious instruction is provided for the people in Gaelic it is necessary that the Inspector should be acquainted with that language.'
> Your memorialists concur in the propriety of acting upon that rule with reference to Highland parishes generally. At the same time they beg leave respectfully to submit that owing to certain specialties in the condition of the parish of Campbeltown it is unnecessary to insist upon a Gaelic-speaking Inspector being appointed there.
>
> Your memorialists further submit that although the Gaelic language is extensively spoken, yet the English also prevails even among the Highland population.
> At a remote period a large emigration of lowlanders occurred. These have still kept up their distinctive language and habit. Owing to this circumstance together with the universality of education in the parish and its containing a Royal Burgh, the English language is cultivated to such an extent as brings Campbeltown out of all analogy to ordinary highland districts. Accordingly the Board are assured by parties who are competent to give a decision on the subject, and who have gone through the parish for the purpose of enabling them to form it, that there are not a hundred persons in the whole population, consisting of upwards of nine thousand, who are unable to speak English so as to transact ordinary business through the medium of that language. Steps will immediately be taken to ascertain how many of this class are upon the roll, that your Honourable Board may perceive that the number is very small.
> In support of this inference, your memorialists can state from their own experience that the instances are extremely rare in which applicants are found incapable of answering in English such questions as may be asked of them. At the last meeting of the Board out of sixty poor persons who appeared only one person required an interpreter. The applicant however was a stranger and it was found afterwards that her ignorance of English was assumed as she conversed in that language with the Inspector.
> These views, as to the prevalence of English among the general population of the parish, are confirmed by many recent proceedings of the Parochial Authorities, proceedings which have been homologated by the Reverend protestor himself. That Reverend Gentleman lately moved and secured the appointment of a gentleman to the situation of session clerk who knows nothing of Gaelic. Within the last few years, seven teachers have been appointed to charity schools where the children of the poorest of the people are taught, and yet it is not known to the Board that the Reverend protestor objected to any of these teachers, on the ground of their notorious ignorance of Gaelic. That language is not taught in any school in the parish, with possibly the exception of Peninver, and the Presbytery of the bounds have found it expedient entirely to dispense with that language as a qualification in one of the ministers of the parish, and even after

this curtailment of the means of instruction in Gaelic had been effected, the protestor Mr McLean endeavoured to introduce English into the Gaelic Church in the afternoon.

On these grounds the Board, with the exception of the Reverend protestor, are unanimously of opinion that notwithstanding Mr Hunter's ignorance of Gaelic, he is fully qualified to discharge the duties of Inspector efficiently.[51]

Peter Hunter continued, despite the fuss, as inspector of poor in Campbeltown. There is, however, a curious postscript to that controversy. When the post was advertised some thirty years later, in August 1879, the qualification − 'must have Gaelic' − was written into the conditions of application.[52] The reasons may be conjectured.

The Gaelic Censuses of 1881 and 1891

Some use − albeit limited − of the Gaelic section of the 1881 Census has already been made, but I have to admit to a reluctance to base, on the findings of that census − the first to take account of the Gaelic-speaking population − any but the most general of conclusions. The Gaelic speakers in some districts − particularly in rural Kintyre − appear to have been fairly accurately represented, but in others − particularly in the burgh of Campbeltown − neglect and incompetence so marred the returns that absolutely no credence may be placed upon them. With most suspected omissions, no proof can be advanced, but what is to be made of such a sample − by no means isolated − as this, extracted from a single enumeration sheet for Lorne Street, Campbeltown? On that sheet appear a 36-year-old blacksmith, native to North Uist; a 50-year-old mason and his 43-year-old wife, both Islay-born; and a 52-year-old native of Luing. None of them is credited with Gaelic;[53] and that sample omits possible native Gaelic speakers, about which less certainty is admissible. One, or two perhaps, of these four individuals could, by some quirk of circumstance, have been born into a solidly Gaelic-speaking community and failed to have acquired the language, but almost assuredly not all.

The defects of that census soon became apparent. The *Campbeltown Courier* was moved to condemn the exercise as 'a miserable failure, if not, indeed, a farce'. In one populous district of Campbeltown, 176 schedules were distributed, and when these were returned, merely 29 Gaelic speakers were accounted for. A subsequent check produced, however, the revised figure of 125, but whether that amendment was incorporated in the census return remains, by the vagueness of the report, uncertain. The *Courier's* unequivocal conclusion was that 'on account of the bungling way it has been carried out, the Gaelic census must go for nothing'.[54] The *Oban Times*, published in the north of the county, was more strident in its condemnation:

> It will be remembered by many that the so-called Gaelic census was a bungle and a failure, very much owing to the inertness of our Parliamentary representatives, who are so much afraid of hampering the Government that they prefer to let matters be muddled. When, yielding to pressure, the Home Secretary agreed to allow a Gaelic census to be taken, the arrangements for such were so utterly inadequate and the instructions so very confusing that the returns are most incomplete and utterly untrustworthy . . . Might the member for Argyllshire (Lord Colin Campbell), who promised to learn Gaelic when wooing his constituency, not do something to get a fresh Gaelic census of the county which he occasionally represents in the House of Commons?[55]

The enumeration forms, in 1881, actually included no provision for the Gaelic census, and the information was simply cramped on to the ends of the regular particulars. That defect was amended in the subsequent census, of 1891, by the inclusion of a separate column in which the definitions 'Gaelic' and 'Gaelic and English' – i.e., monoglot Gaelic speaker, or bilingual speaker – could be noted.

As for the status of Irish speakers, no precise directions appear to have operated. The inclusion or exclusion of Irish speakers was entirely arbitrary, depending on the judgement – or lack of it – of the individual enumerators. Thus, in 1881 the middle-aged sisters Mary and Margaret MacCaig (Campbeltown-born, but of Rathlin parentage) are marked down as Gaelic-speaking; but in the subsequent census the fact goes unnoticed.[56] From the social and geographical origins of the immigrant population in south Kintyre a sizeable percentage of Irish speakers may safely be postulated, but of that there is no suggestion in either the 1881 or the 1891 censuses.

If incompetence, inconsistency and disorganisation blunted the impact of the Gaelic census in 1881, the exercise, nonetheless, was not without its values. These values emerge at the extremities of the material. Thus, for rural Kintyre at any rate, the broad pattern of Gaelic-speaking may be considered accurate, which, accepting that demography is not, and cannot be, an exact science, is adequate enough. Conversely, the individual strands of that pattern – where they can be perceived – may, with cautious handling, be trusted to convey something of the meaning in the patterns.

The returns of Gaelic speakers for the burgh of Campbeltown indicate 1040 in a population of 7693, or 13.5 per cent;[57] but there is that inescapable evidence of the inadequacy of the returns there, and so their implications may be ignored. In any case, the true summation – whatever it may have been – could only, at that late stage, have demonstrated a preponderance of migrant Gaelic speakers, principally from the rural districts of Kintyre. The vital evidence on the state of the language must be sought in these very districts. Two – the first bordering the north of Campbeltown parish, and the second the south – will serve as examples.

In Killean and Kilchenzie parish – its northern portion encompassing Largieside – 901 persons out of 1368, or 65.9 per cent, were returned as

Gaelic-speaking.[58] There is more to it than that, however. Closer analysis of the statistical breakdown reveals, significantly, but not surprisingly, a north to south pattern of reduction in Gaelic-speaking. In Rhunahaorine district 190 Gaelic speakers were counted in a population of 225; in Muasdale district, 221 in 271; and in Glenbarr district, 233 in 298. Going south from Glenbarr, however, the Gaelic totals decline progressively – 117 in 188 the length of Tangy, and 51 in 223 from Tangy to North Craigs, on the boundary of Campbeltown Parish.[59]

For Southend, 121 Gaelic speakers in a population of 955, or 12.7 per cent, were returned;[60] but, similarly, closer scrutiny reveals the predictable. The remote western end of the parish – encompassing Glenbreackerie and the scattered sheep-farms around the Mull – held no fewer than 72 Gaelic speakers in a total of 167, leaving merely 49 accountable for in the three other districts of the parish.[61] That proportional imbalance is entirely attributable to the Lowland presence in the prime farm lands of the eastern end.[62]

Approaching the other end of the statistical pattern – the minutiae of the composite – a couple of trends, deducible from oral tradition, become plain:

1. The failure, by many Gaelic-speaking parents, to transmit the language to their children. That trend was, in 1881, most pronounced in Campbeltown burgh, where erosive forces had most taken hold. Thus, as an example of contrasting attitudes, the five children of Maurice and Jane MacSporran, in 34 Dalaruan, their ages ranging from 22 to 8 years, were all Gaelic speakers, while of the three children of Donald and Barbara MacSporran, living next door in 36 Dalaruan, their ages ranging from 23 to 12 years, none had Gaelic. Both sets of parents were Gaelic speakers.[63]

2. Another characteristic which recurs in the census particulars is the absence of Gaelic in the lower age group of families. This has been explained, no doubt with some measure of validity, as attributable to a progressive disinclination among parents to take the trouble of furnishing later children with two languages.[64] A couple of instances will suffice. The two oldest children of James and Agnes MacDermid in High Street, Campbeltown were credited with Gaelic, while the younger two were not.[65] In Tarbert, the five oldest children of James and Catherine Law were Gaelic-speaking, while the succeeding three children were not.[66]

Anglicisation of Surnames

There is no doubt that for many an ambitious person, seeking an outlet for his energy and ability, and intent on social advancement, the Gaelic stamp on his character was reckoned a misfortune and a handicap. A vernacular manner of speech and the ingrained traits of upbringing may be eradicated, more or less, by conscious self-'correction', but what would one do with such a name as Brolachan or Loynachan?

The answer is, of course, that one would change it. But do motives of self-advancement explain the veritable rash of surname changes which took hold in the eighteenth century and which, by the end of the nineteenth, had radically altered the whole complexion of personal nomenclature in Kintyre? Such an explanation is unacceptable. That there was a definite reaction from native surnames of the type cited above is quite plain, but there is no evidence that the substitution of one name for another was in any sense premeditated. Rather, the changes appear to have occurred gradually and, to some degree, independently of any common agreement.

There were several factors operating in these changes, but all may be traced to a common source – an irreversible anglicising trend. In many cases, no doubt, the transformation of an offending surname proceeded with the acquiescence of individual bearers. There is an account – of uncertain origin, admittedly, but nonetheless with something of the smack of authenticity to it – of how Neil Brolachan came to renounce his distinguished surname and became, instead, plain Neil Brodie. He was born at Campbeltown in 1813, attended Glasgow University, and was ordained a minister in 1842.[67] He is best remembered in Kintyre as one of the reputed authors of the enduring local dialect song *Flory Loynachan.* In his first year at university he enrolled in the Latin class. When Professor William Ramsay was marking the roll, he came to the name Neil Brolachan. He paused, looked up at him, and asked: 'Where did you get that barbarous name?' The students laughed. As soon as the class had been dismissed, Neil, in a state of discomfiture, sought out the professor and told him that henceforth he wished to be known as Neil Brodie.[68] As much as can confidently be said is that he matriculated in 1830 as 'Niel Brolachan', and that by the time of his appearance in the junior Hebrew class in 1834/5, he had become 'Niel Brodie'.[69]

This account is interesting and illuminating as far as it goes, but it leaves unanswered a few significant questions, not the least of them being – why the name Brodie? Did that name already exist as an alternative? The answer must be that it did (p. 208). This example of the adoption, by sudden persuasion, of a substitute surname is quite singular, and will not explain the generality of surname changes. The explanation is, rather, to be found in the social milieu of the times, as a transformative influence operating from both within the Gaelic community, and without it. Accepting that the Lowlanders in Kintyre, and their descendants, disdained, in the main, to acquire a working knowledge of the Gaelic language, or – more likely – were under no necessity of doing so, then those native surnames which they found difficult to pronounce would tend to come under some euphonic adjustment. Call it corruption or call it improvement − the judgement would depend on which side of the linguistic divide one stood.

At the same time, in a society which − in south Kintyre, at any rate − was increasingly succumbing to Lowland ways and in which the Lowland model increasingly represented advancement in that society, Gaelic and the outward marks of the Gaelic character were becoming unavoidably *déclassé*. The reasoning, whether conscious or otherwise, may be expressed thus − if one's surname was being torn out of its Gaelic mould and hammered into something more resembling a Scotch or an English form, then why resist? The greater number of name changes were, therefore, simply the products of a long process of transmutation on the lips of people and at the hands of scribes who were ignorant of Gaelic orthography.

There was not necessarily, in that latter tendency, any sinister or repressive intention. A great deal of weight must be attached to the fact that most of those who acted officially − as notaries, registrars, and reporters of one kind or another − were either non-Gaelic or had learned their profession in a non-Gaelic environment. Registrars, for example, often manufactured English equivalents of Gaelic names. The Dean of Lismore was, in a well-recognised tradition of notaries-public, recording Gaelic names in a Scots framework, although he was enthusiastic and knowledge-able enough to compile the finest early anthology of Gaelic verse.[70]

Yet, a feature which stands out from the confused mass of Kintyre surnames is the persistence of the older, 'homely' forms not just in a traditional, oral context, but also side-by-side, in public records, with the modern forms. Appendix II is largely based on demonstrable surname alternation as found in eighteenth and nineteenth century records.

The notion that surnames prove hereditary association with a particular family or clan in a particular locality may be disposed of at once. The matter is not as simple as that, and 'clan guidebooks', whatever their romantic appeal, are of superficial value only. By exhaustive research one may successfully trace a surname to an expected origin. For the most part, however, the generality of ancestor worshippers will settle on the connections which are both obvious and pleasing. But in many cases the superficially most simple assumption is entirely wrong and misleading.

The whole substance of contemporary surnames is the product of a long simmering in the broth-pot of history, and so entirely mixed and interblended is the broth that the original constituents are difficult to separate. To take pride in one's given surname is a narrow conceit, and ignores the multi-tudinous other blood lines which fed one's unique conception. The paternal surname may deceive − proud Dugald MacMillan, strutting in kilt and brogues, may, in all other lines of descent, be of English − or Japanese − ancestry, while plain John Smith or Robert Taylor may be Gaelic to the root.

The discussion of Kintyre surnames in Appendix II has but one purpose – to demonstrate both the changeability and variability of surnames at work in the eighteenth and nineteenth centuries. A distinction should be drawn between the *existence* of surnames and the *use* of surnames. Surnames were not much used in the clan territories because, compared with patronymics, they were a poor means of identification. But, as the eponymous name was preserved in the collective name of the clan, it was always available, should need arise, to provide the surname of an individual member. Thus, a man might be known and best identified as *Iain mac Sheumais* ('John son of James', his patronymic), but he and his neighbours would know that he belonged to *Clann Mhaolain*. To obtain the surname, all that was necessary was to substitute *Mac* for *Clann*, thus *Mac Mhaolain* (MacMillan). Surnames, in that category, may therefore be dated from the period of the eponymous ancestors, which in the Gaelic west is usually the twelfth to the thirteenth centuries.[71]

In actuality, however, hereditary surnames were uncommon in the Highlands until the sixteenth and seventeenth centuries. When surnames came to be required for legal documents, some individuals adopted the name of their chief, or a recognised variant of it, and some settled for their own patronymic, while the surnames of others had an occupational origin or described personal characteristics.[72]

Adherents of particular clans were sometimes the victims of coercion, and motives of expediency – for example, the desire for the protection of a powerful family – frequently dictated individual affiliations. Many surnames, individually examined, are thus of spurious origin. Add to these factors the veritable muddle of corruption and disguise of surnames, and the historical pattern – where it can be defined – is a very thin one.

REFERENCES AND NOTES

1. *NSA*, Vol. 7, 428.
2. '. . . The Lowlanders complained of the occasional absence of the parish minister . . .' *Ib.*
3. A. J. MacVicar, *The Book of Blaan*, Oban 1965, 25, 33. The first Relief Church minister, the Rev. Alexander Laing, was ordained in June 1799.
4. A. J. MacVicar, *The Rev. Dr. John Smith of Campbeltown*, Campbeltown 1934, 2-3.
5. *Argyll, Volume 1: Kintyre*, 'An Inventory of the Ancient Monuments', HMSO 1971, 103.
6. C. Mactaggart, *The Lowland Church of Campbeltown from its Foundation in 1654 till the Disruption*, Campbeltown 1925, 3 (quoting from 'an old minute, which was recorded by the Managers of the Longrow Church, when the Longrow Congregation seceded from the Lowland Church in 1767').
7. *Ib.*
8. MacVicar, *The Rev. Dr. John Smith, op. cit.*, 3 (quoting minutes of the Presbytery of Kintyre, 1 Dec. 1790).

9. *Ib.*, 4.

10. *OSA,* Vol. 10, 546.

11. MacVicar, *The Rev. Dr. John Smith, op. cit.,* 4.

12. *Argyll, Vol. 1, op. cit.,* 105.

13. A. McKerral, *Kintyre in the Seventeenth Century,* Edinburgh 1948, 150-1.

14. Min Bks TC Cam, e.g., 'As there is a prospect that at May next Mr Thomson the Doctor to the English Schooll will succeed Mr Mollison as Rector . . .' (4 March 1788). Also 27 May 1768, 4 April 1777, 15 March 1784, and on until 1 July 1795.

15. *History of Kintyre,* Campbeltown 1930 (3rd edition), 11.

16. N. M. Holmer, *The Gaelic of Kintyre,* Dublin 1962, 131.

17. Translation by Mr K. D. MacDonald, 1981.

18. H. L. Mackenzie, 'A Country School a Hundred Years Ago', *TKM* No. 12, 10.

19. C81 K & K Par/d4/p1. At the School House, Ballochantee, with his wife Margaret, aged 46, a native of St Ninians, Stirlingshire, six children, and a housekeeper, also of St Ninians. None of the household had Gaelic.

20. M. MacDonald, archivist, Argyll and Bute District Council, Inveraray, letter to author, 17 Jan. 1983.

21. Log-book of Drumlemble General Assembly/Public School, 4 June 1873, 165.

22. *Ib.,* 26 May 1874.

23. M. MacDonald, letter to author, 25 Jan. 1983. In 1886 and 1887 Thomson was living at Overnewton, Glasgow.

24. Log-book of Rhunahaorine School, 461.

25. *Ib.,* 472.

26. Undated cutting pasted on to the front cover of a minute-book of the School Board of Kilcalmonell and Kilberry, in Argyll and Bute District archive, Inveraray. Other like cuttings, referring to both Clachan and Whitehouse schools, in the period 1895 to 1899, and recommending an 'ability to teach Gaelic', are preserved in the same minute-book.

27. Min Bk School Board of Kilcalmonell and Kilberry (above), 6 April 1889.

28. He wrote *A History of France* in three volumes, and contributed chapters to the *Cambridge Modern History* − Obit., *CC,* 24 Sept. 1921.

29. *The Times,* 21 July 1906.

30. J. A. Smith, 'Gaelic and Education', in *The future of the Highlands* (ed. D. S. Thomson and I. Grimble), London 1968, 62.

31. *The Ring-Net Fishermen,* Edinburgh 1981, 44.

32. *NSA,* Kilcalmonell and Kilberry, 410.

33. Obit., *CC,* 11 Feb. 1939.

34. 15 July 1977.

35. *Dialect of South Kintyre,* Campbeltown 1934, 3.

36. C81. John Houston, 52, shepherd at Lailt, So Par, d1/p7; William Mitchell, 56, drainer at Low Rhunahaorine, K & K Par, d1/p3; David Watson, 57, fisherman, Seafield Cottage, K & K Par, d2/p15; Archibald Watson, Cam Par, d14/p13 − all born in Campbeltown parish.

37. *WHT,* 5-6.

38. C81. *Armour* − Archibald, 66, farmer in Rosehill, K & K Par, d3/p15; Archibald, 29, farmer in West Killarrow, K & K Par, d5/p2; John, 59, farmer in Monebacach, Skip Par, d1/p2; Robert, 26, distillery workman, Dalaruan Terrace, Cam, d12/p26; William, 61, 'malster', Broad Street, Cam, d13/p28; John, 43, carter, Longrow, Cam, d17/p4. *Blackstock* − John, 41, ploughman, East Killarrow, K & K Par, d5/p4; Duncan, 60, shepherd in Glemanuillt, So Par, d1/p3. *Colville* − Robert, 54, distillery workman, Millknowe, Cam, d14/p21. *Mitchell* − Charles, 24, distillery workman, Millknowe, Cam, d14/p15. *Wallace* −

Archibald, 56, labourer, Mill Hamlet, So Par, d3/p17; Robert, 84, agricultural labourer, Saddell Village, d1/p3; Donald, 48, distillery workman, Dalaruan, Cam, d12/p15.

39. *Ib. Bruce* – Colin, 44, fisherman, d1/p18; John, 35, fisherman, d1/p43; James, 43, fisherman, d1/p46; William, 61, fisherman, d3/p9. *Hay* – William, 38, fish-merchant, d1/p5; Robert, 28, fish-merchant, d1/p5; George, 36, herring-buyer, d1/p17. *Law* – Archibald, 46, fisherman, d1/p27; George, 35, fisherman, d1/p45; James, 45, fisherman, d3/p13; John, 42, fisherman, d3/p16.

40. *Ib. Allan* – Richard, 25, fisherman, Torrisdale Square, Sad Par, d2/p4. *Blackstock* – Gilbert, 60, farm manager, High Ugadale, Sad Par, d1/p1. *Bruce* – Duncan, 40, fisherman, Lephenbeg, Sad Par, d2/p2. *Mitchell* – John, 27, fisherman, Waterfoot, Sad Par, d2/p1; Neil, 55, crofter, Upper Torrisdale, Sad Par, d2/p3; John, 53, maltman, Broad Street, Cam, d13/p26. *Muir* – John, 54, fisherman, Kirk Street, Cam, d21/p7. *Wallace* – Archibald, 60, distillery workman, Kirk Street, Cam, d21/p8.

41. Holmer, *op. cit.*, 1.

42. James MacDonald, AD14 56/199, 27 – '. . . I was one of the party at the "caelach" or harvest home in MacMillan's house.' The *cailleach* celebration took its name from the last sheaf of corn cut from the harvest field. There was great competition to secure that prize, and even when reaping with machine 'it was a race to see who would get the last sheaf' (Alexander MacDougall, Clachan, 3 March 1977). That corn would be taken home, plaited, adorned with ribbons, and hung in the house.

43. Precognition against Duncan MacConochy, AD14 56/199.

44. C K & K Par, d2/p10.

45. Obit., *CC*, 11 Feb 1939.

46. *Ib.*, 22 Oct. 1910.

47. 'The Alleged Fire-Raising at Tarbert – Trial of Douglas', *ib.*, 12 May 1888.

48. *Fasti Ecclesiae Scoticanae*, Vol. 4, Edinburgh 1920, 51.

49. 'Reasons of Protest and Appeal', dated 1 April 1848, Min Bk PB Cam, 3 April 1848.

50. *Ib.*, transcript of letter from Board of Supervision, Edinburgh, dated 14 April 1848.

51. *Ib.*, 2 May 1848.

52. *CC*, 30 Aug. 1879.

53. C81/d20/p13.

54. *CC*, 9 April 1881.

55. Quoted *ib.*, 3 Sept. 1881. The Census Bill for Scotland was introduced into the House of Lords on 16 July 1880, and quickly passed to the House of Commons, obtaining Royal Assent on 7 September of that year. During that brief period, very little debate concerning the issue of the Gaelic census appeared in *Hansard*, or any other parliamentary record, up to Sunday, 3 April 1881, when the actual census was taken. From the available evidence it seems clear that the pressure to secure a Gaelic census originated outwith Parliament – the Federation of Celtic Associations of Scotland and the Committee of the Free Church of Scotland are specifically mentioned in *Hansard* (2 August 1880). But as late as 10 January 1881, the Home Secretary, Sir William Harcourt, was arguing that 'the question whether such a Census should be taken had been considered, and it was thought, on the whole, that the advantage of doing so would not be correspondent with the trouble and expense of it'. He saw 'no reason for altering that decision'. By then, the census date was less than three months off. That decision was altered, but when and by what means remains obscure. There is little doubt, however, that the delay in yielding to the Gaelic interest spawned the troubles which largely invalidated the exercise.

56. C81/d15/p13; *ib.*, 91/d15/p9.

57. *Census of the Population of Scotland 1881*, HMSO 1892, Vol. I, 142.

58. *Ib.*, 115.

59. C1881, Registration District 519, Enumeration Divisions 1-5.

60. *Census of the Population of Scotland 1881, op. cit.,* 115.

61. C1881, Registration District 532, Enumeration Divisions 1-4.

62. The point is worth emphasising that Lowland immigration to Kintyre did not begin and end in the seventeenth century. It continued intermittently, and continues still. The censuses provide evidence of an extensive nineteenth century immigration of Lowland farmers to Kintyre, and particularly to Southend Parish. From the 1881 Census of that parish: Division 2 – Janet Craig, 57, farmer's widow in Cattadale, from Mearns, Renfrews. (p. 1); George Macrae, 54, in Cattadale More, from Tarbolton, Ayrs. (p. 1); John Galbraith, 57, in Drumavuling, from Dalrymple, Ayrs. (p. 2); James Hislop, 34, in Brecklat, from Lanarks. (p. 7); Thomas Young, 42, in Knockstaple, from Beith, Ayrs. (p. 7); Andrew Ronald, 36, in Dalmore, from West Kilbride, Ayrs. (p. 8). Division 3 – William Hunter, 63, in Machribeg, from W. Kilbride (p. 9). Division 4 – John Wilson, 30, in Blasthill, from Kilbride, Ayrs. (p. 2); John Barbour, 38, in Aucharua, from W. Kilbride, (p. 3); Andrew Ronald, 71, in Pennysearoch, from Cumnock, Ayrs. (p. 4); James Cuthbertson, 55, in Kilmashanachan, from Stewarton, Ayrs. (p. 4); Robert Wylie, 55, in Macharioch, from Kilbirnie, Ayrs. (p. 6); James Gibson, 66, in Glenaharvy, from Ayrs. (p. 7); James Smillie, 74, in Eden, from Ardrossan, Ayrs. (p. 10).

63. C/d12/pp 22-23.

64. Nan (MacNab) Cowley, a native of Minard, Lochfyneside, recorded 16 Feb. 1977, observed that she and her sister – the oldest two of the family – spoke fluent Gaelic, but that the degree of capability in the language diminished child by child, leaving her two youngest sisters entirely without Gaelic – 'they hadn't even a *blas* (accent)'.

65. C/d12/p5.

66. *Ib.*/d3/p13.

67. *Fasti, op. cit.,* Vol. 3, 111.

68. MacVicar, *The Book of Blaan, op. cit.,* 60. He refers erroneously to 'John Brollachan'.

69. M. Moss, University of Glasgow archivist, letter to author, 25 March 1983.

70. Prof. D. S. Thomson, letter to author, 11 Dec. 1983.

71. Rev. W. Matheson, letter to author, 14 Dec. 1983.

72. R. W. and J. M. Munro, 'Clans', *A Companion to Scottish Culture* (ed. D. Daiches), London 1981, 67.

CHAPTER 3

George Campbell Hay: Bard of Kintyre

The accomplishments of George Campbell Hay have not, it may fairly be claimed, been accorded the degree of recognition which they deserve – not least of all in his native Kintyre. The reasons are not difficult to deduce. The poet, while generally acknowledged to be working language to its highest level of expression, has, since the ascendancy of the novel in the nineteenth century, been increasingly obliged to direct his talents towards a circumscribed readership. This observation is the more relevant applied to a poet such as Campbell Hay, whose preferred languages are Scots and Gaelic. There is, thus, in the matter of communication, limitation within limitation.

The need for publication of a fairly comprehensive collection of Campbell Hay's poetry – incorporating the bulk of his three volumes, which have since become rarities on the book market, and the best of his later work – is long overdue. These three volumes appeared within a six-year period after the war – *Fuaran Sléibh* ('The Hill Spring') in 1947, *Wind on Loch Fyne* in 1948, and *O na Ceithir Àirdean* ('From the Four Airts') in 1952. There followed a long recession, which ended only in 1970, with the appearance of stimulating selections from these three books in *Four Points of a Saltire*,[1] now out of print. Six years later, a further selection – from the two Gaelic volumes, and supplemented by a later, uncollected poem, *An Ciùran Ceòban Ceò* (p. 59) – was published in the bilingual anthology *Nua-Bhàrdachd Ghàidhlig* ('Modern Scottish Gaelic Poems'),[2] which remains in print and will serve as a valuable, if limited, introduction to Campbell Hay's work.

The restoration to public notice of Campbell Hay's verse was further advanced by the publication, in 1982, of his long poem *Mochtàr is Dùghall* by the Department of Celtic at Glasgow University, and by Campbell Hay's receipt, in October of the following year, of An Comann Gaidhealach's Gaelic Writer's Award.[3] That award generated a good deal of media interest, but Campbell Hay himself, characteristically, kept out of it. Nonetheless, he confessed privately to be 'pleased and proud about the award'.[4]

The publication of *Mochtàr is Dùghall* gave George a good deal of personal pleasure, though the poem remains unfinished. On 29 December 1980, just a month after George had approved the poem's publication, I received a letter from him in which he reported that he was 'working on *Mokhtar and Dougall* and [had] already added a few lines to it', but that happy momentum was lost and, in the end, the poem was issued in substantially the form in which it had slumbered, chrysalis-like, in his keeping for almost forty years. Of that unfinished state, Iain Crichton Smith remarked, in a review of the book:

The poem we have here, if completed, would have been one of the most important poems in modern Scottish literature. But even as it stands, its close detailed imaginative description of the desert, its insight into the Arab mind and traditions and history, its compassion, and many beautiful lyrical passages haunt one with a grave beauty.[5]

The poem opens with the deaths, on the Tunisian *jebel* (mountain), of the Arab Mokhtar and the Gael Dougall, representatives of disparate cultures, who 'have met in an everlasting fellowship without conversation' (*Mhochtàir is Dhùghaill, choinnich sibh an comann buan gun chòmhradh*). The poem was a product of the Second World War, which took Campbell Hay to North Africa. It was begun while on active service in Italy, towards the end of that war, and added to in Greece and in his native Tarbert.[6]

I first encountered Campbell Hay's poetry in 1967, as a boy of fifteen years, who, quickened by a creative stirring, had begun to read eagerly. I found my way to *The Oxford Book of Scottish Verse* and in that anthology read, with a thrill of association which I can recover still, his poem *The Two Neighbours*, on the dying of an old Tarbert skipper, and the vigil kept at the bed of death by the man's fishing partner, or 'neebor', of a time past. I wrote immediately to Campbell Hay's last publishers, Oliver and Boyd, who were able to supply an address at which, they suggested uncertainly, I might be able to contact the poet. I wrote to George, in what manner of boyish exuberance I cannot now recall, and waited. He replied, and immense was my delight and pride – indeed, disbelief, for I had not really expected that I should ever hear from him – on that morning when I took the letter out of its envelope and realised that George Campbell Hay had written to me!

We became friends. The formative elements common to our backgrounds – love of Kintyre, a fascination with herring fishing and its traditions, and the poetic practice – assured such a bonding. This account is, therefore, an appreciation of one whose being and, properly, whose poetic faculty, have contributed an indefinable something to my own being, a spiritual infusion. When I return, as I often do, to his poetry, I am that boy again, astounded by the magic of the familiar, transmuted mysteriously by that power which all art generates.

John MacDougall Hay

He was the son of John MacDougall Hay, whose literary reputation – established on a single, irresistible novel, *Gillespie*, set in nineteenth century Tarbert – has recently emerged from a long eclipse. The Hay family in Tarbert was founded by William, who was of Ayrshire – probably Dunure[7] – origin, and whose settlement in Tarbert may be dated approximately to the 1830s.[8] He married a native of the place, Margaret MacFarlane.[9] He was a fish merchant, as were three of his four sons after him. These sons were all Gaelic-speaking (p. 34), but that language endured in the family only a generation and was lost with them. John MacDougall Hay, therefore, was without Gaelic – a want which he ever regretted[10] – and it was left to his son, George, to repair the break, and, by an extraordinary interaction of circumstances – not the least of which was his father's early death – to ensure that the last Gaelic bard of Kintyre (and a major one at that) was, nominally at least, of Lowland ancestry. That the Gaelic literary tradition of Kintyre should have so ended is, perhaps, hardly surprising, viewed within the crumbling hall of mirrors in which is reflected the cultural physiognomy of that diverse stock.

John MacDougall Hay was born in Tarbert on 23 October 1879, the fourth child of George Hay and Mary MacDougall, who was the daughter of Alexander MacDougall, fisherman, and Mary MacKinlay.[11] After schooling in the village, he entered Glasgow University in 1898 on an open bursary.[12] His academic achievement was extraordinary,[13] the more so considering that he had already dedicated himself to writing. A university colleague remarked of him: 'He wrote many articles in those days, and we often used to wonder how he got time to gain class prizes. I asked him once, and his answer is worth recording: "I cannot tell, for a university is an institution where one must not on any account be original. A professor is a man who has learned the art of stealing from the printed labours of some scholar; the prize-man one who has learned to steal from the professor."'[14]

Having taken an M.A. degree in 1901,[15] he decided on a teaching career, and in March 1902 took up an appointment as headmaster of Lionel School in Lewis. His employment there ended in February 1905.[16] His teaching career also ended there, for he had resolved to become a minister. He enrolled in the Church of Scotland Divinity Hall, and distinguished himself academically there too. He was licensed by the Presbytery of Inveraray in 1908, and ordained a minister of the parish of Elderslie, Renfrewshire on 12 May 1909.[17] He remained there, increasingly debilitated by ill health, until his death, ten years later, of tuberculosis.[18]

Gillespie, which was published in 1914, was MacDougall Hay's first novel (his second, and last book, *Barnacles*, followed two years later, but has remained unpopular). It was received with almost unified critical acclaim, both in Britain and in the United States. The *Campbeltown Courier*, even, had its say, and concluded on the cheerful assumption that 'it must be pleasing to Argyllshire folks to hear that their old western county has produced another novelist of first rank [a reference, no doubt, to Neil Munro], and one who is likely to go far . . .'[19] The novel was not, however, received with such generosity in MacDougall Hay's native Tarbert. There was too much reality in it . . . or too much disfiguring invention, as some of its detractors maintained. The shock which that book's appearance sent through the community has only recently passed from living memory.

In an early article, published anonymously in the *Glasgow Evening News,* MacDougall Hay set out what amounted, virtually, to a blueprint for the uncompromising social realism which characterised *Gillespie* and which, in parts, by its excess, came close to critically weakening the work. The article was published in 1903. He was just twenty-four years of age, and the publication of his masterpiece was eleven years off:

> To the sceptical Englishman or American, who has doubts as to the reality of Scottish life depicted in the incisive pages of *The House with the Green Shutters,* a Saturday night in a Lochfyne fishing village would do much to show that George Douglas Brown's directness in the Balzacian sense (if the phrase can be used) is no mere trick of the trade of making books, but the outcome of what he saw and heard. Barbie is inherently Scottish, and if there are rather too many gallons of whisky on the pages of the book, it is a fault to be condoned, in respect of the sentimental slush of the lesser kailyairders.[20]

That article was titled 'With the Lochfyne Men' and described in the most uncompromising of language, heavily seasoned with the vernacular of Tarbert, the revelry and brutality of a village Saturday night. The tone and content of the piece were dourly disputed by a local laird, James Campbell of Stonefield, who ended his complaint on the judgement: 'Anonymous contributors are seldom worth much.'[21]

George Campbell Hay was born on 8 December, 1915, at Elderslie, during his father's ministry there. After John MacDougall Hay's death in December, 1919, two days after his son's fourth birthday, the little family – Catherine Hay, George, and his eight-year-old sister Sheena – removed to Tarbert.[22]

MacDougall Hay was a divinity student when, during a vacation in Tarbert, he met his wife.[23] They were married at Knap House, Tarbert, on 29 October, 1909.[24]

Maternal Antecedents

Catherine Hay's connection with Tarbert was not, however, solely the result of marriage. Her mother, Jessie MacMillan, was a native of Tarbert. She was the daughter of Hugh MacMillan in Tarbert – separately described as 'feuar' (i.e. one who rents land in perpetuity) and 'ploughman'[25] – and Catherine McIntosh.[26] Hugh MacMillan himself was the son of Angus MacMillan, farmer, and Janet Johnstone.[27] The family tradition, as George has it, identifies Kennacraig, on the southern shore of West Loch Tarbert, as the place in which Hugh MacMillan and his family were established, but of that I have been unable to find evidence. He was said to have worked a croft there,[28] and he may well have done so in his earlier years.

Of his father's people (the Hay line in Tarbert is now extinct) George knew very little. The family traditions of his mother's line understandably were the more immediate to him. She was a Campbell, whence George's middle name, his Gaelic stamp as it were. Her father, Duncan Campbell, was a native of Knapdale – the son of Archibald Campbell, farmer, and Jane Fletcher[29] – though brought up at Gruinard, on the west side of Islay. He farmed in early manhood, first with his father, and later independently. During the religious revival which swept across Scotland in 1859 and 1860, Duncan Campbell experienced, as his obituarist loftily put it, 'the realities of eternity'. He became an evangelist and finally, in 1863, took his hand from the plough and enrolled at Glasgow University.[30]

After completing his divinity course at the Free Church College, Glasgow, following an Arts degree, he went to Tarbert and ministered to the Free Church congregation there during the final illness of the Rev. John Campbell. His meeting with Jessie MacMillan belongs presumably to that period. Upon John Campbell's death in 1874, Duncan Campbell was one of those chosen by a majority of the Tarbert congregation, but simultaneously, however, he was unanimously 'called' by the Free Church congregation of Kilfinan, which call he accepted.[31] He was ordained at Kilfinan in 1877.[32] Four years later, in Tarbert, he married Jessie MacMillan, then a shopkeeper.[33]

He would conduct a service in Gaelic, and, immediately after, a service in English, through both of which Catherine Campbell – who was born in 1883 at Auchenlochan, near Tighnabruaich[34] – had to sit as a child.[35] The extent of that parish – incorporating, as it did, three churches – finally broke him down physically. On the day before his death, on 1 June 1891, 'he had the most unbroken peace and joy, and seemed completely loosened from all human concerns, wholly resigned to the Father's will. Early on Sabbath morning he exclaimed in the language of Hugh McKail: "Farewell all earthly delights, welcome blessed Jesus, welcome eternal glory."' He died that day, and was buried in the graveyard of Kilfinan, Lochfyneside.[36] One child only was born of the marriage.

Duncan Campbell was possessed, perhaps, of less of that moral ascerbity which characterised many of his counterparts of the time. George is fond of relating an apposite little story which belongs to the period of his grandfather's ministry at Kilfinan. Campbell had been accustomed, on certain weekdays, to crossing the Cowal hills and conducting services in outlying farmhouses:

> One late evening he went over the hill to a farm called Stiallaig, which is well known, and he came in the dusk and he knocked on the kitchen door, and the serving lassie was expecting her boy, and she opened the kitchen door and in the dusk she saw the figure of a man standing outside the door, and she flung her arms round his neck and she kissed him, and . . . *'Bi falbh, a ghràidh, tha'm ministear a' tighinn a-nochd'* (Away, love, the minister's coming tonight). I daresay he would laugh at it.[37]

Tarbert: The Formative Years

At about the age of ten years George was sent to Edinburgh to attend John Watson's College. He was scarcely pleased with the arrangement, and would have preferred to have 'stayed in Tarbert and been a fisherman'.[38] He attended that school for four years and then, in 1929, went with a scholarship to Fettes College, also in Edinburgh. Another scholarship took him to Corpus Christi College, Oxford in 1934.

Tarbert, however, he considered his true home, and it was to the village he returned during vacations. There he was sedulously acquiring another more personal and more passionate education. He was gathering into himself the foundation of a Gaelic knowledge which would later, structured by study of the literature and grammar of the language, furnish him with the materials of the major branch of his art. George was not a native Gaelic speaker; neither was he, however, a 'learner' in the accepted sense of one who adopts, in maturity, a supplementary language. His acquisition of Gaelic began in early childhood, facilitated, no doubt, by the easy, unselfconscious receptiveness of the child and by his own exceptional linguistic aptitude. He claims that his awakening to Gaelic began at the age of six years.[39]

The primary inclination was stimulated by his mother, he believes. Though not herself fluent in the language, she had some knowledge – her parents had both been native speakers – and enough to open a door for him on that other culture which, in Tarbert then, was nearing its end. That interest which his mother unwittingly stimulated his grand-aunts, Elizabeth and Ann, were to foster. They were then both old women. Ann had been the wife of the Rev. Duncan MacLean Black, a native of Tarbert, to whom had been attached the undignified nick-name 'the Dooker Minister', in recognition of his passion for the shooting and eating of guillemots,[40] known in Tarbert as *dookers*. He was Free Church minister at Eccles, Berwickshire until his retirement in 1912. Some time after his death, in 1916,[41] Elizabeth moved into Ingleside, and the sisters were again, as in their distant childhood, together and companionable.

George would be asking them continually what was Gaelic for this and for that, and so his knowledge broadened steadily. Though native Gaelic speakers, the sisters did not use the language habitually in their home. George's sister, Sheena, once heard them sing, one to the other, the verses of a Gaelic waulking song, but the Gaelic content of their everyday speech was limited to occasional intrusive words. George explained: 'They weren't speaking it, because they would be brought up in the old tradition, the Gaelic language is a terrible thing, ye know. The old tradition – it's gone. And they thought – This boy is keen on Gaelic; we'll spoil him; we'll teach him some Gaelic.' Three peculiar old words he recalled particularly from their instruction: *croidhe,* for *cridhe* ('heart'); *eisge* for *uisge* ('water'),[42] and *cursta* ('accursed').[43]

He found his way, in time, to Gaelic literature, of which the bookshelves at Ingleside contained some volumes. The Gaelic Bible he read, and sermons in the language − arid stuff for a boy of his years, it may be thought − and a few old anthologies of Gaelic verse.

His cultural debt to the kindly old sisters was a great one, which he repaid generously in his *Cuimhneachan do Ealasaid agus Anna NicMhaoilein* ('In Memoriam for Elizabeth and Ann MacMillan'), in which Sorley Maclean found a 'quiet grace'.[44] George himself left the poem untranslated in the volume in which it appeared, *O na Ceithir Àirdean,* and the following is my own English version, which is partly a fusion and partly a reworking of translations provided for this book by Iain Crichton Smith and by George himself. I quote the entire poem, for it says much of George's attachment to the two old ladies − much that, otherwise, might not have been expressed:

> Lying in Cill Aindreis[45] are two old women who nurtured me; women who, though old, made this life beautiful with their deeds; Eliza together with Ann, they had breadth of spirit and kindliness and liberality; they devoted a whole lifetime to giving, but a single year took them to the graveyard.
>
> Nobility of bearing, gentleness of speech, affability, cheer and greatness of heart − who would have thought that old women would have been a cause of wonder for these? So were Elizabeth and Ann, with a zest more natural to youth; the old generosity of the Gael came alive again in their ways.
>
> The old kind world that opened itself through you at every step − we may say, alas, it was but 'a dream of the past'. We would be fortunate if the two of you had left behind you as a gift, and if the people of this sore world could get, a half of the blessings you had to give.
>
> You never bent head or mind, Eliza, to anything that was worthless; and Ann, liberal, loving and happy, you never closed hand or door. I see you with your smile at the head of the table, distributing to the rest; and if you are still about the old place, you are a generous and welcoming spirit.

Calum Johnson

George was still a boy when there entered his life someone else who was to exercise a shaping role on his eager venture into that diminished Gaelic world which lay, submerged for the most part, around him. That such a role was given to him, as it were, would have surprised that man, for Calum Johnson died while George was abroad, during the war years, and before the publication of the three collections of verse in which, were he to have read them, he would have recognised something of his own experience and knowledge which George had taken and reserved for − but did he know it then, himself? − the poetic course which lay before him.

Calum Johnson was 66 years old when he died at Springside, Tarbert, on 25 April, 1944.[46] His grandfather, John Johnson, and his father, Malcolm Johnson – better known in Tarbert as 'Calum Pheigi',[47] or 'Peggy's Malcolm', after his mother, Margaret Sinclair – were fishermen before him. Mr Ronald Johnson, Lochgilphead, has provided a few personal memories of Calum, who, though a grand-uncle of his, was invariably known to him as 'Uncle Malky':

> Malcolm Johnson, like the rest of his six brothers, was about six feet tall, well-built and never overweight. To me, he was always of a fairly serious disposition and, like many fishermen of his day, superstitious. I remember him sending me for matches (he smoked a pipe) and being told to bring 'Pearl' matches and not 'Swans'. He hated me to whistle on the boat.[48]

The superstitiousness, as Ronnie Johnson has described it, of Calum Johnson, and, it may be agreed, the majority of his contemporaries, was sustained at a much deeper level than these two examples – which are common to the cultural fabric of most Scottish fishing communities – would suggest. The phenomenon of the *céinteach* I shall illustrate here, with a story of the late Hugh MacFarlane's, both because it concerns some brothers of Calum Johnson's and because Campbell Hay himself employed the little wailing woman of the Gaelic supernatural tradition (p. 60).

Five or six of these Johnson brothers were walking on the hill to the south of Tarbert and stopped to refresh themselves at the spring known as Jacob's Well or Tobar an Tighearna. One of them there was confronted – whether 'materially' or by some projection of his own unconscious – with the vision of a 'wee wife' weeping incessantly. The intensity of the experience, however it may be explained, was such that he put his brothers – who could neither see nor hear anything uncanny – into a panic, and the whole company dispersed off the hill in a blind rush. Hugh was returning that evening to his home at the Battery when he encountered two of the brothers running towards him. They were shouting to him, 'Oh, bolt, bolt quick – ye'll be nelled (nailed)!' They entreated him to 'come on up tae the gate wi' us', and he left them home, in what state of unreasoning fear he could merely guess at.[49]

George described Calum Johnson simply: 'He had grey eyes and a rugged face.'[50]

Dougie Leitch's boatshed stood on the south side of Tarbert harbour, below the grassy patch which was called Earrann Ghoineach (the Sandy Portion). In front of that shed lay an old log on which the men of the village would seat themselves to take a smoke, and gaze out across the harbour, and talk in the easy ways of those accustomed to the liberality of time, and familiar, one with the other, so that neither passion nor constraint put its mark upon their tongues. They would gather, too, in the shed, and stand talking, or busy themselves with the whittling of wood. The conversation was often in Gaelic, and George was drawn to the shed and took his quiet place among the men, asking no questions, and seeming not to listen.

The boatbuilder, Dougie Leitch, was usually there himself. He understood the Gaelic conversation, but would seldom venture on speech. One day George was listening to the men on the log talking away in Gaelic, and when he broke clear and was passing the window of the shed, Dougie appeared and declared: *'Chan 'eil an duine glic ag ràdh diog'* (The wise man is not saying a thing).[51]

It was there that the young George encountered Calum Johnson, whose skiff, the *Liberator,* lay at moorings a little distance offshore, below the stark, upright frames of the net-poles, or *croich.*[52] George would sit beside Calum on the log and talk with him, and so got to know him well enough to declare one day: 'Oh, I'll go to the fishing.' Thus was conceived the great and informed interest in herring fishing which cuts a sure course through the current of Campbell Hay's verse. Some of his finest verse had its origin in the experiences which opened to him in the summer and autumn night fishings with Calum Johnson in his little *Liberator.*

George was about 16 years old when his apprenticeship – informal and incomplete though it was – to the sea and fishing began. Calum Johnson worked at ring-netting, in partnership with Archibald MacCaig, whose *Seònaid* was the *Liberator's* neighbour-boat (*commanach* or *coindeag,* as that was in the Gaelic of Tarbert).[53] George's work, with each set of the net, was to haul in the 'bow corks', which is the buoyant upper – or 'back' – rope of the net, from which the enclosing walls of netting hang. His role would certainly not have been one contrived to satisfy a boy's enthusiasm, for the Tarbert ring-net skiffs carried minimal crews of four men, unlike those of Campbeltown and, in the main, Carradale, on which an additional, fifth, member was carried, customarily a boy. His function, in the fishing operation, was to do just what George did – haul in the back-rope.

George was going to sea most nights throughout his summer vacations. During those years he maintained the self-imposed discipline – both unexplained and inexplicable – of asking no questions, but for a single exception. He decided to ask Calum Johnson a question, 'to try it out', and that question was on the meaning of *crùisle,* a word which he had acquired in his reading. Calum replied, 'a family vault', which was exact, and satisfied George.[54] Despite his shrinking from active enquiry, the sum of the knowledge which he assimilated was both substantial and diverse. That knowledge encompassed the practice and the lore of herring fishing, the Gaelic and Scots nomenclature of the community at Tarbert, and the intimately sustained chain of fishermen's place-names along Lochfyneside and around the village. These many and varied elements were later to be built, purposefully and conscientiously, into the structure of his verse, as a verbal embodiment of that old Tarbert from which he was separated (by distance and by the aftermath of a war from which he returned altered in mind) and which he sought to perpetuate in the workings of his craft.

Campbell Hay's relationship to his homeland, as expressed in his verse, differs markedly from that of his contemporaries in Gaelic poetry, all of whom explore that relationship to greater or lesser degrees. He is patently less interested in the demonstration and analysis of his sense of belonging to a specific community. His feelings appear to be directed primarily to the physical reality of his homeland rather than to its people. In *Luinneag* (p. 59), for instance, his nostalgia feeds upon his feeling for nature, as embodied in the physical Kintyre, rather than on thoughts of a community.

This is no doubt explicable by his separations (however incomplete) from Tarbert – first as a schoolboy, then as a student at Oxford, and finally as a soldier in the war years. That detachment from his community was, perhaps, early intimated by his reluctance to move into an active social role, exemplified by his reticence and by his passion for solitary hill-walking around Tarbert.

His minimal social involvement allowed him the freedom to accept, rather than question the community ethos, which he worked from to create his verse, rather than worked into the verse itself. 'Inheritance', in the Gaelic sense of *dùthchas*, is a more central fascination for him than for his contemporaries, and he conceives his homeland and home community as part of that broad tradition, rather than as a separate set of relationships to be explored.

The Poetic Value of Place-Names

The recurrent device of summoning into his expression the place-name, as a kind of ready-made poetic form within the larger form of the poem proper, is a distinctive mark in the verse of Campbell Hay. That traditional device has served, for him, to bring on to the stage of language the support of an extant tradition, with all its inherent – if inherently personal – poetic values. The practice not only gathers benefit into itself, by the enrichment of the verse, but projects benefit also, by the perpetuation of these names in contexts far removed, and more widely assimilable, than the localised origins out of which they were taken.

Analysis of the internal symbolism of literature – the vital organs, as it were, which sustain a work from within, essential to it, yet concealed beneath the skin of it, and (the point) neither intended nor required to be laid open – has become increasingly the preoccupation of a certain class of critic, for whom the creation itself is subordinated to the riddle of its conception. This operation has its fascination, and may well recognise its antecedents in the scientific tradition, but I have no intention of dissecting, part by part, the body of Campbell Hay's poetic work, even if that were possible and if the scope were available in this chapter.

The potency of the place-name in the poetic work of Campbell Hay is no more plainly realised than in his English poem *Kintyre*, which is a model of impeccably controlled sentiment. The conjoining, in the penultimate verse, of six place-names, rather as concordant notes in a musical score, is perhaps rather the celebration of remembered names than of remembered places. The poet conceives this as a 'litany', and with candour confesses it to be for his delight alone:

> Leaving those men, whose hearts
> are hearths that have no fire,
> my greetings, westward go
> to lovely long Kintyre.
>
> Her uplands draw my thoughts,
> till over lands and seas
> my dreamings go like birds
> that seek the leafy trees.
>
> Of names sweet to the mouth,
> of names like the sounding sea,
> for my delight alone
> I'll write this litany.
>
> Ròaig and Airigh Fhuar,
> words from some fairy tale,
> the Grianan and Davaar,
> Carradale, Sunadale.
>
> These on my mouth, I walk
> among grey walls and chill,
> these are a flame to warm,
> a sain against all ill.[55]

In his Gaelic poem *Luinneag* he evokes by name a succession of the places familiar to him from his Tarbert youth, but here the naming is of a more intimate character, and as the poem strikes its climax he has returned, in spirit, to the West Shore, that high, rocky coast which reaches in bends and bights to Skipness in the south, and which was the haunt, *par excellence*, of the Tarbert herring fishers. The poet is writing in England, and is reminded that the 'hard wind' which kept him from sleep in the night (no gastric disorder alluded to!) would have visited its power on Lochfyne too, blowing in from the south, a bad airt for men at fishing on the loch:

Hug ó hoireann ó,
gura fada, cian fada,
hug ó hoireann ó.

B' e gairbhe na gaoithe
chum an raoir mi 'nam chaithris.

Gaoth á deas air Loch Fìne,
teachd gu fìochar le tartar,

Na tuinn chaoirgheal mu Gharbhail,
neart na fairge s a farum.

Is ann an raoir a bha'n nuallan
'na mo chluasan s mi 'n Sasuinn.

Gu'n tig fuaim an Uillt Bheithe
eadar mise s mo chadal.

Abhainn nan Gillean s a gaoir aic'
bho Loch a' Chaorainn 'na cabhaig,

Lagan Ròaig s tràigh na Lùibe
eadar mo shùilean s mo leabhar,

Agus Rudha Clach an Tràghaidh
a' snàmh air a' bhalla.

IT WAS THE HARDNESS OF THE WIND

It was the hardness of the wind that kept me awake last night.
A wind from the south of Loch Fyne, coming fiercely with uproar.
Waves blazing with foam round Garvel, the might of the sea and its clangour.
Last night its roaring was in my ears, and I was in England.
The sound of the Birch Burn comes between me and my sleep.
Abhainn nan Gillean with its outcry, hastening from Loch a' Chaorainn.
Lagan Roaig and the strand of the Bight between my eyes and my book.
And Ebbing Stone Point swimming on the wall.[56]

More intimate still his introduction of Am Paiste Beag ('The Wee Patch')
into the poem *An Ciùran Ceòban Ceò*. The name does not appear on any
map, and it has vanished entirely – as have so many other such names –
from living tradition. Am Paiste Beag – a scrap of arable ground on the
deserted farm of Lagan Ròaig – was a fishing mark among ring-net
fishermen, and George acquired the name one night at sea. 'We're on the
run o' the Paiste Beag', remarked one of the crew, and George looked in on
the land and saw what was meant.[57]

In *Còmhradh nan Rudha* – 'The Talk of the Headlands' – the
promontories Ebbing Point (Rudha Clach an Tràghaidh) and Laggan Head
(Rudha Lagan Ròaig) are invested with the power of speech and converse
companionably in the darkness of a night. They talk of the fishermen who
are absent from their waters, wondering where they might be:

Says Ebbing Point to Laggan Head:
'Where do they watch their nets to spread
on the black lifting of the sea,
that laid their homeward course on me?'

'When the sun stoops and leaves the sky
the loch lies dead, with not a cry
or torch to mark from far or near.
It leaves me lonely watching here.'

Says Laggan Head across the bight:
'What sounds the men must rienge tonight,
not Holy Isle or Ailsa know,
who flashed farewell and saw them go.'

'They search dark seas they never kent,
seeking out death, ill-rested, spent;
yet sweet it drones aye in their ear,
the swell that breaks upon us here.'[58]

Poems of Fishermen and Fishing

To turn to Campbell Hay's poems of fishermen and fishing is to turn to one of the vital themes of his early work. In *Wind on Loch Fyne* (1948) are gathered ten such poems, and these form the living heart of his expression − as so far collected − on that theme.

The Three Brothers is a tragedy of drowning in which the prescient silence of women and the keening of a *céinteach* (for *caointeach*, a spirit harbinger of death) conjoin to register the end of the brothers, 'whose lair was laid in the wrack an' seaweed'.[59]

The Fisherman Speaks is set in 1938, when the fortunes of the industry were low, and, as Campbell Hay remarks in a footnote to the poem, 'the loch was alive with herring, and the men, "unemployed", were set to mending the road that runs along its shores':

Along the shore the solans strike,
and rise, and strike again in spray,
and I myself, and all my like,
can curse our fate and look away.

On sheltered rocks the black scarts bask
full fed, and rise to feed again;
we bend our shoulders to the task
they threw to us like beggar men.

The skiff I had for thirty years
has gone to pay her debts and mine.
My son a stranger's cutter steers.
I delve the roadway by Loch Fyne.

From Kenmore south to Saddell Bay
the blind shoals wander in the sea.
I ply my spade and watch them play −
God, what is it but mockery?[60]

Three poems in the group – *To a Loch Fyne Fisherman, The Old Fisherman,* and *The Fisherman* – celebrate the skills and durability of individuals, and the pervasive influence of Calum Johnson may not be far away in these. In the first of the poems, which begins, 'Calum thonder, long's the night to your thinking', the tribute may, indeed, be a direct one:

> Calum thonder, long's the night to your thinking,
> night long till dawn and the sun set at the tiller,
> age and the cares of four and a boat to keep you
> high in the stern, alone for the winds to weary.
>
> A pillar set in the shifting moss, a beacon
> fixed on the wandering seas and changing waters,
> bright on the midnight waves and the hidden terrors;
> the ancient yew of the glen, not heeding the ages.
>
> Set among men that waver like leaves on the branches,
> still among minds that flicker like light on the water.
> Those are the shadows of clouds, the speckled and fleeting;
> you are the hill that stands through shadow and sunlight.
>
> Little you heed, or care to change with changes,
> to go like a broken branch in the grip of a torrent;
> you are your judge and master, your sentence unshaken,
> a man with a boat of his own and a mind to guide her.[61]

The most accomplished, it seems to me, of these three convergent poems is *The Old Fisherman,* in which the poet's veneration is expressed in language both spare and unfaltering. The poem is a minor masterpiece of sentiment contained and distilled to wholesome essentials. With three others from the same collection, it was put to music by the Scottish composer of song-settings, Francis George Scott: [62]

> Greet the bights that gave me shelter,
> they will hide me no more with the horns of their forelands.
> I peer in a haze, my back is stooping;
> my dancing days for fishing are over.
>
> The shoot that was straight in the wood withers,
> the bracken shrinks red in the rain and shrivels,
> the eyes that would gaze in the sun waver;
> my dancing days for fishing are over.
>
> The old boat must seek the shingle,
> her wasting side hollow the gravel,
> the hand that shakes must leave the tiller;
> my dancing days for fishing are over.
>
> The sea was good night and morning,
> the winds were friends, the calm was kindly –
> the snow seeks the burn, the brown fronds scatter;
> my dancing days for fishing are over.[63]

The strength of Campbell Hay's feeling for the fishing skiffs of Lochfyne
charges three poems − *Ardlamont, The Kerry Shore,* and *Seeker, Reaper* −
in that collection. Boats he conceives as living, spirited things, and this is a
wholly acceptable conception to any who have sailed in the smaller kinds of
craft and appreciate the individuality invested in what, to others outside
that appreciation, may seem a mere construct of nails and timber. The
living potential of the boat is no more fully realised than in the exhilarating
contest with risen wind and water, and that contest is notably conveyed in
The Kerry Shore:

> Blow, good wind from westward, blow against the dawn,
> blow across this livid loch with shadows strawn.
> Sweetly blew the breeze from westward, o'er she lay,
> coming down the Kerry Shore at break of day.
>
> Up from hills of dreaming Cowal came the sun,
> clear he stood and struck with fire the waters dun,
> waves green-sided, bright, white-crested glittered gay,
> coming down the Kerry Shore at break of day.
>
> Branches rocking, waves of shadow, all the trees
> becked and swung in Glennan to the singing breeze,
> Caisteal Aoil, the Bròg, the Buck to leeward lay,
> coming down the Kerry Shore at break of day.
>
> Head on Tarbert, through the seas she raised a cry,
> jewels of foam around her shoulders tossed on high,
> green waves rose about her bows and broke away,
> coming down the Kerry Shore at break of day.[64]

Seeker, Reaper is a long, gusty poem, urgent and resounding as quickened
water. It is written for the most part in Scots, with passages in Norwegian
and Gaelic breaking into its middle section. The germ of the poem was
received one night at the fishing when George noticed the name of a passing
motor-skiff, the *Sireadh* of Minard,[65] one of the last of the herring fleet out
of the upper loch. Her name, *Sireadh* − 'Seeking' − is echoed in the poem's
title, and the whole piece is of a boat's ceaseless questings. The final
passage:

> Though they come from the world's rim
>   along wi a livin' gale,
> she'll gap and batter through them
>   and teer her chosen trail.
> She's stieve, thrawn, light, quick,
>   fast, wild, gay;
> she'll curtain the world wi hammered seas,
>   she'll drench the stars wi spray.

> They can tower between her and the sky −
>   she never felt their awe;
> she'll walk them aa, thon trampin' boat,
>   she'll rise and walk them aa.
> She's a solan's hert, a solan's look;
>   she canna thole a lee.
> I'll coil her ropes and redd her nets,
>   and ease her through a sea.
> She's a seeker, she's a hawk, boys.
>   Thon's the boat for me.[66]

As for the practicalities of ring-net fishing, there are relatively few descriptions in the work of Campbell Hay, but that is not to be wondered at. The wonder is that he so successfully wrought into hard and satisfying poetic form such seemingly intractable stuff.

In the following extracts, Campbell Hay evinces a sure understanding of the complexities of the ring-netting operation − the skilled assessment of wind and tide essential for the surrounding and containing of the discovered shoal − and he has expressed that understanding with remarkable acuity of language. Indeed, his choice of key-terms − '... the *master glance* ... the *curve* of the outgoing net ... the *drift* of the wind and sea ... we *mark* them, *shoot* and *round* them wheel ...' − communicates such a sense of absolute rightness that I think only one who had experienced ring-net fishing could wholly appreciate these passages. The final half of the second extract conveys, with bare realism, the gruelling labour of a ring-net haul in adverse conditions:

> Dark and daybreak, heat and hail had tried
> and schooled the two in the master glance for esteeming
> the curve of the outgoing net, the set of the tide,
> the drift of wind and sea, the airt where the prey was swimming.[67]

> And if Fortune chances on us
> in the dark, and swings our keel
> into the airt where shoals are swimming,
> we mark them, shoot and round them wheel.
> Then a foot for purchase on the gunnel,
> numb hands that have lost their feel,
> the ebb tide straining, the steep seas snatching
> a backrope like a rod of steel.[68]

The broader themes of Campbell Hay's verse − his tender celebration of the natural world, his nationalism, and the intensely philosophical poems which were the hard, reflective fruits of his wartime experience − I shall not venture upon. The full measure of his accomplishment has been carefully weighed by Derick Thomson.

George Campbell Hay has the interests and talents that are, on one level, very useful to a poetry which is making a major change of course, as Gaelic poetry has been doing over the past thirty years. He is a wide-ranging linguist and scholar, and an accomplished poet: he has combined these gifts in translations from and poems in the styles of Early Modern Irish, Welsh, French, Greek, Icelandic and a number of other European languages. And reciprocally, he has translated into English, French and Norwegian from Gaelic. This varied range of work appears in his three collections, two in Gaelic and English, and one in Scots and English, published to date. No one in Scottish Gaelic has written so delightfully in the tone of the Irish poets of the *amour courtois* as Hay has done in his 'Trì rainn is amhran' series.

Hay's most original, and surely his most enduring, work is of a different kind. It is in non-traditional metres and rhythms, and concerns personal experience and political and philosophical principals. This poetry, with its greater philosophical and dramatic power, appears mainly in his second Gaelic collection, *O Na Ceithir Àirdean*, and includes poems on Scottish Nationalist themes, love poems, and some fine war poetry, the poem 'Bisearta' being one of the most vivid and emotionally charged pieces of writing in Gaelic, and making a strong impact also in Hay's own translation. His main published work was written before 1950.[69]

School and University

George Campbell Hay had gone to Fettes College, in 1929, as a foundationer, that is on a full scholarship. The distinction was duly noted in the *Campbeltown Courier,* whose correspondent intimated that 'the career of this exceptionally promising young man ... will be watched with much interest by a wide circle'.[70]

Robert A. Rankin – formerly Professor of Mathematics at the University of Glasgow – is well qualified to write of the earliest part of that career, for he shared with Campbell Hay a study during their last two years at Fettes College, and 'got to know him very well'. Indeed, the two became close friends. Professor Rankin writes of those years:

> In some ways he was quite a wild character and when doing OTC (Officers' Training Corps) duty one kept out of his way if he had a bayonet in his hand. It was he who stimulated my interest in the Highlands and in Gaelic and we went on several walking holidays and cruises up the West Highlands together. He had a phenomenal capacity for picking up languages and, in addition to Gaelic, Latin and Greek is at home in Serbo-Croat, Norwegian and other languages. When we were studying Homer, which is an older form of Greek than classical Greek, he would ask me to open the Homeric dictionary at random and ask him the meaning of any word I saw and he always could tell me. We used to play a similar game later on with a Gaelic dictionary ...
>
> He could be a very colourful figure. I remember before the war walking with him and a friend in Lochaber. After a very strenuous and wearisome walk from Loch Ossian through to Loch Laggan we were walking very wearily on the hard road by the lochside still some miles from our destination. George was dressed in a plaid – a Campbell tartan rug that he had folded and wrapped round himself in the traditional way. He presented such an interesting sight that a private coach full of old ladies stopped and gave us a lift for the last few miles.[71]

George apparently was not athletically inclined, although he played in his House rugger team. He was a corporal piper in the school pipe-band,[72] but of his interest in that most apposite, for him, of musical traditions he had little to say retrospectively, other than that he had been self-taught and that his involvement with piping ended with the war.[73]

When he left Fettes, in July 1934, it was with a major classical scholarship. This, too, was noted in the *Campbeltown Courier*, in a generous report headed 'NOVELIST'S SON WINS OXFORD SCHOLARSHIP'. The announcement expanded into a résumé of J. MacDougall Hay's career and a discussion of his literary status, which contains the eccentric suggestion that he 'promised to become a second Crockett'.[74] The piece ended on an account of Catherine Hay's return to her birthplace: 'Mrs Hay, whose home is in Edinburgh, has been on a visit to Portavadie lately, her first time in the Kyles [of Bute] since her girlhood days. She had the pleasure of being received at her early home, Auchenlochan Manse, and had a kindly welcome from old friends in the district.'[75]

Campbell Hay was matriculated at Corpus Christi College on 13 October, 1934, took Honour Moderations in Classics in Hilary Term of 1936, and the final examination in the Honour School of Literae Humaniores in Trinity Term, 1938. The B.A. degree was conferred on him on 16 December, 1939.[76]

George enjoyed his years at Oxford. He befriended there a native of Kintail, Christopher MacRae, and they 'used to sit and sing Gaelic songs and play the pipes until two o'clock in the morning'.[77] That George had nothing more to recount of his Oxford years is perhaps indicative of the cultural magnetism which already had begun to draw him from his early classical affinities. Professor Rankin maintains that 'by the time he left Fettes for Oxford I think his interests had passed away from Latin and Greek, which no doubt explains why he finished with Honours of the Fourth Class'.[78]

Literary Beginnings

Campbell Hay began to write verse seriously at the age of sixteen,[79] while in his second year at Fettes, though at the age of twelve he had made a start on a Gaelic song:

> *Soraidh slàn le Cinntìre*
> *'S le Loch Fìne mo ghràidh . . .*[80]

('A long farewell to Kintyre and to Loch Fyne that I love . . .'). Gratifyingly for this biographer – if not for George himself – the young poet had, in the school magazine, *The Fettesian*, a ready vehicle for his work, and he availed himself unstintingly of it. To Robert Rankin I owe the meticulous identification of Campbell Hay's pseudonymous contributions to the magazine, for none of the numerous poems and articles carried his own name. George evidently delighted in the invention of bizarre and ridiculous pen-names, some apposite to the character of the piece – as with *Eggmoan,* a spirited denunciation of eggs, signed 'Leghorn'[81] – and others not. A complete list of these pseudonyms may not be without interest, and if justification were required, then the list will serve others in the identification of the entire body of his adolescent work which reached print in the pages of *The Fettesian.* Chronologically, then: The Permanent Feature, Y.A.H., Noggs, ''Ικη, Seorus Ciotach (Left-handed George), ΚΡΑΙΠΑΛΗ, Ciotach, Brasso, Barebones, Pinko, J. Bogie Spooner, Leghorn, and Jehu.[82]

Most of these *Fettesian* contributions are of a comic or sarcastic nature. Indeed, his first-published composition – in the April, 1931 issue – is a tilt at himself. Titled *Maths,* it begins:

> Five terms I've graced the bottom set
> Without a hope of a punt[83] as yet,
> For when I should be doing Maths
> My mind will run on other paths . . .

And, indeed, his mathematics ratings were consistently low. In the 1932/33 term he occupied the bottom placing in his class, yet he rallied sufficiently in the succeeding year to gain a Scottish Leaving Certificate in the subject, albeit in the lower grade.[84]

Of these *Fettesian* contributions – 19 poems, including two in translation, with three prose pieces – only one, the poem *Homer,* of December 1933, was to find a place in his English collection, *Wind on Loch Fyne. The Hind of Morning,* also published in that collection, was written at Fettes, but was turned down by the editor of *The Fettesian.*[85] The two versions of *Homer* appear below, and though the final published form retains the structural integrity of the original, the maturer craftsman has chiselled away the weaker parts. These alterations scarcely require my elucidation, but, in the phrases 'dawn's bright smile', 'the torrents swirling', and 'the lightning-flash', there was no doubt perceived, in later and more critical readings, the deadening touch of the commonplace:

> They say that you were blind: but from the shore
> You saw the long waves gather out at sea;
> Before the dawn's bright smile from heaven's floor
> You saw the dark night flee.
>
> The torrents swirling in the spring-time thaw,
> The shady slopes of Ida many-pined,
> The lightning-flash of falling swords you saw,
> They lie; you weren't blind.[86]

> > (*The Fettesian*)

They say that you were blind, yet from the shore
you saw the long waves cresting out at sea;
before the climbing dawn from heaven's floor
you saw the dark night flee.

The torrents whirling in the springtime thaw,
the shady slopes of Ida many-pined,
the curving flash of falling swords you saw –
they lie; you were not blind.[87]

(*Wind on Loch Fyne*)

In few other poems may be heard the sure, resonant tones of his later work. *A Lament for Ruaraidh Mór MacLeod* suffers by an excess of stock romantic imagery, but, then, the work was that of a very young man whose critical faculty had scarcely developed. Yet, in the final lines of these otherwise undistinguished verses, the tone and phrasing are at once compelling:

For what can we see or hear again with Ruari sleeping,
But the grey rain on the dreary hills, weeping, weeping,
And the sea's mouth mourning along the shore?[88]

Compelling, too, is the theme which he approaches in the evocative short story, *Home,* which is the fictional account of a man's return, after long absence, to the township of his birth. I do not doubt that the final passages, closely detailed as they are in their description of the wilderness and ruin to which the sentimental exile unsuspectingly returned, were the products not of an imaginative fixing on vague remembered things, but of a mind which had been moved, and powerfully moved, by that indescribable atmosphere of desolation which enfolds remote and long-abandoned habitations.

George was familiar with such ruins as lie out on the hills to the south of Tarbert, for he was fond of taking the old track which leads down to Lagan Ròaig. Reading these passages, it was of Lagan Ròaig that I thought, at once – a roofless, long ruin standing with its back to the hill, and facing across the wasted fields eastwards to the sea and the hills of Bute and Cowal:

There was no smoke climbing into the still air there, and no sweet songs – only a few broken ends of houses dripping with the western rain, and tumbled stones scattered through the long grass. And in all places were the rushes, and the brackens, and the thin sheep-grass growing. From the clefts in the walls tufts of grass were springing, and over threshold and hearth crowded nettles, nettles everywhere. The doorways were blocked with damp, trailing brambles, and through all the croftland round about tall weeds were spreading.

When I saw that I felt weak like a sick man, and for a long while I stood there listening to the wet wind wailing through the chinks of the ruined walls. But there was no help in my standing there, for all I loved the place; and I turned and went back my way down the path. And at the place where the track turned I looked back – a last look at Bail'

Imheir. And what I saw was the jagged, broken end of a house standing out black against the grey sky. And at that seeing, I tell you, there was little between me and tears. And that is the way I came home.[89]

On 15 January, 1983, George Campbell Hay came home. His return to Tarbert deeply surprised his friends, not least by the impulsiveness of his decision. On 18 January I had a brief letter from him at Tarbert, in which he explained: 'Last Friday I was sitting in the flat in Edinburgh and I thought: "I'll go back to Tarbert for good." So I went out and transferred my pension to Tarbert and bought some clothes and a rucksack, and on Saturday I came to Tarbert. And here I am *gu bràth!* The old Tarbert is still there, although a host of familiar faces has disappeared.'

He himself became a 'familiar face' in Tarbert. He had made the choice of spending the remainder of his life there. The academic and artistic promise of that life was impaired in 1946, when, as a sergeant in the Education Corps, stationed at Salonika, his association with working-class Greeks precipitated an assassination attempt on him by right-wing activists. The attempt failed, but he has since carried with him the indelible scars of mental collapse. He was retired on a full disability pension,[90] and since then has worked periodically as a translator and reviewer, and at his poetry. The legacy of that trauma has been the sporadic nature of his literary activity, following the immediate post-war run of publications, and his difficulty in undertaking sustained literary work. Whether or not his return to Tarbert could have restored to his art a measure of past power will not be known. Unable to find a house of his own there, he decided to go back to Edinburgh. On 31 August, 1983, George Campbell Hay left Tarbert.

Postscript

On 26 March, 1984, the body of George Campbell Hay was found in his home at 6 Maxwell Street, Edinburgh, by a visiting social worker. The loneliness of his dying makes it all the harder to think on.

An Lagan

Có chunnaic an lagan tosdach,
s a' ghrian mochthrath air a shlios,
ag òradh cromadh réidh an ruighe,
nach do chaill a chridhe ris?

Tha toirm nan stuadh s nam bliadhna eadar
mi fhéin is fear a' mholaidh thall.
'Nan déidh am faighear leam san lagan
na dh'fhàg mi uair de m'anam ann?

The Hollow

Who saw the silent hollow,
with the early sun upon its flank,
gilding the smooth sweep of the lower slope,
that did not lose his heart as he looked?

The thunder of the waves and the years is between me
and the one who made the praise, beyond them.
After them will I find in the hollow
that part of my soul which I left there?

REFERENCES AND NOTES

1. Edinburgh. Containing also verse by Sorley Maclean and two others.

2. Ed. D. MacAulay, Edinburgh (Southside Publishers Ltd.) 1976. Containing also verse by Sorley Maclean, Derick Thomson, Iain Crichton Smith, and Donald MacAulay.

3. *The Scotsman*, 13 Oct. 1983.

4. Letter to author, 22 Oct. 1983.

5. *Oban Times*, 29 July 1982.

6. D. S. Thomson, editor's note, *Mochtàr is Dùghall*, 63.

7. G. C. Hay, 3 Oct. 1980.

8. C 1861 Tar/d1/p13. William Hay (56), fish merchant; wife Margaret (59), sons William (19), fish merchant, George (16), John (13), and Robert (11), with a 13-year-old domestic servant, Susan McDougall, all in Elder's Land.

9. *RM* Tar, 4 Feb. 1873, George Hay and Mary MacDougall.

10. H. Reid, '*Gillespie* – our forgotten masterpiece', *The Scotsman*, 21 Oct. 1972.

11. *RM, op. cit.*

12. Obit., *Glasgow Herald*, 11 Dec. 1919.

13. *Ib.* He was prizeman in classes of natural philosophy, moral philosophy, education, logic, English literature (ordinary and honours), and won the Lorimer Scholarship in logic, moral philosophy, and English literature.

14. *Ib.*

15. Michael S. Moss, archivist, University of Glasgow, letter to author, 30 Aug. 1983.

16. A. M. Morrison, chief librarian, Western Isles Libraries, from logbook of Lionel School, letter to author, 16 Dec. 1981.

17. Obit., *op. cit.*, and *Fasti Ecclesiae Scoticanae*, Synod of Glasgow and Ayr, Edinburgh 1920, 138.

18. H. Reid, *op. cit.*

19. 7 Feb. 1914.

20. 19 Sept. 1903.

21. *Glasgow Evening News*, 2 Oct. 1903.

22. G. C. Hay, 3 Oct. 1980.

23. H. Reid, *op. cit.*

24. *CC*, 30 Oct. 1909.

25. *RD* Tar, 11 Feb. 1883 (Hugh MacMillan) and *RB* Tar, 5 March 1864 (Catherine MacMillan, his daughter).

26. *RD, ib.* Hugh MacMillan's death – at the age of 84 – was both certified and registered by his son, Dr. Duncan MacMillan.

27. *Ib.*

28. G. C. Hay, 3 Oct. 1980.

29. *RM* Tar, 8 Feb. 1881.

30. Obit., *CC,* 6 June 1891.

31. *Ib.*

32. C. M. Ferguson, Free Church of Scotland, Edinburgh, letter to author, 14 Oct. 1983.

33. *RM* Tar, 8 Feb. 1881.

34. *RB* Kilfinan, 4 Feb. 1883.

35. J. C. Hay, note on draft ms. of this chapter, returned 10 Dec. 1982.

36. Obit., *op. cit.*

37. G. C. Hay, 14 May 1979.

38. *Ib.,* 15 Nov. 1980.

39. *Ib.,* 3 Oct. 1980.

40. *Ib.*

41. *Fasti of the United Free Church of Scotland,* 1900-1929, Edinburgh, 76.

42. G. C. Hay, 3 Oct. 1980.

43. *Ib.,* note on draft ms., *op. cit.*

44. *The Nairn Star,* 5 April 1952, in review of *O na Ceithir Àirdean,* credited to R. M. Robertson, at whose request Maclean produced the piece.

45. The graveyard in Tarbert, which G. C. Hay now believes should be *Cill Ainndreann.* There is, however, a *Sloc Aindreas* at the head of Tarbert harbour. Letter to author, 10 Dec. 1982.

46. *RD* Tar.

47. Margaret Johnson, Lochgilphead, letter to author, 3 Dec. 1981.

48. R. Johnson, *ib.*

49. H. MacFarlane, 16 Feb. 1977.

50. 3 Oct. 1980.

51. G. C. Hay, *ib.*

52. R. Johnson, *op. cit.*

53. *Commanach* recorded in Tarbert by the author; *coindeag,* G. C. Hay, note on draft ms., *op. cit.*

54. G. C. Hay, 3 Oct. 1980.

55. *Wind on Loch Fyne,* Edinburgh 1948, 2.

56. *Fuaran Sléibh,* Glasgow 1947, 17.

57. G. C. Hay, 3 Oct. 1980.

58. *Wind . . ., op. cit.,* 6.

59. *Ib.,* 5.

60. *Ib.,* 10.

61. *Ib.,* 5.

62. M. Lindsay, *Francis George Scott and the Scottish Renaissance,* 1980, 158-161. Also *To a Loch Fyne Fisherman, The Kerry Shore,* and *Alba.*

63. *Wind . . ., op. cit.,* 12.

64. *Ib.,* 7.

65. G. C. Hay, 15 Nov. 1980.

66. *Wind . . ., op. cit.,* 40.

67. 'The Two Neighbours', *The Oxford Book of Scottish Verse,* ed. MacQueen and Scott, Oxford 1966, 585.

68. 'At the Quayside', *Wind . . ., op. cit.,* 17.

69. *Contemporary Poets of the English Language,* London 1970, 484-5.

70. 20 July 1929.

71. 2 Jan. 1982.

72. R. A. Cole-Hamilton, keeper of the register, Fettes College, letter to author, 17 Dec. 1981.

73. G. C. Hay, 15 Nov. 1980.

74. S. R. Crockett, 'Kailyard' novelist of the late nineteenth century.

75. 1 Sept. 1934.

76. R. A. Bowyer, administrative officer, Graduate Studies Office, University of Oxford, letter to author, 2 Dec. 1981.

77. G. C. Hay, 15 Nov. 1980.

78. 2 Jan. 1982.

79. G. C. Hay, 3 Oct. 1980.

80. *Ib.*, note on draft ms., *op. cit.*

81. *The Fettesian,* June 1934, 343.

82. *Ib.*, April 1931 – July 1934, but primarily in issue of June 1934, of which he was editor!

83. Fettes slang for a promotion to a higher set – R. A. Rankin, letter to author, 14 Oct. 1982.

84. R. A. Cole-Hamilton, letter to author, 13 Jan. 1981.

85. G. C. Hay, note on draft ms., *op. cit.*

86. Dec. 1933, 128.

87. *Wind, op. cit.,* 1.

88. *The Fettesian,* Dec. 1933, 131.

89. *Ib.*, July 1934, 432-4.

90. G. C. Hay, 15 Nov. 1980.

CHAPTER 4

John Campbell: Tradition-Bearer

I spoke to John Campbell for the first time in the summer of 1980. The year is perhaps irrelevant, because I believe that the encounter was inevitable, by which I do not imply predestination. Simply this, that I had for several years been noticing him with increasing interest, and was – as I now realise – only waiting for a chance to make his acquaintance. I saw him first as a small man walking the roads of south Kintyre, an old black beret pulled tightly over his head and sandshoes on his feet.

I like to believe that the folk-historian develops a kind of intuitive ability to identify the potential informant within a community of mere faces and figures. The more usual means of coming to such a state of recognition is, to be sure, by the recommendation of others, and by that means, too, no doubt I would eventually have reached John Campbell. But I had noticed him and marked him as one who could perhaps be a storyteller, a bearer of local tradition, and I was not mistaken.

On the day that I first spoke with him, by way of opening a conversation I remarked that I had been missing him lately on the Kilchousland road, which was his familiar trail. Obviously wondering who I was, he asked my name. I gave it to him, and to forestall the inevitable, 'And who are you for a Martin?', I volunteered the information that my people were from Dalintober. He 'got me' immediately, and surprised me by announcing a connection between our families (p. 78). The personal interest, genealogically, of the information was such that I immediately suggested that I visit him, to which he consented, and an arrangement was made.

Thus began a succession of visits to John Campbell's house in Hillside Road. The genealogical preoccupation of the initial visit was soon supplanted by an enlarging awareness of the man's stature as a local tradition-bearer. That awareness was stimulated by his recital of a number of old riddles and by his continual evocation of events and personalities which, I could guess, only required unlocking from the safe of memory. He would later reflect, with a kind of wonder, on that unabating process of recall of which I became the conscious agent. The phenomenon is, of course, familiar to all experienced oral historians. It requires but a repository of tradition and a recipient (for all storytellers need an audience, even should that 'audience' be one person). By my third visit I had decided that John merited tape-recording, and I put the proposal to him. He was delighted by it and at once agreed. As yet, however, there was no indication that he was in possession of tales, but his fund of social history was of such promise that to have expected more would have seemed unreasonable.

I visited him with tape-recorder for the first time on 17 October, 1980, and committed to tape such material as had interested me on my earlier visits. Two stories also emerged that evening. Neither was particularly momentous, but they suggested the possibility of a greater store.

The liberation of a submerged mass of tradition is generally a prolonged undertaking, which is the more difficult in an area such as Kintyre, where the vitiation of the Gaelic culture has removed the *seanchaidh* (storyteller and historian) from his traditional role. Had John Campbell lived a hundred and fifty years ago in the area of Kintyre, Skipness, where his father's people originated, then he would undoubtedly have been a notable story-teller. To his house would have thronged old and young, men and women, to hear his stories, of which he would then have possessed innumerably more. In short, he would have had an audience, an audience for which the ceilidh − on winter nights especially − was the surest source of entertainment. To that audience he could have given his tales, by demand told and retold, and from other storytellers he would have taken other stories and so enlarged his repertoire.

There is, however, no actual audience for John Campbell and his like, a void which has opened even in the areas − of the Gaelic west particularly − which have been supportive of the *seanchaidh*. The folklorist, however appreciative, is no substitute for a responsive audience. The collector may return, but seldom for the same tale, which has been told and committed to the cold tape which threads its dispassionate coils through that instrument which must fail to catch the larger gestures of the man. Yet, people, as people, have not altered so very greatly that the charm of the tale is lost to them. It is that the storyteller's place has been usurped by the disembodied actors of a larger culture who have entered the ceilidh house and filled it with an alien clamour. Indeed, every house is now a ceilidh house, but the 'seanchaidh' is a mindless box in a corner of a room.

Sensing the probability of John's having further − and perhaps more valuable − tales, I took the unusual course of suggesting to him that he note the outlines of any stories which he might remember in my absence. Without much hope of his being able to satisfy the request, and not unhappily resigned to the likelihood of having to rely on prolonged conversational stimulation, I left it at that. On my return, four days later − 21 October − I was, however, presented with a scrap of paper on which he had noted a series of headings. These, he told me, represented stories which he had recalled. An intriguing compilation it was, and I quote some of the titles as he formulated them with his sure sense of essentials.

The Grog still (a tale of illicit whisky-making and evasion of detection at Grogport); *John Ruadh and the piano* (a comic story relating an old Grogport man's unfavourable reaction to the first piano which he heard);

At the sheep-clipping and what followed (an account of an old shepherd's outrageous battle of wits with two sarcastic daughters of the farm). In an uncommon state of excitement, I let merely three days pass before I again visited him, and once again he had taken the exceptional trouble both to recall and to note his tales.

Merely two of John Campbell's tales appear in this book, in contexts proper to their themes, and I do not propose to introduce any to this account, gratuitously as it were. The purpose of this account is to isolate, from the mass of informants whose knowledge – to varying degrees – has served this work, a single person as representative of the whole. There could have been no choice but John Campbell. He is unquestionably the most accomplished storyteller, and probably the most knowledgeable tradition-bearer left in Kintyre, and this is the more remarkable considering that he was born and brought up within the burgh of Campbeltown. That apparent anomaly – for, without exception, all other able storytellers in Kintyre have been, at least in my own experience, of farming and shepherding backgrounds – will later be explained. What, essentially, his facility demonstrates is the tenacity of inherited culture.

John McFadyen Campbell was born on 23 March, 1904, at number 10 Saddell Street, Dalintober. That building in which he entered the world has long since disappeared. He was the seventh and last child of Robert 'Ruch Rob' Campbell and Agnes Keith McFadyen, who had married in 1889. Robert Campbell was a native of Grogport. He was a son of Robert Campbell, fisherman, and Margaret MacKinven, and a grandson of Colin Campbell, crofter, and Catherine MacLarty.[1] He came in early manhood as a fisherman to Dalintober. Gaelic had been his first language, and from him and his brother Colin Campbell – remembered still in Campbeltown as 'Colin Grogport', and remembered too as both a fisherman and storyteller of redoubtable abilities – John acquired the greater part of his fund of tales. That these tales were products not of the English, or more properly Scots culture, scarcely requires explanation. What may, however, be emphasised is that the legacy was an indirect one, having been communicated in translation, because John, to his unceasing regret, was denied access to the language of the originals. That cultural deprivation, if the matter may so be expressed, is a familiar tragedy. To parental unwillingness to perpetuate Gaelic may be ascribed, in great part, the language's present failing state.

There were, however, it is fair to record, other significant factors acting against John Campbell's acquisition of Gaelic. The first had a general application and was his upbringing within an effectively non-Gaelic-speaking community. That circumstance, though unquestionably disadvantageous, need not have been insurmountable, for children have been raised as bilingual in more hostile environments than the south Kintyre of the early twentieth century. A second adverse factor, no less prevalent, was the incompetence in the language of one of the parents, in John Campbell's case his mother. That factor was, however, less absolute than is ordinarily the case, because his mother acquired in childhood a certain familiarity with the language.[2]

That familiarity she owed to her maternal grandmother, Agnes 'Nanny' MacCallum, a venerable woman who died in December, 1893. Her age at death is officially recorded as 100 years,[3] but she herself claimed, shortly before her death, to be 'going on' 103 years.[4] She was born in Barr Glen, at the farm of Arnicle, the daughter of Archibald MacKeich, which name has entirely disappeared from Kintyre and is perpetuated in the forms 'MacKeith' and 'Keith'. (That Archibald MacKeich was evidently the first of the name of which – in 1797-8, at Arnicle – there is record in Kintyre.[5] Oral tradition in Kintyre maintains that the family appeared from Aberdeenshire in the aftermath of the Jacobite Rebellion of 1745.[6]) Her mother was Margaret MacBride, an old Kintyre name which has completely gone (the family McBride in Carradale arrived in Kintyre from Irvine, Ayrshire, c. 1880[7]).

When the young Agnes MacKeich arrived in Campbeltown her entire English vocabulary, it was said, consisted merely of the words 'yes' and 'no'.[8] She kept a public house near the junction of Longrow and Roading. By 1922, it was the last thatched house in Campbeltown.[9] She spent the greater part of her long life in that house, and died in it. Until within months of her death, she had been 'in the habit of rising early and sitting at the fireside, where she enjoyed a talk in her native language (Gaelic)'. Her husband, Edward MacCallum, predeceased her by 13 years. She left, at death, three sons and three daughters, 23 grandchildren, and 18 great-grandchildren.[10]

John's interest in Gaelic developed in boyhood. His father was not, in fairness to him, unsympathetic to that interest, but a positive response to his son's linguistic fumblings was missing from the relationship, which is regrettable, because if John Campbell is a cultural asset to his community without that Gaelic inheritance which might have been his, then how much greater an asset would he have been with it. But such speculation is pointless. As it was, Rob Campbell, on country rambles with his son, enjoyed explaining to him the Gaelic names of 'farms an landmarks on the rodd an on the coast'. When his father would 'come away' with a phrase or a saying in Gaelic, John would eagerly attempt to reproduce the sounds. He would enquire of his father: ' "Is that, is that hit?" – "Naw," an he'd laugh, ye know. Of course, 'e liked tae kinna torment me a bit, ye know. "Aye, that's hit." Sez I: "Wid ye know hoot A wiz sehin?", an A wid seh it agane, hootever it waaz. "Well," 'e sez, "*I* would know, but A don' know if anybody else wid know." An he'd laugh.'[11]

In High Street, Dalintober, where the Campbell family later removed, their house attracted visitors from among the Carradale fishermen, for whom it became something of a ceilidh house. These customary visits owed much to the sense of community between the Carradale people and the people of Grogport. For many of the older Carradale fishermen, to whom the Gaelic language remained a vital, living force, the Campbell house provided a kind of cultural resort, a 'home from home'. A meal would be shared by the assembled company, and then would commence a round of song, dance, and story. Rob Campbell was a fiddler until his fingers got crooked with the work of fishing. He was also a noted exponent of 'cantering',[12] and his richly timbred voice would charm to dancing many a guest in that hospitable home.

By exactly what conditions the tradition-bearer is shaped and set in his role as custodian of the unwritten 'book of the people' is something of a puzzle. Intelligence and a retentive memory are certainly prerequisites. An environment − usually, but not invariably the home − in which he or she may come into contact with a living, vigorous body of tradition is a certain requirement. Finally, he or she must possess or acquire that intensity of interest and involvement in tradition which characterises the finest of the type. All of these basic requirements are satisfied in John Campbell.

He has been referred to repeatedly as a 'storyteller' or 'tradition-bearer', and these terms require elaboration. He assuredly does not belong to the great tradition of storytelling which, if the attributes of art may strictly be ascribed to interpretative as also to creative expression, is undeniably an art form. In such tales as John Campbell inherited may be perceived the poor remnants of that tradition, in spirit if not in substance. His tales, if an analogy with football may be used, are not of the 'first division'. To carry the analogy further and to attempt to place them in a lower division of that hypothetical league would be an absurdity, but the point has been made and reflects no discredit on John Campbell.

Of the old, complex Gaelic tales no trace now remains in Kintyre, at least to my knowledge. The following − which is scarcely an outstanding example of the genre − was taken down in the Muasdale district, probably in the 1920s. It was set in Dùn Ach' na h-Àtha − or 'Muasdale Fort', above Bealach a' Chaochain − which was held by none other than Fionn Mac Cumhaill himself. He had occasion to leave with his Fenian warrior band, and gave the fort to the care of a henchman, Gille Cochull nan Craiceann[13] (the Lad of the Hood of Skins). In the middle of a night the lad was visited by a hideous monster, a kind of supernatural bull. He met the thing at the fort entrance and the two fought with such violence that the clash could be heard 'beyond the seven glens and the seven bens and the seven moor mountains'. The beast seemed invincible. The lad, with a stroke of his sword, swept off its head, only to see it rise and reunite with the colossal trunk. He took the head off once again, whereupon a voice came to him in his desperation: 'Lay the flat of the sword against the marrow.' This he instantly did, just before the head could rejoin, and down it fell and struck the ground with a terrific thud and sank deep into the earth. The lad won great fame by his feat.[14] (Stories about battles with bulls are fairly common both in Gaelic hero-tales and in local legends. The motif of the sword held against the marrow – sometimes held until the marrow 'froze' – is also common in hero-tales. The name of Fionn's servant is usually associated in Scotland with the Ceudach/Céadach story, for which see Alan Bruford's *Gaelic Folk-tales and Mediaeval Romances*.[15]

In pockets of the Irish and Scottish *Gaidhealtachd* where the culture has persisted vigorously, the old order of *seanchaidh* could be found into the present century. (Indeed, genuine representatives of the type continue to occupy the attention of folklorists.) The late Calum Iain Maclean, who was pre-eminent among Scottish folklorists, encountered a storyteller who took from seven to nine hours to narrate some of his tales, and in County Kerry J. H. Delargy of the Irish Folklore Commission heard of a beggar who required seven nights for the telling of a single story.[16]

These stories of John Campbell's are not characterised by strictness of narrative form. A particular story may, therefore, vary considerably in both structure and content from one rendering to another, although invariably its vital elements will remain intact. John's narrative technique is an accomplished and effective one. Once his consciousness of the microphone has been swept away by the impetus of the tale, his speech and gestures and facial expressions with a gathering expansiveness mirror the intensity of his identification with the characters and events of the story. He becomes, for the duration of the tale, a helpless actor in its unwinding drama.

A characteristic of his story-telling is the susceptibility of his concentration to stray from the course of the narrative. He is liable to break a tale to pick up and discuss an intrusive place-name or personality, or whatever, a trait which may serve as a sustaining device, to forestall the final tightening of the thread on which his tale is hung.

His command of local dialect is an undiminishing wonder, and not a visit passes without my being able to add substantially to my word-lists. These acquisitions remain unsorted, but constitute a body of words and phrases – both Scots and Gaelic – numbering several hundreds. Their significance, in the frame of local cultural inheritance, is quite as remarkable qualitatively as quantitatively, yet that significance is undermined by the very fact of their unrepresentativeness – in totality – of local dialect. The Gaelic elements are uncharacteristically prominent, reflecting his father's bilingual influence. A number of these unmistakably Gaelic elements survive, in a strictly local relation, with John Campbell alone.

If his Gaelic vocabulary is extraordinarily rich for one who is both a native of south Kintyre and a non-Gaelic speaker, strictly defined, then his Scots vocabulary too demonstrates a vigour and diversity which is uncommon within that same geographical frame. The two blocks of vocabulary co-exist without complication, as no doubt was the case three and four generations ago in south Kintyre, when the influence of each language upon local speech was decidedly more marked.

To attempt to represent the weight of these languages on the everyday speech of John Campbell would be wearisome and, for one who is essentially unskilled in linguistics, unwise, but their impingement on a single theme may here be examined. John is a moderate and appreciative whisky-drinker, and the following words belong to the honourable ritual of offering and dispensing that most marvellous of spirits. He is able to summon no fewer than five terms which describe − if loosely − a measure of whisky, and which equate with the common 'dram' or 'half'. With the exception of the fourth word, I have heard none of these from anyone else in Kintyre.

1. *Feejag.* This appears to be *fideag,* the common Gaelic word for a whistle. John relates it to a receptacle for whisky, in particular a small horn vessel which an aunt of his kept for dispensing liquor.[17] The late Donald MacDonald in Gigha − the only other person from whom I heard the word − firmly maintained, however, that the meaning was 'just a wee taste, a wee drop in yer mouth'.[18] 2. *Bolgam.* From G. *balgam,* a mouthful of any liquid. This word is perpetuated in the Campbeltown street-name, Bolgam Street − significantly, 'Balgom Street' in the earliest records − which owes its origin to the dram-shops formerly located there.[19] 3. *Jerrag.* This may be G. *deurag − deur,* 'drop', with a feminine diminutive ending − so, 'a drappie'. It may, alternatively, be *dearg* − 'red', etc. − in some extended sense. 4. *Tait.* Scots, 'a small quantity of anything'. 5. *Drooglan.* Presumably connected with G. *drùdhag,* 'a sip, a small drop'.[20]

Three of John Campbell's stories have been substantiated in newspaper reports. Two contain pronounced elements of supernatural forewarning,[21] which do not, of course, occur in the printed sources. The third story − which, to be fair to John Campbell, is much slighter and sketchier than the generality of his stories − has genealogical interest and will serve for comparative analysis. It concerns the drowning − at Ardglass, Ireland, in 1868 − of his maternal grandfather, Alexander MacFadyen, who was also a brother-in-law of my own great-great-grandfather, John Martin, in whose smack he was fishing at the time. First, a report of the drowning, from the *Downpatrick Recorder:*

A melancholy accident, which has resulted in the loss of two lives, took place on Tuesday evening in Ardglass harbour. About five o'clock that evening, the fishing-boat *Elm*, master John Martin, was coming into Ardglass, having a punt in tow; and while the mainsail was being lowered, the punt was upset, and the line by which it was made fast to the smack broken, so that the punt went adrift seawards. Alexander McFadden and John McKie (McKay), two of the crew of the *Elm*, having borrowed a punt belonging to another fishing-boat, started off to recover their own punt, in spite of the remonstrances of several parties present, who warned them of the extreme danger of their undertaking, as a very heavy sea was running in the harbour at the time. They succeeded in getting their own boat, which was floating keel up, and attaching it to that in which they were, and tried to go outwards rather than into the harbour, in consequence of the sea being so high. Unfortunately, they got among breakers at Ardtole, in which their punt was upset, and both were drowned. The body of McFadden has since been recovered . . . (He) was a married man of about 48 years of age, and leaves a wife and five children. McKie had been married only about six months. Both the deceased were natives of Campbellton, Scotland, and were favourites with their fellow-fishermen. Yesterday evening we learned that the body of McKie was recovered.[22]

John Campbell's version has the name of MacFadyen's companion as MacNicol or Nicolson, and he has them launch a punt in an attempt to secure a boat which was dragging her anchor and in danger of going aground:

They got this punt, an A canna mind the name o' the man that gied them (it) . . . A heard tell o' his name, too, that gied them the punt. An whether 'e sez, 'Ye'll naw make it', A don' know. But they went out anyway in the punt an, oh, it wiz gettin worse an worse aa' the time. Thir beltin aweh at it the two o' them, beltin aweh at it, an she's stannin up on end. Here, this sea took 'er, put 'er right ower. An the few men that wiz on the beach, thir lookin at them. Well, it wiz eether the nuxt deh or two dez (days) efter that they got them rowed (rolled) in the wreck (wrack) on the shore. They come in, ye see, wi' the wreck. They got them rowed in the wreck.[23]

The conclusion of his story is the appearance of his grandmother, Margaret MacFadyen, before the Parochial Board in Campbeltown: 'It *waaz* a poor law. An she had nawthin. She wanna even haiv the money laikly tae take the corpse hame. It wid be wile (wild — terrible). They wir beeried there. An they said tae 'er, "Well, Margret, ye've plenty rich freens. They'll look efter ye aa' right." — "Och well," she sez, "freens is freens, but ye don't waant 'ae be at anybody's cott-tells (coat-tails)." This committee, the three or fower men, an them blowed oot wi' drink laikly . . . If ye'd jeest a mallet an hit ev'ry wan on the heid, jeest squerr (square) there. That's the feelin A've got, ye know. Me mother used tae tell me aal aboot it. "We're only allowed 'ae gie ye three shillins." '[24]

In fact, Margaret MacFadyen was awarded 6/6d (32½p) weekly on 8 September, 1868, almost six weeks after her husband's drowning.[25] The 'rich freens' referred to were on her own, MacCallum side (p. 75). Her brother John — or 'Jeck' — MacCallum was a prosperous baker in

Campbeltown. John McKay's widow, Isabella Loynachan, had to wait until the birth of the child she was carrying before that 'disablement' qualified her for poor relief. On 10 November, 1868, at the age of 22 years, she was awarded a shilling (5p).[26]

John Campbell bobbed in and out of jobs with the determination of a boxer evading blows – no arbitrary comparison, for one of his many occupations was boxing. His fundamental motivation was not the pursuit of material comfort (to which he has never been accustomed), but of a degree of individual freedom, no more manifest than in his travels through the Highlands, hill-walking and climbing when these were, in the main, the privilege of the leisured and professional classes. He has been a fisherman, deckhand on a sailing ship, whaler, coalminer, farm labourer, general labourer, gardener, night-watchman, winkle-picker, and whatever else besides.

Each of these parcels of experience has contributed, to some degree, to the sum of the man's character; but his real strength as a storyteller is not an anecdotal one. It is invested in the great and varied fund of social tradition and traditional tales which he possesses. That fund – the potential of which can scarcely be considered exhausted – is contained in a series of tape-recordings exceeding 20 hours. These recordings contain some 30 stories, and these, though with two exceptions (pp. 112, 124) unavoidably absent from this work, will survive John Campbell as a record of his status as the last of the conscious tradition-bearers in Kintyre.

REFERENCES AND NOTES

1. *RB* Sad, 13 July 1863 – Robert Campbell Jr.; *RD* Cam, 14 Dec. 1901 – Robert Campbell Sr.

2. J. Campbell, 24 February 1981.

3. *RD* Cam, 11 Dec. 1893.

4. J. Campbell, *op. cit.*

5. *HTL*, 6.

6. D. MacKeith, 25 Jan. 1977. He has the tradition that the family landed at Carradale, crossed over to Barr Glen, took the farm of Arnicle, and then nearby Garvalt.

7. In C81 Skip/d3/p5 the family was living – presumably in a hut – on 'Garchroit Shore', near Grogport: William McBride (34), fisherman, born Troon; Ann (35), his wife, born Irvine; their children William (15), Laurance (12), Lilias (9), and Ann (1), all except the last of whom were born in Irvine.

8. J. Campbell, *op. cit.*

9. *CC*, 29 July 1922. It had lain for years unoccupied and the roof was beginning to collapse.

10. Obit. notices, *CC* and *Argyllshire Herald*, 16 Dec. 1893.

11. J. Campbell, 30 Dec. 1980.

12. Mouth music of a sort, but lacking meaningful words.

13. More usually *Gille nan Cochall-Chraiceann.*

14. Rev. D. J. MacDonald, 'Antiquities of Killean and Kilchenzie', in *CC*, 8 Oct. 1932.

15. Dublin 1969, pp. 123 ff.

16. A. and B. Rees, *Celtic Heritage*, London 1961, 359.

17. J. Campbell, 19 Nov. 1980.

18. D. MacDonald, 16 Dec. 1978. (Dr. A. Bruford notes – letter to author, 10 Jan. 1984 – that the related *feadan* can mean a spout, a barrel, and 'discharge of a still'.)

19. C. Mactaggart, *Life in Campbeltown in the 18th Century*, Campbeltown 1923, 14; agreed with by D. Colville, 'A Survey of the Place-names of the Burgh of Campbeltown', pt. 3, in *CC*, 1 May 1937; also in oral tradition, e.g. J. Campbell, 2 Feb. 1982.

20. These words recorded at various times, but all – except *tait* – brought together on 2 Feb. 1982, as part of a comprehensive recording of J. Campbell's Gaelic-derived vocabulary, for the *Historical Dictionary of Scottish Gaelic.*

21. The foundering of the smack *Lizzie* of Carradale (*CC*, 26 April 1879), on passage to the Kinsale mackerel fishery in the south of Ireland, presaged by inexplicable lights along Port na Cùile shore and by the refusal of the skipper's dog to accompany him on the trip (J. Campbell, 21 Oct. 1980). The foundering of the lugger *Pass-by* of Campbeltown (p. 210), presaged by the appearance of a phantom lug-rigged boat (J. Campbell, 24 Oct. 1980).

22. The *Downpatrick Recorder*, 1 Aug. 1868 (courtesy of Mr Michael McCaughan, Ulster Folk and Transport Museum).

23. J. Campbell, 24 Oct. 1980.

24. *Ib.*

25. *RP* 535.

26. *Ib.* 549.

CHAPTER 5

The Irish in Kintyre

The extent of the Irish influence, socially and culturally, in south Kintyre during the nineteenth century is an absorbing, if problematic, question. That the native population was itself just beginning to close the cultural divide opened by the seventeenth century plantations of Lowlanders demonstrates the complexity of the fabric which awaits unravelling.

The Irish immigrant population was, for the greater part of the nineteenth century, singularly unstable. By about 1850, it is true, the majority of those families which did actually settle – and whose descendants remain – had already begun to 'dig in', but outwith that stable nucleus continual flux prevailed. The explanation is inextricably bound up with the social status and condition of many of those Irish who arrived in Kintyre. They were not merely poor, but quite destitute.

There are no means of establishing when, in Kintyre, vagrancy lost its social acceptability (p. 3) and came to be considered an evil, to the extirpation of which public funds could justifiably be directed, but there is record in 1763 of £1 7s (£1.35p) being paid to one Dugal Campbell of Auchrossan for 'searching for, apprehending and committing to the Tolbooth of Campbeltown two vagrant persons who had come from Ireland to Kintyre in November last'. These unfortunate men were later pressed into naval service,[1] an expedient – if morally questionable – means of disposing of vagrants, if not of vagrancy.

In 1832, two special constables – John Stewart, son of Andrew Stewart in Calliburn, and Hugh MacTavish, wright in Stewartfield – were appointed by a committee of heritors in Campbeltown to 'patrol the Parish and to apprehend and bring before any of the resident Magistrates such public beggars, vagrants and unlicensed hawkers as may be found following their unlawful courses within the limits of the parish'.[2]

There is abundant evidence that, during and after the disastrous Irish potato famines of the late 1840s, the problem entered a critical phase. By then, however, firm legal provisions existed for the deportation of Irish paupers. These provisions were contained in the Poor Law Amendment Act of 1845,[3] which, however, was but a reinforcement of the very old and curiously titled 'Act for punishment of strange and idle beggars, and Relief of the pure and impotent', passed by the Scottish parliament in 1579.[4] That Act of 1845 – which remained the basic legislation for the relief of the poor until the Local Government (Scotland) Act in 1894 replaced the parochial boards with parish councils[5] – will require fairly close examination if the complexities of illegal immigration and the problems of the immigrants themselves are to be understood.

The Act was not – ostensibly, at least – designed to halt immigration. Rather, its object was to ensure that immigrant arrivals – of Irish, English, or Manx extraction – in any Scottish parish did not immediately become a financial burden on that parish. To that effect, an immigrant was required, as a condition of eligibility for poor relief, to have lived continuously in a particular parish for five years, 'without having (had) recourse to common begging, either by himself or his family, and without having received or applied for parochial relief'. Retention of that 'settlement by residence' was conditional on his remaining in that parish for at least one year entire in every subsequent period of five years.[6]

The Act, then, was quite clearly aimed at those immigrants who had left Ireland destitute and who arrived in Scotland unable to support themselves. For those families which arrived in Scotland and found work and housing, there was relative security, providing accident or death in the family did not plunge them into destitution within the statutory five-year settlement period. But for many other families and individuals there was merely the prospect of judicial arraignment and – sooner or later – of expulsion by court order. In the decade following the legislation of 1845, on a national scale, 'the numbers removed by judicial proceedings were very numerous',[7] but, in the records of the Parochial Board of Campbeltown for that period, there is absolutely no evidence of a stringent policy of expulsion. The explanation is not that there were no Irish paupers in and around Campbeltown during those years. There were, for their cases are in the same records, but in such limited numbers that the problem may have been reckoned so slight as to warrant only minimal action.

The Board more often allocated sums of money to assist passages back to Ireland than actually instituting legal action to have paupers forcibly removed (which is not, however, to suggest that the 'assistance' was entirely disinterested). Thus, in February 1847, Rose Dunian (?Durnian) – 'an Irish pauper' – was granted a free ticket to take her by steamer to Greenock, and 2/6d (12½p) to pay her passage thence to Derry.[8] In 1849, 'Andrew Corbet and wife, natives of Ireland, applied for a passage to Ayr, on their way to Belfast, which was granted'.[9] In 1850, 'Application having been made by Widow Samuel Galacher for Parochial aid – refused, as she has no claim upon this Parish, as she has only come to this Parish three months ago from Ireland, with three orphans in a state of destitution – 1/6d (7½p) given to aid her to go home'.[10]

Deportations

Only three removals by warrant arc on record: Hugh Delary (?Delargy), with his wife and family, Mary Delary with her two children, and Maria Grier Newland with her child, were all shipped from Campbeltown to Belfast in August, 1851.[11]

Hugh Delary first appeared in the records of Campbeltown Parochial Board on 3 June, 1851. His family were then 'in fever', and assistance was granted until they had recovered sufficiently 'to be removed to Ireland as they have no claim on this or any other parish in Scotland'.[12] That interim relief was in accordance with the terms of the Act, which directed that no persons could be removed without medical certification of their fitness.[13] In 1851 Delary was aged 55 years, and his wife Nancy 54 years. Until his family was stricken by fever, he had been working as a labourer[14] and presumably managing on his earnings.

Mary Delary – probably his eldest daughter[15] – appears on record earlier. On 12 February, 1851, she applied for assistance for her illegitimate child and was refused in the standard terms, '. . . having no claim upon this Parish, nor any Parish in Scotland'.[16] On 9 April she again applied for aid and was again refused, but with the additional instruction to the inspector that she be deported.[17] On 19 June she once more applied, pleading that her two-year-old child was 'ill . . . in the Ark'.[18] She was provided with 'an empty house at Big Kiln for a short time'.[19] Her final appearance is the record of her removal.

The final case – of Maria Grier Newland – is the best documented of all. On 7 May, 1850, her husband James, a mason[20] – 'in bad health, having a wife and two children and having no claim upon this parish' – was granted temporary aid of 2/- (10p) weekly.[21] Some time between then and 3 July, James Newland died. The temporary aid was continued to his children, but the inspector was in some doubt as to his next move and was obliged to 'correspond with other parishes as to the practice in similar circumstances'.[22] The nature of that doubt was unspecified, but it most probably hinged on the birth, in Campbeltown, of one or both of Newland's children. His first wife, Mary Darroch – a native of Campbeltown – died in Glasgow. There was one child of that marriage, Archibald, his birthplace unknown. Newland remarried in 1848 and a second child, Maria, was born in Kirk Street, Campbeltown.[23] The argument that although natives of Ireland were legally removeable, their children, born in Scotland, could not be included in the warrant[24] was widely used to frustrate removal actions. The legitimacy or otherwise of such an action may have been the cause of his indecision.

Maria Newland remained on the poor roll until her removal in August, but by 9 April a decision on her case had already been taken. As her husband had no claim on the parish at the time of his death, she was to be 'removed with her child to Ireland without delay'.[25]

The story of Maria Grier Newland does not, however, end there. In March 1855 she turned up again in the Parochial Board records, 'applying for aid to relieve her clothing from pawn, that she may go to service'. She was refused on the grounds of her having returned from Ireland after removal there by warrant,[26] an action which could have put her into prison for two months.[27]

In fact, she remained in Campbeltown, and in 1889 was admitted to the poor roll on 1/6d (7½p) a week. She was born in County Donegal in January 1822. Her father, William Grier, was a weaver. Her mother's name was Margaret Kerr. Maria Grier Newland died in Kirk Street, Campbeltown on 18 July 1901.[28]

The evidence of Irish destitution in these parish records, though unquestionably so fragmentary as to be useless for any but the most limited of purposes, nonetheless does demonstrate that there was no definitive approach in dealing with such cases as came before the Board. Some Irish applicants, without any claim to assistance, were helped out – albeit temporarily – without threat of deportation, viz:

> 2/6d (12½p) to Martha Davidson, Dalintober, in 1847, 'her legal claim on Londonderry';[29]
> 2/6d to Peter Dillon, 'Irish pauper', in 1848.[30]

However, the removal clause in the Act of 1845 was interpreted in the parish of Campbeltown so that few cases got the length of prosecution; by 1858, on a national scale, the Act had virtually broken down.[31]

Irish Settlement

Of those Irish families which came to Kintyre and settled, much more, obviously, is known. Selected families and their histories, generation by generation, where the lines are clear, form the substance of Appendix I. But that substance is diffuse and, at its furthest edges, touches obscurity and will elude definition. The Irish immigrant population in south Kintyre was an amorphous body – Roman Catholics and Protestants, English speakers and Irish speakers, returning descendants of Scottish settlers in Ireland and true natives, the whole lumped together and having but a single common distinction: its Irish immigrant status. No doubt they brought their national conflicts – religious and political – with them, but of these there is no record. Some maintained their Irishness, in name and by the unifying agency of the Roman Catholic Church, while others abandoned it readily, by discarding both name and religion. Those families which compromised are the most elusive of all. They have disappeared, as it were, beneath the surface of history.

An historical fabric, and the patterns that form with it, are only as durable as the materials which go into the fabric. The historian's fundamental duty is to ensure that the patterns are consistent with the materials. This is more easily said than done. The Irish poor left no personal records of when, and why, and how they came. These reasons may be deduced, with reasonable certainty, from contemporary records and from later histories, but the individual voice, the personal testimony are entirely lacking. Oral tradition offers nothing at all, and one must suppose that, Ireland behind them, with its sufferings and injustices, was Ireland struck from memory.

The present subject, in its specifically local frame, has hitherto been entirely neglected. The preparation of this account has, therefore, involved an extraordinary cost in time and energy, so thinly spread and slender were the strands of the material. These sources are, of course, detailed at the chapter-end, but I will mention three: the population censuses from 1851 to 1891, the records of births, marriages, and deaths, and the poor rolls of Campbeltown. That last-mentioned source was unquestionably the most vital, for therein names ceased to be mere names. The people stepped out, as it were, of their case histories and became the embodiments of their social and racial history. As the principal Lowland settling families are traceable in the Kintyre rentals – from which their distribution may be defined, and the social and economic weight of their presence inferred – so the Irish settling families may be traced in the poor rolls. Hardly an Irish family escaped that end.

Origins

The first question which may be asked is: from which parts of Ireland did the immigrants come? The answers will not be completely reliable, but will certainly provide a broad indication. Two sources have been analysed – the 1851 census, which is a fixed representation of the Irish population in the month of April in that year, and the poor rolls of the period 1848 to 1927, both sources limited to Campbeltown burgh. The fundamental flaw in each of these sources is the very incompleteness of the evidence. In the census enumerations, more than 75 per cent of the immigrants are simply described as Irish. The poor rolls specify place of birth more consistently – less than 50 per cent are described by nationality alone – but comprise a slighter body of examples. All in all, the disparity of the two sets of evidence ought to have been such as to have minimised their comparative value, but, in fact, the two exhibit a remarkable degree of correspondence:

County	1851 Census (total 100)	Poor Rolls (total 81)
Antrim	56	50
Donegal	14	6
Down	9	5
Derry	9	5
Fermanagh	5	4
Tyrone	4	3
Armagh	2	—
Louth	1	—
Others	—	8

The most striking features of these tables, whatever their inherent deficiences, are (1) the preponderance of northern Irish origins – all but nine individuals in a total of 181 belonged to Ulster – and (2), by a narrower perspective, the predominance of specifically Antrim origins – more than 50 per cent from each sample. Neither of these features is particularly surprising considering the proximity of the north of Ireland to Kintyre, and the historical and cultural connections of the two peoples.

To narrow the analysis further by attempting to locate these families more specifically is not altogether feasible. For many of these families, the county of their origin only is given, and while it has been possible, in some cases, to fill the gaps by using extra sources – e.g. the registers of births, marriages, and deaths and later censuses – the most convenient method of handling the material will be to analyse it selectively, as attempted in Appendix I, and so, perhaps, bring into historical focus the composite character of the Irish community.

The Glens of Antrim

The area of Antrim which supplied the heaviest influx of immigrants was the coastal margin of the north-east known as the Glens of Antrim, described thus in 1586:

> The Glynnes is a Countrie so called because it is full of rocky and woody dales; it stretcheth in length 24 miles, on the one side being backed with a very steep and boggy mountain, and on the other part with the sea, on which side there are many creeks between rocks and thickets where the Scottish galleys do commonly land; at either end are very narrow entries and passages into the countrie, which lieth directlie opposite to Cantyre, from which it is 18 miles distant.[32]

Until the laying of the Antrim coast road in the mid-1830s,[33] access to the Glens was impeded by the necessity of following narrow routes through mountainous, wooded country, or of negotiating ways between the forbidding bogs which top the inland plateau.[34] These factors likewise hampered internal communication, and undoubtedly tilted the social and economic structure of the Glens communities towards a peculiar dependence on Kintyre.

The Glens area is formed, from north to south, by the island of Rathlin and the civil parishes of Ramoan, Armoy (both partial), Culfeightrin, Layd, Ardclinis, and Tickmacrevan (Map 2).

Of the society from which the immigrant stock in Kintyre was drawn, the following description – written in 1835, as an Ordnance Survey memoir for the Parish of Culfeightrin – will serve as a reasonable introduction:

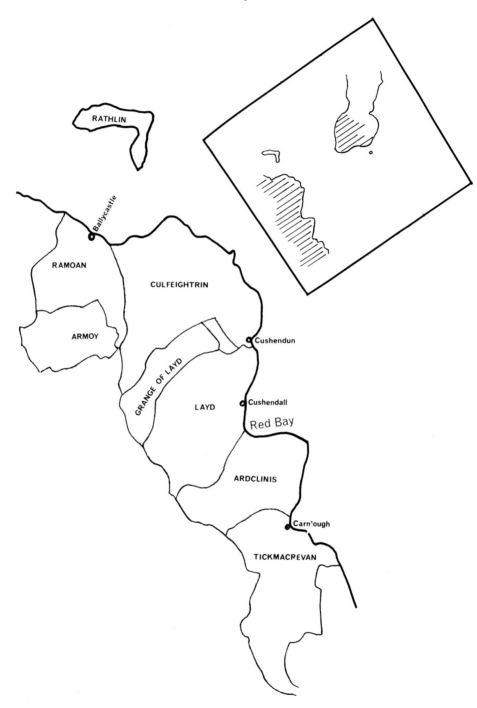

2. The civil parishes of the Glens of Antrim, with inset map showing the Glens in geographical relation to Kintyre

The houses of the lower class are all one-storey, thatched, and built of stone. Those in the more cultivated part of the parish are tolerably comfortable and consist of from two to three apartments. They are rather cleanly and receive light from two or sometimes three glazed windows. The houses in the more remote and mountainous districts are not near so cleanly or comfortable and seldom consist of more than one apartment. There are several . . . farmers' houses, the planting about which gives them a very comfortable appearance.

Meal and potatoes, with a little fish, form the only articles of food. In the mountainous districts very little meal is used. Tea is becoming an indispensable article, particularly with the older persons. Turf, which is very abundant, is the only fuel. Their dress is very good and comfortable, particularly in the more cultivated districts. They marry rather early and are rather long lived . . .

Dancing forms their principal amusement and of it they are passionately fond. A dancing master is kept in constant employment by them and many of them come to the fairs of Ballycastle for no other purpose. St. Patrick's and St. John's are their only patrons' days. Their traditions respecting them are absurd and ridiculous. The only custom now existing is that of burning fires on St. John's eve . . . They are very honest and peaceable and industrious and hospitable. The Roman Catholics are very superstitious, having a firm belief in all manner of ghosts, fairies and enchantments.[35]

Work

What work did they find when they arrived in Kintyre? To say that the great majority of them were 'unskilled' would, in the accepted sense, be accurate enough, yet, at the same time, an over-simplification. Their predominantly rural background undoubtedly equipped them with diverse skills, many of which have become so rare as to enter the category of specialist occupations. Many of the immigrants would be adept at thatching, basket-weaving, rope-spinning, etc., in addition to whatever knowledge they had of fishing and farming and general land work, such as peat-cutting and draining.

Indeed, a great number of the Irish did turn to the land and were feed as farm-servants, working from place to place as conditions suited. A single example will suffice. Elizabeth Kiargan or Cairns − born in Ballycastle in 1842 − in the late 1850s was feed at Belloch and other farms near Campbeltown for ten months, was at Feochaig for two months, and at Drumnamucklach in the parish of Killean, Balligroggan near Machrihanish, and Machremore and Gartloskan in Southend for six-month terms in each case.[36] Those farm-servants lived mainly in the landward districts of Campbeltown Parish and in Southend Parish, and are thus outwith the present survey; but, even in Campbeltown itself, the number of individuals − both male and female − who described themselves as farm labourers was fairly high − 22 in a total of 262 occupations stated in the 1851 Census. That figure is probably reduced by numbers of farm labourers included in the general class of labourers, which is the predominant one, as would have been expected. Occupational lists, compiled from the Census of 1851, appear over page:

labourers	72
servants (mainly domestic and female)	28
farm labourers	22
hawkers	21
fishermen	19
lodging-house keepers	8
seamstresses	8
carters	8
spinners (female)	7
sewers (female)	6
masons	6
merchants	6
maltmen in distilleries	5
nail-makers	4
cobblers	4
weavers	3
gardeners	2
tin-smiths	2
slaters (one master)	2
net-workers	2

In addition, there were: a dyer; a watch and clock-maker; a 'web flowerer'; a miner; a lime-burner; a cartwright; a seaman; a joiner; a tailor; a laundress; a pig-dealer; an umbrella-maker and an umbrella-repairer; a shopkeeper (employed in, but not owning the premises, by deduction); a 'sand retailer'; an errand-girl; a brassfounder finisher; a pawnbroker; a clerk; a porter; an errand-boy; a stocking-worker; a cow-feeder; a quarryman; a washing-house keeper; a stone-cutter; and a stone-quarrier.

The most significant feature of these statistics is the disproportionately small numbers of businessmen and tradesmen. The professional classes are entirely unrepresented. The business by which, perhaps, the Irish were best known in the community was that most public of occupations, hawking or 'general dealing' as it is still sometimes euphemistically described. To be a hawker then was, as a rule, to be poor, and the poor rolls demonstrate that equation. Whereas, in the census returns, hawkers number 21 in a total of 262, in the poor rolls the figure is 22 in 97 stated occupations. Hawkers were, in the main, women, and usually middle-aged or elderly. They dealt in most goods which were at once inexpensive, in general demand, and portable: stone and delf ware, bread, fish, and the like. Some peddled their goods through the countryside, while others – fishwives principally – confined their trade to the town. In 1873, Margaret O'Hara (p. 205) forfeited a deposit of 2s 6d (12½p) at Campbeltown Police Court when she failed to appear on a charge of 'obstructing a crossing by leaving a herring barrow unattended on the street'.[37]

Fishing

The occupation in which, however, the Irish rose to prominence and by which they gained a sure and lasting economic foothold in the community was that of fishing. In 1851, only 19 fishermen of Irish origin were recorded. The explanation is probably that the time of year in which the census was taken – April – was a notoriously slack one. Line-fishing was then failing, and the herring season proper was two months off. Some individuals who would have worked as fishermen for the greater part of the year had no doubt taken jobs ashore, and so were absent from that group at the time of the census.

But the Irish commitment to fishing was essentially a late nineteenth century development, and it occurred at a crucial stage in the growth of the industry in Kintyre. A new method of herring fishing, unrivalled in its efficiency and productivity, had been pioneered about Tarbert, and by the early 1860s, though still illegal, had caught on among a few of the Campbeltown and Dalintober fishermen. That method was ring-netting, and following its legalisation in 1867 there began, in Campbeltown as elsewhere in Kintyre, a steady shift away from the traditional drift-net method. Until then, the industry had been dominated by an aggregation of wealthy boat-owners who hired skippers and crews for the drift-net fisheries in both home and distant waters. Skipper-owners were generally a depressed class, working in small boats and rarely earning much more than a subsistence wage.

With the advent of ring-netting, however, boat-ownership and a degree of real prosperity came within the reach of careful and ambitious fishermen. In the 1860s, about £36 would purchase a ring-net skiff and the necessary fishing gear, whereas investment in a drift-net smack and a fleet of nets required £140 or more.[38] Self-determination had clearly become viable for the man who was able to set some money aside after a good season. Some first time boat-owners invested in second-hand boats, at minimal cost, while others – in partnerships of two and three, or more – pooled their savings and so, at once, secured their independence and reduced their investment risk. The greater profitability of the ring-net method and its fairer system of reward – crewmen received a share of the week's profits, rather than, as at drift-netting, a fixed wage, and so occasionally took quite outstanding wages out of a successful week's fishing[39] – together raised the ring-net fishermen, as a whole, into a wage-earning scale far above their drift-net counterparts.

By the 1870s, increasing numbers of fishermen were loosening themselves from the economic grip of the boat-owning consortia and were making their way independently. By the 1880s, Irish fishermen and (predominantly by then) the descendants of immigrant Irish were heavily represented in the boat-owning class. By the early years of the present century, the advance was complete, and a few of these Irish families – notably the McKay brothers, Archibald, Denis, and John – had, by their phenomenal ability, attained pre-eminence. The Irish presence in the Campbeltown fishing community has declined as the industry has declined, but with such families as the Meenans and the Finns that illustrious tradition is perpetuated.

I cannot suggest that the biographical and genealogical accounts of the Irish families which constitute Appendix I are in any sense complete. Some, to be sure, are complete within the strict confines of the exercise. I have dug at the deepest roots of the Irish community in Campbeltown and have been content to uncover the progenitorial sources and a generation or two on either side. The knotty entanglements of subsequent generations I have largely avoided, to curtail both the scale of the material and the work involved in compiling it. I have further limited the survey by examining only those families which were involved in fishing. In most cases, involvement was continuous through several generations, but, in a few cases, families which appeared and disappeared rapidly have been examined for the special insights which they bring to the social substructure of the material.

A remarkable feature of these family histories, yet one so obvious that it might have been overlooked, is that the majority of these families stem from the settlement of a single parental unit. These instances – e.g. Meenan, Finn, O'Hara, Morrans – serve as a reminder of how rapidly a name may proliferate within a community and – by migration – beyond it.

The figure of 473 Irish-born individuals compiled from the 1851 census enumerations – in a total burgh population of 6,880[40] should, in strict accuracy, be closer to 500. Irish-born Inland Revenue officers, not being strictly classifiable as immigrants, were excluded. Additionally, a few of the enumeration sheets were so illegibly written, or had become so faded and indecipherable, as to necessitate omission. Whatever the true figure, in real terms it cannot but be reckoned unrepresentative of the full impact of the Irish presence in Campbeltown. Immigrant children, though born in Campbeltown, would undoubtedly have been locally classed as Irish. The real figure is thus further inflated.

Family Names and Cross-Migration

Many surnames introduced from Ireland were already current in Kintyre. The following list – by no means exhaustive – of Irish-born families in nineteenth century Kintyre will indicate the extent of the correspondence and the inherent difficulty of distinguishing 'native' families from Irish: Black, Brodie, Darroch, Duncan, Gillies, Graham, Hamilton, Hattan, *Mac*

-Allister, -Donald, -Geachy, -Gill, -Gougan, -Innes, -Intyre, -Isaac, -Kay, -Kerral-Kiargan, -Kinven, -Lean, -Millan, -Neill, Martin, Mitchell, Morrison, Murray, Reid, Sharp, Smith, Stewart, Wilkison.[41] Some of these names were products of parallel development, and so may be considered native to both Ireland and Scotland. Some others − both in that list and out of it − which superficially appear to be of English or Scottish origin actually prove more likely to have been formed by translation, pseudo-translation, or simple borrowing.[42] But the greatest section of these names above, containing some of the most extensive and influential family groups, belonged to the descendants of Gaelic settlers in the north of Ireland. A number of these may be identified with reasonable certainty as of specifically Kintyre origin.

In the study of relations between the peoples of Kintyre and the north of Ireland, a single compelling factor emerges − that the intermixing of the contiguous populations cannot be explained solely in terms of specific migratory surges. Political and social pressures undoubtedly did periodically impel large-scale migration, but the historical frame must be regarded as a very open one, in which migration and counter-migration operated continuously.

Nonetheless, between the fourteenth and the early seventeenth centuries, three substantial movements of Scots into Ireland have been identified. The first and second movements − of mercenaries from Argyll and the Western Isles (*gallóglaigh*, or gallowglasses) − effected a fairly general dispersal and settlement throughout Ireland, but the final influx was of a more concentrated character, and, moreover, was not confined to the military class. It took the form of a gradual shift, increasingly impelled by political and social pressures, of the southern confederacy of Clan Donald in Argyll. That transference of its power base from Argyll to Antrim was the consolidation of an inheritance forged in 1399 by the marriage of Eoin Mór MacDonald of Dunnyveg in Islay to Marjorie Byset, heiress to the Glens of Antrim.[43] That territorial extension, which was reinforced by subsequent intermarriages, opened up the Glens as a place of refuge and resettlement for Clan Donald and its associate families right down to its disintegration in the seventeenth century.

The contribution of Kintyre to the Gaelic stock in the Glens was a heavy one, and most of the old names native to Kintyre are represented there. Not a few of them, indeed, are present in greater numerical strength in the Glens than in their historic homeland. An extreme example of population movement and its distributional effect occurs with the name MacCambridge, in Irish *Mac Ambróis*.[44] That name was formerly current in Southend, and survives in the romantic tradition of the district through Flora MacCamrois who is supposed to have saved the infant son of

Archibald MacDonald of Macharioch from the bloody aftermath of the siege at Dunaverty in 1647.[45] The name vanished entirely from Kintyre in the nineteenth century,[46] but retains a hold in Antrim. In the Glens itself there were, in the electoral role of 1963, 41 McCambridges,[47] making it the twenty-third most numerous name there,[48] while in the burgh of Larne, farther south, 30 McCambridges were enumerated.[49] The Argyll surname *Mac Gille Ghuirm* was translated as Blue (p. 208) and its original form has entirely vanished, but in Antrim it survives as McIlgorm.[50]

The principal Kintyre surnames in the Glens of Antrim are McAllister, McKay, and McNeill, and all of these were returned proportionately by nineteenth century immigration to Kintyre.

MacAllister: The family of Loup, on West Loch Tarbert, was the main branch in Kintyre. Its involvement in Irish affairs is indicated by the deaths, in military action, of two men of the name – one of them described as 'the Laird of Loop' – in Antrim during the late sixteenth century. Twelve MacAllisters were recorded in the Glens in 1669.[51]

MacKay: One of the oldest Kintyre families, it appears on record in 1329.[52] In the Glens of Antrim the name is particularly concentrated about Red Bay. Thirteen of the name were recorded in the Glens in 1669, one of them being 'ffennell McCaye'[53] of Ballytearim, near Cushendun, whose land was granted, probably to his grandfather Daniel, in 1615.[54]

MacNeill: There were three landed branches of the family in Kintyre, of which that of Carskey was the earliest, appearing on record in 1505.[55] In 1669, eleven of the name were recorded in the Glens.[56] For a brief reference to the Tirfergus branch see page 5.

Each of these names is now more numerous in the Glens of Antrim than in Kintyre. Thus, in an electorate of 5,170 in the Glens (1963), compared with an electorate in Kintyre of 7,063 (1970):

	Glens	Kintyre
McAllister/McAlister	168	68
McKay	97	52
McNeill	158	38[57]

It would be as well, at this stage, to consider the long-term historical implications of immigration and counter-immigration between Kintyre and Antrim. Taking, hypothetically, any family from any of these three representative surname groups, an absolute minimum of three cross-channel shifts may be postulated.
1. The initial migration of Gaelic stock from north-east Antrim to Argyll around the sixth century A.D. (remembering, of course, that the system of hereditary surnames was then undeveloped).

2. Departure from Kintyre and resettlement in Antrim in the seventeenth century.

3. Return to Kintyre in the nineteenth century.

Historical truth will not be too badly served by that hypothetical outline; but it does treat the possibilities minimally. Additional shifts would have been likely, so that if it were possible to delineate the successive locations of a particular Gaelic family in either Antrim or Kintyre, from the twentieth century right back to the fifth or sixth century, five or six or more shifts between the two areas might appear. Add to this the continual accretion of familial and territorial associations by marriage, across a span of 1500 years, and the network of connections between the two peoples becomes marvellously complex.

In emphasising the fundamental importance of the proximity of Antrim to Argyll, the observation of an Irish writer may be quoted with effect: 'The tracing of recorded and organised movements from one to the other must not be allowed like the sea mist to blot out the very obvious sight of the opposite coast. It is possible to go from one side to the other without losing sight of land . . .'[58] The sea connections between the two will later be discussed, but within an implicit context of decided immigration. There were, however, frequent comings and goings, particularly of migrant labour, which annually – and temporarily – inflated the Irish population in Kintyre. Many of these workers liked Kintyre, or thought that they could better themselves there, or married locally, and so remained. They were attracted mainly by land work – ditching and draining, harvesting, and the like. From about 1785 until the famine years, 1845-1848, the Irish immigrant had been an 'indigent labourer meeting the demand created by the expansion of industrial and agricultural Scotland . . .', but the onset of that cataclysm – which decimated, through death and emigration, the Irish population by more than two millions[59] – reduced him to 'a starving peasant escaping from the wrath that was, or was to come'.[60] J. E. Hanley expressed the distinction succinctly: 'Self-improvement was the impulse that transported him to Scotland in pre-famine days. Self-preservation was the urge that drove him onwards in the black night of pestilence.'[61]

For as long as thatched houses remained commonplace in Kintyre – that is, in general, until about the mid-nineteenth century – thatching skills were imported from the north of Ireland. That custom is preserved in the song *The Thatchers of Glenrea,* and with it is preserved a good deal about the conditions and attitudes of the Irish thatchers. It is, despite its patently comic intentions, an interesting social testimony, the more so for its authorship. It was composed by a Ballycastle thatcher, Hector ('Hecky') McIlfatrick, and was preserved entirely in the oral tradition of Southend until written down some time after the turn of the century by Archibald

McEachran, a farmer at Kilblaan and, besides, an avid collector of folk tradition. Of its remarkably circuitous survival, Hamish Henderson of the School of Scottish Studies has remarked: 'With "The Thatchers", there-fore, we traverse the Mull in both directions; it was written by an Irish labourer while working in "the shire of Argyle"; was learned by a Kintyre man[62] direct from the author; was passed on by the Kintyre man to a local collector, and later transmitted by this collector to Sam Henry in Coleraine.'[63] It has as its theme Hecky's rueful service at a notoriously inhospitable farm, Glenrea, which is now ruinous and lies within a rising forest, above Glenbreackerie. The entire song is reproduced in Appendix IV.

The Maintenance of Kinship Ties

As the proximity of Antrim and Kintyre facilitated migration between the two, it also favoured the maintenance of kinship ties to a degree perhaps unparalleled elsewhere. The separation of families by the emigration of a branch to, say, Glasgow or Dundee, engendered, for the most part, prolonged if not final separation. But the removal of a family from Antrim to Kintyre − and, at earlier periods, vice-verse − was in no sense much different from a shift to the opposite end of the parish, in a society in which prolonged travel was not much indulged in, and a trip to the market town − on a fair day, for instance − was a rare and memorable event.

Both of my own grandmothers were of Irish extraction. My paternal grandmother, Caroline Stewart, was born in Southend, in 1864, and spent her childhood there, but her parents were from Ardclinis in the Glens of Antrim. She had two maternal uncles who were seamen, and they occasionally sailed from Antrim to Southend to visit. One of them wore in his ears tiny anchors of gold, and my grandmother, then a child, was fascinated by these and wanted a pair for herself. Her uncle promised to have a pair for her on his next visit, anticipating which she and a brother cheerfully pierced their ears with sewing needles. But she never got the golden anchors.[64]

The Irish link was maintained into the present century, but has since almost entirely lapsed, though boat parties from the Antrim coast do still visit Kintyre, and there is a strong association − formed in recognition of the affinities which this chapter attempts to explore − between the Campbeltown yachting club and its counterpart in Cushendall, which is maintained by reciprocal inter-club competitions staged annually.[65] The McKay fishing families (p. 202) occasionally crossed by fishing skiff to their native Cushendon to visit friends and relations. Of one such trip, in Denis McKay's *Annunciata*, in 1911, it was reported that 'a splendid day was spent among friends, everybody enjoying themselves immensely. At 2 a.m.

on Monday, to the strains of "Come back to Erin", the anchor was weighed and the return journey commenced, Campbeltown being reached about 8 o'clock'.[66] The last trip reported was in August, 1914. A party of sixteen representatives of the local Catholic population crossed in John McKay's *Little Flower* for the dedication of a new chapel in the village of Cushendall.[67]

Sea Links

The earliest reference to a regular ferry service between the north of Ireland and Kintyre appears to be the record of Edward Lhuyd's cross-channel movements in 1699/1700 (p. 12). The ferry then operated between Ballycastle, on the north coast of Ireland, and Southend.[68] The earliest steamship connection began – and ended – in 1818 with the *Rob Roy*, which called at Campbeltown on passage from Greenock to Belfast. In 1819 the sailing became a direct one.[69] Regular weekly sailings from Glasgow to Londonderry were introduced in 1824 by the Glasgow and Londonderry Steam Packet Company with the *Argyll* and the *Britannia*.[70] In 1825, these vessels were sailing from Campbeltown to Londonderry every Friday evening and returning on Monday evening, presumably in alternation, additional to a daily service, from Monday to Thursday, to Greenock and Glasgow, calling at Rothesay and Port Glasgow.[71] During the 1830s and '40s a steady sequence of new steamers maintained a service which varied in frequency from two to three weekly sailings, and calls – which were discontinued at an unknown date – were made at the Giant's Causeway, Campbeltown, and Rothesay.[72] By 1847, there was evidently no direct steamer link with Ireland, because an Irish pauper, on assisted passage, had to sail to Greenock from Campbeltown to secure a connection (p. 83).

From the records of recurrent disputes between Campbeltown Town Council and the Glasgow and Londonderry Steam Packet Company, over harbour dues levied on that company's ships, a little more about the service is known. The dispute began in 1833 with the refusal by the masters of the vessels *Foyle* and *Londonderry* to pay the harbour dues demanded, and their threats to legally contest these demands. On 18 June the council itself threatened legal action unless a debt of £1 10s (£1.50) was settled. Two days later, the company, from its Glasgow office, denied that the dues had ever been refused, but stated an objection to 'the system adopted by the Magistrates of Campbeltown in raising the dues from time to time from one sum to another, as is again attempted . . .' Payment would continue to be resisted until legal proof of the council's right to adjust the dues had been established. On 22 June the council issued the company with the ultimatum that, if the dues were withheld for eight days more, legal action would be taken. In July a settlement was reached. It was agreed that the annual harbour dues, commencing at Whitsunday of 1833 and fixed for the succeeding two years, would be £15 for the *Foyle* and £12 for the *Londonderry*, these sums to be modified in the event of the withdrawal from service of either ship.[73]

Four years later, in November 1837, the dispute erupted once more. The company objected to the dues imposed, on the grounds that the *Foyle* 'had not plied during the whole year ending Whitsunday 1837', and that the *Rover* − a recently commissioned vessel − 'did not begin to ply until the 7 September 1836, tho she is charged for a year as at Whits. 1837'. A compromise was reached,[74] but in the following year the parties again found themselves at odds. The full year's dues for 1836 had been charged against the *Foyle*, 'whereas the Boat plied only for 4 months & a half having been laid up under repair'. A reduction of dues was requested, to which the council consented. The registered tonnage of the *Foyle* was given as 136 (annual dues accordingly set at £15), the *Rover's* tonnage as 200 (£22 1/2d, or £22.05), and the tonnage of the *St Columb* − an additional vessel which had also gone into service on the run − as 153 (£16 17/6d, or £16.87½).[75]

There is little doubt, however, that the ferryboats which plied between Southend and Cushendun conveyed the bulk of the immigrants. The preponderance of Antrim families in that immigration was no accident. Kintyre was their obvious destination both because a convenient and − presumably, by the very shortness of the distance − inexpensive crossing was available, and because, by reasonable supposition, that destination was less remote and forbidding than the industrial centres to which the majority of their compatriots were drawn. The history of that ferry is almost as sketchy as that of its steam-powered, later rivals.

The earliest extant record of the ferry is the petition, in 1710, of John McIlreavi, ferrier at Machrimore, to the Justice Court of Argyll, applying for protection against encroachments on his right of ferry between Kintyre and Ireland,[76] which suggests the activity of unlicensed competitors. In 1730, John McShenog was granted the tack of the half-merkland of Machrimore, with the change-house − or tavern − and ferry attached to it. A condition of McShenog's contract was that he should 'obey what Statutes or acts shall be made by the Duke (of Argyll) or his Baillie depute of Kintyre for the time being in relation to the passage at the ferry'.[77] In 1770, Archibald Lamont was granted, on a 19-year lease, the half-merkland of Monroy, 'with the right and priveledge of ferrying from the said land to the Coast of Ireland as now and formerly in use'. By that agreement he was obliged to 'hold and keep in constant rediness and sufficient repair and order a good Boat with hands proper for ferrying from the coast of Kintyre . . . to the Coast of Ireland'.[78]

A few of the practical implications of the contract are revealed in a petition to the Duke of Argyll from the ferryman at Monoroy, Kenneth Morrison, in 1792. He affirmed that he had 'always kept up two half Deckt boats for the Accomodation of the publick passing to and from Ireland', but complained that during the eighteen months past he had lost, with onshore winds, two boats on a pair of dangerous rocks which lay at the entrance of the ferry channel at 'Machrimore water foot' (i.e. the mouth of Conieglen Water). These losses prevented his continued operation of two ferryboats and explained the lapse in the punctuality of his rent payments. He recommended that the rocks be removed, and suggested that 'a safe and commodious harbour' would thereby be created.[79] The petition was successful. In 1794 Morrison was granted £15 for the blasting and clearing of a rock from the harbour at Machrimore, which little port was of such importance that it could, in 1808, be reckoned 'the principal communication betwixt this country and Ireland from whence there is daily intercourse'.[80]

A ferry service was evidently conducted from the Irish side also – in 1802 Charles McAllister was running the open boat *Rattlesnake* from Cushendun to Southend[81] – but of its history virtually nothing is known. The year in which the Southend ferry service ended is also unknown. 'About 1840' was the opinion of one local historian, while the evidence from Ireland states more exactly that 'by 1834 the ferry had been abandoned'.[82]

Sea links with Ireland were not, however, confined to ferries. By the late eighteenth century, most of the merchants in Campbeltown – then the biggest trading port in the West Highlands – had centred their interests on Ireland, and were sending ships not just to the major ports of the country, but also to such smaller Antrim ports as Larne, Ballycastle, Cushendun, and Cushendall.[83]

Additionally, there was a commercial traffic – often in illicit goods, for smuggling was rife – between Ireland and such primitive ports as Machrihanish, Carskey, Feochaig, and Glenahervie. In 1817, the tenant in Glenahervie, Colin MacEachran, petitioned the Duke of Argyll for some compensation for the expense of building a 'harbour' there. That harbour – which was begun in 1810 – had since become much used by the farmers round about, especially in the importation of limestone from Ireland. The facility no doubt had been designed to harbour a smack of 24 tons which he built in 1807.[84] That same Colin later built, on the shore at Glenahervie, with his brother Neil's assistance, a 50-ton sloop, the *Two Brothers*, which they launched in 1828. She was built entirely by their own hands, with larch boated from Carradale and Ayr, and they traded mainly between Kintyre and Ireland. She was sold in 1835, to Killough near Ardglass, when the brothers decided to emigrate.[85]

That numbers of Irish reached Kintyre as passengers on trading vessels, or even in boats chartered on the Irish coast specifically for their conveyance, is a possibility. In 1798, Campbeltown Town Council proposed, as a measure against 'the great inundation of Irish stragglers who are daily coming over to this part of the Country', the stationing of two revenue cutters – ordinarily engaged in the prevention of smuggling – 'betwixt the Mull of Kintyre and the Coast of Ireland to relieve each other in order to intercept every Boat and examine the same'.[86] The council, in 1821, was still tackling the problem and had directed its attention to Southend, 'through which parish a number of Vagrants are continually coming from the shores of Ireland to Campbeltown'. A directive was addressed to the minister and heritors of Southend parish, 'that every Vagrant or Beggar who shall in future be ascertained to come in this manner from the Parish of Southend shall immediately be transmitted back to the said Parish leaving it to reconvey them to Ireland if (it does) not take measures for preventing their landing from that Country'.[87] In 1847 the Constabulary Committee of Argyll was advising its officers in Kintyre to 'use every exertion to prevent Irish vagrants entering the country by the ports of the district'. The 'danger of Fever being introduced by the Irish numbers' was vexing the committee.[88] To these 'Irish vagrants (wrote the minister of Killean and Kilchenzie Parish in 1843) who are conveyed by steam-boats to Campbelton, and itinerate through the parish, begging their way from house to house', was attributed the prevalence of 'typhus fever and other epidemic diseases'.[89]

Religious Issues

The immigrant Irish were, in general, unwelcome in Kintyre. Contemporary records indicate as much. An extraordinary complaint, in the minutes of Campbeltown Town Council in 1821, conjoined 'Irish vagrants and swine' as 'an insufferable evil on the streets of the Burgh'.[90] The association of epidemic disease with Irish vagrancy and the financial burden of the Irish poor on parochial resources aside, there were unquestionably other social factors which are less apparent in the records of the times. As late as 1907, the local newspaper could complain that 'Southend is unfortunate in the class of immigrants who have taken up quarters in the village and are giving the place an unenviable reputation by the frequent calls made upon the services of the police . . . Most of the actors in these scenes have a rare fluency of speech and a well-marked brogue'.[91]

The Catholic Emancipation Bill of 1829 – for the removal of remaining civil and political constraints on Catholics – provoked objection in Southend Parish. Five hundred and seventy-six signatures were subscribed to a petition, which was sent to both Houses of Parliament. Of William

MacDonald, proprietor of Ballyshear Estate and the principal heritor in the parish, it was written, with unconcealed admiration, that he 'distinguished himself by his exertions in preparing the petition and by his zeal for the Protestant cause'.[92] The success of that petition may not, of course, have been entirely unconnected with the status of its proponent.

A similar petition, raised in Campbeltown in January, 1779 – 'oposing the Repeall of the present laws Against Popery'[93] – fared less well. When submitted to the local town council for its 'countenance', a special meeting was convened to debate the issue; but so few councillors appeared that the meeting was adjourned until the following day. The council then cautiously declared that, although it was 'far from wishing to give any obstruction to . . . the Protestant Interest', the petition was insufficiently supported and so, in effect, was unrepresentative of public feeling.[94] No more was heard of it.

The root cause of the hostility was, of course, religious opposition, which is entirely in accordance with the national pattern of relations between the overwhelmingly Protestant native population and the predominantly Catholic immigrant population. Roman Catholicism had largely vanished – or been extirpated, more accurately – from Kintyre by the eighteenth century, but there is ample evidence to indicate, in the preceding century, a lingering religious link with Ireland. That link, not surprisingly, persisted longest in the Mull area of Southend, into which came Irish priests to perform baptismal and wedding services, and from which went natives of the place to Ireland to have these services performed there.

That religious link with Ireland has come down through tradition in one fragmentary tale, recorded from Calum Bannatyne. The problem here – as with a good deal of orally preserved material – is the lack of any internal evidence by which to date the account. The story, whatever its value in strict historical terms, tells of an Irish priest who came across by boat to officiate at a marriage in one of the coastal communities between the Mull and Machrihanish. His boat was 'catched in a tide' and swept round into Carskey Bay, whence he had to find his way on foot to the township.[95]

In 1646 the Protestant Synod of Argyll expressed its alarm at the 'number of freiris and seminary priests' who were 'going about Kintyre and some of the Isles using all diligence and endeavour to seduce the people to poprie . . .'[96] By that year, however, the great missionary drive had evidently ended. A good deal is known about these daring priests from reports which they sent to Rome during the period of their active service, 1619-1637. They belonged – those that are known, anyway – to the Franciscan order, and their mission was to revive the Roman Catholic faith in the Highlands and Islands. In 1629, one of them, Cornelius Ward, reported that there were many places in the southern Highlands and in the Hebrides in which neither a priest nor a minister had been seen, since the Reformation in 1560, and that in such places some of the people had memories of Catholicism which had not been infected by the teachings of the Calvinists.[97]

From 1626 to 1637 the entire personnel of the mission comprised Patrick Brady, Patrick Hegarty, Edmund McCann, and Cornelius Ward. Both McCann and Ward were captured and jailed for two years, but returned to the mission after their release. Hegarty was later (in 1641) jailed for five years. All were from the province of Ulster, and their knowledge of the Irish language fitted them ideally for their work among the Gaelic-speaking people of the Highlands and Islands. The mission was dogged by financial constraints, and seems to have effectively ended in 1637, when the last priest, Cornelius Ward, returned to Ireland. The mission was formally re-established in 1647, but whether or not its members were active in or after that year is not known.[98]

Those reports which describe the mission's work in Kintyre are worth examining selectively. In July of 1624 Hegarty and his companions landed on Sanda Island. He explained to the islanders the meaning of the sacred vestments and preached to them. They had been instructed in the faith four years before by another Irish Franciscan, but had seen no priest since then. Hegarty and his companions baptised four children, and fishermen who had crossed to the island from Kintyre were 'instructed in the faith'. Forty went to confession and received communion that day, and in the evening the missionaries crossed to Kintyre. They had to spend that night in the open, but on the evening of the next day a Catholic welcomed them to his house, and they stayed there overnight. On the following morning Hegarty's companions left him to go to labour elsewhere. During the eight weeks Hegarty spent in Kintyre, he converted 206 persons and baptised twelve adults and two babies. His days were spent hiding in caves, and by night he preached, baptised, and administered other sacraments. He would say mass twice daily before the sun rose, and at places ten miles apart.[99]

During 1625, Hegarty visited 21 'villages' in Kintyre, converting 426 and baptising 58 persons there.[100] A list of 132 of Hegarty's converts in Kintyre has survived.[101] Hector MacNeill, laird of Carskey, was described as 'very well disposed towards Catholics'.[102]

In 1650, Lachlan McCawish and More ncNeill confessed to having been married by a priest, and though that marriage was subsequently validated by the Synod of Argyll, they were ordained to 'stand three severall Lords dayes in the place of publict repentance in the kirk of Lochead for takeing away the scandall of marieing with ane priest'. McCawish not only confessed his own guilt, but also informed on another couple – John McMath of Gartavaich and Jonnet ncConochy – who had likewise undergone a Catholic marriage ceremony.[103]

Recource to the Catholic Church was no doubt, for many, a matter of convenience – or even necessity – because the parish of Southend was without an incumbent from c. 1645 until 1672.[104] The moral dangers posed by the vacancy troubled the Synod, which in 1658 resolved to 'take mor nerow inspection of the south ends vacant paroach in Kintyr, whence sevrall scandalous persons go over to Irland for mariag and baptism'.[105]

The exposing and stigmatising of 'papists' was serious business then, and the scattered adherents of the old faith were ruthlessly pursued. In the correction of 'ane obstinat papist', Anna ncDonald, 'great paines' were taken, but to no effect. She refused to relinquish her Catholicism, and in 1652 was ordained by the Synod to be excommunicated. Two years later, the Synod heard reports that 'sevrall persons in the cuntrey conversed with' her, and proscribed all further communication with 'any excomunicat person (except such as naturall tyes binds) under the pain of condingne censure' and civil punishment.[106]

The Riot of 1851

There is on record but a single case of violent anti-Catholic demonstration in Kintyre, and that occurred in Campbeltown in 1851. The uproar was triggered by a drunken spree involving mineworkers from the Drumlemble district, who, 'some of them being Protestants, and some of them Roman Catholics . . . began to fight about their religion'.[107] Three of the brawlers – Protestants, presumably – were arrested and taken to the tolbooth of Campbeltown to sober up, but while they were being removed a crowd gathered. The crowd was mostly made up of boys, but one of the adults there, Donald MacCaffer, assumed the role of rabble-rouser and was subsequently charged with assault and riot.

The crowd were subdued enough until the three were locked up; then they set off through the streets, on a circuit of the town and Dalintober, gathering support as they marched, and chanting 'To hell with the Pope', 'No priest, no Pope, no holy water', and slogans of the kind. They converged on Kirk Street and gathered outside the house of Charles Reid, the young Roman Catholic priest in Campbeltown. There they kept up a noisy demonstration.[108]

Their vocal protest exhausted, the crowd dispersed; but some thirty minutes later a fresh and altogether more menacing design was unleashed. The mob reassembled, invaded the courtyard of the chapel house and broke open the door of the house. The house and adjacent chapel were stoned and windows smashed. By then, Reid had collected the church plate and secured it in his house. He 'sat up till a late hour, but was not disturbed any more'.[109]

During the riot, a Roman Catholic bystander, John McMenemy – 27 years old and master of the smack *Pioneer* of Campbeltown[110] – was the victim of a vicious assault. He was approached by Donald MacCaffer, who was heard to remark, 'There is an Irish bugger'. MacCaffer felled McMenemy with a punch to the right eye and while he was down kicked him in the head. Nancy MacGowan, a Southend woman of Irish parentage,[111] intervened and protested, 'Donald MacCaffer – don't kill the man!', but MacCaffer turned to her and replied: 'Yes – and I will kill you too.' She ran off and found a policeman, Donald MacDonald. When they got there, McMenemy was being lifted, and she helped carry him to the house of Neil Campbell, fisherman in Kirk Street. McMeneny was losing much blood, and she 'got (her) clothes very much abused by it'.[112]

The five burgh policemen were unable to contain the demonstration and decided to retreat towards Main Street, 'expecting the crowd to follow us and get them away from the priest's house'. The strategy was successful, but the officers were stoned all the way along Kirk Street and had to take refuge and let the mob pass. At the cross in Main Street Provost David Colville and other civic leaders addressed the mob and finally persuaded the people to disperse.[113]

In May of 1913, the Catholic Church properties in Kirk Street were vandalised in the early hours of a Sunday morning. The culprits were never found, but the police did 'not attribute it to any anti-catholic feeling or religious bitterness, of which there is at present no evidence in the community'.[114] That statement exemplifies the difficulty in approaching such a highly charged issue as religious discord. '. . . of which there is at present no evidence in the community . . .' communicates nothing very positive. The absence of evidence is not necessarily, of itself, evidential. That 'anti-Catholic feeling' and 'religious bitterness' prevailed in Kintyre, and linger still, is not a matter of dispute. If the traces of bigotry have all but vanished, then that may be attributed to the diminished relevance of sectarian religion in an increasingly irreligious society.

In a fatal affray[115] which disrupted the Old New Year's Day* shinty match on the Strath Mor of Southend in 1836, the incitement to violence was supplied by 'a big Irishman named Robert', who interrupted play to announce that 'he would fight any Scotch or Highland bugger who stood on the strand'.[116] The overtones here are racial, rather than religious, but the two, fundamentally, are seldom distinguishable in the irrationality of embitterment.

Racial rather than religious motives also characterised – ostensibly at least – the crusade of a Dalintober 'worthy' whose nickname was 'Kipples'.

* Footnote: New Year's Day was traditionally celebrated on 12 January, and that remained a
         holiday in Kintyre into the final half of the nineteenth century.

He died in 1913 and was accorded a couple of posthumous tributes in the local newspaper. He was no doubt an extraordinary character – uproarious, erratic, witty – but he had his objectionable side and was incapable of containing it:

> His dislikes were not many, but if he had a pet aversion at all it was against anything Irish. It was a strange part of his nature. He always fought with more zest if his antagonist happened to display a bit of the brogue. That he called the 'raw bit'. 'Kipples' was always ready to do his best to knock the 'raw bit' out of anybody.
>
> One night at the weigh-house he was apostrophising natives of the Green Isle in general, when one of them, who could stand it no longer, gave 'Kipples' a lusty blow on the back of the head. Quickly wheeling round he failed to discern his attacker, and he asked – 'Was there no Scotsman in the crowd to give me warning o' that. Am I no' standing on my own grun'?' That was his outlook.[117]

Conclusion

That Irish immigration to Kintyre was well under way by the beginning of the nineteenth century is implicit in the founding, in 1809, of a Roman Catholic mission at Campbeltown. The construction of the present chapel – St Kieran's – was begun in 1849 and completed in 1850,[118] and that chapel has remained the pivot of the Catholic community in Kintyre.

That community retains its distinctive character, but its awareness of its predominantly Irish origin has diminished to the level of a vague tradition, and – more significantly – its religious unity is gradually breaking down. Inter-marriage within the Roman Catholic faith remained customary throughout the nineteenth and well into the twentieth century. Deviation from that custom was exceptional, as the hastiest examination of Appendix I will demonstrate in the intermixing of the entire Roman Catholic immigrant stock in south Kintyre. But the diminishing relevance of not just religious distinctions, but of religion itself, before a head-tide of social liberalism, has all but destroyed the taboo of the 'mixed marriage'.

This undoubtedly admits a welcome element of social balance, but the end of it will be the end of a community within a community, aware of its Irishness and secure in its religious commitment.

REFERENCES AND NOTES

1. Minutes of the Commissioners of Supply (Argyll and Bute District Council archive), 4 May 1763.

2. Min Bk, Heritors of Campbeltown, 25 Feb. 1832.

3. An Act for the Amendment and better Administration of the Laws relating to the Relief of the Poor in Scotland (8 & 9 Vict., c. 83).

4. *Ib.* Cited s. LXXIX – 'Persons again becoming Chargeable to be Punished.'

5. M. MacDonald, archivist, Argyll and Bute District Council, letter to author, 7 May 1983.

6. An Act for the Amendment . . . *op. cit.*, s. LXXVI – 'Settlement by Residence of Five Years.'

7. *Poor Law Magazine*, Vol. I (1858), No. II, 66.

8. Min Bk PB Cam, 2 Feb. 1847.

9. *Ib.*, 20 Nov. 1849.

10. *Ib.*, 19 Feb. 1850.

11. *Ib.*, 5 Aug. 1851.

12. *Ib.*

13. An Act for the Amendment . . . *op. cit.*, s. LXXVII – 'Removal of English and Irish Paupers.'

14. C51 Cam/d5/p39.

15. *Ib.* Then aged 26 years, and a 'sewster'.

16. Min Bk PB Cam.

17. *Ib.*

18. A Town Council property in Bolgam Street. Its unsanitary condition was causing the council concern in 1848: 'All the pigs to be removed and the pig stys (sic) and ash pits pulled down.' Min Bk TC Cam, 4 Dec. 1848.

19. Min Bk PB Cam.

20. *RP,* 1280.

21. Min Bk PB Cam.

22. *Ib.*, 3 July 1850.

23. *RP, op. cit.* A Maria Nolan, who died in February 1950 at Hamilton, Lanarkshire, two months after attaining her 100th birthday (*CC*, 23 Feb. 1950), was almost certainly that daughter.

24. *Poor Law Magazine, op. cit.*, 67.

25. Min Bk PB Cam.

26. *Ib.*, 16 March 1855.

27. An Act for the Amendment . . . *op. cit.*, s. LXXIX.

28. *RP, op. cit.*

29. Min Bk PB Cam, 19 Oct. 1847.

30. *Ib.*, 4 Jan. 1848.

31. The reasons were several. Two have been discussed in a case detailed above – Maria Newland's children (hypothetically), and her return from Ireland after removal. That latter flouting of the law was an especially sore point with the parochial authorities, as the following diatribe – which appeared in the *Poor Law Magazine* (*op. cit.*, 69) in 1858 – will confirm: 'In 1847-8 and 9, when deportation was the rule . . . the experience of parochial officers taught them that as fast as they sent the paupers to Ireland, Ireland returned them with interest. Officers transmitting paupers in custody to Ireland had the satisfaction of returning with them as passengers in the same boat. And while Parochial Boards were paying large sums in Scotland to fit the paupers for their voyage – and the passage money for each was two shillings and sixpence [12½p], and sometimes five shillings [25p] – the steamboat companies brought them back for the very moderate sum of sixpence [2½p] a head, which sum was supplied them on landing by parties who, by some secret arrangement with others whose object may be guessed, were thus actually engaged in handing back to Scotland the legitimate burdens of Ireland. These paupers on their return knew well that to apply for relief again to the removing parish would subject them to the penalty of imprisonment; but they also soon learned that this could only be carried out where they applied to the *same* parish that had deported them. The penalty was thus easy of evasion, as there was nothing so simple or so gratifying to them as to change their residence and attentions to the neighbouring parish, and thus they might, and did, ring the changes on the several parishes of Scotland with impunity.'

32. Marshall Bagenal, *Description of Ulster,* quoted by B. S. Turner in Distributional aspects of family names study illustrated in the Glens of Antrim (unpublished Ph.D. thesis, Queen's University, Belfast, 1974), 16.

33. J. Irvine, 'The Port of Machrimore', *TKM* No. 11, 10. Mr Cahal Dallat, Ballycastle, Co. Antrim, in a letter to the author (22 Nov. 1983), elaborated: 'Previously there was a road which did not run so close to the sea and which had to climb over each succeeding headland. These steep hills were almost impassable in winter weather. At the head of each glen lay a flow-bog, which helped to cut off the Antrim glens from the rest of the county.'

34. Turner, *op. cit.,* 18.

35. James Boyle, 'Habits of the People', *The Glynns* Vol. 5, 1977, 54.

36. Let Bk PB Cam, 6 June 1868.

37. *CC,* 2 Aug. 1873.

38. *Sea Fisheries Commission – Minutes of Evidence* (1864), London 1865, 1147.

39. A. Martin, *The Ring-Net Fishermen,* Edinburgh 1981, 40.

40. *Census of Great Britain,* Vol. II, HMSO 1852, 104.

41. C Cam and So, 1851-91; *RP* Cam, 1865-1920.

42. E. MacLysaght, in *The Surnames of Ireland* (Shannon 1969), examines – reliably or otherwise – the various anglicisation processes.

43. Turner, *op. cit.,* 21.

44. MacLysaght, *The Surnames of Ireland, op. cit.,* 41.

45. A. McKerral, *Kintyre in the Seventeenth Century,* Edinburgh 1948, 163.

46. The last instance of the name which I have happened across in Kintyre (undoubtedly there would have been later instances) is in *ORB* I: 1 Nov. 1795, the birth of Donald McCambridge, son of Donald McC and Margaret McKerrall (specific location unstated).

47. Turner, *op. cit.,* App C, 267.

48. *Ib.,* 273.

49. *Ib.,* App E, 381.

50. *Ib.,* App C, 264 – in 1963 four occurrences in the Glens; App E, 387 – six occurrences in Larne and one in Ballymena. Dallat, *op. cit.* (1983) – 'There are still McIlgorms in Co. Antrim – Larne, Carrickfergus, Mosside.'

51. Turner, *op. cit.,* 133.

52. McKerral, *op. cit.,* 10.

53. Turner, *op. cit.,* 239.

54. Rev. George Hill, *An Historical Account of the Macdonnells of Antrim,* Belfast 1873, 440.

55. McKerral, *op. cit.,* 11.

56. Turner, *op. cit.,* 129.

57. *Ib.,* App C, 273; App F, 445, 448, 451.

58. *Ib.,* 113.

59. Gearóid Ó Tuathaigh, in *The Irish World,* ed. Brian de Breffny, London 1977, 189.

60. J. E. Handley, *The Irish in Modern Scotland,* Cork 1947, 1.

61. *Ib.*

62. Hugh McMillan, Kilbride, Southend.

63. 'Willie Mitchell', *Tocher* No. 31, 1979, 4.

64. Caroline (Martin) McCallum, 31 Oct. 1980.

65. J. Mactaggart, Campbeltown, noted 24 Aug. 1983, and confirmed by letter on 26 Aug. In that letter the commencement of the association is reckoned at c. 1971.

66. *CC,* 26 Aug. 1911.

67. *Ib.,* 5 Sept. 1914.

68. J. L. Campbell, *Edward Lhuyd in the Scottish Highlands,* Oxford 1963, xvi.

69. A. W. H. Pearsall, *North Irish Channel Services,* Belfast undated, 23. In 1816 — two years earlier — the *Greenock* had made a crossing, partly under sail, from Glasgow to Belfast, stopping on passage at Campbeltown — Handley, *The Irish in Scotland,* Cork 1943, 8.

70. Pearsall, *op. cit.,* 26.

71. Pigot & Co.'s *New Commercial Directory of Scotland, 1825-6,* London and Manchester, 209.

72. Pearsall, *op. cit.,* 27.

73. Min Bk TC Cam, 22 June and 19 July 1833.

74. *Ib.,* 29 Nov. 1837.

75. *Ib.,* 14 June 1838.

76. *Minutes of the Synod of Argyll,* Vol. I, 1639-1651, Edinburgh 1943, 65.

77. *AP,* Bundle 1984.

78. *Ib.*

79. *Ib.,* Bundle 1955.

80. J. Irvine, *op. cit.,* 9.

81. *Ib.*

82. Rev. A. J. MacVicar, *Surnames Common throughout Kintyre, Islay and Arran in the 17th Century,* Campbeltown 1931 (pamphlet), 1; J. McCann, 'Ferry Me Across the Water', *The Glynns* Vol. 2, 1974, 27.

83. S. MacDonald, 'Campbeltown's Overseas Trade, 1750-1775', *The Glynns* Vol. 7, 1979, 10.

84. *AP,* Bundle 2009, 16 Oct. 1817. Four years later — on 16 Nov. 1821 — he again petitioned the Duke of Argyll for direct aid or a reduction in rent. *Ib.,* Bundle 1956.

85. A. McEachran, notebook, Kintyre Antiquarian Society library, ref. 348.

86. Min Bk TC Cam, 4 May 1798.

87. *Ib.,* 13 Feb. 1821.

88. Min Bk (Argyll and Bute District Council archive), 7 July 1847.

89. *NSA,* Vol. 7, 379.

90. Min Bk, 29 Sept. 1821.

91. *CC,* 11 May 1907.

92. Min Bk, Kirk Session of Southend, 18 May 1829.

93. No specific bill, at that time, dealing with repeal of the popery laws can be traced. The first Catholic Relief Act had, however, been passed in 1772, and was followed by another such Act in 1776. It is likely, therefore, that the petition was not directed against any specific repeal measure, but against the general concept of Catholic relief which was then intensifying. D. Ó Luanaigh, keeper of printed books, National Library of Ireland, letter to author, 5 Aug. 1983.

94. Min Bk TC Cam, 26 Jan., 2 Feb., 3 Feb. 1779.

95. 17 March 1977.

96. McKerral, *op. cit.,* 45.

97. C. Giblin, *Irish Franciscan Mission to Scotland, 1619-1646,* Dublin 1964, viii.

98. *Ib.,* x-xv.

99. *Ib.,* 32-33.

100. *Ib.,* 79.

101. *Ib.,* 38-39.

102. *Ib.,* 24.

103. *Minutes of the Synod of Argyll, op. cit.,* 162.

104. Rev. A. J. MacVicar, *The Book of Blaan,* Oban 1965, 23. The year 1645 is an estimate only. The Rev. Duncan Omey was still minister at Southend in 1641, but the year of his demission of the charge or his death is unknown.

105. *Minutes of the Synod of Argyll*, Vol. II, 1652-1661, Edinburgh 1944, 178.

106. *Ib.*, 5, 26-27, 69.

107. Donald MacDonald, police constable, 14 March 1851, Precognition against Donald McCaffer, AD14 51/188, 29.

108. *Ib.*, 29-31

109. Rev. C. Reid, 14 March 1851, *ib.*, 25-27.

110. J. McMenemy, 13 March 1851, *ib.*, 1.

111. C51 Cam/d11/p29, Shore Street.

112. Nancy McLeary McGowan, 13 March 1851, Precognition, *op. cit.*, 5-7; J. McMenemy, *op. cit.*, 2-3.

113. D. MacDonald, *op. cit.*, 32.

114. *CC*, 10 May 1913.

115. A 34-year-old farm servant at Gartvain, John McCoag, was beaten about the head with shinty sticks. He died on the morning after, 13 January 1836. Duncan McMillan, farmer in Culinlongart, and Duncan McDougall were suspected of his murder, but they evidently were never brought to trial. On 11 February 1836 the procurator-fiscal at Campbeltown, Dan Mactaggart, reported: 'Every exertion was made to apprehend the accused, but it is believed that they crossed over to Ireland and have absconded.' Precognition against Duncan McDougall and Duncan McMillan, AD14 36/113.

116. James McMillan, blacksmith at Drimavulline, aged 32; *ib.*, 29-30.

117. 'Dalintober' (pseudonym), *CC*, 6 Dec. 1913.

118. J. Webb, 'Centenary of St Kieran's Roman Catholic Church', *ib.*, 5 Jan. 1950.

CHAPTER 6

Destitution, Disease, and Death

In April 1933, the *Campbeltown Courier* published an article titled 'The Good Old Days in Kintyre'. The author – 'extremely well-known in Kintyre' – evidently chose not to be associated publicly with these reminiscences, which were attributed to 'An Octogenarian'. The article is both readable and informative, but quite what was 'good' about these 'old days' somehow fails to materialise. There are accounts of diet, clothing, housing, bedding, and so on, but these imply a difference of standards not a decline of standards.

Nostalgia obscures the reality of the past it may evoke, but cannot recover. The twentieth century produced a spate of personal and local histories in Kintyre. The horrors of the Great War, accelerating mechanisation in even the most traditional of industries – as farming and fishing – and presentiments of an unprecedented force of technological change accentuated that sense of break, of sudden – as it seemed – estrangement from a system of living and a moral order which had seemed essentially immutable.

It may have been that, contrasted with what was and what was yet to be, the 'old days' indeed seemed 'good'. That quality may, in the end, be weighed up fittingly not on a scale of material values, but on one of spiritual values. What of this account – of the heating of the old thatched houses – in 'The Good Old Days in Kintyre'? – 'On calm days the smoke was not unsuccessful in making its way out at this aperture [in the thatch], but on windy days, and especially with certain airts of the wind, it had no escape, and gathered in the room till everything was in a darkness that might almost be felt.'[1] The fingers of romance grope in strange parts!

The damp, smoky, unventilated atmosphere in most houses, the dirt and vermin in and around them, and the endemic overcrowding, all combined to break down and destroy human health. A visit to any of the old Kintyre graveyards will reveal, in infant mortality and the sudden decimation of families, the toll which sickness and disease levied on the population.

The infant mortality rate in the burgh of Campbeltown – 6.5 per 1,000 of total population – was four times greater than in the landward areas of the parish during the period 1855-75. The causes were detailed thus: the overcrowding of families in tenements, poverty, improvidence, drunkenness, and 'the almost constant prevalence . . . of contagious disease'.[2]

These epidemic diseases have been contained or eradicated in the present century, by preventive medicine and by the rapid improvement of sanitary and housing provisions. Such diseases as typhoid, smallpox, scarlet fever, measles and whooping cough have scarcely any contemporary relevance; yet, not three generations past, all were dreaded. Epidemics of scarlet fever, whooping cough and measles in the years immediately preceding 1875 claimed 247 lives in the parish of Campbeltown alone – and that figure was reckoned to be much lower than it would have been without the immediate isolation of first cases.[3]

The most devastating outbreak of epidemic disease in Kintyre, of which there is record, was the 'plague' of 1647, to which Andrew McKerral, in *Kintyre in the Seventeenth Century*, devoted an entire chapter. More recent scholarship tends, however, to refute his assumption that the disease in question was bubonic plague, and the evidence, inadequate though it certainly is, suggests an outbreak of typhus fever.[4] Whatever disease it actually was, nothing approaching such a scale of suffering and death recurred until the nineteenth century plagues of cholera.

The Plague of 1854

Of epidemic cholera in Kintyre there is no record during the eighteenth century, but in 1854 the disease – which is acutely infective and characterised by severe diarrhoea, muscular cramps, and the rapid collapse of the victim – broke out violently on Lochfyneside, particularly about Tarbert. Its ravages ended that season's fishing, and the villagers were said to have believed the epidemic 'a judgement of Providence on trawling',[5] a method of herring fishing which had recently been proscribed, but which was carried on defiantly by the men of Tarbert.

It was on the traditions of that epidemic, there seems little doubt, that J. MacDougall Hay based his account, in Chapter XXI of the novel *Gillespie*, of the coming of plague to Brieston, his fictional Tarbert. That narrative is characterised by an almost hallucinatory intensity. All spring, persistent easterly gales had 'darkened the land'; then came parching drought and a chain of eerie phenomena: 'dry summer lightning' flickered about the hills; 'the thunder ran moaning and rumbling out to sea, and died away like the whimper of far trumpets'; 'the atmosphere went mad, rising and falling in a great wave beneath the furnace of the sky'; 'the horizon was ringed with a hard red in the evenings, and twenty suns danced and slid over the sky'.

And then, on a Sunday, a 'tall, mysterious, dark ship' drifted silently into the harbour – a plague ship. Five corpses were brought out of her, and the village doctor ordered the destruction of the ship. A keg of gunpowder was brought and as the charge was prepared there rose, out of the hush of the transfixed crowd, the strident voice of the old fish-buyer, 'Quebec', declaiming frenziedly from an open bible. That the plague ship had come as a scourge of the Divine Will was his message, and as the ship erupted in flame and smoke, his cry was 'Fire to burn and to cleanse'. There followed the ravages of the disease through the whole community.[6]

The historical record attests to a popular belief in the epidemic as 'a judgement of Providence', which, paradoxical though the expression be, is just another expression of the concept of divine intervention with punitive ends. The oral tradition of Tarbert, as far as it goes, supports the central frame of MacDougall Hay's story – that a ship brought plague to the village; that the epidemic ran free in the intense heat of that summer, and that many people died. There is also a persistent tradition of a plague-cloud suspended over the village,[7] which cannot but bring to mind Peter MacIntosh's account of the great plague of 1647 coming to Kintyre from Ayrshire 'in a white cloud'.[8]

MacDougall Hay's son, George Campbell Hay, received a plague tradition from one of his MacMillan grand-aunts (p. 53). A family in the township of Allt Beithe (Birch Burn) abandoned their home. The man of the house took the door on his back and led his family down into Tarbert, and 'the fog was rising up out of Tarbert'.[9]

On the coast between Lochranza and Catacol, on the west side of Arran, in a field called Achnamara, is the grave of a Campbeltown fisherman, John MacLean, who contracted cholera during the plague of 1854, and died at sea. MacLean had been fishing out of Tarbert when cholera 'struck in'. There was a mass evacuation of Campbeltown fishermen, who abandoned boats and gear and got on the road south – 'a wile fright took possession o' the people aaltegether'. MacLean had already sickened, and lay on board his boat. Only one man of the crew, John Conley, remained with him, and MacLean entreated him not to go. Conley decided to try to manage the boat single-handed back to Campbeltown. The wind suited a passage and he set sail, but before he had got the boat far into the Kilbrannan Sound the wind fell away. MacLean had already died, and Conley put into Lochranza intending to bury his friend in the graveyard; but when the people there heard of the appearance of a plague-ship, Conley was turned back to sea. He carried on a little way south, and – apprehensive that rejection also lay ahead of him at his home port – he beached the boat at Achnamara. In darkness he dug a shallow grave and put MacLean's corpse in it. Before he left he laid the foundation of a cairn which became well known as 'the Sailor's Grave'. A slab, on which was painted simply the name MacLean, was later raised on the cairn by local people.[10]

If ships figure prominently in plague accounts, then that is hardly surprising, for ships were the customary means of trade, and the means, too, of the introduction to remote communities of foreign influences, benign as well as malignant. The black rat, or ship rat (*Rattus rattus*), to which may be attributed the bubonic plagues which ravaged Europe recurrently, is commonly supposed to have entered Europe in the ships of returning Crusaders.[11]

The role of ships and their crews in the spread of disease was widely recognised. At the onset of the second cholera epidemic which gripped Campbeltown in 1854, the medical officer of the parochial board advised 'as to the necessity of not allowing any vessel or fishing boat in which cholera has been to come to an anchor in the harbour or near to any other vessel', and that such craft should be 'scuttled and placed in deep water for a short time'.[12]

That order followed the salvaging of a local fishing boat which had been reported disabled at sea by an outbreak of cholera on board. Four Campbeltown men were hired to search for and bring to harbour the drifting boat. They set out, on their unsavoury mission, on 9 September, and by the following evening had brought the vessel to port, buried the dead, and salvaged the nets. The vessel's owner, James Brown of Lochend in Campbeltown, was charged for that work 'which few men were found willing to do'.[13]

In the records of Campbeltown Town Council there is a dramatic instance of decisive measures taken to forestall an outbreak of cholera. In 1720, plague was rampant in Marseilles and other ports of the Mediterranean, and cases – or suspected cases – of the disease had occurred at Douglas in the Isle of Man.[14] The Town Council, therefore, imposed stringent quarantine regulations on all ships entering Campbeltown Loch, and prohibited all intercourse between Campbeltown and the Isle of Man. Despite these orders, a Campbeltown vessel, commanded by Dugall McNaghtan, put in at Douglas.

On her arrival at Campbeltown, the contravention became known, and the council ordered the vessel and everything in her to be burned without compensation to her owners or to the owners of her cargo. The unfortunate Dugall McNaghtan and his crew – James Robison, Lachlan McQuorkadell, and Hugh McConachy – were 'stript to the skin of their cloathes', and immediately banished to tiny Sheep Island, off Sanda – this in the month of December, 1720. Of the provision of shelter, food, and clothing to McNaghtan and his crew, during the 40 days of their isolation, there is no record,[15] but one would hope that the rudiments, at least, of creature comfort would have sustained them in their profound ignominy.

Of the cholera epidemic at Tarbert in 1854 no contemporary records appear to have survived. That deficiency is, however, more than compensated for by the completeness of the documentation on the two epidemics which ravaged Campbeltown in that same year. The first broke out on 20 January and lasted fully a month, claiming 25 lives. A recurrence in September brought 35 deaths during its two-month course.[16]

The appearance of cholera in Kintyre had been anticipated, and in October, 1853, precautions began to be enforced. On the 26th of that month a special meeting of the parochial board was convened, at which an 'active and efficient' committee was appointed. That committee met on the following day and began its preparations. An 'inspector of cleansing' was chosen; the town and parish were divided into districts, and a supervisory committee appointed to each district; a depot was established, from which supplies of lime were to be issued free to the poor, 'for washing their houses'; medicines for bowel complaints were, by arrangement with the town 'druggists', to be given free not only to the poor, but also to 'any person whose ability to pay was doubtful'; a proclamation was issued, 'calling upon the inhabitants to cleanse and purify their houses and premises'.[17]

By 1 February, 1854 – with the community gripped fast in the epidemic, and 17 deaths already accounted – the cleaning of the burgh was well advanced; but the scale of the operation had been almost overwhelming, and even then remained unfinished. More than 700 cartloads of dung had been removed, and numerous derelict buildings cleared out and bricked up; two medical officers had been employed at the remarkable fee of two guineas (£2.10) each per day, and a soup kitchen had been established 'with the happiest results'. Legal action had been taken against no fewer than 24 individuals for the removal of swine and pigsties. The number of pigs kept in the town alone was calculated at between 1500 and 2000.[18]

Pig-Keeping

The keeping of pigs – in south Kintyre, *doories* or *doorkies* (p. 217) – occupied a special role in the domestic economy. The custom proved difficult to break, because pigs were not merely food and income for the people, but in many households were treated as pets and gained the favour and affection of children especially.

The company of a black and white fattening pig at Port na Cuthaig, Saddell, kept by the ferryman there, Lachie Galbraith, was much indulged by the Galbraith children, who would romp and play with it on the shore. A day came when the loved pet disappeared, the victim of an arrangement with a Campbeltown butcher. Soon after, a parcel arrived at the ferryman's house. Inside was the Galbraiths' share of the doomed animal – a ham and a half of the head. The parcel was opened on the white-scrubbed kitchen table – 'We wir all howlin when we seen the pig's head'.[19] John Campbell's grandmother, on the family croft at Grogport, would invariably walk out into the hills towards the farm of Narachan on the day of the family pig's slaughter, so to be out of sight and hearing of its death.[20]

According to William Smith (1835), an epidemic of cholera at Campbeltown in 1831/2 impelled the town council to 'greatly reduce' the pig population. 'It is now,' he wrote, 'comparatively rare that they are met with',[21] an observation which is certainly belied by the estimate in 1854 of between 1500 and 2000 pigs in the town alone. A reversion to old habits would seem to have occurred in the interval between the epidemics of 1832 and 1854.

A great many pigs enjoyed complete freedom and, rather as dogs, prowled the town as they pleased. No doubt they performed a useful service as scavangers, but the quantity of dung which they dropped through the streets must have been great, and as great a nuisance. In 1835, at Dalintober, pigs were 'still allowed to be kept in the houses of the poorer inhabitants, and may be seen revelling in all the luxury of accumulated mud and filth upon the road, and in a few minutes afterwards enjoying themselves stretched before the fire, their filthy carcasses steaming . . .'[22]

The free-ranging pigs of Dalintober relished 'pottle' – 'pot-ale', or the effluent from the first distillation of whisky – and were frequently seen indulging that taste at the Pottle Hole, a sandy basin in the Mussel Ebb opposite Princes Street. Dalintober distilleries discharged their waste into a stream which welled up at the Hole, and the pigs would go into it to drink. Piglets – locally *galach-plockachs* (p. 218) – were prone to drown in the effluent if the banks of the Hole – which disappeared with the reclamation of the Mussel Ebb (p. 116) – were soft and slippery after rain.[23]

Mactaggart (1922), with his claim that the pig's 'privileges were curtailed, and he ceased to be a household pet in Campbeltown in consequence of the cholera epidemic of 1832', is simply perpetuating Smith's precipitate assessment. Of greater interest are a couple of little anecdotes which Mactaggart records. He remarks on a tradition that pigs 'often met with fatal accidents through falling from attic windows', and recounts a story about an old Campbeltown woman who kept a massive boar in her attic. Its face was seen one day, peering out of the attic window, by a passer-by. Fascinated, he asked the woman how she had managed to get the pig up the stair. 'Up the stair?' she exclaimed in disbelief – 'He's never been doon!' That custom continued in Campbeltown as late in the century as the 1860s. In 1866 Mary McMillan or McKinven – 'a widow presently in the custody of the police' – was charged that she 'did keep swine in the house occupied by her as a dwelling-house in or near the lane between Kirk Street and Shore Street'.[24]

The first blow in the campaign against the burgh pigs was struck in 1821, with the appointment of an additional policeman, Hugh Speirs, one of whose duties was to 'use his utmost endeavours to destroy all the swine found upon the streets of Campbeltown, and when with all his exertions he shall be unable to kill such swine, he shall discover the owner, or owners, and bring them before the Magistrates that they may be fined for the offence of suffering their swine to go at large through the streets . . .'[25]

The second stage of the campaign, in 1848, was an attack upon the very custom of pig-keeping. Pigs – as also cattle – were being kept in 'confined and badly constructed premises, and generally near to dwellings, sometimes even inside, the dung and liquid waste generally lipping about the doors without any regard to cleanliness'. The Council recoiled, however, from any suggestion that 'poor persons should be compelled to put away their pigs or cows except where kept in confined and densely inhabited localities', reasoning that 'where these animals are well attended to and in proper houses for the purpose, though it may be near to dwellings, they may give rise to nothing filthy or unwholesome and besides . . . their removal would take away a principal stimulus to industry and economy from the poorer classes'.[26]

That argument was echoed more than 60 years on, in 1911, when Peter McGown in Dalaruan, Campbeltown, appeared in the Police Court on a charge of 'keeping in the vicinity of his dwelling-house sixteen pigs which are a nuisance and an annoyance to the inhabitants of the neighbourhood'. The case provoked an angry response from one A. McLeod, who divined 'victimisation' in the action. His letter to the *Campbeltown Courier* was headed 'Man's inhumanity to man':

> These two poor old people have been in the habit of keeping a number of pigs for years back, and no one ever objected to the 'intolerable nuisance' caused by the swine until one or two extra fastidious personages got anchored in Dalaruan, and their patrician code of morality did not include the herding of swine in their immediate environment. Now, when these apostles of sanitation have succeeded in taking away the means of livelihood from these poor old folk, what steps are they going to take to help them eke out an existence, precarious at all times, but more so now than ever . . .[27]

The practice of pig-keeping lingered on in the domestic economy of Campbeltown until the Second World War, and some of the older people of the town will recall earning, as children, a few coppers by the collection of 'brock' – household food scraps – for the last of the town swine. The confinement of pigs – and, earlier, cattle – in cramped and filthy outhouses is one custom of which no humane person could have regretted the end.

The Mussel Ebb Reclamation

The Mussel Ebb – that expanse of shore which now lies beneath Kinloch Park in Campbeltown – was for long recognised as a bed of filth and disease. In February, 1854, in the middle of the first plague outbreak of that year, the Ebb was described as 'a flat shore upon which the whole refuse of the Town as well as the refuse of 20 distilleries fall, upon which there is always a very great amount of decomposed organized matter, and in summer when the sun acts upon this mass the stench is often very great'.[28]

Towards the end of that year, the Town Council, by petitioning the Duke of Argyll, secured 'a professional engineer to report upon the best mode of reclaiming that part of the harbour from the sea, keeping in view the sanitary improvement of the town'.[29] Nothing more was heard of the project until 1875, when Campbeltown Town Council set out plans for the reclamation of the Ebb.[30]

That reclamation – using earth, rubbish, and stone carted from the quarries at Kilkerran and Dalaruan – began in 1877.[31] By June, 1878 an embankment – extending from Dalintober Quay to the Old Quay of Campbeltown – had been built, and a wooden bridge laid across the culvert which discharged Lochend Burn.[32] The bridge was hardly up, however, when a part of the supporting wall subsided and the bridge collapsed. In the few days for which it had stood, it had 'become the favourite route to and from Dalintober',[33] and not until August was the convenience restored.[34]

In June of 1880, the reclamation work was completed and the embankment bridge removed.[35] In the following summer, the muddy flats were sown with rye-grass, and ash paths were laid on the lines of the cardinal points – north to south and east to west – on which they remain. The reclaimed shore had come to be known as 'the Mussel Ebb Park', but so vulgar a name – perpetuating as it did the memory of a vanished evil – could not be sanctioned, and in June of 1881 the council recommended the name 'Kinloch Park'. At least one councillor was sceptical and remarked that 'the Town Council may call it what they like, but the people will call it the Mussel Ebb'. The roadway linking Campbeltown with Dalintober, behind the new sea-dyke, became the grand-sounding 'Esplanade'.[36]

All was not well, however, with the new park. In the winter of 1882 it had deteriorated into a state of unsanitariness and ugliness. At the junction of Kinloch Road and the Esplanade lay a massive heap of sludge which had been dredged from the harbour and dumped there, on top of which was a crown of 'old chaff, old boots, bottles, dead rats, dung, and a variety of other substances in a state of putrefaction'. On the opposite side of the road was another heap – of human excrement. On the Dalintober side of the Esplanade yet another midden had accumulated, to which clung a 'green foetid substance, from which is exhaled a most pestiferous odour, which is absolutely sickening'. The 'park' itself was 'but a mighty stretch of mud, on the surface of which are scattered miniature lakes, composed of an inky black fluid'.

At its west end, however, 'a slight show of green vegetation' had appeared. Some sheep, which had been put there to graze, were making short work of it, and the council at last issued a proclamation forbidding the grazing of sheep and cattle on the park. 'The authorities,' remarked the *Courier* wickedly, 'were so fond of their little oasis in the midst of the mud that they were afraid the sheep would extinguish it, and then where would the "Park" be?'[37]

E

The *Courier* argued that the council had spoiled the project, by its fear of spending money and being criticised for so doing. The entire reclamation scheme was condemned as unnatural interference, because the Mussel Ebb had formerly been washed twice daily by a flood tide, which 'acted as a deodoriser to the decaying matter lying about'.[38]

In fact, the scheme was no final solution, and the nuisance was merely shifted further out. Deposits of sludge accumulated on the ebbing shore between Dalintober Quay and the Old Quay, and stank abominably, summer in and summer out, until the sewage of the town was piped, in 1973, to an outfall beyond Trench Point. The park itself became, in time, a valuable amenity, though its area has been reduced by successive building on it, a despoliation which, I hope, has reached its limit.

The completion of the reclamation work had several immediate effects. The most significant of these was the rapid decline of the ferry between Dalintober and Campbeltown, which had eliminated the circuitous route around Lochend.[39]

Sanitation and Housing

If the incursions of disease from without were feared, then as great a source of fear ought to have been recognised at the people's own doors. Literally, for the habit of keeping dung and household waste outside dwelling-houses was endemic throughout the eighteenth century, and remnants of the practice lingered into the final quarter of the nineteenth century.

Householders in Campbeltown were expected to keep in a clean condition that part of the street opposite their houses, but, habituated to their foul state, and – to be strictly fair – hampered by the utterly inadequate sanitary provisions, they certainly failed in that public duty. An order of the Dean of Guild of Campbeltown, dated 1751, suggests that the nuisance was both extensive and inveterate:

> Such [inhabitants] as keep dunghills or filth upon the streets or the foresides of their houses that they cause carry them away [before] the 25th current [or] such dunghills or rubbish shall be forfeited and they be made pay for the carrying away of the same, and that no such dunghills or middens are to be laid upon the streets or foresides of their houses under a severe penalty that they will be made liable for.[40]

More than a century on, the custom persisted. In 1874, a complaint was lodged against one John Colville, in whose yard a dungheap had accumulated against the wall of a dwelling-house. To the 'foul air' rising from that heap was attributed the illness of a young girl who had languished all winter in an upstairs room of the house.[41] A year later, the burgh medical officer, William Gibson, in stressing the necessity of public toilets in the town and of compelling landlords to instal lavatories in their properties, reported that 'at present every quiet street and lane is covered with human filth'.[42]

In 1884, the problem had scarcely receded, and Gibson was warning of the threat of cholera. He divided the unsanitary tenements into four categories. The most extreme of these comprised 'those [tenements] without punds or middens or privies as well as being without W.C.s and water in the houses. There is a number of tenements in such a condition. In one of them the population is over a hundred. Four have close upon that number, six have from 40 to 60, and a number more have from 20 to 40. The persons inhabiting these houses are entirely without any place to put their night-soil. They are forbidden to empty it on the streets and on the shore, and the town carts refuse to take it unless mixed with ashes, so as to render it somewhat dry, which in many cases is not possible, and the result is that these persons are forced to keep a collection of night-soil in their houses for 24 hours, or until late at night, when, by watching the police, the wives and children steal out with the 24 hours collection, and deposit it in some quiet corner of a street or on the shore, or in the pund or midden or privy of some neighbouring property'.[43]

His concern was to compel, by existing legislation, the owners of unsanitary tenements to instal lavatories and water supplies and to 'do away with all punds or middens and privies that may be certified as injurious to health, which would include the greater number'. As an example of the feasibility of his proposition, he cited one 'land' containing seven families dependent on a single lavatory. That lavatory was 'kept clean and in good order', and was considered by the tenants 'indispensable for health, comfort and cleanliness'.

'The question,' he continued, 'may pertinently be put − if such a plan works well in one tenement with so many families, why should it not do so generally?' Gibson evidently was not an unfeeling man. He fully appreciated the predicament of those tenants who, while aware of the sanitary regulations by which they were bound, were nonetheless unable to comply with them. He voiced, on their behalf, the very fundamentals of that predicament: 'How can we help it? What can we do? Give us water-closets and water in our houses and you will soon see a change for the better.'[44]

Such tenements as had been condemned repeatedly as unsanitary were not, as a whole, the crumbling monuments of a long discredited housing policy. Many of them, certainly, were old and dilapidated, but even into the 1870s, in Campbeltown, new buildings were going up 'on the old plan of having only one common stair without ventilation, a single jaw-box (sink) at the bottom of the stair for the whole land, and no water-closet'.[45]

Cramped and squalid though these tenements were, none of them lacked its fill of tenants. Indeed, the problem was an altogether different one −

there were not enough of them to contain the population of shifting poor in
Campbeltown. The Whitsun Term – a traditional flitting day for towns-
folk, as for their rural counterparts – annually occasioned the evacuation on
to the streets of hundreds of the poorest families. Many of these families
would fail to find alternative lodgings. The misery of that hopeless minority
was described in the *Campbeltown Courier* of 29 May, 1880: 'Many of these
[families] were unable to find a place of shelter on Wednesday night, and
were to be seen wandering dismally along the streets, while women and
children, sobbing and crying, were sitting on their household goods which
had been turned out. Altogether the scene was a most pitiful one, and for
the relief of these poor people and the honour of the burgh something ought
to be done speedily by those in authority towards providing at least some
temporary accommodation for them.'

Some of these families would have found their way, no doubt, to the
miserable shacks – some of them converted pig-sties – which littered the
back areas of the town, out of the sight of the comfortable citizenry. Two of
the most notorious of these poor quarters were described – and
unequivocally condemned – by Dr. Gibson in 1882.

At the back of Longrow were four hovels: 1. A wooden hut, 13' 6" by 11'
10", and 7' in height, housed a family of five and a lodger. There had been
two lodgers, but one – a woman – sickened and 'lay ill in this wretched
den for about eight days, and when she died her corpse remained with the
inmates until buried'. 2. A shed, 9' by 8' and 8' 9" at the highest point of its
sloping roof, occupied by five persons, a father and three children, and an
unmarried woman. The floor was earthen and the roof leaked. 3. A shed,
11' 10" by 9' 4" and 8' 9" at its highest point, occupied by a husband and
wife. 4. An (?) 'old sleep', 7' by 8' and 6-7' high, occupied by one woman.
Its floor, too, was earthen.

In High Street, Dalintober two houses which were formerly pig-sties.
The first, 12' 2" by 9' with a 7' ceiling. The floor was wooden and was sunk
about a foot below ground level. The second was of near identical
dimensions and its floor – of bare earth – was likewise sunken. Each of
these buildings housed a family of six. The sewer there was choked and
pools of sewage fouled the ground about.[46]

All of these houses were the property of Mr Angus MacDonald. Mr
MacDonald was a town councillor and as such was present during the
hearing of these reports. Not surprisingly, he asked to be allowed to say 'a
few words'. These were his words:

> As a member of the Dean of Guild's Committee, I am glad the matter has been
> referred to the Council. I can say that a good deal of Dr. Gibson's report is drawn from
> his imagination. He took the statements of a poor half-witted woman and put them down
> as facts. As an instance, he asked her age and she said she didn't know. He asked if she

was 70 and she said yes. If Dr. Gibson had asked if she was 90 he would have got the same answer. The tenants in the houses referred to took possession of them without my authority. They have all been warned to leave. They are outside and I will bring them in and you can question them. (The Council: 'No, no.') I was out in the storm myself yesterday and I had compassion on the poor people. I did not act on Dr. Gibson's human(e) suggestion that I take down the roofs and leave them in the cold, but they have all got notice to leave and I will see that they do so. I get nothing from them, and I could not turn them out on such a day as yesterday.

(His colleagues were less than reassured by the statement and a bitter exchange ensued.)

Mr Martin: I don't know about that. I am told that MacNeill pays you three shillings (15p) a week for the wooden hut.

Mr MacDonald: It is not true. He is outside there and you can ask him.

Mr Martin: I would as soon believe him as you.

Mr Muir: We are as guilty as Mr MacDonald in allowing this state of matters to exist. I am sorry that a member of this Council who, time after time, has spoken here of making this a model burgh, should be guilty of such a deplorable thing.

Mr MacDonald: Did you see anything?

Mr Muir: Yes, I went and saw it.

Mr MacDonald: And what did you see?

Mr Muir: I saw a great deal more than I would like to see, or could have believed.

Mr MacDonald: I was out in the storm myself yesterday and had compassion. I could not turn the people out.

Mr Brown: We are all aware that there are a good many poor people in the town requiring shelter, and I believe that Mr MacDonald in his kindness of heart may have given them that; but I also believe that Mr MacDonald is as fond of the money as anybody else, perhaps even more so. Could some of our wealthy friends not erect some place of shelter for them, because they must be put out of where they are at present.

The council agreed to take legal action against Angus MacDonald to compel him to have the shacks evacuated, unless he had done so, of his own accord, within a month.[47]

An Eviction

Paradoxically, in the face of increasing public concern and the unremitting efforts of the sanitary authorities to eradicate all such hovels and the misery and squalor rooted in them, their occupants were singularly reluctant to budge. Neither comfort nor convenience, nor even the shackles of habit deferred their going – the reality was that they had nowhere else to go. An account of one eviction – of the tenants of 'some old ramshackle buildings' at Lochend – is on record. That eviction was carried out in August, 1891, at the instance of the proprietor – unnamed – who had 'long been anxious to get the premises pulled down'. The account, which appeared in the *Campbeltown Courier* under the matter-of-fact heading 'A Local Eviction', is curiously at odds with that paper's usually sympathetic approach to the condition of the poor of the town:

> . . . the tenants . . . obstinately refused to leave. This deadlock was brought to a crisis on Monday morning when a squad of workers, among the jeers and taunts of the tenants, made an attack on the roof, which they commenced to pull rapidly down. The work proceeded steadily, and the tenants occasionally varied the entertainment of abusing the workmen by having free fights among themselves, encounters which seemed to be enjoyed by the assembled spectators. It was only when the bricks and mortar began to rattle about their ears that the tenants bethought themselves of removing their belongings to other quarters . . .[48]

As to what and where these 'other quarters' were, the writer is singularly reticent. No doubt he did not trouble himself to find out. Such an ugly weight of realism hung on the end of his descriptive balloon might have pulled the whole thing to earth. If the fate of these people is unknown, then it may, with reasonable certainty, be conjectured. Most of them would have taken to the streets, and some, perhaps, remained there. Driven from one night resort to another, sleeping in stairways and outhouses, in derelict buildings and in caves, veritably they had descended into an 'underworld'.

Cave-Dwellers

Human occupation of caves originates in remote prehistory. Approached thus, the subject is properly the province of archaeology; but cave-dwelling as a social necessity persisted into this century, which means that, hypothetically, persons born or (no matter how briefly) raised in Kintyre caves may yet be living. Such, in the scale of time, is the proximity of the final phase of cave-dwelling.

The persistence of the custom was demonstrated by the archaeologist J. Harrison Maxwell, who, in 1934, reported human occupation of Keil Cave, Southend, during an interval in his excavation of it. A dug-out pit had been filled with straw and used as a bed. He concluded that 'this and empty whisky bottles indicated the life and habits of the modern cave-dwellers'.[49]

Tradition in Southend district connected Keil Cave with the activities of nineteenth century itinerant blacksmiths. Those smiths were remembered particularly for the casting of side-plates and socks for ploughs, and very rough products these reputedly were.[50] Certainly, in the Census of 1881 two tinker families – John MacFee, tinsmith, and Alexander MacCallum, basketmaker, with their wives and children – were recorded in that cave.[51] In 1835, the cave was noticed as an occasional resort of 'ragged crews of Irish wanderers'.[52]

The caves of Kintyre, without exception, harboured a diversity of social groups, from tinkers, tramps and destitutes to inveterate recluses who, although numerically the least significant of all, achieved a kind of celebrity by their long association with particular caves and by the curiosity which their simple lives engendered. The two best known were women, Esther Houston and Janet MacCallum.

'Queen Esther' lived and died − in December, 1885 − in a cave on Pollywilline shore, Southend. She was sufficiently well known to merit an obituary in the local newspaper:

> On Sunday morning Esther Houston, a somewhat eccentric old woman, who for many years occupied a rude hut in a cave on the estate of Macharioch, Southend, was found dead in her primitive dwelling. Esther, who was known about the Southend district as Queen Esther, was a harmless person, and the farmers and others in the district never allowed her to want; but for some time back her health was giving way. She resisted every attempt made to induce her to leave her lonely and comfortless abode, and always maintained that she was far happier as she was, with the company of her cats and fowls, than she would be in any of the surrounding villages . . . Esther had a boat on the shore near her cave, and when she was stronger used occasionally to go out fishing.[53]

She was evidently not as old as that account would suggest. The rigours of her existence probably gave her an aged appearance. In 1881, she gave her age as 40 years. Her habitation was described as a 'rock house or hut'. She was unmarried, gave her occupation as an 'agricultural outworker' − though probably not in quite these terms − and claimed Irish birth. With her was a 17-year-old son, James McNeill, born at Southend.[54] Her age, at the time of death, was reckoned at 53 years. She was then described as a 'wilk-gatherer'. Her father − forename unknown − was a seaman, and her mother's name was Hannah Bowman. James McNeill, her son, registered the death.[55] Nothing is known of him thereafter. Poor Esther achieved undeserved posthumous notoriety. One of the photographs in a series titled 'Kintyre Beauty Spots', which appeared in the *Campbeltown Courier* in the late 1930s, was a view of Pollywilline shore. It was captioned: 'The Witch's Cove is among these rocks. Some years ago an old woman used to live there with about twenty cats.'[56]

Jenny MacCallum, a native of Carradale, was reckoned to have spent half-a-century in the cave at Sunadale, farther north along the coast from her birthplace. Popularly known as *Cailleach na h-Uamh* ('the Old Woman of the Cave'), she too availed herself of charity, but was not entirely dependent on it, for she made money by hawking. She had 'always appeared to be in the utmost destitution', but when, in 1875, she was admitted to Lochgilphead poor-house and, in accordance with the house rules, was stripped of her clothing, beneath her bodice a large and unusually heavy bag was discovered. That bag, which day and night she kept secured to her, contained the astonishing sum of £98 − £45 in silver, £6 in gold, and a Union Bank deposit receipt for £47. The coins alone weighed 11 lbs, and she carried, additionally, a 'pock' (sack) weighing 40 lbs, and containing 'everything required in a kitchen and larder' − cooking utensils, beef, several pounds of braxy mutton, pickled herrings, various kinds of bread, besides some small articles of clothing. In the final years of her independence, she had taken a house at Cape, near Sunadale, 'desiring,' it was supposed, 'to be in the neighbourhood of help, should she ever be attacked for the sake of her store of pelf (money)'. Latterly, she got into the habit of leaving her 'pock' in a neighbour's house for safety during the night, but her horde she always kept with her. 'Perhaps . . . Janet's idea was that however safely the braxy might be kept, the money might not fare so well.'[57]

She had a considerable reputation as a healer. As conventional medicine was already, in her lifetime, advancing rapidly as a science, and as the services of professional doctors were, by then, generally available, she may with certainty be recognised as one of the very last of the traditional healers and herbalists in Kintyre. Her reputation has survived in oral tradition, and there is an account – from John Campbell – of her curing a case of acute dermatitis, in the treatment of which standard medicines had failed. She had been in Carradale to get some herring for herself, and, at one of the houses there, was appealed to by the wife of a fisherman whose life had become unbearable by an inflammation of the hands. He felt himself a 'leper' among his fellow fishermen – he had been expressly discouraged from handling food on board the boat, and ate from a particular plate and drank from a particular cup. Jenny prepared a lotion for him and instructed him in its application. He was to immerse his hands in it repeatedly and let it dry naturally, until a 'milky glaze' formed on the skin. After five or six treatments, the condition vanished.[58]

The best known of the caves along the Leerside is popularly known as 'the Wee Man's (Cove)', or 'Mecky's (Cove)', which is a fishermen's name. 'Mecky' is the local diminutive of Malcolm, and the 'Mecky' of the cave was identified as one Malcolm MacCallum.[59] That cave lies a quarter of a mile south of New Orleans, and is the larger of the two caves there. There is no tradition, far less documentation, which would indicate prolonged occupation by any individual. Fragmentary references to families and individuals for whom that cave provided refuge are concentrated in the final decade of the nineteenth century, when official concern with the welfare of the homeless began to intensify.

The case history of one Martha Huie C———, in the register of poor for Campbeltown, presents, entry by entry, across a span of sixteen years, a wretched catalogue of destitution. She first entered the register in 1890, at the age of 24, when abandoned by her husband. In October, 1894, she and her five children were 'houseless, sleeping on stairs, and are becoming town's talk and public scandal with the present severe weather'. On 13 April, 1897, her infant daughter Janet 'died in cave on Kildalloig shore'. On 10 December of that same year, with her children Mary, Martha, and Caroline, she was admitted to the poor-house from a 'cave at New Orleans'. The entry continued: 'Police were to raise an action against the occupancy.

She was a little the worse of drink. Husband going about – she is pregnant.' The last entry is dated 2 April, 1906: 'C——— sentenced to 30 days for attempted housebreaking. Wife applied for relief. Offered Poor-house but refused to go in.'[60]

John Garvie, a seaman and labourer, was admitted to the poor-house at Campbeltown in July, 1895. He was then 22 years old and suffering from 'pleurisy of right side'. His home – 'a cove at New Orleans'.[61]

A Sheriff Court report, which appeared in the *Campbeltown Courier* of 6 January, 1894, detailed the conviction of Thomas Dunsmore, charged with day trespass on the farm of Auchenhoan. He had been seen setting four rabbit snares. His address – 'the Cave, New Orleans'.

St. Ciaran's Cave, at the base of Auchenhoan Head, is traditionally associated with the sixth century Irish missionary, Ciaran Mac an tSaoir, abbot of Clonmacnois and titular of the former parish church of Kilkerran. There is no tradition of the occupancy of that cave during the nineteenth century, but in 1772 the traveller Thomas Pennant wrote of it: 'On the floor is the capital [head[62]] of a cross, and a round bason, cut out of the rock, full of fine water, the beveridge of the saint in old times, and of sailors in the present, who often land to dress [cook] their victuals beneath this shelter. An antient pair, upwards of seventy years of age, once made this their habitation for a considerable time.'[63]

Despite the efforts of local government officials to eradicate cave-dwelling, the practice continued into the second decade of this century. Although no policy statements appear to survive, the main concern most likely would have been the welfare of children subjected to the regime. The Great War seems to have effectively ended the practice.

In March, 1915, under the Defence of the Realm Act restriction on visible lights on the coast, cave-dwelling was declared 'strictly prohibited'. A warning, issued by the chief constable of Argyll, was directed at 'persons dwelling in or using as an habitual abode caves or hollows along the shores, or any rocks facing the sea'. The newspaper report which carried the warning predicted: 'As cave-dwellers are still common in Argyllshire, particularly at Lochgilphead, Knapdale, and Kintyre, many families will be rendered homeless.'[64]

The only reported breach of that regulation occurred that very month, when a 70-year-old tramp, Thomas Price, was discovered living in Smerby – or Stackie – Cove (p. 195). The charge against him was deserted upon his agreement not to return to the cave, but the unfortunate Thomas was jailed that summer for having lit a fire in the wood called the Maidens Planting, near Campbeltown. Two policemen, passing along the lochside in the late evening, saw a light up among the trees and found Thomas beside his fire. They maintained that the fire could have been seen from seaward, and Thomas was put away for 14 days.[65]

Stackie Cove was the only habitable cave between Campbeltown and Saddell. In 1900 and 1901 a family O——— was lodged there. On the sanitary inspector's recommendation, legal action for their removal was instituted.[66] In 1913 the parochial board in Campbeltown considered an application for relief transmitted from Greenock on behalf of a 20-year-old hawker, Isabella H———. Her birthplace was recorded as 'Smerby Cave'.[67] A 'glib of the tongue' fern-gatherer, James H———, when he appeared before Campbeltown Police Court in 1906, on a charge of drunkenness, introduced himself as 'a native of the district, having been born and brought up at Smerby Cave'.[68] He was a brother of Isabella's.

The H——— family appeared in the Census of 1891, living at 'Smerby Cove'. The family had evidently long been accustomed to the road – the eldest son, William (15), was born at Balfron, Stirlingshire, Hugh (10) at Lamlash, Arran, and John (7) at Fort William. Mary (3) alone was born in Campbeltown Parish. Isabella and James followed. The father, Robert H———, a 'general labourer', was born in Eaglesham, Renfrewshire, and the mother 'at sea, between Cumbraes and Arran'.[69]

The earliest recorded housing of a tinker in Kintyre – in 1872 – was motivated by a desire to get him and his wife out of 'a cave at Smerby'. The site of the house, at Ardnacross, was provided by the Rev. H. McNeill, 'that honest, warm-hearted philanthropist'. The arrogant idealism of that scheme would be hard to surpass: 'It is to be hoped that from motives of humanity the example of the laird of Airdnacroish will soon be followed by others who possess the valleys of the west and mountains of the north, and when tinkers have become located, let their civilisation form one of the schemes of the Church for heathenism at home.'[70]

The following account – which may incline towards dramatisation, but which, even allowing for that, is appalling enough – belongs to the year 1886:

> For several years back a family have been residing in a cave on the shore at Smerby . . . Flora W——— or M———, whose husband is at present engaged in the fishing, is well known in Campbeltown, and has been brought before the court on several occasions for neglect of her children. She is the mother of a considerable family, most of whom, however, have died, and she is now left with three miserable children, who, along with herself, occupied the very primitive dwelling we have just referred to. As far as we can learn at present, Flora left her home on Friday night of last week, and remained away. On Saturday, while some women were gathering wilks on the Smerby shore, they were accosted by the children, who were in a very miserable and poorly clad condition, and begged the women to give them something to eat, as they were starving. On visiting the cave it was found to be in a most deplorable state of filth, the stench that proceeded from it being unbearable. The straw on the floor was in a rotten state, and everything around indicative of misery and squalor. The oldest boy was without any covering but a small jacket, and the other two were in rags. The youngest, a child of two years, was in a very helpless condition, and so ravenous was it for food that it had eaten the embers from a

small fire-place. The women went to Campbeltown and reported the matter to the police, who arrested the mother on Saturday night. The doctor visited the place, and ordered the children to be taken to the hospital.[71]

In October of 1901, the father of these wretched children, Dugald M———, risked his life to rescue the crew of the Campbeltown fishing skiff *Red Ribbon*, which grounded on an offshore reef at Smerby.[72] A heavy sea was running, and he lost his own boat in the effort, but, by public subscription in Campbeltown, a replacement was built for him. That skiff – aptly named the *Rescue* – was ceremoniously presented to him in April of the following year. A great crowd gathered at the New Quay Head, Campbeltown for the presentation, after which 'a couple of horses were yoked to the lorry, and a procession of fishermen formed, those in the van carrying flags, and the boat preceded by the pipe band of the Artillery Volunteers. Mr M———, clad in his oilskins, sat at the tiller, and at various points along the route was loudly cheered as the hero of the hour'.[73] Several photographs of the presentation have survived. In all of these, the bulky figure of Dugald M———, in his bright oilskin suit, presents an almost ghost-like appearance. He did not live to profit by his fine new boat – in November of that year he died.[74]

A tramp, known as 'Covie', is reputed to have suffered the loss of half a moustache while lying asleep in Stackie Cove. He had treated himself to a 'black pudding' before he bedded down for the night, and some audacious rats of the place made a meal of the grease on the exposed half of his whisker, and by their greedy attentions did away with the appendage.[75]

Boat-Dwellers

Redundant fishing boats – in the main, smacks and luggers discarded with the decline of the distant drift-net fisheries for which they had been built[76] – were also occupied by destitutes. The following admissions to the poor-house were of boat-dwellers:

Archibald MacE———, labourer, 52, in 1879, from a skiff at New Quay Head, suffering from an eye injury;

Jane MacA———, 34, in 1879, from a boat at Old Quay Head – 'near confinement';

Archibald G———, fisherman, 66, in 1892, from 'a boat at the quay, now sold';

William and Christina S———, first admitted to the poor-house in 1901, she pregnant and he ill with boils – 'They live on the shore'. In 1905 Christina was again taken into the poor-house, unwell 'after a recent confinement' – 'They live in a boat at Kilkerran from which they are being evicted and thrown out on the road, she being practically helpless';

Charles J———, labourer, 32, in 1908, from 'a boat at the New Quay', suffering from diarrhoea.[77]

Some of these hulks of boats were floated across to stances on the Kilkerran and Glenramskill shores of Campbeltown Loch, and there served a succession of homeless people. Repeated evictions, on sanitary grounds, were of little avail – no sooner had a boat been vacated than another family occupied it. These boats no doubt were used until they broke up, or were broken up. In 1901 the sanitary inspector was complaining of 'five people living in an old boat at Glenramskill, unfit as a place of human habitation',[78] and, in 1903, served a notice of eviction on the occupants of 'an old boat on the shore at Glenramskill, whose owner is unknown, and which is being taken posession of and occupied at times by different people as a dwelling'.[79]

A female child was born, in February of 1887, in one of these house-boats. The *Courier* thrilled: 'Considering the peculiar circumstances, both mother and child are doing well. An extra effort has been made, with the use of bags and other articles, to make the novel habitation as comfortable as possible.'[80]

Rural Squalor

Housing and sanitary conditions were little better in the rural districts of Kintyre. As late in the century as 1892, 52.3 per cent of the rural population lived in one- and two-roomed houses, and 15.6 per cent in single apartments:

> No improvement has taken place in farm workmen's cottages, many of which are in anything but a satisfactory condition. The principal grounds of complaint are damp floors and walls, roofs not rain-proof, too small windows, which often do not open, and which cannot be used for ventilation, unsuitable sites, filthy surroundings and no conveniences. As a rule there is no such thing as a properly formed midden or privy, and where there is a family, household refuse and excreta may be found deposited around the cottages. There are no places for coals or potatoes, and it is no uncommon thing to find one or other under beds, or in some corner of an apartment in which some of the family sleep.

Only in 'very rare instances' did cattle continue to be 'kept in an apartment of the dwelling-house'.[81] One such 'all purpose' cottage was fired by boys in 1900 and reduced to charred gable-ends. Known as the 'Ark', the building, which was thatched until the end, stood by the Glasgow road at Tangy. It consisted of a single room and was occupied by two sisters and a brother, with 'a cow, a pig, and a lot of hens' besides. With the death of two of the family, and the removal from the district of the surviving member, the house – 'which has been a source of endless trouble to sanitary inspector and medical officer' – was abandoned.[82]

In Tarbert (1894), many of the houses in the back streets were 'small, badly built, drained and ventilated, while others are in a dilapidated condition'.[83] Three years before as a result of a visit to the village by the sanitary inspector, notices were served on the owners of wooden hen- and duck-houses to have them removed. These 'unsightly hovels' were reckoned detrimental to the village as a holiday resort, and 'some good summer houses have remained unlet on that account'.[84]

One visitor to Machrihanish in 1903 was so shocked by the squalor of the village that he complained to the local newspaper: 'Imagine my disgusted surprise to discover that the houses here are utterly devoid of any sanitary arrangement whatsoever. There is not a lavatory or waste-closet of any description to be found − either inside or outside the dwelling places. The consequent evils and discomforts arising out of such a disgraceful and heathenish state of affairs cannot, and need not, be detailed here. Is this the 20th century or the 10th? I have travelled considerably in the British Isles (and out of them) but I have never seen the like in any civilised place. Certainly visitors will cease to come here if such conditions continue.'[85]

In May, 1884, at nearby Drumlemble, an outbreak of diphtheria prompted an investigation by the sanitary inspector and medical officer. They found that there was no convenient supply of good water to the school there, and that the children had to drink from the adjacent burn. That burn, they discovered, was polluted by sewage and 'filth' from the farm of Torchoillean and a house at High Drumlemble. A branch of that burn was being 'used as a privy' by some of the children and villagers, and a rotting sheep was lying half-buried close to the bank. The village lacked adequate sewage facilities and 'the whole surroundings were in a filthy condition'.[86]

A collier in that village was prosecuted in 1875 under the Public Health (Scotland) Act of 1867, on account of the unsanitary condition of his cottage. The roof at one end of the building was 'completely away', and water ran 'in streams across the floor'. 'Altogether,' the complaint read, 'the whole fabric is in such a bad state that the lives of the inmates is (sic) endangered.'[87]

'Rocky'

In death, even, the social order persists. Tinkers, tramps, destitutes, the parish poor . . . these had no obituarists. The most of them would, anyway, have scorned the very suggestion. Yet, their lives had abundant character, of the rough native kind which, if it brought them few of the material comforts of the world, enlivens social history.

Of that lowest stratum of society, there would − indeed, could − have been no intimate record here, but for the particular fascination invested in one man, who may fairly be reckoned as typifying local 'character' at its richest. His name was Alexander Campbell, but few knew him as such. He was simply 'Rocky'. He was born − probably in Glenbreackerie, but possibly in Ireland – about 1818, and married Barbara McCualsky of Southend, who died in 1866.[88] He slept in outhouses and distilleries, and was reputed never to have 'done two consecutive weeks' work all his life'.[89] It could not be said of him that he resented or resisted his lot, and in that respect he cannot be considered typical of that class which destitution claimed. In 1895 he was certified insane,[90] and five years later died in the Argyll and Bute Asylum in Lochgilphead.[91]

The Rev. Dr. A. Wylie Blue, author of the novel *The Quay Head Tryst* (1915) – which is interesting as a record of the dialect of Campbeltown, but otherwise quite trivial – paid 'Rocky' tribute some forty years after his death:

> He was old and bent. His face was large and studded with bristles that seemed to have stopped at a permanent irregularity of growth. He had a blunt knobbed nose and a mouth large and loose-lipped. His eyes were light and moist, pathetic eyes always full open and with a half wondering and questing wistfulness in their gaze upon men and things.
>
> Rocky's clothes, if they could be called such, seemed to have settled on him for good. They had long served their purpose of covering. The tails, or remnants of tails, of the coat were almost on the ground. The trousers threatened an irregular spiral wilt to the feet. Nothing covered his leathery throat . . . Such was Rocky's outward man, and if the description suggests a scarecrow rather than a poor human this is only because Rocky is not amongst us to make plain the individual distinctiveness that gave him eminence as a character. He was part of our attractions and as important for rounding off seasons of display as Provost or Corporation.
>
> Whether Rocky ever had a home I do not know. In my boyhood days he was a free tenant of whatever spot afforded undisturbed respose, and we understood that in the warm comfort of a killogie[92] Rocky spent most hours of balmy sleep. He looked like it as, hirpling along by the aid of a short crooked stick, he might be seen of a morning making his way to the nearest pump.
>
> Leaning on the same bent stick he sunned himself at a corner and surveyed the human scene. His survey was apt to be a comment, for Rocky was not just a contemplative philosopher. I believe there was a time when no election was considered to be properly conducted until, mounted on a barrel as a hustings, Rocky had delivered himself in oracular utterance. However that might be, he was a weaver of words, but in his use they would often work out in idioms of his own and in forms the dictionary did not acknowledge. They were blended words, multisyllabled and rounded off in a grandiose style, which was the Rocky peculiar – his very own. To exalt him to the heights of his beclouded and transmogrifying eloquence, I suppose there were those among the free and independent of his hustings days who kept him duly befuddled. Poor Rocky, as I remember him, seemed pretty often in the state of quarter half-seas over.
>
> He was a harmless dweller among us and only on rare occasions when the too personal attentions of boys had to be dealt with, was the old stick known to have come into play. Indeed, I do not know that it ever touched a boy.
>
> I have called him harmless. It would be true to say there was a certain benignity about Rocky which showed luminously as he acknowledged 'the time o' day' given by a passer-by. The old head like a cahootchie ba'[93] bobbed as if threatening dislodgement from his shoulders while with smiling and grandiloquent response he called down benisons from the Supreme Divine. This last was a phrase often upon his tongue.

His great day was when Archibald, Duke of Argyll – MacCailean Mor – stepped ashore from the steamer. Such an occasion saw the apotheosis of Rocky. He, Alexander Campbell, was there to receive his chief. The old head was bared, the old face lustrous with tribal pride, and while the MacCailean Mor walked to his carriage, Rocky, head bobbing, kept near as his old body could press and his old legs and the old stick could carry him. The jumbled oratory poured itself out assuring the great one that here at least beat the heart of unchallengeable loyalty . . .

I remember meeting him one day on Lower Askomil Road. He was labouring under a sense of grievance. Someone had had the impudence to suggest that they would soon be giving him, Alexander Campbell, the clap of the shovel. Rocky had sought to relieve his outraged soul in poetry. I can see him as he lifted up his old face and I can recall the fierce scorn and gusto with which he castigated the prophet of final ends.

> Within this town there lives a fop,
> his name you may well know.
> He has a goat's appearance,
> and his physogal so;
> but he doesn't remember the time
> when he picked the wilks
> on an island long ago.[94]

REFERENCES AND NOTES

1. *CC,* 8 April 1933.
2. *Ib.,* 27 Feb. 1875.
3. *Ib.*
4. A. M. Maiden, 'The Great Pestilence in Kintyre', *TKM* no. 6, Dec. 1979, 13-18.
5. A. Martin, *The Ring-Net Fishermen,* Edinburgh 1981, 12.
6. *Gillespie,* London 1914, 291-301.
7. H. Reid, '*Gillespie* – our forgotten masterpiece', *The Scotsman,* 21 Oct. 1972.
8. *History of Kintyre,* Campbeltown (1930 ed.), 35.
9. G. C. Hay, 3 Oct. 1980.
10. John Campbell, 19 Nov. 1980, supplemented by J. A. Stewart's 'Cholera in Kintyre', *CC* 2 July 1953, based on traditions collected from Colin Campbell – 'an aged fisherman in Campbeltown' – who was J. Campbell's uncle.
11. M. Hart, *Rats,* London 1982, 34.
12. Let Bk PB Cam, 13 Sept. 1854.
13. *Ib.,* to James Brown, 13 Sept. 1854. Expenses, charged to Brown, were accordingly: Francis McComb, in charge, £1; William McEachran, 10s; Norman Galbreath, 10s; James Pursell, 11s; William McMillan at Kilkirrean, 5s; R. Alister, burying the dead, 10s.
14. C. Mactaggart, *Life in Campbeltown in the 18th Century,* Campbeltown 1923, 31.
15. Min Bk TC Cam, 5 Dec. 1720.
16. Min Bk PB Cam, inspector's report, 5 March 1855.
17. Let Bk PB Cam, to Sec. of Board of Supervision, Edinburgh, 4 Oct. 1853.
18. *Ib.,* to W. Walker, Board of Supervision, 1 Feb. 1854.
19. Annie (Galbraith) McAllister, 20 Oct. 1980.
20. John Campbell, 29 Oct. 1980.
21. W. Smith Jr., *Views of Campbelton and Neighbourhood,* Edinburgh 1835, 11.
22. *Ib.*

23. J. Campbell, *op. cit.*

24. *A Ramble Through the Old Kilkerran Graveyard, or Some Old Campbeltown Yarns Respun,* Campbeltown 1926 (2nd ed.), 10; Procurator Fiscal's Papers (Campbeltown), Argyll and Bute District Council archive.

25. Min Bk TC Cam, 19 Oct. 1821.

26. *Ib.,* 4 Dec. 1848.

27. *CC,* 14 and 28 Oct. 1911.

28. Let Bk PB Cam, 1 Feb. 1854.

29. Min Bk TC Cam, 22 Nov. 1854.

30. *CC,* 31 July 1875.

31. *Ib.,* 23 June 1877.

32. *Ib.,* 27 April and 1 June 1878.

33. *Ib.,* 8 June 1878.

34. *Ib,,* 3 Aug. 1878.

35. *Ib.,* 26 June 1880.

36. *Ib.,* 25 June 1881.

37. *Ib.,* 11 Feb. 1882.

38. *Ib.*

39. Little is known about the early history of that ferry. In 1851, the ferryman was Archibald McLellan, who lived in High Street, Dalintober, and from whom descended the fishing family of that name in Dalintober. He was the son of William McL and Margaret McMillan, and died in 1860, aged 70 years. His successor evidently was James Robertson − 'Catto' − born c. 1815 at Dalintober, the son of James R, gardener and seaman, and Margaret McKerral. Ironically, in 1875 − the year in which the Mussel Ebb scheme was formulated − a new ferryboat was delivered to him from the yard of Wardrope in Campbeltown. She was 18 feet long and could carry about two dozen passengers − which suggests great beam − and was 'easily pulled with a pair of oars'. James R died in January, 1888, and his successor was John Taylor, a native of Clachan. By then the service had entered the final stage of its decline, and John T's function was confined to the ferrying of Dalintober fishermen to and from their moored skiffs. Captain Samuel Muir − who commanded, successively, the steamers *Kintyre, Gael,* and *Davaar* for the Campbeltown and Glasgow Steam Packet Company − began his distinguished career on the humble Dalintober ferry. M, who was a native of Dalintober, retired in 1889 and died in 1908, aged 78.

40. Min Bk TC Cam, 14 Nov. 1751.

41. *CC,* 30 May 1874.

42. *Ib.,* 27 Feb. 1875.

43. *Ib.,* 30 Aug. 1884.

44. *Ib.*

45. *Ib.,* 27 Feb. 1875.

46. *Ib.,* 25 March 1882.

47. *Ib.*

48. 8 Aug. 1891.

49. *CC,* 14 April 1934.

50. A. D. Cameron, 18 July 1977.

51. So/d3/p19.

52. W. Smith Jr, *op.cit.,* 43. 'These caves are now chiefly used as folds for cattle, for which they are admirably adapted, being quite dry inside; and, occasionally, even yet they resound with the mirth and jollity of a ragged crew of Irish wanderers.'

53. *CC,* 26 Dec. 1885.

54. C So/d4/p8.

55. *RD* So, 19 Dec. 1885.
56. 11 Feb. 1939.
57. *CC*, 23 Jan. 1875.
58. 24 Oct. 1980.
59. Duncan Newlands, noted June 1974.
60. *RP*, 1306.
61. *Ib.*, 1490.
62. This may be in error for the cross-decorated stone which is still in the cave.
63. *A Tour in Scotland and Voyage to the Hebrides*, Chester 1772, 195-6.
64. *CC*, 6 March 1915.
65. *Ib.*, 20 March, 3 April, 12 June 1915.
66. Min Bk Kintyre District Committee, 12 April 1901.
67. *RP*, 2142.
68. *CC*, 19 May 1906.
69. Cam/d9/p4.
70. *Argyllshire Herald*, 11 May 1872.
71. *Ib.*, 9 Oct. 1886.
72. *CC*, 19 Oct. 1901. Her skipper-owner was Malcolm Brown, and her crew were John and Dan McVey, James Smith, and Robert McGown.
73. *Ib.*, 12 April 1902.
74. *Ib.*, 15 Nov. 1902.
75. Jimmy McAulay, noted 21 Jan. 1983.
76. Martin, *op. cit.*, 57-9.
77. *RP*, 906, 916, 1358, 1660, 1948.
78. Min Bk Kintyre District Committee, 17 May 1901.
79. *Ib.*, 16 March 1903.
80. 12 Feb. 1887.
81. Dr R. McNeill, M.O.H. for Argyll, *2nd Annual Report on the Health and Sanitary Condition of the Districts*, 1892, 14-15.
82. *CC*, 2 June 1900.
83. *Ib.*, 12 May 1894.
84. *Ib.*, 15 May 1891.
85. *Ib.*, 15 Aug. 1903.
86. *Ib.*, 31 May 1884.
87. *Ib.*, 6 Feb. 1875.
88. *RP*, 1142.
89. *CC*, 21 April 1900 – 'Death of "Rocky"'.
90. *Ib.*, 23 Nov. 1895 – ' "Rocky" Insane'.
91. *Ib.*, 21 April 1900.
92. The kiln for drying barley in a whisky distillery. Extended in Campbeltown to mean 1) a household cupboard – or 'press' – and 2) a small cabin or forecastle in a fishing-boat. The expression 'killogie linnet' was applied disparagingly to a fisherman who would be heating himself below deck when he might usefully have been working or watching on deck.
93. Gutta-percha ball.
94. *CC*, 7 Feb. 1942 – 'Campbeltown Yesterdays.'

CHAPTER 7

The Resurrection Men

On grave-robbing in Kintyre there has been such a lack of documentation that, had it not been for the discovery of a fully investigated case of the 'violation of sepulchres' – as the charge was couched in the legal terminology of the time – this book would not have contained a mention of it. The sole published account of grave-robbing in Kintyre appeared in a booklet titled *A Ramble Through the Old Kilkerran Graveyard*, written by Col. Charles Mactaggart. That solid little work contains a brief account under the heading 'The Resurrectionists', and that the colonel could have stretched his meagre resources on the subject even to 560 words attests to the obstinacy of his craft.

Mactaggart's booklet having been written in 1922, he was able to draw on oral tradition. He remarks reasonably: 'Many of you, I imagine, think that Kintyre, owing to its distance from the medical schools, and owing to the difficulty which must have attended the secret exportation of bodies from here to Glasgow, would escape the attentions of the "Resurrectionists".' He, however, had 'no doubt that those men did ply their nefarious trade here, and that bodies were lifted from our graveyards and exported to Glasgow'.[1]

'The traditions on the subject,' he explained, 'extending as they do to individual cases, are too definite to be altogether false . . .' He cited the evidence of a Campbeltown-born doctor who, as a medical student in Glasgow, had seen, 'on one of the tables, in the anatomy room in the College, the body of a well-known Campbeltown woman, the wife of a prosperous farmer'.[2]

The starting point of Mactaggart's brief account was his description of the burial place of the Lambs, an old family of lawyers and distillers in Campbeltown. That grave is protected not only by enclosing iron railings, but also by an iron grated roof which, as Mactaggart put it, 'encloses the grave in a kind of iron cage, an expedient which was very commonly adopted in other parts of Scotland, to keep graves safe from the attacks of the "Resurrectionists"'.[3] That explanation of the enclosing of graves has been questioned by Ted Ramsey, who has made a particular study of grave-robbing. He contends that, in the main, the bodies stolen belonged to the poorer classes, which 'makes nonsense of the oft-quoted myth that the rich went to great lengths to protect their graves with expensive barriers'. He maintains that the barriers served to deter strangers from interring, by night, their own dead in the graves.[4] Whatever the explanation, of that ultimate resort in the protection of graves there is no other example in Kintyre.

Although the case to which I have referred was the only one, within my knowledge, prepared for prosecution, there is definite evidence that grave-robbing had been going on in Kintyre, and on a considerable scale. That evidence is contained in a petition which was lodged, in December 1831, by the procurator-fiscal in Campbeltown, against three accused. The petition indicates '. . . that for some years past it was suspected that dead bodies were raised out of different Churchyards in Kintyre and, within the last week, it has been ascertained that different graves in other Churchyards have been violated within the last month'.[5] If the phrasing of that passage is a bit muddled, the meaning is quite plain – grave-robbers were in business in Kintyre, and had been 'for some years past'. There is also the implication that this was the first such case for which there was a sufficiency of evidence to warrant prosecution.

The function of grave-robbers was to supply schools of anatomy with fresh specimens for dissection. That market in corpses reached its peak in the early nineteenth century, before the passing of the Anatomy Act of 1832 provided legally for the supply of bodies. But the assumption that grave-robbing, however morally indefensible in itself, nevertheless facilitated medical advance, is questionable. As one writer on the subject has argued: 'Surgery, the most likely branch of medicine to have benefited, had to await the arrival of Lister and the coming of chloroform before it could move out from being treatment of the last resort. In truth, body-snatching was called into being not for scientific reasons at all but to provide subjects for the private schools of anatomy . . . It was a business.'[6]

The Kintyre grave-robbers' efforts were no doubt concentrated on rural cemeteries, where there would have been a greater chance of their operations being completed without interruption. Certainly, the corpse of the farmer's wife to which Mactaggart refers was 'lifted from a graveyard near Campbeltown – not Kilkerran', and the extant case deals with an incident 'in the Churchyard of Ballochantuy on the Farm of Margmonagach'.[7] That churchyard – or graveyard, properly, there being no church in its proximity – is better known as (Cladh nam) Paitean and stands on the seaward side of the main Glasgow road, little more than eleven miles north of Campbeltown. The graveyard lies within an imposing walled enclosure, set remotely at the northern end of a long stretch of machair between the villages of Ballochantee and Glenbarr. (The name Margmonagach has now disappeared, and that farm is more manageably known as Barr Mains.)

In Cladh nam Paitean, on 30 November, 1831, was buried the body of Mary MacKinven, wife of Robert Munro, formerly farmer at Margmonagach and at the time of his wife's death a cottar in Machrihanish.[8] Two days before, a still-born child delivered of Margaret MacTaggart at

Killocraw had also been buried there, unceremoniously, by the child's father, William, and its grandfather Charles MacDougall, farmer at Auchabraid.[9] Some days later, MacDougall was again in the graveyard, attending the funeral of one Alexander MacEachen. While there, he and others in the funeral party noticed that a new-made grave had been disturbed. The scraws, or turves, at the head of the grave had been removed and part of the grave left uncovered. MacDougall's grandchild's grave was soon afterwards seen to be in a similar state.

MacDougall immediately went across to the small grave and discovered that some of the scraws there were missing, though the grave was 'in a more decent and better condition than the other'. After Alexander MacEachen's body had been buried and the grave closed, MacDougall asked the grave-diggers to clear out his grandchild's grave so to discover whether the body had been removed, 'as some people at the funeral said they were afraid the Churchyard had been visited by resurrection men'. When the diggers reached the coffin, the lid was seen to be broken, and the coffin itself full of earth.

MacDougall's fears had scarcely been realised when he was approached and told that the child's body had been found on Mary Munro's grave. The tiny corpse had been laid on top of that grave and a light covering of earth heaped over it. MacDougall put the body back into the broken coffin and returned it to its own grave. That done, he and the grave-diggers opened up Mary Munro's grave and found that the lid of the coffin had been broken and that her body was gone. Donald Munro, weaver at Margmonagach, put his hand into the coffin and felt some grave-clothes in it. He left them there.[10]

A 36-year-old fisherman, John Carmichael, unknowingly witnessed the grave-robbers' departure from Paitean. Carmichael was almost certainly a member of the noted – and now dispersed – fishing family of that name in Dalintober, for his boat was kept at Dalintober, and while at the fishing he lived with his father there. His wife and family lived, however, at Ballochantee, and he had been there with them for several weeks. Carmichael's statement, in its entirety, is invested with a peculiarly evocative power. There is a sharp quality of atmosphere to it. Though its style undoubtedly owes a good deal to the unknown scribe who wrote it down, its narrative impact suggests that John Carmichael could tell a story well.

Carmichael prepared himself that morning – of Tuesday, 6 December – for departure 'about cock-crow'. The morning was very dark. As he and his wife stepped out of the house, they heard 'the noise of a cart travelling along the high road towards Campbeltown'. He told his wife that he would 'hurry after it and have company with him to town'. He left her and pursued the cart, being put, he said, 'into a heat walking and running after it'. He caught up with the cart about a mile-and-a-half on, at Killocraw:

There was a chest about the size of a sailor's chest in the cart and two men in the cart sitting upon it, and there was a third man driving a white or light coloured poney (sic) ... On coming up with the cart I asked the driver if he was going to Campbeltown, when he answered that he was going to Taynamaol only. I replied that I would be so far on the way with them and would be glad of their company as the night was so dark.

Carmichael and the driver then got into a conversation in Gaelic. The driver told him that he was from Clachan and was going with his sailor brother's chest to Taynamaol, 'that he might have it at hand to put on board of the Londonderry Steamboat as he was going to sail from that place'. By this time, the driver was feeding the pony from a sheaf of corn under his arm, and the pace had slowed noticeably. Carmichael asked the man to drive quicker, but he replied that the pony was tired, and advised Carmichael to walk on and not be detained by them. Carmichael took that advice and carried on, arriving in Campbeltown between five and six o'clock that morning.[11]

The driver's name was John MacLean. He was 25 years old and married with two children. Described as a labourer, he lived in Bolgam Street, Campbeltown. His companions were Peter Clark of Main Street, Campbeltown, and an Irishman, Arthur Donnelly. Clark had for several years been employed as a carrier between Campbeltown and Largie, but had given up that work about a year before and had since then 'been doing little except buying a few fish and sending them to Glasgow'. Donnelly had come with his family to Campbeltown in May of the previous year. Since then he had laboured wherever he could get work, 'and when not better employed, he has been going through the country selling earthenware which he bought from Bernard McGuire who gave him credit when he was unable to pay ready money for the goods'.[12]

Thus did these grave-robbers describe themselves. Whatever virtue they may have shared, they had their poverty in common – the poverty of men without a trade, who may work only when there is work for them, and who may, without that work, think of themselves and their families thrust into such hardship as is now virtually unimaginable.

Clark and MacLean were partners in the enterprise, but the initiative would seem to have been MacLean's although there is no direct evidence of that. Certainly, the organising role was assumed by him. They wanted an assistant, and MacLean it was who – recklessly, as he no doubt reflected from the tolbooth of Campbeltown where, with his accomplices, he languished the winter and spring of 1832 – undertook the recruitment of that assistant. The poor Irishman, Arthur Donnelly, was no first choice. At least three other men – significantly, all 'labourers' – had been approached by MacLean, and all three declined his proposition and subsequently gave incriminating evidence against him.

In the winter of the previous year, MacLean had repeatedly invited 30-year-old Colin Graham to 'join him in raising dead bodies to be sent to the Low Country'. Graham was 'horrified' by the proposal and put MacLean off with the reply: 'God forbid that I should be employed at any such work.' MacLean had told him that from £5 to £7 could be got for each body, and that 'he thought no more of lifting and carrying a dead body than a piece of clay'.[13]

He had also, that winter, approached 35-year-old Farquhar MacLellan of Dalaruan and told him that £7 was the price paid for each body.[14]

Just a few days before the removal of Mary Munro's corpse from Paitean, MacLean had tried to persuade 26-year-old Neil MacLellan to join him and Clark. He had perhaps thought MacLellan a surer prospect, because the two had been acquainted for many years and had worked together, in the summer of 1831, as crewmen on a boat at 'the North herring fishing'.[15] MacLean seems to have been capable of the most astonishing indiscretion, and that he and his accomplices were seized and charged within a fortnight of the Paitean 'job' is scarcely to be wondered at. Indeed, the wonder is that the business got as far as it did, particularly if MacLean and Clark had had a hand in the earlier grave-robbings.

MacLean told MacLellan a good deal about the business, but whether in the persistent hope of enlisting him or whether out of a mistaken faith in their friendship, one cannot be sure. Whatever his reasons, MacLean revealed that Peter Clark had 'been in Glasgow and got instruments . . . which would enable them to do the business with great ease, for he had got a spade which could be separated from the handle – that he could put the spade in his pocket and use the handle as a walking-stick – that he had a small saw for cutting the coffin and a chisel for prising it open'.[16] MacLean's confidences were, however, of no avail. Neil MacLellan was not the man.

These descriptions of the special tools which had been acquired for the business were likely intended to impress MacLellan with the efficiency and professionalism of the team he would be joining. When examined, however, the claims expose MacLean as a garrulous amateur. It is very doubtful if these tools had any existence outwith MacLean's imagination. Of the collapsible spade it will be enough to say that if one is prepared to lug a dead body about the countryside in the hours of darkness, then there is little point in trying to conceal the spade. Similarly, the idea of having a saw and a chisel for opening coffins would seem to betray the amateur. Graves are seldom dug with much side clearance, but to insert a chisel under a coffin lid, side clearance would be necessary. Alternatively, the coffin would have to be raised to the surface. In either case, the robbers would be doing more work than was necessary, and taking more time than was wise. Grave-robbers invariably smashed open the lids of coffins at the head, and then dragged out the bodies by a rope attached to the neck or under the arms.[17] The lids of both of the coffins which MacLean and his accomplices violated at Paitean were simply broken open.

Peter Clark's main role in the undertaking was no doubt the transportation of the bodies to Glasgow. This, theoretically, he was ideally qualified to do. He had his legitimate 'cover' – as a fish-buyer dealing with the Glasgow market. On Wednesday, 30 November, Mary Munro's body had been buried; on the Monday night or Tuesday morning after, her body was raised; on the Thursday, nine days after death, the corpse of Mary Munro, late of Margmonagach, late of Machrihanish, and late of the burial-ground of Paitean – no 'final resting place' for her – was sailing northwards on the steamship *Duke of Lancaster*.

Peter Clark's wife, Agnes Currie, had understood that her husband's trip to Glasgow was to collect money 'due to (him) for fish he had sent to Glasgow'. When he returned on Saturday, he told her that he had 'got the price of the fish, and she saw money with him, but cannot tell how much it was as he kept it to himself to purchase fish'.[18]

John MacLean's denial of the charge against him rested – all too precariously – on a curiously convoluted tale which involved a chance encounter with a whisky-smuggler. The alibi was no doubt cunningly contrived, a smuggler being just the sort of mysterious outlaw who would tender no personal identification and who, therefore, could not be sought out to testify in court.

MacLean claimed to have borrowed a horse and cart in Lochend, Campbeltown, to go to the farm of Culfuar for potatoes for his family. He claimed to have worked for the farmer there, Donald Sillars, and 'expected to get from him as many potatoes as would load the cart without paying ready money for them'. But, of course, by his account he never did reach Culfuar, and, so, Donald Sillars could not have been called as a witness to the deception.

Instead, he claimed, he encountered at Taynamaol another traveller, who was trying to repair a broken wheel on his cart. The cart held two casks and one jar of smuggled whisky, bound for Campbeltown. The smuggler offered MacLean five shillings to return to Campbeltown with the whisky. MacLean accepted the offer, and they sat together at the roadside for two hours drinking whisky from a flask which the smuggler produced from his pocket.[19]

On 1 May, 1832, at Inveraray, John MacLean pled guilty to the charge of 'violating the sepulchres of the dead' and was sentenced – with uncommon severity for a first offence involving a single corpse – to a year's imprisonment in the tolbooth of Campbeltown. Clark and Donnelly denied the charge, and, on the Advocate-Depute's decision not to proceed with the case against them, were released.[20] There is no evidence that either of these men returned to Kintyre, or that MacLean, after completing his sentence, remained in Kintyre. Most probably they slipped away into obscurity elsewhere. That case evidently has the distinction of having been the last prosecution in Scotland of individuals robbing a grave for profit.[21]

REFERENCES AND NOTES

1. C. Mactaggart, *A Ramble Through the Old Kilkerran Graveyard, or Some Old Campbeltown Yarns Respun,* Campbeltown 1926 (2nd ed.), 6.

2. *Ib.,* 7.

3. *Ib.,* 6.

4. Letter to author, 18 May 1983.

5. Petition attached to Precognition against John McLean and others, AD14 32/170.

6. Ted Ramsey, letter to *Sunday Standard,* 15 May 1983.

7. Petition, *op. cit.*

8. Agnes Munro or McMillan, widow of Malcom McMillan, sailor in Greenock, and daughter of Robert Munro, Precognition, *op. cit.,* 1.

9. Charles McDougall, *ib.,* 4-5.

10. *Ib.,* 5-8.

11. John Carmichael, Precognition, *ib.,* 9-14.

12. Declarations of John McLean, Peter Clark, and Arthur Donally, taken at Campbeltown on 16 Dec. 1831, *ib.,* 57, 72, 81-2.

13. Colin Graham, *ib.,* 18-19.

14. Farquhar McLellan, *ib.,* 54-5.

15. Neil McLellan, *ib.,* 20.

16. *Ib.,* 21.

17. T. Ramsey, letter to *Sunday Standard, op. cit.*

18. Agnes Currie or Clark, Precognition, *op. cit.,* 28-9.

19. Declaration, *op. cit.,* 57-61.

20. *Glasgow Herald,* 7 May 1832.

21. T. Ramsey, letter to author, 9 Nov. 1983.

CHAPTER 8

The Western Shore

The Eenans

'The Eenans' – the name's plural probably acknowledges the twin townships there, long abandoned and now ruinous. Innean Mór is on the Atlantic-facing slope of Cnoc Maighe, south of Eenans Glen. Innean Beag is on the northern shoulder of the glen. Its remains are sparser and less defined than those of its neighbour, and when the virulent bracken has risen chest-high the scattered ruins are hidden.

Near each township stands a massive fank, or fold, raised with the coming of sheep, and stone-plundering from the ruins almost certainly occurred. Confronted with such massive material requirements, the labourers who built these fanks – now themselves disused and entering a ruinous future – would likely have utilised without sentiment the drystone shells of the townships.

An *innean* in Kintyre 'generally appears to comprise a grassy area on the coast bounded by steep rock-strewn slopes in the form of an amphitheatre'.[1] But such definitions seldom satisfy the imagination, and to see the Eenans is, perhaps, to realise why it is the Eenans. It is quite simply the finest of the few bays which indent the high coast between Machrihanish and the Mull of Kintyre. Much of its charm is, no doubt, the charm of the singular, for it is without comparison on that coast which raises itself, as it were, against the unrestrained violence of the Atlantic, lifting in unchecked between the islands of Rathlin and Īslay.

One's first sight of the Eenans, from no matter which direction one approaches, is invested with a kind of awe which seems never to diminish, as though time were suspended in that clear landward drift of the Atlantic air. One of my own favourite approaches is from Ballygroggan, a hill farm above Machrihanish. The walk is a slow, moderate one across uneven moorland, sectioned here and there with the shaded hollows of old peat workings, marking the toil of unremembered people.

Leaving the moorland – and leaving, too, the backward vista of the plain of Laggan, the sanded bow of Machrihanish Bay which is its westerly margin, and the northerly rising hills of Kintyre – the descent into the bay begins. Eenans Glen is moulded by the steep, stony shoulders of Cnoc Maighe, in the south, and Beinn na Faire (the Watch Hill) in the north. A peaty burn falls down between. Keeping to the course of the old road to Innean Beag, well above that burn, the prospect is of the wall of mountain rising to the south, and, right ahead, the neat V of the glen's extremity, with the sea's blue caught in the notch, like water in the bottom of a glass. And then the first glimpse of the bay itself . . . the sudden revelation of the whiteness of sand.

141

Kintyre

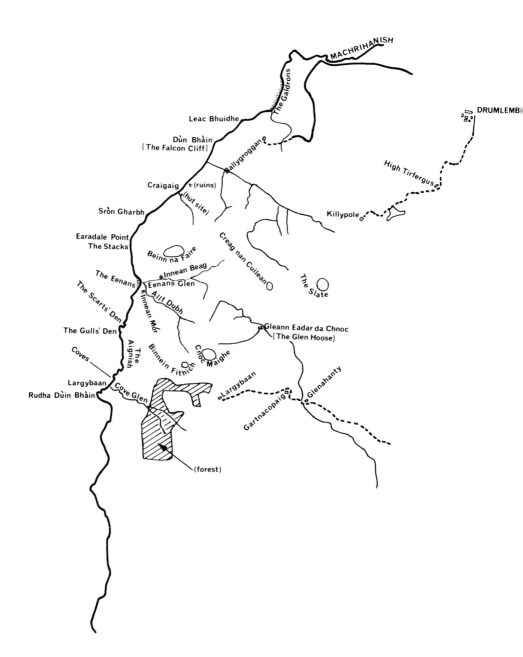

3. The Western Shore

The bay is level and grassy right to the walls of the glen. Visible from a height above the bay, in the subdued light of early morning or evening, are broad rigs, aligned vertically from the shore, and transversing the length of the bay. The sandy, sparse earth has since been undermined by the innumerable rabbits which now thrive there.

Wherever man goes he leaves, in some form or other, an expression of himself to the place, unlike his fellow creatures which offer, in the end, only their poor mortality to the haunts which they knew with an intimacy and vibrancy of spirit which we fugitives from our natural being dare not now contemplate.

These expressions may be material – dwellings, fortifications, burial sites, artifacts, and so on – or they may be marks on his landscape – cultivations, drains, peat-banks. They may even, by their very absence, testify to his past presence – forests felled and marshes drained to yield him crops. In the remotest of places may be found his mute expressions across the span of transient cultures.

Or he may leave vestiges of his language in the names which he put, with intimate sureness, on the places which filled his landscape, his visible world. The process is unending. As a culture and its language break down, the ascendant culture will hoist itself on to the wreckage and rebuild, fusing new materials with the old. That renewal goes on.

If one but thinks the process through, unsentimentally, there is, at the end of it, a kind of justice. On a summer night in 1981, an archaeologist friend, Norman Newton, was seated with me in the Eenans, beside a blazing driftwood fire. We had eaten before darkness came, and were sipping whisky in the glare of the fire. I spoke to him, in a mood of regret, of the Gaelic people of the place who had gone with their culture; but he reminded me of the pre-Gaelic sites which we had visited that day, and asked: 'What of these people, and what of their culture?'[2]

The Gaelic place-names of the Eenans have mostly gone, leaving, as one would have expected, only those attached to major features of the landscape. Cnoc Maighe and Beinn na Faire have already been mentioned; Innean Mór and Innean Beag, too, and there are few names to add to these. An Cìrean – the Crest or Ridge[3] – arches the skyline to the sea on the south side of the bay. Allt Dubh – Black Burn, for the gully down which it runs is shaded constantly – comes off Cnoc Maighe and enters the fuller Eenans Burn before merging with the sea. An Cìrein and Allt Dubh properly belong to the six-inch Ordnance Survey maps on which they are recorded, and I have heard them only from those acquainted with these maps. Effectively, the names are as dead as the people who propagated them.

But the need to name and to comprehend by names is persistent, and a useful, if very meagre, crop of compensatory names has grown up. All are

English, and all are of fairly recent origin, having appeared perhaps within the last century. Their existence is owed to the successive generations of men – mainly miners from the village of Drumlemble – whose liking for the Eenans and the style of living which they evolved for themselves in its remoteness, will form the heart of this chapter.

Rising from the grassy level at the north end of the bay is the Needle Rock, a stack distinctively formed, if of unimpressive height. Behind it rises the bluff seaward brow of Beinn na Faire, the base of which is known as the Singing Rock. That name, though explained to me by individuals long acquainted with the Eenans, remained essentially a wonder until, one night after sunset, I wandered with a companion across the shore.

It was he who, unaware though he was of the tradition and the name embedded in it, drew my attention to the sound. It was difficult to describe, as I later noted in my journal, and I am content to reproduce here what I noted at the time: 'A continual muted roar, which sounds as though it is coming from within the rock.'[4] It induced in us both, listening intently in the dark, a sense of awe and unease. The theories on the cause of the 'singing' vary between reverberation of the breaking sea and resounding of the wind, but the likelier explanation is wind.

Horseshoe Bay – a rocky indentation south of the Eenans – completes the stratum of English names, but for the Sailor's Grave.

The Sailor's Grave

That grave, with which the Eenans is inseparably associated in the minds both of those who have seen it and those – the greater number by far – who have simply heard or read of it, was made on a day in May, 1917. Though traditionally known as 'the Sailor's Grave', there is absolutely no evidence to substantiate the name. It would appear to have emerged out of supposition – the unconfirmable, but not at all improbable association of the nameless victim with some wartime shipping casualty in the western Atlantic.

Accounts of the discovery and burial of the body conflict in their detail, not least in the matter of responsibility. It is quite possible, of course, that the body could have been 'discovered' several times over, but it certainly could not have been buried several times over. The find is generally attributed to some men from Drumlemble,[5] but the strongest evidence suggests that the finders were not men, but dogs.

A young shepherd from Ballygroggan, Duncan Sinclair, was in the Eenans early in May attending to lambing ewes. His dogs disappeared on to the shore and were sniffing about the rocks. He called to them repeatedly, but they would not respond. Puzzled, he went down to them and there saw what had attracted them – a decayed and incomplete human corpse. He left it as he had found it and notified the police constable at Machrihanish, John MacDonald.

On 16 May, some days later, a small open boat put into the Eenans from Machrihanish carrying a burial party: local lobster fisherman, Robert Rae, whose boat it was; his daughter, Nellie; Duncan Sinclair's sister, Annie; and John MacDonald. A grave was dug in the foreshore and the assembled remains, enclosed in a makeshift coffin, laid in it. Duncan Sinclair himself, preoccupied with lambing on the hills above, missed the little ceremony.[6]

The grave is marked by a border of sea-rounded quartz stones and a wooden cross. A succession of crosses has stood at the head of the grave, sharing the feature of date, 16 May, 1917, and inscription, 'God Knows', a reminder that the broken man beneath had surrendered, upon death, not just his individual being, but his very history.

The Eenans crosses have numbered at least four. The cross which stood when John Campbell first visited the bay, in the early 1920s, was gone from the grave on a later visit. He and his friends searched, but failed to find trace of it. Then appeared a band of 'Drumlemmle lads', who had been about the bay earlier. They came across to speak. 'Wherr's the wudden cross wiz there?', asked one of John's companions. 'Aw,' was the reply, 'we got hoot we thought wiz a bit o't – burnt!'[7]

The back of a small snapshot of the grave, shown to me,[8] was dated 'about 1930'. If the chronology implied by John Campbell's account and by that dated photograph can be trusted, then that cross which stood 'about 1930' was the second, or possibly third, memorial on the grave.

Some time in the mid-1950s a new cross was provided by mineworkers at the now redundant Machrihanish colliery. Peter McDougall, a Campbeltown joiner, made the cross from oregon pine, and the late Willie Mitchell varnished and lettered it. A Drumlemble man, Willie Brown, had, however, the honour – and the labour – of carrying the new cross to the Eenans and erecting it.[9]

It was succeeded by a fine teak cross, wheel-headed and in a simple manner representing a Celtic type. That cross had been replaced, on a grave in Kilkerran Cemetary, Campbeltown, by a new headstone, and so was acquired by Duncan MacLachlan (p. 179). A painter and signwriter to trade, Duncan put his practised hand to the lettering of an inscription on the cross, following the traditional form. The completed cross was taken by road to Machrihanish, and later carried to the Eenans in a small motor-boat belonging to John Kelly.[10]

That cross itself was replaced on 29 July, 1981, by a tall, slender, altogether more ascetically proportioned cross, fashioned from the hard uncommon keruing wood by a Campbeltown joiner, Neil Brown. He, with his young son Stephen, his brother-in-law George MacKendrick, and Teddy Lafferty, travelled by car to Glenahanty and entered the Eenans through Gleann Eadar da Chnoc, resting on the way by the kindly ruins of the old 'Glen Hoose'. The cross, shouldered alternately by Neil himself and Teddy Lafferty, was set up on the grave soon after noon that day.[11]

According to a tradition once current in Machrihanish, a ship grounded and broke up to the north-west of the Eenans Bay, on a reef which is called Sgeir nan Gall (the Reef of the Strangers). The dead among the crew, washed into the bay, were said to have been buried there in a mass grave, supposedly within a low-walled rectangular structure in the north-western corner of the foreshore.[12]

The feature had intrigued me for as long as I had been visiting the Eenans, but I could find out nothing more about it. That tradition was all that there was, and it seemed somehow inadequate. The problem was, however, resolved by Norman Newton in August of 1981. Improvising with a broken plank as a spade, he made two soundings, one in the centre of the feature and the other in the centre of the north-west quadrant, exposing four inches of undisturbed black soil on top of undisturbed natural.[13] The rich black soil's being consistent with the structure's use as a stock enclosure disposed of the tradition of a mass burial there, a tradition which, to my knowledge, is unsupported by documentary evidence and which must, for all its interest, remain, in the final assessment, 'not proven'.

Making Camp

The Eenans, for all its grandeur, is both remote and exposed, as any unfortunate who has huddled out there on a grey day of wind and rain will testify. The early coasters nevertheless took their chance with the weather and lay out in the open bay, unprotected and often without even a blanket in which to wrap themselves.[14] A small tent, now within the means of most people, was then, for these poorly paid miners, a financial impossibility.

Shelters of various descriptions have, however, been and gone in the Eenans Bay. A ship's lifeboat, which drifted in there some time before 1920, was presumably unseaworthy beyond repair, for she was upturned and secured on a turf base – to increase the limited headroom within – and a small door cut into her side, with a flap of canvas over it. When John Campbell went first to the Eenans, 'rascals' had already been active in the destruction of the boat, and only a 'wing' of the bow remained. He and his companions, not to be beaten, incorporated on to that remaining bit a small windbreak of turf and stone, behind which they lit a fire and later got some sleep. On subsequent visits, however, sleeping out in the open around a constant fire, by drawing always to the heat they were uncomfortably 'toasted jeest lik' a scone, this side an then that side'.[15]

Teddy Lafferty was a young man of about twenty when he ventured first to the Eenans in the company of three friends, only one of whom had been there before and knew, if hazily, the way. Lacking a tent, they set up two oil-drums, seven or eight feet apart, and placed a beam across them. They propped sloping planks against that beam and then 'cut some bits o' scraa oot the hillside', and these sods they inverted on the wooden frame to absorb such rain as might fall during their nights there. The customary fire was lit at the back of the open space between the drums, and the four lay with feet extended towards its glow, which, by repeated stoking, got so hot that the tar in the wood began to melt.[16] The work involved was, however, prolonged and tedious, and on a subsequent visit there Teddy simply formed a crude 'lean-to' by setting up overlapping planks against a rock and placing here and there a stone upon the planks to stabilise them.[17]

There have been, in more recent years, two attempts at providing permanent shelter in the Eenans. In the 1960s the Hamilton brothers, Malcolm and Stewart, pitched a spacious conical tent by the burnside there. I saw it first, as a boy of fifteen on passage to and from the trawling grounds on the west side of Kintyre. That tent is magnified in the memory of my first, unhappy, experience of the Eenans. I had gone with my firm companion of those years, Iain Campbell. We set off on a Sunday afternoon in September 1967, loaded with a small tent, pots, and provisions. By the time we had reached the head of Eenans Glen, a dismal smirr was blowing into our faces from seaward. In the darkening bay we could not get a fire started and so had to improvise a meal with tinned cream and tinned mixed fruit – grim fare for two wet and weary boys.

There was no ground sheet to our tent and so we lay that night in our wet clothes, on wet grass, and slept little. Persistent in our thought, as we huddled in our tiny dripping prison, was the vision of that great white tent standing in its splendour across the burn. We listened intently, from time to time, for some human voice, but there was no voice. We talked of going across to the tent, entering, and announcing ourselves to its unknown occupants, but the inhibitions of two teen-aged boys prevailed, and we lay where we were throughout that dreary night, regretting the misery we had brought ourselves to.

When morning came, a grey drizzly morning, and we warily crossed to the big tent and tentatively drew the flap aside, we found its dry comfortable interior as empty as it had been that evening before and all that night through. I keep a tiny snapshot, taken from the foreshore of the bay, of that tent standing against the wet hazy mass of Cnoc Maighe. Having succeeded in making a fire and cooking a meal, we left soon afterwards. My journal records 'a most miserable homeward journey; progressed painfully slowly over moor and bog, soaked, despondent, and tired'.[18] Such was my first experience of the Eenans. I did not return there until many years afterwards.

That tent was succeeded by a neat little hut, built with sloping walls of overlapped planking, which could accommodate two sleepers comfortably. Teddy Lafferty first saw it, completed, in the early 1970s, while in the Eenans for a day. He decided then that the hut would serve ideally for an overnight stay in the bay, and would remove the necessity of lugging a tent there and back. When he returned to the Eenans in late summer of that year, he noticed that sheep had been using the hut. As a precaution against tic-infestation, he cut armfuls of dry bracken and spread these on the floor. He laid a ground sheet across that mat and slept soundly in a survival-bag. He kept the door of the hut closed from within – excluding such sheep as might have fancied the place as a shelter for themselves – by propping a length of plywood, lifted from the beach, against the door and securing it with a stone. He spent several comfortable nights in the hut, during two successive summers, but later heard that it had been destroyed by fire.[19]

The Natural Diet

Willie McArthur began visiting the Eenans regularly about 1948. In those years he would accompany four or five friends and remain in the bay for a fortnight. The provisions, during that period, cost each man merely £3 or £4, including the cost of a load of fresh meat, which, however, had to be eaten within a few days of their arrival. The remaining provisions would be supplemented by snared rabbits and by fish taken with rod and line from the shore.

Rock fishing was generally an evening diversion, and was most productive during August and September. The rods were of bamboo and extended about 15 feet. The standard lures were rubber sand-eels and flies, but Willie discovered, by chance, a quite novel alternative which he has since preferred. He was trying, one evening, with one or other of the usual lures, bound on with sheep wool, and noticed that even after the lure had been 'sooked off', fish continued to strike. He has subsequently used sheep wool, lashed with thread to a plain hook, and attests that 'they'll go for that before they'll go for the feather'.[20]

Gleshans (young saithe – p. 218) and lythe (pollack) were the commonest of the fish taken from the bay. Saithe, however, he cared little for – 'They're aa' right if ye're hungry', his laconic verdict – preferring 'golden lythe',[21] which is the immature pollack, reddish-tinged in the skin, before, in adulthood, it assumes its characteristic greenish sheen. These smaller fish were preferred for the sweetness of their flesh.

The heaviest lythe which Willie himself landed there weighed about six pounds. He might carry back with him from a trip to the Eenans four or five fish, most of which he would give away to 'the ould fellas' who frequented the public house at Machrihanish, where he would stop to appease the thirst of the hike. Fish were frequently eaten in the bay, with potatoes boiled in sea-water. As Willie succinctly put it: 'They jeest got caught an got thrown on tae the pans.'[22]

Rabbit meat – invariably cooked in a stew, with potatoes and vegetables – was a satisfying addition to the diet of the men who favoured a long stay in the Eenans. The rabbits were taken in copper wire snares, set along the runs which intersect the level bay and terminate among the higher rock outcrops. Having set a batch of snares, the trappers would retreat into their tent until the unsuspecting rabbits, bold again, reappeared. Then a sudden rush from the tent would send them scattering along the runs. Willie McArthur: 'There that many o' them . . . Wance ye got them started runnin, they're easy meat – ye canna miss.'[23]

The Time of the Gull Eggs

The time of the gull eggs spanned the final days of April and the early days of May, but generally fell on the first Sunday of that month, when enthusiasts were free for the adventure. Adventure it was, and the plunder at the day's end mattered less, for most, than the accomplishment of their dizzy contest with rock and sea.

The harried nests were mainly those of the herring gull (*Larus argentatus*). The birds lay their eggs on a vegetal deposit, primarily withered grass or bracken, piled on a rock base. The nesting sites might often be more readily located by smell than by sight, because a bitter stench of guano pervades the air around.

Few gulls nest within the Eenans itself, but the bay serves as a base from which harrying parties strike out north and south along the coast. Nests are to be found at Earadal, the promontory to the north of the bay, on and around the two great rock protrusions which tower above the sea and which are called the Stacks.

The main locality lies, however, to the south, and a more formidable undertaking beckons those who would take that way. The singular object was to gain the inner fastness of the breeding birds, a cliff-bound inlet of the sea which is named on no maps, but which coasters call the Gulls Den.

The descent to the broken shore usually begins above a narrow sea-cave to the north, enigmatically known in Gaelic as Uamh Ròpa (Rope Cave), but renamed the Scarts Den, for always about its entrance perch black throngs of shags and cormorants. A few gull nests could be found in the area of the cave, and any eggs gathered there and along the approaches to the Gulls Den would be piled conspicuously in a harried nest, for easy retrieval during the climb out.[24]

F

Reaching, from the northerly point of the Den mouth, the inner boulder-massed shore where the nests are concentrated, was the climax of the entire undertaking. The weight of the incoming seas was the ruling factor. A heavy sea, breaking and spraying the rocks over which the gatherers would have to make their entry, increased the risk of accident by slipping and falling, and the singular concern of the gatherers, once inside the Den, was that the swell would not increase and so threaten their exit.

At the outer extremity of the Den is the most hazardous stage of the venture, a low rock ledge, swept by the sea. Teddy Lafferty: 'Ye've got tae pass it, try an run over it an up the other side before the wave comes in an hits the rock face . . . If ye make a slip ye could be caught on it. It's the worst bit o' the whole lot . . . but once ye come along it an up the other side, ye're actually lookin intae the Gulls Den then.'[25]

Easily accessible nests abounded within the Den – on and under rock shelves at the cliff bottom, among the massive boulders, and in recesses below the boulders. Teddy Lafferty's principle was to select only single eggs in nests, and then, should he require additional eggs, to begin to remove clutches of two eggs. Clutches of three he would take only as an ultimate necessity, believing that, generally, one egg in that maximum clutch would be liable to be 'on the turn', or clocking.

He would pack his eggs – normally four or five dozen, a modest take by normal standards – into a haversack carried with him for that purpose. He had then to try to manage the bag out of the Den without breakages, and this he facilitated by roping the load up and over the more difficult rock obstacles. That method was not, however, infallible, and on one foray he lost the greater part of his haul when a sudden wave caught the haversack and swung it against a rock face. 'A wiz only half-way out, and that wiz most o' them gone,' he remarked ruefully.[26]

Baskets were more commonly used for carrying out eggs, and the usual practice was to spread grass between the layers of eggs to reduce the risk of damage.[27] For those who lacked a box or basket, eggs could be freely carried in a shirt or jersey knotted at the sleeves and neck,[28] or against the body, in the slack of a jersey tucked securely into the belt at the waist.[29]

Considering the risks attached to the gathering of eggs, surprisingly few of those who repeatedly faced these risks relished much the harvest of their effort. Willie McArthur expressed, with characteristic brevity, the sentiments of many: 'I might eat wan or two. If ye're hungry ye'll eat anythin, right enough, but a kinna fishy taste off them.'[30] Such eggs as had been cracked on the way back to the Eenans were usually cooked and eaten on the shore. 'I winna eat them at that time,' remarked John Campbell, 'but aboot the thurd time A'd be ower, sez I: "A'll need 'ae sample them there." Thir strong, certainly, but A'd boil it very hard an dip it in saalt before A could . . .' He later discovered the eggs more palatable cooked as an omelette, 'scutched' (switched) with milk, butter, and a little self-raising flour, seasoned liberally with pepper, and turned frequently in the pan. 'Well,' John declared, 'if a man wiz hungry, my heavens, there naethin wrang wi' that.'[31] Teddy Lafferty preferred to fry his eggs as they were, and broke the yolk in the pan. For baking purposes, gull eggs were considered serviceable, and reputedly produced pleasing sponges.[32]

But human taste is a fickle master, and the decline from favour of that seasonally preferred bounty of nature, the gull egg, perhaps has much to do with the relative ease with which our society now receives its nourishment, in quantity and variety unprecedented. Duncan MacLachlan remembered, however, a time when the gathering of eggs provided a welcome lift to the resources of his family, and of other families, too, because the yield of the day's work would be shared with others less able or inclined to undertake the hazards. 'I climbed the whole o' that shore . . . climbt roon the rocks, tryin 'ae get as many eggs as ye could before some'dy else got there before ye. The times wiz hard, mind ye. Tae get a dozen eggs, it wiz grett.'[33]

Leac Bhuidhe

Along that harsh coast were few other haunts of coasters. Three may be mentioned. Leac Bhuidhe – 'Flat Yellow Rock', more popularly known as 'the Lake', a corruption guaranteed to mislead a few first-time visitors as to the nature of the feature – lies below the farm of Ballygroggan. It was, with Dùn Bhàn headland, still farther south, a favourite spot for rock fishing. Bamboo rods were used there, as at the Eenans, with 'eel-tail', 'sea-fly' and limpets the customary baits. Gleshans, lythe and 'rock cod' were taken.[34]

Lobster- and crab-fishing was carried on at the deep tidal holes between the big rocks. That form of fishing was always more popular with the younger visitors, for whom the myriad life of the pools provided an inexhaustible source of fascination. The bait was usually a cluster of limpets tied to a large stone and sunk to the bottom of the pool on a rope. The crabs and lobsters were snared using a 'snig', which was a hand-held length of fence-wire with a noose of snare-wire attached to it. Thus equipped, the fisherman took up his station and gathered his reserves of patience.

The whole skill of the method was to cautiously manoeuvre the loop over the crab's main – or crusher – claw. Lobsters were less easily taken, being more apprehensive when emerging from the cover of the rocks, and being quicker in their reactions. They had to be snared around the tail, because they were loathe to be taken by a claw and would cast it immediately they felt the noose tighten. Quite often the pools would be visited by a conger eel, 'which soon made a mess of any bait'.[35]

An overhang of rock at 'the Lake' served as a shelter, and there meals would be cooked and tea brewed. That recess was known as 'the Devil's Kitchen', and an apt description that must have seemed to any travellers, looking down into the smoking den from the steep hillside above.[36]

Craigaig

Craigaig (pronounced 'krajag') lies between Leac Bhuidhe and the Eenans, and the name – Creagaig: Rocky Place – is surely a measured description. It, too, has its ruined dwellings, altogether better preserved than those at the Eenans, and communicating more poignantly the message of man's transience. These cluster on the crown of a headland, whose modest cliff and scree face looks to Sròn Gharbh and the rising land south.

From the foot of that headland extends a level grassy bay, hard and unyielding underfoot, but scarred still by the marks of cultivation. The beach is wholly formed of dull stones. Craigaig has nothing of the beauty or amenity of the Eenans, but has drawn its share of visitors, to some extent, no doubt, by its proximity to Machrihanish. A burn of good water runs off the hill slope at the south end of the bay, and a wooden hut – similar in size and construction to that which was in the Eenans – stood by the burn there, on a grassy flat above the shore, and was maintained until recent years. It was rather grandly named 'Hamilton House', as a painted sign, nailed above the door, proclaimed. The sign is gone and the hut lies wrecked now. It was a favourite resort of Martin Dunsmuir, who loved these hills, and who is buried now in Campbeltown. I met Martin there on many a Sunday, and many a cup of smoke-flavoured tea I supped with him there.

The Craigaig hut was built in the early years of the 1939-45 war by a team of young men comprising Jimmy Thomson, Calum Galbraith, Ian Munro, Donnie McShannon, and the youngest of the Hamilton brothers, Stewart and Ian, all of them from the Drumlemble-Machrihanish district. Stewart was the architect of the scheme and assembled all the sections. Timber for the construction was hauled from the shore, occasionally from as far as Dùn Bhàn, and the work took about a year to complete.[37]

Of its situation, Jimmy Thomson remarked: 'It was on the best site at Craigaig, with a running burn beside it and vast views of the Atlantic.' The hut was hardly completed, however, when the Argyll Estates manager in Kintyre got to hear of it and demanded that it be dismantled and the site restored to its former state. Jimmy Thomson visited him at his office in Campbeltown – 'He was very kind, but he had his duties to carry out . . .' Happily, however, nothing of the threat materialised, 'and the hut lived on in its original form for more than twenty years and gave pleasure and shelter to hundreds of visitors during that period'.[38]

One of its most frequent occupants was an elder brother of Stewart Hamilton's, Malcolm, for whom it served as a base for his ploys to the Eenans and Largybaan. Indeed, Malcolm knew the terrain of that coast so intimately that he could – and often did – travel it in darkness. Malcolm renewed the roof of the hut, and, other renovations and repairs included, in the end little of the original building remained. A visitors' book was kept for long in the hut.[39] Interesting and nostalgic reading it would undoubtedly now have made, but it is, regrettably, untraceable.

Below that camp is an intriguing feature, which is essentially of the shore, but which exhibits marks of human occupation. A spacious rock hollow, its entrance has been built across with turf and stone, leaving a narrow doorway. Into the inner walls have been driven iron pins, and a natural chimney opens above. I had for long assumed that the walls were of some antiquity, but in fact the whole work was done by some of the boys who later built the hut. Of that primitive shelter Jimmy Thomson remarked: 'The walls were similar in construction to drystone dykes. There wasn't a great deal of daylight and if the wind was blowing the wrong way it could also be smoky!'[40]

Largybaan

Largybaan – Leargaidh Bàn, 'the light-coloured slopes'. Thus one translation.[41] Enclosed by stupendous walls of cliff and scree, and choked with rocks from end to end of its shore, a more inhospitable place could scarcely be found in all Kintyre – but it is unforgettable in its majestic desolation and exercises an undeniable attraction, which is attested by the scores of names, some of them dating from the late nineteenth century, which have been incised into or pencilled on to the lime-coated walls of the southernmost of the three caves there.

It was to that desolation that a Machrihanish fisherman, Alexander McM———, retreated in mid-March of 1907, a time of storms. He had set out on a Monday for Killellan Quarry – midway between Campbeltown and Southend – to take a temporary job there. He carried a week's provisions and a change of clothing, intending not to return until the following Saturday. He was last seen setting out along the Knockhanty road, but upon reaching Tirfergus Glen – motivated by whatever impulse, he never declared – he hid his bundle and turned his face west.

His non-arrival at Machrihanish on Saturday generated such concern that search parties were on the hills throughout the succeeding week, and a 'fresh-water loch near Machrihanish' – Killypole, presumably – was dragged. On the Saturday of that week – fully seven days overdue – he casually walked into his house 'as if nothing had happened', as the

Campbeltown Courier reported. 'He was in good enough spirits, and although he did not attempt to explain his strange conduct, he was able to tell where he had been. It appears that he spent the fortnight in that lonely part of the coast known as Largiebaan Caves . . . and he existed entirely on shellfish which he gathered along the shore.'[42]

There is a mysterious sequel to the story of Alexander McM———. In July of that year he again disappeared. The *Campbeltown Courier:* 'Largiebaan Caves, where he lived during his former absence from home, have been visited by his relatives, but he was not found there.'[43] There, obscurity must close on the fate of Alexander McM——— and whatever discontent consumed him.

REFERENCES AND NOTES

1. *The Place-names of the Parish of Southend,* Campbeltown 1938, 20.
2. *AHJ,* II, 1 Aug. 1981.
3. The most direct meanings, applied to a geographical feature, but Alasdair and Agnes Stewart, who have long been familiar with the Eenans, prefer the more imaginative 'Cock's Comb', and 'often refer to the ridge as "the Comb"'. Agnes Stewart, note on draft ms. of this chapter, Dec. 1982.
4. *AHJ,* II, 29 Aug. 1981.
5. Mr H. T. Munro, Paisley, has the tradition that the body was discovered and buried by his father, Donald Munro, along with Duncan McPhail and John Lambie – all of Drumlemble – who had been camping in the bay. Letter, 9 Oct. 1983.
6. D. Sinclair, as dictated to his daughter, Mary Sinclair, Sept. 1981.
7. J. Campbell, 29 Oct. 1980.
8. By Alex. Colville, Campbeltown, Aug. 1982.
9. A. Colville, noted 12 Oct. 1982; P. McDougall, noted 24 Dec. 1982.
10. D. MacLachlan, 6 Feb. 1981; W. McArthur, 4 Feb. 1981.
11. E. Lafferty, noted 7 Oct. 1981.
12. James McMillan, 7 Aug. 1977.
13. *AHJ,* II, 2 Aug. 1981.
14. W. McArthur, *op. cit.*
15. J. Campbell, *op. cit.,* and 6 Oct. 1981 (noted).
16. E. Lafferty, 28 Jan. 1981, and 7 Oct. 1981 (noted).
17. *Ib.,* 28 Jan. 1981.
18. 24 Sept. 1967.
19. E. Lafferty, 24 Aug. 1981.
20. *Op. cit.* First noted at the Eenans, *AHJ,* I, 31 Aug. 1980.
21. J. Campbell, *op. cit.* – name only.
22. *Op. cit.*
23. *Op. cit.*
24. E. Lafferty, 12 Oct. 1981.
25. *Ib.*
26. *Ib.*

27. D. MacLachlan, *op. cit.*
28. W. McArthur, *op. cit.*
29. E. Lafferty, 6 Feb. 1981.
30. *Op. cit.*
31. *Op. cit.*
32. R. Armour, E. Lafferty, 6 Feb. 1981.
33. D. MacLachlan, *op. cit.*
34. James Thomson, letter to author, 7 Jan. 1983.
35. *Ib.*
36. *Ib.,* 20 Jan. 1983.
37. *Ib.,* 7 Jan. 1983.
38. *Ib.*
39. *Ib;* Stewart Hamilton, 13 Dec. 1982 (noted); Agnes Stewart, note . . . *op. cit.* – 'When I went there first, about 1950, [the hut] contained a visitors' book.'
40. J. Thomson, 20 Jan. 1983.
41. *The Place-names of the Parish of Southend, op. cit.,* 23.
42. *CC*, 23, 30 March 1907.
43. *Ib.,* 20 July 1907.

CHAPTER 9

Wild Goats

A trip to the Western Shore would scarcely be complete – indeed, scarcely possible – without a glimpse of the most intriguing of its resident species, the goat. These goats, which inhabit the coast between Machrihanish and the Mull, are popularly designated 'wild', but in strict terms they are not truly wild, for their ancestors were domestic goats. The distinction is, however, a slim one, because domestic goats have always an innate and irrepressible strain of wildness to their character, and can readily adapt to a feral state.

The history of man's association with the goat would reach very far back, if only it were known. From the wild Bezoar of south-west Asia – which survives, in uncontaminated form, from Turkey to the Persian Gulf – is descended the domestic goat (*Capra hircus*), and from the domestic goat is descended the feral goat. The history of the goat in Scotland begins about 5000 years ago, with the arrival from the Continent of neolithic herdsmen, who introduced livestock. The imported breed was of the Alpine breed group. There was no native wild goat in Britain after the last glaciation.[1]

No record exists, to my knowledge, of how these Kintyre goats attained their feral state. The original goats 1. may have been abandoned; 2. may have escaped; 3. may have been released. My own belief is that they had been attached to the townships of that coast and were left behind when these settlements were abandoned, either because they could not be gathered or because they were not considered worth that trouble. The late Calum Bannatyne, who for many years shepherded about the Mull, shared that theory: 'They jeest originated fae these crofts (sic); they wir left tae go wherr they laiked. That's the descendants that's there yit.'[2]

There is, however, solid evidence of the prohibition of goat-keeping on the Argyll Estate lands in south Kintyre (as elsewhere), undoubtedly on grounds of that animal's notorious destructiveness to woodland plantations.[3] The late Duncan Colville noted some 83 farms – both coastal and inland – the leases of which forbade goat-keeping on a penalty of 10s per goat per annum. That condition evidently was enforced between 1751 and 1857.

The following is a transcript of the clause in its entirety, from a lease dated 1772 (the inclusion of sheep in the prohibition lends it a special irony): 'That no sheep or goats shall be allowed to pasture on farms, except where the Duke grants special liberty. If any are found, the tenant shall on conviction be obliged to pay ten shillings sterling of yearly rent for every one kept on the grounds.'[4]

Nevertheless, goats – as also sheep – were kept on certain farms about the Mull. In a manuscript dated 'Cameltoun 26 Novr 1769', compiled by one John Campbell and evidently part of a stock valuation survey, three farms are detailed as carrying a stock of goats: 'Ballin Mool' (*Baile na Maoile*) had 'a few goats' valued at 10s, besides 14 cows (£2 10s) and 40 sheep (£1 10s); 'Inungouh' (*Innean Gaothach*) likewise had 'a few goats', identically valued, and also 12 cows (£3) and 40 sheep (£1 10s); 'Ballahmakvicker' (*Baile Mhic a' Bhiocair*) carried 20 goats (16s 8d) and 60 sheep (£2 5s).[5]

Whether these goats (and sheep) were kept within the terms of lease, or in defiance of that specific prohibitive clause, remains uncertain. In general, leases had a common form, with only the names of farms and tenants altered, but there may be some reason to suppose that the ban would not have affected the farm-towns on that treeless coast between Machrihanish and the Mull.

Goats were certainly a marketable commodity in the eighteenth century – for each goat 'slaughtered and brought to market' in Campbeltown a penny was levied by the council there[6] – but whence they came remains unclear from that reference.

There may well have been stocks of feral goats on that coast for long before the people dispersed. Occasional escapees there no doubt would have been, and some of these would almost certainly never have been recovered. The high, rocky nature of that coast would tend to favour the success of such 'refugees'. A shepherd with a couple of nimble and well-trained dogs would be hard put to capture a single mature goat on that terrain. What likelihood, therefore, that the subsistence farmers of the place could, without the aid of trained dogs, have brought rogue goats back into captivity? No doubt, however, such feral stocks as may have persisted on that coast could have been relied upon to supply, if need dictated, meat or skin, or kids for rearing. In short, they may have been of ancient stock, free-ranging, and accepted common property. The question is altogether a difficult one.

Of the scale of goat-keeping in south Kintyre, and of the practice itself, at any time, little is known. Place-names testify to the former presence of the goat, but almost certainly fail to represent the density of that presence. The explanation is no doubt that when the people left the coastal and hill town-ships, the greater part of their place-names went with them. Among these more intimate names for smaller features on the ground – hillocks, fields, rocks – would almost certainly have been several more to supplement those which have survived:

1. *Cnoc nan Gabhar* – 'The Hill of the Goats', south of Homeston.
2. *Bodach nan Gabhar* – 'The Old Man of the Goats', a hill above the ruined township of Ballymacvicar.[7]
3. *Cnocan Leum nan Gabhar* – 'The Hillock of the Goats' Leap', a little distance north-west of the farm of Amod in Glenbreackerie.
4. *Leth-pheighinn Gabhar* – 'The Goat's Half-pennyland', on the opposite side of the road to the smithy formerly at Low Cattadale.

Goats were kept for the skin, meat, and milk which they provided, and for the cheese and butter into which the summer milk surplus was converted. The making of cheese and butter − essential winter provisions − was largely carried on at the shielings, which were clusters of small, crude turf-and-stone huts to which the folk of the townships removed for the summer. Their livestock would be driven with them to the shielings, which lay out on the hill ground beyond the townships, and there let loose on the fresh grazings.

These shielings − in Kintyre Gaelic signified in place-names by the element *airigh* (as in Arinascavach, Arinarach, etc.) − may be found scattered throughout the hills, and are often traceable by the greener land in which they lie.

An increasing cash trade in black cattle to England in the course of the seventeenth century[8] no doubt significantly reduced the goat stocks in Kintyre, and may account for the decline of that essentially domestic tradition. That economic shift is to some extent supported in oral tradition. Calum Bannatyne, discussing the shieling system: 'I wiz told that's wherr they put the cattle in tae milk. An before that it wiz goats they drove in there, an they had a high place (milking platform), ye see, for tae milk the goats. The goats jumped up on this high place and ye could milk them withoot bendin.'[9]

There is a counter tradition that goats were introduced to that coast by early shepherds, who recognised their value on the precipitous and rocky terrain, which they will graze with minimal risk and to the deterrence of sheep. As one shepherd put it: 'There would be no encouragement for the sheep to go down in dangerous places, because the sheep aren't as good among the rocks as the goats.'[10] That principle has been applied elsewhere, but conclusive documentary evidence is lacking. The two theories are not, however, mutually exclusive. The liberation of goats by shepherds could well have been calculated to infuse with fresh blood, and so reinforce, an existing strain.

Characteristics and Distribution

None of the goats is entirely white, but in many − the majority, perhaps − white is prominent in their colouration. Some are predominantly white, but with black or brown on the neck and head only, while others have an additional dark patch about the rump. Some are almost uniformly of a dingy grey or brown colour, but with darker coloured heads or necks, or dark-coloured patches or streaks about the body. In short, the goats exhibit complete individuality of appearance.

As to numbers, an estimate only can be ventured. I would reckon the total stock, distributed from Ballygroggan in the north to the Mull in the south, at 70, more or less.

The goat stock has, unquestionably, been much more numerous in the past. Indeed, in the 1950s the population had so multiplied that feeding competition along their habitual coastal territories was forcing increasing numbers of goats out on to the hill grazings where they came into competition with the Ballygroggan sheep stock. A cull was made by a party of Argyll Estates gamekeepers. The herds were driven towards the guns by the shepherds of that place, and upwards of 40 goats were shot and dumped among the rocks between the Galdrans and Eenans Bay.[11] One of the shepherds at Ballygroggan, Donald Sinclair, skinned a nanny, which skin his wife Jenny cleaned and cured with household salt and alum. The Sinclairs, who have since removed from Ballygroggan, retain that skin – which on the underside bears still the perforations of the fatal shot – as a novel, if rather grisly, fireside rug.

Donald Sinclair was born and raised at Ballygroggan, the only son of Duncan Sinclair, shepherd there (p. 144). Donald worked for some 23 years (1953-76) as a shepherd at Ballygroggan. He herded the shore 'hirsel' (or sheep stock) between Ballygroggan and the Eenans Bay, and his invaluable knowledge of the goats of that coast is the cumulative product of regular observation throughout that period. His colleague at Ballygroggan for 12 years (1961-73), Duncan Jackson, a native of Gruinard on the west side of Islay, had the hill hirsel, from Creag nan Cuilean to the march with Glenahanty in the south. He, therefore, had less frequent opportunity of observing goats – except when, in summer, numbers would rise out on to higher ground, or when he would be gathering sheep along the shore – but his experience, too, has served to supplement the singularly meagre published material on the feral goats of Scotland.

Donald Sinclair and Duncan Jackson share the opinion that the goat population comprises distinct 'packs' which keep to their own territories and seldom intermingle, except in the breeding season when some billies will roam off their habitual ground in search of mates.

The most northerly herd ranges between the Galdrans and Craigaig Water. Donald Sinclair saw that herd fully a score strong. There is another 'puckle' between Craigaig and Earadal, also as numerous as a score in some years. Farther south still, in the area of the Eenans, is another herd, perhaps the most numerous of all. Its strength has exceeded 30 individuals. In the area of Largybaan is a fourth sizeable herd, which will range south towards the Mull.

In the presence of humans, goats will exhibit a degree of confident detachment uncommon among sheep. They will not start away immediately, unless one surprises them at close quarters. Rather, they will coolly regard the oncoming intruder and make an orderly and timely retreat. Frank Fraser Darling has expressed that coolness thus: 'The goats never appear to be in a hurry and they seem well aware of their tactical position in relation to a human being.'[12] In Donald Sinclair's experience, goats may become accustomed to a familiar and regular human presence on their territory – but only 'tae a certain extent', a significant qualification. If that person adopted a threatening attitude or approached too close – about 30 yards was as close as he himself was generally able to go – then the herd 'wid jeest take off'. That positional sense to which Darling referred was noticed, too, by Donald Sinclair: 'It depends jeest wherr ye were, or wherr *they* were. If they were near a face, or that, wherr they knew you cou'na follow them, they wid wait longer. They had the advantage . . . they could jeest go doon the side o' the rock at any time.'[13]

There are times when the indifference of goats is especially noticeable. During the mating season they become not so much indifferent as quite reckless (p. 165). Extremes of weather may subdue their reactions. The intense warmth of a summer's day will drive them into shade, usually under rock shelves or into the cool recesses of a bouldered shore; and, once settled, they will move only with reluctance. Wet, stormy weather will also rather immobilise them, a particular instance of which is worth relating here. On 12 November, 1982, Teddy Lafferty was hiking to Largybaan when a storm broke out. The gale was westerly. Incoming seas obliterated the shore with surf and spray, and lumps of spindrift were carried right up the gully and into the forest. He was scarcely able to stand in the face of the gale, and halted on a hillock midway down the glen. Below, in a hollow close to the westerly boundary of the forest, were ten or eleven goats grazing. He was little more than 40 yards from them, and sat looking at them for some fifteen minutes. From time to time one or another would lift its head and gaze nonchalantly at him, but they carried on feeding, out of the force of the wet wind, as though he did not exist.[14]

Misadventure and Death

The carcasses of adult goats are very seldom found on open ground. During 1982, I came upon two only, one a billy and the other a nanny. The nanny was on the shore of Eenans Bay and the billy was lying in Largybaan Glen. In neither case was there any obvious indication of the cause of death. The nanny's carcass had deteriorated almost to a skeletal state, but the billy was just recently dead and bore no visible evidence of wounding or of sudden and accidental death. Mature goats are not, by nature, accident-prone. They command their precipitous domain with a haughty agility. Some of their customary paths can be attempted only with the utmost caution, and, having negotiated a particularly tortuous part, one may look in vain for a sight of the retreating goats.

I have heard of only one instance of the witnessing of the natural death of a goat. That extraordinary experience was described to me by Duncan Brown, a native of Drumlemble and a regular visitor to the Eenans. He was there with his companions of the day, and they noticed a lone billy standing on a rock right at the edge of the sea. Supposing him to be trapped there by a hoof, or otherwise disabled, they went down to him to investigate – whereupon he dropped dead in front of them. He was an 'old scraggy beast',[15] and perhaps shock had much to do with his fatal collapse.

Instances of goats stranding themselves on cliffs are surely rare, yet I can attest to one such occurrence. On 16 June, 1982 I called at the house of a friend, Donny McLean, at Machrihanish. Donny was then working as a lobster fisherman. He had something to tell me. Since the previous month, two goats had been seen daily, from the sea, midway down the cliff to the south of Rudha Dùin Bhàin, and appeared unable to withdraw. This was extraordinary information and I could scarcely credit it.

Next day, with another MacLean friend, Ruari, I went to Largybaan to check the report. We had with us a thirty-foot length of rope and two slings, but little use these proved to be. I climbed on to Rudha Dùin Bhàin that afternoon and looked from the edge of the cliff – nesting fulmars no more than twelve feet below, sitting unconcerned on their tight ledges – and saw, first, the unmistakable evidence of the goats' presence. All accessible vegetation had been cropped bare, leaving a parched and yellowed wall. One goat alone – a billy – I saw, but on a later visit,[16] scanning the cliff with binoculars, I sighted the two together (the other was a nanny), standing out of the heat within a cramped recess, which they had no doubt adopted as their nocturnal lair.

On 24 July the goats were still on the cliff. I was, on that occasion, in the company of a nephew, Donald Docherty, who was eager that we should, together, attempt the rescue of the goats. His theory was that the track which had taken the goats on to that section of cliff might have collapsed at a critical point and left them helpless – more likely, perhaps, they had jumped down from a ledge, and were unable to manage the upward leap, a misfortune to which sheep are occasionally prone[17] – and his plan was to scale the cliff and see, if his theory was confirmed, what repair could be made.

The afternoon was intensely warm and our progress round the foot of the cliffs was slow and lingering. Perhaps, too, we were holding back from what was ahead of us – certain failure. When we had got around to the rock shore below – so very far below – the goats, and taken stock of the prospect, we decided to begin our ascent on a grassy slope. I had scarcely gone fifty feet up when – simultaneously and inexplicably – I lost footholds and handholds and suddenly took off down the slope, bumping

and bouncing over protruding stones. The fall was accomplished − in a
perverse spirit of exhilaration − in mere seconds, and I found myself back
on the shore, cut and bruised about the elbows, knees, and stomach. My
spectacles, which had been dislodged midway down the slope, I found,
marvellously intact, beside me. I started up again, mustering a fierce
concentration and steeling myself with the conviction that such a mishap
could not possibly recur. There was no recurrence, but at the top of the
slope we were thwarted by a vertical rock face which, from below, had
appeared deceptively simple to scale. We returned to Largybaan shore and I
bathed in the cool sea to soothe my injuries. By the time we had eaten and
extinguished our fire, the day had darkened and a sea-mist had fastened on
the land. We left the goats to their own devices, or to death.[18]

Lairs

That abortive venture did, however, produce an interesting discovery. On
our way around the foot of Rudha Dùin Bhàin we surprised five little she-
goats and drove them before us along an obviously well-trodden pad. That
pad came to an end at a sloping green grassy corner of the shore, bounded
north and south by massive rocks. Above the shore rose the sheer, bird-
resounding cliff. Donald disappeared over the slope and, shortly, I heard
him call to me. I followed him and found that the slope fell away again,
under the cliff, forming a shallow cave. We had chanced upon a goats' lair.
Little light penetrated there; indeed, the mouth of it was virtually closed by
the ridge of the incline. The cave floor was entirely bare within, and packed
firm with accumulated droppings. More interesting still, we counted eleven
goat skulls and associated skeletal remains, one adult corpse at the mouth,
and the decomposing corpse of a kid within.[19]

   That goats inhabit that den nocturnally is a certainty, which would
suggest that the living lie with the dead. This takes me back to the
earlier speculation (p. 160) on why so few corpses are found on open
ground, and the evidence seems to suggest that goats − in common,
admittedly, with many another species − will seek to die in a familiar lair,
failing which they will retreat into some narrow rock gap and lie down there
to die. Such is the theory also of Duncan Jackson and Donald Sinclair.[20] I
have chanced upon two such corpses. On 6 September, 1981, on the
seaward face of Cnoc Maighe, I happened upon, and photographed, the
corpse of a mature billy lodged in a rock cleft hardly broader than the beast
itself. The corpse was in a crouching position, and the spine had already
burst the fleece apart. On 7 March, 1982, south of Craigaig, a young
companion, John MacDonald, stumbled − literally − on a cranny which
contained a skeleton.[21]

Each of the various herds along that coast has its customary lairs. These lairs may be caves or simply the recesses beneath rock shelves. Goats are not particular what form their shelter takes, if only it is dry. Indeed, goats will quite readily occupy abandoned houses, which they no doubt find compatible with their high standards of comfort. The herd of white feral goats on Cara took over the upstairs bedrooms of the island house[22] – now restored – and David Mackenzie found, in an abandoned shepherd's cottage in the Galloway hills, that goats there had lain down a bed of droppings which was no less than four feet deep.[23]

Mackenzie has suggested that goats originated the principle of underfloor heating![24] Certainly, their droppings will be found in any place where they resort – to a greater or lesser depth, depending on duration and frequency of use, and on the numbers of animals involved. Largybaan Coves – the southernmost of the three, in particular – are probably the best-known lairs of goats. Even the person who knew only that goats are on that coast could deduce that they are accustomed to occupying the caves. Dugald Macintyre, the Kintyre-born gamekeeper who made quite a prestigious secondary career for himself as a writer of naturalist books and articles, described 'the floors of the caves . . . carpeted with the caked dung of the goats of ages . . .', and remarked that 'the dried goat manure makes splendid fuel'. It could, he said, be raised in sheets from the floor, and he 'once spent quite a comfortable night in the cave, warmed by a huge goat-dung fire, which gave out an intense heat'.[25]

North of Largybaan there are no capacious lairs of which I am aware. The herds of that area probably split and retreat below sheltered rock overhangs. At the north end of Craigaig Bay goats will lie on the beach below the cliff. The base of the south face of the Falcon Cliff is another nocturnal retreat. On warm summer nights they may be encountered on the high rocky ground above the shore. When disturbed there, they will 'scatter away doon, back on tae the shore'.[26] In the warmth of summer each goat has its separate bed, but if conditions are cold, then the goats tend to lie together, so that only one flank of each goat is exposed to the night air.[27] Goats have no liking for dampness and are extremely fussy as to where they settle for the night. Sheep tend to rise out on to higher ground with nightfall, but the goats generally obey a contrary motion, and may be seen, just before sunset, trooping down to the shore to occupy their lairs. Duncan Jackson and Donald Sinclair agree that when goats are seen on high ground, then that is an indication of fair weather.

The Breeding Season

Goats mate in early autumn, and the kids are usually born in January or February. There could be no harsher season for entry into the world, and the mortality rate is undoubtedly severe. Yet, the winter climate of Kintyre is relatively mild and one may postulate a higher − if marginally only − survival rate there than in the more northerly parts of Scotland which goats inhabit. Winter birth no doubt effectively removes the weakest offspring, leaving only those which are best suited to the testing conditions, and which will perpetuate a strain of hardiness in the stock.

The billies break away from the herd about June, leaving the nannies and that year's kids to their own resources. At that time the billies, in detached groups, are inclined to rise out on to high ground. They will rarely, if ever, venture on to the damp moorland plain, but will forage, for days at a time, close to the head of Eenans Glen[28] and the Cove Glen, which runs down to Largybaan.

With the commencement of the breeding season, the billies will descend from their lofty isolation and seek mates. Donald Sinclair has observed a greater interaction between separate herds during that season. The billies will roam off their habitual territories and pursue the she-goats of neighbouring herds. The movement is fundamentally a south to north one, with billies from the more numerous Eenans stock encroaching on the Craigaig and Ballygroggan herds.

The breeding season, in Kintyre, begins in August, but September is, as Donald Sinclair put it, 'the busiest time'. For the duration of the season, the greater part of the billy's energy is channelled into his sexual drive. There is much rivalry among the billies at that season and contests are frequent, but these will rarely, if ever, end in injury. These butting sessions look, and sound, terribly earnest − dramatic spectacles they undoubtedly are − but in actuality they are mere sham and display, and probably serve to relieve sexual tension. I listened some years ago to an old shepherd − now dead − describe the antics of billies in the breeding time, 'fightin an throwin wan another ower the rocks', but such stuff may safely, I think, be consigned to the waste bin of invention. That the otherwise companionable billies should maim and kill one another would scarcely be conducive to the interest of the herd.

On 6 September, 1981 I witnessed for the first time the courtship activity of goats. I was camping in the Eenans with John MacDonald and an American friend, John Hathway. I had slept badly the previous night and decided, about 2 p.m., to retreat to the tent for a nap. I had not long been inside my sleeping-bag when young John opened the flap of the tent to announce that a herd of goats had trooped by the camp and had halted not far off. I was half-asleep and scarcely heard − let alone heeded − his words, but an hour later, however, I woke and left the tent and saw that the goats were still in the bay. What I subsequently saw seems to be of sufficient interest to merit fairly full adaptation from my journal entries of that day.

A group of goats was gathered at the south end of the bay. I grabbed my camera and hurried across. The majority of the goats – all billies – began to move off up the slope, but one large billy continued pawing and nuzzling a much smaller greyish-coloured she-goat, which was lying among the rocks. While trying to rouse her, the big billy was emitting a curious wail which was entirely strange to me, and which young John later pronounced 'ghost'-like. When she had raised herself, the billy pursued her along the rocks and mounted her briefly – and ineffectually – several times. A few other billies tagged along, in attendance, but the main group kept higher up, and rejoined the others in Horseshoe Bay.

I realised later that I had probably precipitated these hasty and awkward attempts at copulation by my pursuit, which introduced an element of urgency and alarm into what would otherwise have been a more orderly affair. The entire herd began to climb the slopes, and I took a circuitous route up, hoping to encounter them again, which I did. There, on the slopes above the sea, the spectacle was an altogether more composed one. The dominant male appeared to be making up to an altogether more responsive female, though he did not have his way while I was there. A few billies carried on across the gorge, but the majority remained on the periphery of the courtship scene, grazing or simply resting. The dominant male continually followed the young female, whose tail wagged briskly from time to time – a certain sign of oestrus – and when she finally lay down, he too lay and simply watched her. The smell was incessant and almost over-powering – a heady odour.

I decided, after a cup of reheated tea and a final sandwich, to try to re-approach the goats. The Johns agreed to the proposal and we set off up the hill. We found the goats virtually where I had left them. Around the dominant billy were two or three other billies, one of which bounded away down the steep slope to a rocky hollow above the shore. There the entire herd re-assembled. The dominant billy was standing over the nanny, with the other billies here and there about. Several times these males began contesting with one another, butting hard – each hollow crack resounding – and then wheeling full round and butting again, but the most determined of the combatants – who had a fairly protracted go at it (perhaps five minutes of sparring) – immediately afterwards made up by nuzzling one another.

One billy tried to mount another billy, which brought the leader rushing across to intervene. The female shifted across the little bay, followed by the dominant male, and they disappeared from sight behind a rock. Four or five of the others crowded round the rock to look at them. None challenged the dominant male's authority or attempted seriously any approach to the female. The stench rose on the onshore wind from time to time. So pervasive was it that I thought I smelt it now and again during the walk home.

Remarks:

1. The dominant billy manifestly exercised a prior mating right over the solitary female. The other weaker or less mature billies – seven in all – merely maintained a hopeful attendance.

2. The female seemed, at first, surprisingly young to be the object of sexual attention, but the evidence is that female goats can conceive at less than a year old, and billies probably also become sexually mature before their first year is out.[29]

3. The infrequent wailing of the billies was entirely new to me. These prolonged high-pitched cries no doubt expressed acute excitement or agitation. Goats are, compared with sheep or cattle, notably silent creatures. The most characteristic vocal expression of goats is a forceful 'sneeze', occasioned by suspicion of danger and delivered repeatedly for as long as the threat remains. Personal experience of that response eluded me, however, until a day in May 1983. Returning from the Eenans with Ruari MacLean, we encountered two billies grazing near Earadal. The larger, startled suddenly at close range, began sneezing repeatedly, without for an instant taking his eyes from us. Having stood for some five minutes watching him watching us, and heeding the sound, uttered over and over again, we finally had to move, and sent the pair into retreat.[30]

4. Never before had I experienced such an intense drift of odour. The effect was almost nauseating, yet – paradoxically – somehow compelling. My enthusiasm to retrace the goats was in no small part due to the inexplicable allure of that sweet, musky scent, the uncommon strength of which was no doubt attributable to the concentration and proximity of the animals. The main musk glands of goats are positioned behind, and along the inner edge of the base of each horn. The glands are present in both sexes. Being activated by the presence of male hormones in the blood, their activity is seasonal in the male and unusual in the female. (Domestic goats may be rendered inoffensive by the cauterisation of these glands.)[31] During the mating season the billies are at their strongest-smelling, and may be detected by the nose long before the eyes perceive them.

Most kids are born in February, but a few may arrive in late January or in early March.[32] Whichever of these months a kid is born in will, generally, make little difference to its chance of survival. Heavy snowfalls are, in Kintyre, just as likely to come in early spring as in late winter, and the early kid might just, in such conditions, have an advantage over a later arrival, by its greater maturity and its relative inurement to the vicissitudes of the weather.

Goats, like sheep, seem able to accelerate or postpone the birth of their young in order to take advantage of favourable weather. Older goats are especially adept at timing the arrival of their offspring. An ideal kidding day is a mild and humid one, with little wind.[33] Most nannies will withdraw under cover of a rock to kid. Many no doubt give birth within their customary lairs, in some of which, in different years, a pathetic little corpse will be found.

Predations

Predators on new-born kids are few. Hooded crows and gulls will no doubt take the eyes and tongue out of a helpless kid, given the chance. There are sentimental types who would consider these violations 'cruel', but the motive is nothing of the kind – hunger is the motive. The practices which man inflicts on the multitudinous animals which he confines in laboratories and battery production houses are infinitely more cruel than the opportunist strike of a hungry bird. Morality fattens on a full belly. There are no priests or legislators in the natural world – there are the living and the dead alone.

In the Eenans Bay in June, 1982, two companions and I sat and watched a herring gull capture and kill a very young rabbit. The bird, by repeated pecking, and seizing and dropping, succeeded in killing the creature after about ten minutes' effort, and swallowed it whole. None of us considered intervening to save the rabbit. We distanced ourselves from the spectacle as though we had not been there.[34] We were mere spectators in the world of the victim and the predator; we had eaten; the gull, too, had to eat; and the poor rabbit, in the order of nature, had to die.

Foxes, which have rather proliferated throughout Kintyre in recent years, are certainly re-established on the ground between Machrihanish and the Mull, and very probably a few kids will fall to them in most years. Donald Sinclair once came across the corpse of a kid which appeared to him to bear the evidence of a fox's work. Much blood had issued from the neck, and a hole had been eaten in the animal's side. Duncan Jackson's opinion was that a fox could take a kid easily and that the mother, if present, 'wouldn't put up much of a fight'.

Desertion

Goats seem not to be particularly protective mothers. Whereas a ewe will confront a threatening presence and will 'stand over' her lamb, a goat will invariably retreat and abandon her kid. In three successive years – 1980-82 – I happened upon abandoned kids, in each instance at the south end of Craigaig Bay. On 7 March, 1981 I saw a herd shift south. The kid must already have been separated from his mother, for we encountered the little creature on the side of the burn opposite to where the herd had been grazing.

My companions – Ruari MacLean and John McFadyen – and I kept well clear of the kid, hoping that he would have the sense to follow the departed herd, but, instead, he wandered down after us and stood for long on a crag above our camp, watching us quite fearlessly. We encountered him again on our way out of the bay, and he obligingly permitted close-range photography before retreating behind a rock. When we left him, evening was already well advanced, and we wondered whether he would survive the night. Exactly one year later – 7 March, 1982 – John MacDonald and I encountered twins in that same area. I noted: 'We saw two tiny kids together on a knowe and decided to climb to them, but as we climbed up we saw the two little heads appear over the ridge of the knowe, looking down at us, and then the creatures were away.'[35]

Duncan Jackson was in the Eenans on a winter's day with two dogs. There was a nanny with twins in the bay, and she deserted them without hesitation. The kids were very poorly, and it seemed to Duncan that they lacked enough milk.[36] He remarked, however, that 'sheep, when they're lean, will bolt an leave their lambs, too', and was prepared to attribute that goat's behaviour to some extent to her debilitated condition.[37] Winter is a lean time for goats, literally. Vegetation is dry and tough, and scarce.

Donald Sinclair frequently witnessed the desertion of kids, but he noticed, too, that naturally if the kid was left alone its mother would return before long. Often, the abandoned kid would simply lie down where it had been left. 'They (the nannies) don't seem tae gie a call tae the young tae follow them – they jeest take off . . . A've seen them goin maybe two hunner yards or so . . . but headin oot the top o' the hill agane, an jeest sorta watchin, ye'll see 'er headin tae wherr she had left it.'[38]

Duncan Jackson once set his dogs on four billies which he spotted out on high ground. His action was as much an expression of curiosity as of mischievousness, and he discovered thereby that goats rapidly exhaust their stamina – 'they'll go lik' a hare for a while an then they're puffed out'. The billies scattered in different directions, and one, conscious of losing ground, and of a dog's getting nearer, hurled himself into a capacious ditch and backed away, his head down for a charge. 'Of course, I just went to have a look at it. I didn't interfere much with it. The smell that's off them sometimes would drive ye away, anyw'y. He was safe enough where he was.'[39]

In Donald Sinclair's experience, 'some dogs winna bother wi' goats, wid hardly look at goats', being – presumably – unacquainted with the working of them. A shepherd many years ago succeeded, with exceptionally 'tight' dogs, in herding a dozen or more goats out of the head of Largybaan Glen and into a fank, where the unhappy creatures were treated to the first – and undoubtedly the last – dipping of their lives.[40]

Goats would occasionally be gathered along with sheep. A pair of billies several times arrived in the fank at Ballygroggan amid a pack of sheep. They seemed to have accustomed themselves to grazing among the sheep on higher ground and came along with them without resistance. Donald Sinclair remarked that 'they thought when they wir among the sheep they wir kinna secure . . . If they'd been near the shore ye winna've got them in'. Once in the fank, however, they refused to accompany the sheep through a foot-bath. Foot-rot or no foot-rot, they hopped on to a beam along the side of the bath and cunningly side-stepped the offensive wash.[41] The Sinclairs keep a snapshot of one of these wily billies tripping nimbly along the beam.

Duncan Jackson once saw a young she-goat come in with sheep to the fank. She was a 'loner' who had attached herself to the sheep, possibly as an outcast from her own herd. One of her legs was twisted and stunted, and Duncan reckoned that she had perhaps suffered a fracture among the rocks, which prevented her stepping with her own kind. The shepherds let her go back out, but she was never seen again.[42]

The Mingary Goats

In 1942, John McMillan gave up shepherding and moved from Summerhill to the hill farm of Mingary, at the back of Drumlemble. He took with him a pet she-goat which he had captured as a kid of three or four months on Ballygroggan shore. At Summerhill, the goat 'ran' with the cattle and was soon adopted by an old brown cow. That cow would brook no interference with the goat, and absolutely refused to go into the byre unless her little companion was in before her. The goat enjoyed the run of the place, and would satisfy her love of heights by climbing the roof of Summerhill house and walking around the chimney-pots.

When John McMillan arrived in Mingary, two more goats – both domestic nannies, and both black in the fleece – were waiting for him. The previous tenant, Bobby Mauchline, had kept them there for milking and had decided to leave them. The two black nannies and the younger grey goat were less than two years together at Mingary when John McMillan himself decided to leave. He could not take them with him; could not conceive of being able either to sell them or to give them away; and would not consider killing them – so he decided to liberate them. Leading one of the goats, and with the others following, he walked across the hills to Craigaig and left them there. He saw them occasionally afterwards, always together, and was satisfied that they had adapted, despite a recurrent inclination to linger wistfully about Ballygroggan house.[43]

There was an old belief that a billy-goat kept with cows reduced the incidence of abortion among them.[44] The belief most probably was founded on the goat's reputation for resilience and robust health, qualities which have long been recognised. Marion Campbell of Kilberry has written of a similar belief in a 'form of sympathetic magic' which protected cattle from infection, tuberculosis in particular.[45]

Diet

The goat has the toughest mouth of all the ruminants and can, in proportion to its size, eat more than twice as much fodder daily as either the sheep or the cow. Almost one-third of its total body capacity is available to accommodate digesting food, so that it can thrive on a large quantity of coarse fodder in which the actual nutrients are very dilute.[46]

The feral goats are comprehensive feeders and will forage extensively along the seaward hill slopes, tackling areas of cliff and rock on which grazing is thin and patchy and which their neighbours, the sheep, could tackle only with difficulty or danger. They will eat most plants – heather, blaeberry and bog myrtle included[47] – and are certainly less choosy than sheep.

Seaweed constitutes an important element in the diet of the goats, but just how important remains a matter for speculation. Donald Sinclair certainly believes that goats resort regularly to the shore to feed.[48] I have seen them often enough taking seaweed to venture the opinion that the tidal zone may well be a food source of major importance. Weed is probably most frequently eaten during the winter months, when an abundance of it is cast ashore by gales, and when sufficient grazing is harder to find, but it is certainly also eaten extensively during the remainder of the year.

It has been suggested that, in the activity of coastal goats in general, a daily cycle – 'perhaps corresponding to the tidal cycle' – moves them between shore and cliff.[49] If the suggestion is that the feeding activity of goats is actually dependent on tides, then I would tend to dispute that thesis, tentative though it is. I have never seen goats feeding from rock-fast seaweeds at ebb tide. The goats of south-west Kintyre, in my own experience, take only weed which has been washed ashore and lies along the high-water mark, and so may feed there at any state of the tide.

Goats will eat most seaweeds and can digest pieces three inches square. From samples of stomach contents taken from goats on Rhum, the favourite species there were *Laminaria digitata* and *L. saccharina*.[50] An analysis – on a dry basis – of *L. hyperborea*, a tangle which grows down to about 15 fathoms and which is rarely exposed, even at the lowest tides, will indicate the value of seaweeds, in general, in the provision of protein and energy. The analysis, in percentages, was: total ash (21-38); iodine (0.5-1.0); crude protein (9-13); crude fat (0.6); cellulose (6-9); carbohydrates – alginic acid (14-24); mannitol (7-16); laminarin (0-18); fucoidin (4-7).[51]

The sheep of that coast also feed on seaweed, but less frequently.

A favourite 'ploy' of the goats which frequent the Ballygroggan shore is to mount the seaward field dykes and eat the tufted lichen *Ramalina siliquosa* from the drystone. The goats are to be seen on the dyke-tops particularly in the spring of the year, when the growth in the lichen is returning fresh,[52] but will also feed on that lichen — which forms distinct grey zones well above tide levels[53] — along the coastal rocks.

Other Stocks

The two other free-ranging goat stocks in Kintyre may be dealt with briefly. Neither has any claim to comparison with the stocks on the south-west coast. That on Carradale Point is of Saanen (a Swiss type) origin, 'introduced many years ago, perhaps even in the eighteenth century',[54] an estimate on which I would reserve judgement, though the antiquity of the name Goat Island — earlier *Eilean nan Gobhar*[55] — off Carradale Point certainly implies a tradition of inhabitation by goats of some description. That white-fleeced stock, the strength of which varied between 25 and 30 goats, has not recovered from a mass slaughter perpetrated in March, 1976. The greater part of the herd — including the old billy — was shot and decapitated, presumably by 'trophy-hunters'. Despite an appeal by Naomi Mitchison,[56] the heroes were never found. It had been hoped that the survivors could, unaided, have replenished the stock, but the reverse happened, and there are now (1983) as few as half-a-dozen goats,[57] with an adverse ratio of age and sex. New stock will have to be introduced, and it is intended to secure three young nannies from the Holy Island (Arran) herd, which is of the same Saanen ancestry.[58] Since 1974, Carradale Point has been managed as a nature reserve by the Scottish Wildlife Trust, by agreement with the landowner, Naomi Mitchison.

Goats have been on Davaar Island since at least the mid-nineteenth century. The late Duncan Colville acquired the mounted head of a dark-coloured billy shot on the island in 1872. It is supposed that the original stock was introduced 'to prevent the sheep from being tempted on to dangerous ledges'. Fifteen goats were considered adequate for that purpose. The 'original' stock was exterminated some time in the 1960s, but was replaced soon after.[59] The existing stock, though exhibiting feral characteristics — in hair and horn — certainly owes much to the infusion of domestic strains.[60]

There were feral goats about Glenahervie and the Bastards until the 1950s,[61] but little information is available on the origin and range of that stock, which is now extinct. In January, 1931 a shooting party saw a dozen goats in the Glenahervie area, and killed three billies and two nannies.[62] The remainder were, presumably, shot out. Donald Sinclair, while shepherding at Auchenhoan, c. 1953, saw the last of these goats, which he described as having been grey-brown in colouration, and of 'the same breed' as the stock about Ballygroggan.[63]

Conclusion

The several goat stocks between Ballygroggan and the Mull have, as yet, required no urgent protection, though the most northerly herd has suffered recent culling which has been both erratic and unprincipled. If, however, protection should ever be required, I hope that public opinion will demand it; but the status of the goat as a wild animal has first to be accepted. As J. A. Gibson put it: 'Although originally descended from domestic stock, some of these herds . . . certainly ante-date some introduced species, e.g. rabbit and brown rat, which have long been regarded as part of our wild fauna. As such, I feel that these herds of feral goats now have a perfect right to be regarded as part of the *ferae naturae* of the British Isles.'[64] No less important is the need to retain the genetic purity of these goats. That 'contamination' has already occurred is suggested in the account of the Mingary goats (p. 169), which may not be an isolated example of the well-intentioned liberation of domestic stock into a feral population. Whether that domestic strain has penetrated the southernmost herds remains conjectural.

I conclude with an appeal. The Scottish feral goat, in general, must be protected from the attentions of irresponsible 'sportsmen' and from contamination by imported or modern strains of goat. It is a unique form of the Alpine breed group, and, in fact, may be the last surviving primitive breed in that group.[65]

REFERENCES AND NOTES

1. J. C. Greig, The Ecology of Feral Goats in Scotland (unpublished M.Sc. thesis, University of Edinburgh, 1969), 1-5.
2. 12 June 1977.
3. For example, in 1783 John, 5th Duke of Argyll, penalised his tacksmen in Liddesdale, Morvern, to the extent of £15 'for keeping 60 goats contrary to the lease' and £50 'as damages done to my woods by these goats . . .' E. R. Cregeen, ed., *Argyll Estate Instructions, 1771-1805*, Edinburgh 1964, 120.
4. *AP*, Bundle 1934.
5. *Ib.*, Bundle 1937.
6. Min Bk TC Cam, 24 Aug. 1795.
7. N. M. Holmer, in *The Gaelic of Kintyre* (Dublin 1962), 73, recorded the form *Bodach nan Gobhar* from Jessie Todd in Baile na Maoile. *Gobhar*, rather than *gabhar*, which occurs on the six-inch Ordnance Survey maps, may in that case − as also in the other cases − have been the standard spoken form.

8. A. Fenton, *Scottish Country Life*, Edinburgh 1976, 127.

9. 17 March 1977.

10. D. Jackson, 18 Jan. 1983; tradition also attested by John McMillan, 23 Feb. 1983 (noted).

11. D. Sinclair, 19 Feb. 1983.

12. 'Habits of Wild Goats in Scotland', supplementary to H. B. Watt, 'On the Wild Goat in Scotland', *Animal Ecology*, Vol. 6, No. 1, 1937, 22.

13. *Op. cit.*

14. E. Lafferty, noted 14 Nov. 1982.

15. *AHJ*, III, 16 June 1982.

16. *Ib.*, 17 July 1982.

17. D. Sinclair, *op. cit.*

18. *AHJ*, III, 24 July 1983.

19. *Ib.*

20. *Op. cit.*

21. *AHJ*, II and III.

22. J. H. McCulloch, 'Cara Island', article in *Scottish Daily Express;* reprinted *CC*, 24 Sept. 1953. The herd to which McCulloch referred has since died out. An attempt to reduce the numbers by shooting was overdone. Jura goats were later introduced, but these were multi-coloured, and the herd is at present kept white by the killing of coloured offspring: J. A. Gibson, letter to author, 6 Dec. 1983.

23. *Goat Husbandry*, London 1970 (3rd ed.), 119.

24. *Ib.*

25. 'District Rich in Memories of St. Columba and Robert the Bruce', article in *Oban Times;* reprinted *CC*, 21 May 1938; letter to *Oban Times*, 8 Jan. 1949.

26. D. Sinclair, *op. cit.*

27. D. Mackenzie, *Goat Husbandry, op. cit.*, 120.

28. D. Sinclair, *op. cit.*

29. Greig, *op. cit.*, 166.

30. *AHJ*, III, 8 May 1983.

31. Mackenzie, *op. cit.*, 240.

32. D. Sinclair, *op. cit.*

33. Mackenzie, *op. cit.*, 231.

34. *AHJ*, III, 5 June.

35. *Ib.*, I and III.

36. Noted 15 Dec. 1982.

37. 18 Jan. 1983.

38. *Op. cit.*

39. 18 Jan. 1983.

40. C. Bannatyne, 12 June 1977; R. McInnes, letter to author, 28 Feb. 1983. The former named Sandy Helm as the shepherd responsible; the latter named Alasdair Beattie.

41. D. Sinclair, *op. cit.*

42. 18 Jan. 1983.

43. J. McMillan, *op. cit.*

44. *Ib.*, and D. Sinclair, *op. cit.*

45. *Scottish Studies*, Vol. 9, 1965, 18.

46. Mackenzie, *op. cit.*, 22.

47. Greig, *op. cit.*, 205.

48. *Op. cit.*

49. Greig, *op. cit.*, 207, citing suggestion.

50. *Ib.*

51. Dr A. A. Dobbie, company chief chemist, Kelco/AIL International Ltd., Girvan, letter to author, 15 April 1983.

52. D. Jackson and D. Sinclair, *op. cit.*

53. J. Laundon, Department of Botany, British Museum (Natural History), letter to author, 5 April 1983.

54. N. Mitchison, Carradale, letter to author, 13 Dec. 1983.

55. 'Island of Goats.' Graham MacKinlay, 23 Feb. 1977.

56. 'I am sure no local person would have had any hand in this. It stinks. But if anybody has any idea of who did it, I hope they will help. The goats were shot; somebody must have heard. The criminals must have used either a boat or a car; somebody must know. It is a shame on the community if we get no information.' *CC,* 1 April 1976.

57. On 5 Nov., during an evening walk around Carradale Point, I saw just six goats together.

58. J. A. Gibson, letter to author, 25 Nov. 1983.

59. J. A. Gibson, 'The Wild Goats of the Clyde Area', in *The Western Naturalist,* Vol. I, 1972, 11. Teddy Lafferty remembers the last of that stock, an old grey nanny which was 'jeest movin an nae merr'. That would have been in the late 1950s. Noted 29 Nov. 1983.

60. There was one white nanny (liberated from Kildalloig Estate), with white kid, on the island in 1983 – from photograph by E. Lafferty.

61. D. Sinclair, *op. cit.*

62. Gibson, *op. cit.,* 10.

63. *Op. cit.*

64. Gibson, *op. cit.,* 6.

65. Greig, *op. cit.,* 4.

CHAPTER 10

The Coasters

There occur, in Chapter 8, occasional references to 'coasters'. That term remains as yet, however, unexplained, for the reason that, though convenient and not without relevance applied to the men who frequented the Eenans, its true locale was the stretch of shore between the glen of New Orleans and the bay of Corphin. That coast – to which this chapter turns – though barely two miles in extent, has generated a density of recent tradition and place-names which is quite unparalleled in all Kintyre.

What, then, was a 'coaster'? Such a definition as I would offer – 'A frequenter of the south-east Kintyre shores; one who habitually removed himself from ordinary society, there to spend time alone or in company with others similarly motivated' – would fail to touch the secret core of the coasting tradition.

'Hoot we cried coasters wiz . . . well, ye went wi' big heavy boots on an wi' haversacks an waalkin-sticks. Emdy else wiz "tourists". Now, we wir real coasters, oor wey. Tourists an coasters. Ye wir never dressed . . . an ye wir supposed to be merr professional than the rest. This wiz aa' in the mind, of course. But ye seemed tae look the part better.'[1] Such was Teddy Lafferty's description – or caricature, as he himself would no doubt cheerfully concede – of the typical coaster. Between these poles – the 'academic' and the intimate – shall appear the real coaster, tramping towards some immutable horizon, in the magical hour of a fading evening, shouldering cheerily his queer bag of codes and customs.

That there should have been anything written, far less published, about the coasting tradition – an essentially casual and uncomplicated diversion which, in the way of these things, ought not to have attracted the slightest attention – would have been remarkable; yet, by a marvellous chance, such an account does exist, and may, indeed, approximate to the very origins of coasting, as now understood. That account is incidental to a local press report of the theft of potatoes from a roadside field on the farm of Kildalloig.

On a Sunday in September, 1912 Robert McCaig, son of the tenant of Kildalloig Farm, saw, from a wood above the field, a band of men enter the field and begin lifting potatoes. He intercepted the band farther along the road. One of the number, James McArthur, a young Campbeltown labourer, carried potatoes in a muffler, and McCaig accused him of having stolen them. McArthur denied the accusation and protested that he had carried the potatoes from town. McCaig, however, was insistent, and asked to be shown what was inside the muffler. McArthur refused, and McCaig tried to seize the bundle, and had it in his hands long enough, he said, to satisfy himself that it did contain potatoes. He could also see potatoes, caked

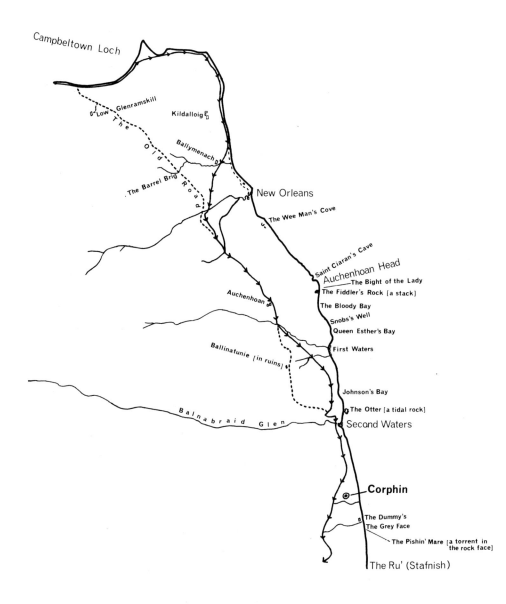

4. The Coast. The arrowed line represents the main road to Southend

with fresh earth, through the openings in the scarf, and he was convinced that they were of the variety – 'British Queens' – which were growing in his father's field. He cycled to Campbeltown and lodged a complaint with the police.

When McCaig and a constable McCallum caught up with the coasters they were brewing tea on the Auchenhoan shore. The potatoes had disappeared – perhaps, wisely, the incriminating evidence had been eaten – and the band, aggrieved no doubt by this inauspicious intrusion, strongly 'denied having been in the field'. Nonetheless, James McArthur later found himself in the dock of Campbeltown Sheriff Court charged with theft of the potatoes, valued at about a shilling (5p).

A 'formidable procession' of his fellow coasters – John McKellar, John McIntyre, Archibald McEachran, Archibald McArthur, James Hunter, and William Hughes – entered and left the witness-box, 'all wearing more or less an expression of injured innocence'. James insisted that he carried in the muffler no potatoes, just tea, sugar, bread, butter, and a *melon*, at which laughter broke out in the courtroom. When asked later by the sheriff if he could suggest anything in the muffler which might have been mistaken for potatoes, he hesitated and then ventured, 'Maybe the melon', provoking another burst of mirth. With humour though the case unfolded, at the end of it James McArthur was sentenced to a fine of 15s (75p) or five days' imprisonment.

Thus the essentials of the case. Of greater interest here, however, is the introduction to that report:

> . . . In the course of the evidence led it transpired that a number of the casual labourers who make the Quay Head their rallying point have an interesting way of spending Sundays and holidays. At a sheltered spot on the shore near Auchenhoan they have what they call a 'camp', where pots, pans, and other cooking paraphernalia are stored, and thither they resort when the weather is favourable and the spirit moves them, carrying provisions sufficient to give them a repast more or less royal, according to the state of their finances at the time. The outing is known as going to 'the coast'.[2]

The Coast

For the coaster there was but one Coast, dominated by the long headland of Auchenhoan, which lies easterly towards the low hills of Ayrshire. To north and south of 'the Heids', as the point of Auchenhoan is popularly known, were the sheltered bays and bights which were the haunts of coasters. The true limit of the Coast was the bay of Corphin, *The Second Waters* as they knew it, for a burn – which rises on Arinarach Hill in the west – reaches the sea there. *The First Waters*, half-a-mile by shore to the north, was the other burn – and bay also, because there too the nominal sense was extended – which coasters laid claim on.

From wooded New Orleans to Feochaig, three miles south by the shore, there are no other comparable burns. There is, as it were, no 'Third Waters'. Feochaig, essentially, was outwith the coasters' customary range. It was a far place, visited from time to time, but not true 'Coast'. The coaster was not – and this, obviously, is a generalisation – at heart a hiker. Being there, not going there, was his primary motivation.

The main rendezvous of coasters was the Second Waters. For those coasters who, from time to time, or habitually, shunned the company of their fellows and took a solitary way, there were – appropriately – smaller bays in which they might linger, alone and undisturbed.

The Dummy's – a fractured name, typifying the facility of dropping the terminal word, which is invariably the geographical definition: fishermen knew the place as the Dummy's Port, but for coasters it was just 'the Dummy's' – is the only bay, of sorts, which breaks the hard-going shore between the Second Waters and Feochaig. A tiny ruin – no more than a single, cramped room – stands at the south end of the bay, and there two mute brothers were said to have lived 'a very simple and poor life', growing potatoes and fishing.[3]

That tradition tends to be supported by documentary evidence. In the Census of 1861, a 68-year-old unmarried fisherman, Donald MacIsaac, was recorded at Corphin. Against his entry is the note, 'deaf and dumb from birth'.[4] It seems likely that he was 'the Dummy' (there is no evidence of a similarly afflicted brother), and that he seasonally occupied the house which commemorates him. Two 'ports' – in local usage, a passage cleared to the sea, over which small boats could be dragged – are visible there, intersecting the stony shore. The MacIsaac family had farmed Corphin since the mid-eighteenth century, or earlier. By 1861, Donald was the last of them left there. A shepherd, James Cook, and his wife occupied the holding.[5] In 1851, however, ten persons – four of them MacIsaacs, and the others employees and relations – were recorded there.[6] In 1865 Donald, still at Corphin, was on the Southend poor roll, receiving 9d (4p) per week.[7] Four years later he was being paid his allowance in Campbeltown.[8] In November, 1871 Donald MacIsaac was found dead on the farm of Dunglas, Southend. The cause of death was registered as 'hypertrophy of the left ventricle of the heart'. His age was estimated at 81 years. His parents' names were unknown – no relative was present at the registration of his death.[9]

Johnson's Bay, lying just around the northern end of the Second Waters, was another secluded retreat.

Farther north still is tiny *Queen Eester's Bey*, which is squeezed between the spacious Bloody Bay and the First Waters. Truly a concealed spot, from within its grassy cavity, vision, both north and south, is blocked by enclosing rock. The late Sandy Morrans frequented that bay, and there would 'brew up' alone on his days at the Coast, taking water from a meagre surface flow nearby. The shallow 'well' which he scooped and cleared for himself, in the marshy ground above the shore, has overgrown, but the flow – piped, more recently, by Teddy Lafferty, where it falls to the shore, and still serving its cool water to the few who know it – commemorates Sandy in its name, Snobs's Well.[10] Sandy was a shoemaker in Campbeltown, and in Scots – as in colloquial English – a shoemaker is a *snob*.

It was from Sandy Morrans – during his final years on the Coast, and before advancing age ended his wanderings – that Teddy Lafferty learned the name, Queen Eester's Bey. Other coasters of whom Teddy – intrigued by the name and wondering at its meaning – later enquired could offer no explanation.[11] The name caught my own interest, but a satisfactory explanation eluded me until, reading through the bound issues of the *Campbeltown Courier* for the year 1885, under the heading 'Death of a Cave Dweller', its origin was incontrovertibly disclosed (p. 123).

As to specifically how that bay – which is five miles by shore from the Macharioch district – acquired its association with 'Queen Esther' Houston will doubtless never be known. The exact location of her 'lonely and comfortless abode' likewise presents difficulty, but it was probably that cave north of Pollywilline Bay, familiar to coasters as the Cats' Cove, and now inextricably associated with the solitary coaster, Colin MacArthur, who lodged in it during his frequent visits to that shore.[12] The name most probably commemorates poor Esther's numerous cat companions (p. 123), which no doubt resisted any attempts to remove them, following the death of their benefactress, and lingered about the cave, forced increasingly into feral independence.

Only two coasters of the traditional school still tramp the shores. The elder is Duncan MacLachlan, who was born at Dalintober in 1908. He 'served his time' on the Coast with his father, Bob MacLachlan, confirmed socialist, controversial town councillor, and occasional poet. Duncan, a small sprightly man, with a round appealing face, maintains a little caravan in Feochaig Bay, to which he resorts – more often than not with his companion, Robert Armour – in fine weather. He will still walk the seven miles by road down to the bay, though usually he goes by bicycle or is content to be conveyed by car.

Edward Patrick Lafferty – or 'Teddy', as he invariably 'gets' in the community in which he takes his unassuming place – is that other coaster. As his name abundantly proclaims, his paternal origin is Irish. The Lafferty line in Campbeltown is a brief one (p. 201) by usual standards – he is second generation born out of Donegal. Nothing in his immediate family background predisposed him to his coasting passion. He discovered that passion and has been claimed by it ever since.

Coasting, in its origin, was probably the diversion of a day. Later, however, 'the brotherhood' – a pleasingly apposite, if ludicrously intended description, for which credit is due to the anonymous *'Courier* man' (p. 177) – began to camp overnight on the shore. Teddy's first camping venture to the Coast was about the year 1951, as a seventeen-year-old serving his apprenticeship as a bricklayer in Campbeltown. The suggestion originated with James 'Loafs' Morran, whom Teddy had fortuitously encountered on his exploratory outings to the Second Waters. Jamie – a big, affable man – was then a 'heid yin' (head one), as Teddy put it, among the coasters,[13] as his popular title, 'the Laird o' Corphin Glen', would suggest. Jamie removed to England to work in the post-war years, but, unlike the majority of his fellow-townsmen who took the road south, he was unable to bear his exile. He was toiling in the noise and the heat of a factory one Sunday, while the summer sunshine, streaming through the skylights, filled the workshop. Thinking continually of the Coast, he resolved finally: 'Jamie Loafs, ye'll naw be here *next* Sunday – ye know wherr ye're gan.' Sure enough, he appeared at the Second Waters a week later, and never returned to England.[14] James Morran became an esteemed companion of the young Teddy, who remembers him – a quintessential image – on the shore, his bulky frame stripped to the waist, trouser-bottoms tucked into long stockings above his heavy boots, and a black beret atop his head, in the blue heat of a summer's day.[15]

The other estimable influence upon Teddy during his formative years at the Coast was John Smith, or 'Smeesh', the bye-name by which he was familiarly known, and by which his son and grandson still are known. Jock was tough and sturdy, the physical legacies of half-a-lifetime's coal-hewing. He is reputed to have cycled to England in the 1920s, in search of work, his pick and shovel lashed to the frame of the bicycle.[16] He was a maker of horn-handled hazel walking-sticks. When Teddy inherited his personal stick, following his death in 1964, he found it too long to let him hold it by the handle. He contemplated cutting a six-inch length from the shaft, but decided, sentimentally: 'That's the wey ye got it, and lea' it the wey it is, jeest for a keepsake. So A changed ma mind, A never touched it, an that stick's hingin in the hoose yit.'[17]

'Smeesh' remained an active coaster until within a fortnight of his sudden death, instructing his young companion in the ways and customs of the Coast. Teddy became an habitual visitor to the old man's house in Parliament Place, Campbeltown, and on one such visit was astonished to find a tent pitched in the middle of the living-room. The extraordinary spectacle was soon, however, explained. Jock had acquired a new tent, for which, in his anxiety to see it erect, he had improvised a pitch by attaching the guys to the legs of furniture. That tent which then pleased the old man so much was, however, to bring him little subsequent pleasure. On its first night of service – pitched on the foreshore of Johnson's Bay – it caught fire, and Jock was extricated from the blaze only in time to spare him serious injury. He and his companions of that night – James Morran, Billy Russell, and Teddy himself – watched in darkness the destruction of the little tent and all that it contained, to the almost surrealistic sound accompaniment of exploding bean cans.[18]

The Caravan

In 1952, however, the necessity of camping was removed. In January of that year a 'caravan' providentially appeared at the Second Waters. That 'caravan' – as it later became – was, in fact, a converted Ford ambulance which had been in service running technicians to and from the radar station at Ru Stafnish. On 6 January, the vehicle skidded on ice at the top of the Corphin hairpin bend and hurtled into the burn below. Of the four occupants, only Roderick MacKenzie Ross, a twenty-eight-year-old technician, failed to escape from the vehicle before it plummeted, and he had to be stretchered, with difficulty, out of the snow-filled glen.[19]

The abandoned vehicle was later secured, at the nominal cost of £5,[20] by Charlie McMillan, himself a radar van driver, and was hauled out of the burn and set up, wheelless, on planks at the burnside. Jock Smith, particularly, expended much time and energy in the conversion of the metal shell. The hardboard-lined interior was coated with paint, two wooden bunks and a card table were installed, a new door was attached, and a small stove was set up in a corner. Teddy assisted Jock with the splitting and flattening out of tin drums, and the resultant sheets were nailed to the wall behind stove and stove-pipe to minimise the hazard of fire. 'Then,' remembered Teddy, 'we stopped the tent, we could dae withoot a tent. We dinna even cerr whether it rennt or naw. We had this caravan, an it wiz jeest *perfect*. In fact, we wir quite happy tae sit in it wi' the dorr open an the stove fuull a' sticks an jeest look at the renn ootside.'[21]

So the little Second Waters caravan became, for a time, the main rendezvous of the coasting fraternity. But if, in the initial years, its effect was a unifying one, drawing, in foul weather as in fair, the solid nucleus of the committed coasters, in the end lay division and dispersal. As knowledge of the caravan spread, there began to converge on the Second Waters those casual visitors – disparagingly referred to as 'tourists' – who appeared for several hours, exchanged talk and perhaps supped a cup of tea, and then left. The old intimacy of the coasting regulars, increasingly subjected to disruptive pressure from without, was breaking up. Teddy Lafferty, perhaps more than most, sensed the impending dissolution of the little

G

fellowship. When travelling to the Coast one Sunday morning as a passenger in the radar van – a customary means, among coasters, of rapid access to the shore – he remarked to the driver as they neared the Waters: 'Ach, A'll jeest carry on tae Feochaig this moarnin an A'll waalk back an meet them at the Saicond Waters.' As the van ascended the steep hill out of the bay, Teddy, looking back, could see the little caravan below, and smoke rising from it, blue in the sunlight. He had assured the driver – and reassured himself, remembering the companionable days there with his friends, the coasters – that he would return and join the company, but: 'A never ever came back tae meet them.'[22] He had broken with the coasters, and though their values would continue to sustain and inspire him, and though from time to time he would walk the shores with individual friends from among their number, his way thereafter would be a solitary one.

Whether his decision, on that day, to carry on and be alone, suprised him then, he did not declare. If he were now to consider the impulse, he would no doubt understand and accept its inevitability. The solitary strain characterised many of the coasting fraternity. Suppressed it might be, temporarily or indefinitely, to admit the company of fellow-coasters, but that impulse, tugging at the sleeve like the lost child of the unresolved self, would linger always. Even in his earliest coasting years, as one of a cheerful band, sharing in and making free with fun, Teddy could not quite put away that longing to be free from the claims of companionship. That conflict he has now resolved. 'Tae be truthful,' he said, 'if I had the choice in the moarnin, tae make a decision – go wi' this crowd or go masel' – A wid enjoy the crowd, but A wid still go masel'.'[23] The tendency to aloneness he considered an inevitable progression: 'Tae me, the coast or the hill, it's somethin ye've really got tae spen' a certain amount o' time on it on yer own. Ye've got tae. Ye probably wid end up doin' it anyw'y.'[24]

There was a story told among coasters which exemplifies that conflict. Three old coasters enjoyed one another's company sufficiently to walk together to the Coast and back, but on the shore each insisted on making and tending his own fire. And at his individual fire each would sit, apart from the others and yet within talking range, and each would berate another, in turn, with such denunciations as: 'A winna sit wae ye, 'cause yer piece (sandwich) is naw good enough!' By such a perverse compromise the pride of each was satisfied, and home together they would go when evening came.[25]

Routes to the Coast

There were two routes to the Coast, the Ould Rodd – untarred and little better than a cart-track – and the main road which replaced it, and which follows the coastline to Southend. The Ould Rodd begins at Glenramskill, where it turns inland towards the farm of Low Glenramskill. A little distance from the farmhouse, however, a track diverges and is routed around the perimeter fence of the unsightly N.A.T.O. oil storage base which, c. 1964, annexed the more direct original section of the track. The Ould Rodd extends, in its entirety, no more than a mile-and-a-half before it rejoins the main road on Ballymenach brae, but the greater part of it traverses open moorland and scenically rewards the traveller on it.

For myself, I delight, returning at evening from the Coast, to rest at the quiet place which coasters called the Barrel Brig. Two barrels were formerly set into the road to carry through the waters of the wee burn which rises a little way above on the hill. An enduring rowan shakes its head in the evening wind there.

The Ould Rodd presented a quicker route to the Coast, and many coasters took that way, avoiding the circuitous main road, unless the weather was fine and daylight prolonged. The coasters would generally set out in a band from the town early on a Saturday afternoon, so to arrive at the Second Waters with enough daylight remaining to enable them to organise their camp – pitch tents, gather driftwood, kindle a fire, and bring water to the camp. The principle of organisation was fundamental to the coasters' schooling, and Teddy Lafferty maintains the practice of gathering into his tent before darkness a pile of dry sticks so that a fire may be started quickly at daybreak, notwithstanding overnight rainfall.

Having taken the main road along the lochside and south by the bird-haunted shore of the reach of sea which fishermen call the Loaden, coasters might decide to continue by the shore, and would leave the road at the foot of Ballymenach brae, where it twists inland. The state of the tide was usually the deciding consideration. When flood tide is well advanced, the shore around the foot of Auchenhoan Head becomes impassable, though a fairly negotiable 'sheep pad' ascends the conglomerate bulk of the Head and leads one on to and over the top, whence the shore may be regained by descending into the Bloody Bay below. Coasting tradition attributes the origin of that name to a deadly combat waged there by seven brothers, who slew one another until few remained living.[26]

Returning by the shore, the practicability of negotiating the base of the Head was determined by the state of the incoming tide as evidenced about a little nameless reef between Queen Eester's Bey and the Bloody Bay. That invaluable gauge was revealed to Teddy Lafferty by one of his elderly coasting companions of the early years, and his initial reaction was one of incredulity. His own later experience confirmed, however, the reliability of the reef. He explained: 'If the waater's well below it, ye can carry on; but if it's jeest almost covered, the waater startin tae turn white roon aboot it, change yer mind an cut up the top o' the hill.' Satisfied of the inaccessibility

of the shore, the coaster had simply to get on to a sheep-track which leads to
the top of the Head, thus removing the folly of his walking the length of the
Bloody Bay and then having to turn back and undertake a direct climb out.[27]

Some coasters were nocturnal in their habits and would seldom be
encountered on the shore. Such were the shy MacTaggart brothers, Dan
and Charlie, of Campbeltown. They would emerge after darkness, walk to
the Coast and remain there until the approach of dawn. They scorned
haversacks, but carried their night's provisions in their pockets. Dan was a
small, slender man who dressed himself entirely in black – waistcoat,
trousers, and overcoat were cut from the blackest of cloth – which rendered
him the more elusive on his nocturnal rambles. He might be heard from
time to time by coasters returning home in the early hours of night, his
squeaky voice summoning from hill or shore the black dog 'Tiger' which
invariably accompanied him.[28]

Fire and Water

No greater concern was exercised, among coasters, than with the
antipathetic elements fire and water. Each was essential to the fulfilment of
the day's expectations, and to each attached a cluster of principles and
procedures, which, though for the most part universally accepted and
applied, nonetheless admitted elements of contention and divergence. At
the centre of that universe of ritual, and the governing force of all its great
motions, was one thing – tea: the consoler, the reviver, the warmer, the
social catalyst *par excellence.*

The initial requirement was a fire-place. At the customary camps of
coasters there would, of course, be one or more fire-places in regular use,
but the solitary coaster might make a stop at any little bay which pleased
him, and in or close to which a good water source was available. The
coasters' ruling principle – if it requires doing, find out the very best way
of doing it, and then improve on that! – is perhaps no more plainly
exemplified than here.

The site of a fire-place required careful choosing. A slightly elevated site
was preferable to one in a hollow, over which flame-enlivening wind would
pass. Teddy's method was to build the fire-place simply, with no more than
four flattish stones laid in the form of a square and with a little gap between
each. Of fire-places constructed of a great ring of stones he assuredly does
not approve! In the selection of stones the criteria were not confined to
shape and size. The nature of the rock also merited attention. His
experience taught him that the hardest of rock is more liable to violent
fission when subject to intense heat, and so he invariably chooses the softer
kinds of rock, usually sandstone, of which, on the Leerside shore, there is no

scarcity. Such rock may crack when fired, but will seldom shatter. The hazard of exploding stones persuaded him also of the wisdom of building the fire-place on grass – 'Ye don't have so many stones tae worry about' – rather than on beach.[29] The value of these considerations was dramatically impressed upon me one summer evening in Queen Eester's Bey. My niece, Barbara Docherty, and I were seated beside a fiercely going fire, waiting patiently for a kettle to boil, when, with a shocking bang, one of the stones of the fire-place suddenly burst asunder and sent the little black kettle flying. We had to refill and reheat, and marked the lesson.

The business of kindling fire was likely to raise among coasters an uncommon degree of animation. The debate would invariably concern the relative merits of heather, bracken and twigs. The essentially solitary Donald MacCorkindale was an unyielding advocate of heather, and between him and Bob MacLachlan would swing a comedy of interplay, no less intense for all its triviality. When the role of camp organiser devolved on Donald he would unfailingly fix his sight on heather and direct Bob to it: 'Bob, ye see these wee clumps o' heather . . .?' Bob, however, had his own theories on the constitution of a good kindling and would conceal beneath the gathered heather a layer of little sticks. This deception Donald would have none of, and he would advise gravely: 'No use, Bob.'[30]

In my own experience – and certainly in that of Teddy Lafferty, whose habit is to lift a clump of withered heather and carry it from hill to shore – there is no more effective material than heather for the kindling of a brisk and rapid fire.

Bob MacLachlan's coasting know-how earned him credit in the *Campbeltown Courier* as one who had 'improved the lot of humanity'. A football match at Kintyre Park, Campbeltown, between two local teams, United and Glenside, in August 1939, occasioned the tribute: 'The midges were carrying on a successful war against the spectators when Councillor MacLachlan lit a dead branch of whin bush and waved it about his head for a little. Others followed suit, and soon tiny smoke fires were seen round the ropes, successfully keeping the pests away.'[31]

Along the entire Coast there was but one spring in known use by coasters. (Snobs's Well, already mentioned, was not a true well, but the gathering of a thin stream of surface water.) Its location was the Second Waters, at the base of a bank close to the burn. Its origin is unknown, but it probably served the occupants of a nameless steading, the ruin of which lies nearby. By whatever hands that well was laid open, the coasters made it their own and kept it clean. Summer and winter it liberated its cool subterranean waters, though disuse and neglect have long since seized upon it, and there are few alive who know its place. The coasters who foregathered at the Waters would faithfully bypass the burn, which ran conveniently beside the caravan, and would fill a kettle from the farther well, although for washing purposes, of course, burn water would suffice. When camped on the shore, however, the distance to the well would be greatly increased, and though the older men would insist on the boys nonetheless taking the well water, expedience would invariably decide the issue, and the boys would fill the kettle from the burn and wisely say nothing of the deception.[32]

At each of the other haunts of coasters were one, or more, convenient water sources. Indeed, a waterless bay − and of these, on that shore, there are few − would exercise little attraction to the coaster, whatever natural appeal might otherwise recommend it.

At the First Waters are two burns, of which the smaller, quick-flowing southernmost one was preferred. The other courses closer to Auchenhoan farm-house and was considered a carrier of waste.[33]

In Johnson's Bay the waters of the little burn there were gathered into a scooped-out basin, into which was placed a pot. Into that pot a bottomless bottle was laid neck outermost, and kettles and cups could be filled conveniently from the water which ran out through it. That burn abounded in dainty watercress, and Jamie 'Loafs', particularly, liked to accompany a drink of its water with mouthful after mouthful of tasty cress.[34]

The Bloody Bay is apparently without a fresh water source, but the impression is deceptive. A sufficiency of water for refreshment or tea-brewing could be got at the southern end of the bay by scooping out a hollow in the upper foreshore.[35] In the early 1950s, old Jock Smith repeatedly pressed for the provision of a 'well' there, but nothing came of it. Teddy Lafferty, however, remembered that suggestion, and in July 1982 − some thirty years later − gave the Bloody Bay its 'well', which is a pretty, shell-bottomed basin nestling in the long shore grasses.[36]

The water source at the Dummy's is a dirty-looking stream which spills through the rocks of the shore. Despite its disagreeable appearance, however, it is both palatable and safe.

As I mentioned, the coasters were, to a man, inveterate tea-drinkers. It would not be over-fanciful to suggest that had tea supplies suddenly become unavailable in this country at any time during the coasting heyday, then just as suddenly the shores would have been deserted. The addictive brew was, perhaps, as vital as that. Certain of the older coasters, Jock Smith especially, demanded an exceedingly strong brew, of an almost tarry consistency, and his recommended (if not entirely serious) test of a brew's drinkability was the placing into the cup of a spoon − if the spoon 'floated', then the tea was fit to drink.[37] James 'Loafs' favoured his tea from a big bowl, which had to be held in both hands. When tea was being dispensed, 'Smeesh' would mischievously instruct: 'Better keep the wee bowl for Jamie.'[38] The tea-drinking passion Teddy Lafferty attributed to the saltiness of the shore air. He himself is very much prone to the passion, and can drink eight cups of tea at a single sitting.

A good deal of boozing went on at the Coast, and some of the coasters, far from spending their days there in sublime communion with nature, seem to have gone about in varying states of stupefaction. The subject proved to be a sensitive one, but I have recognised it here and leave it at that.

Food from the Shore

The coasters' diet was partly natural and in part consisted of meat and tinned foods carried with them. Rabbit stew – supplemented with carrot, turnip, and sausages – would occasionally be eaten at the Coast,[39] as at the Eenans. From the two small fields at the Second Waters, in which the late Sandy Helm of Auchenhoan raised crops of potatoes, a meal could be lifted, but the unscrupulous among the coasting company abused that privilege by the removal of quantities for home consumption.[40]

A customary concoction at the Coast was 'wilk brae' (winkle bree, or soup), entirely unknown as a food at the Eenans, the common periwinkle (*Littorina littorea*), which is the edible, and largest, of the four species, being virtually absent from that Atlantic coast. Several minutes' boiling of the wilks, generally in a potful of fresh water, with perhaps a cupful of sea water added, was sufficient, though some coasters would boil the wilks first in a potful of sea water, and then complete the cooking in fresh water. Some coasters relished wilk brae, and some did not. Duncan MacLachlan was very much an enthusiast, comparing the juice, perhaps extravagently, to a malt whisky. The comparison, it need hardly be said, referred neither to flavour nor effect. It was the habit of his father, Bob MacLachlan, to strain the brae through a piece of muslin, which removed sediment. In the sediment, he believed, resided the mischievous power of the brae to 'skoor oot', or induce in the intemperate a bout of diarrhoea. To the brae, before drinking, would usually be added pepper. Teddy Lafferty was rather less susceptible to the appeal of wilk brae, and in his experience the juice would more often be poured away. 'It wiz,' as he remarked, 'actually the wilks they wir wantin, naw so much the brae.' A quantity of juice might, however, be conserved as stock for a potful of soup, with or without the winkles. The wilks, when removed from their shells, could be fried with oatmeal to provide a quick and tasty dish. Onions, chopped on a smooth, clean board lifted from the shore, could be added to the mixture, having first been boiled.[41]

The removal of eggs from the nests of oyster-catchers – locally, sea-pyets – was a common practice among coasters. The account which follows is justifiable only in terms of the integral part which the practice occupied in the coasting tradition, and should not be interpreted as condoning that practice. The taking of oyster-catcher eggs is absolutely illegal, except by special license granted under Section 10 of the Protection of Birds Act, 1954.[42] These depredations, happily, are less prevalent, though certain of the habitual wilk-pickers continue to lift eggs where they find them.

With the contraction of the coasting community, however, there has passed away the energetic determination which characterised such old coasters as Donald MacCorkindale, who would walk the length of the shore from New Orleans to the Second Waters, harrying every nest located. His passion for the eggs was such that he assumed, as his natural right, a claim to every nest along that stretch of coast, and would angrily reprove any other who presumed to gather on his territory.[43]

Teddy Lafferty now abstains from the forbidden delicacy, but retains an interest in the nesting habits of the bird, and has noticed oyster-catcher eggs both in advance of and after the accepted nesting season of May and June. In Feochaig Bay he found, one year, a clutch on 28th April. In that same bay he was surprised, a year later, to chance upon two freshly laid eggs on 22nd July. These he tested for freshness in the customary manner, by scooping out a basin at the burnside and placing them in the slow-running current. The eggs sank to the bottom – fresh! To put the test beyond dispute, he repeated it, and the freshness of the eggs was again demonstrated. An egg which is clocking, or incubating, will generally tilt upwards at one end and float to the surface, while a rotten egg will rise longitudinally, more or less.[44]

The 'skreiching' (screeching) and distinctive flight patterns of nesting oyster-catchers were liable to betray a nesting site to someone knowledgeable in these signs. Gathered eggs would usually be carried home in a knotted handkerchief. The eggs were considered to be at their best 'fried hard' or scrambled, perhaps with bits of pre-cooked bacon or sausage added to enhance the meal. In flavour, Teddy esteemed the oyster-catcher egg above that of the gull or eider duck, which, he reasoned, being primarily shore feeders, produce a strong egg. The oyster-catcher egg, on the contrary, is milder on the palate and yet possesses a richness of flavour which, if regularly indulged, would tend to 'scunner'.[45]

Sleeping Rough

The practice of 'sleeping rough' was resorted to on the Coast, as at the Eenans. Indeed, in Duncan MacLachlan's recollection, 'if ye had a tent you were treated as a softie by the old-timers'.[46] The usual means of improvising a shelter was with fish-boxes. Two boxes would be set up on their sides, facing the wind, and stabilised by rocks placed into them, and by an additional weighted box laid flat on top. A fire would be kindled behind the windbreak, and the company present would, in turn, gather driftwood and maintain the fire throughout the night. Boots would be removed and feet extended towards the heat. A single blanket as a covering and a haversack beneath the head as a pillow completed the requirements. As Teddy Lafferty observed, however: 'Ye never slept much at night, because even in the summer it wiz cowld.' The unfamiliar discomfort of the shore also reduced the likelihood of a satisfactory sleep, but 'when moarnin came, an ye wir lucky enough tae get a good mornin, a good deh wi' plenty sun, ye'd go tae sleep durin the deh wi' the heat o' the sun'.[47]

Some coasters would retreat at night into a cave, at the entrance of which a fire would be lit.[48] North of Glenahervie Bay is a sheltered rock hollow which served occasionally as a resort of benighted coasters. Dan MacTaggart was accustomed to lying nights there, and after he had ceased to travel the Coast, Teddy Lafferty, on his solitary ventures south of the familiar coasting haunts, occasionally passed the brief span of summer darkness within it. He carried with him a fly-sheet, which he would spread over the mouth of the recess.[49]

Scran

Coasters could earn themselves a little money by gathering miscellaneous materials – collectively, 'scran' – from the shore.

Returnable lemonade bottles, washed ashore from shipping or abandoned by the otherwise objectionable 'tourists', could be relied upon to raise a few shillings, though cumbersome to carry back.

Sheep wool was a more conveniently carried form of scran. Teddy Lafferty took with him to the Coast a small sandbag for that purpose and would pluck the wool – if sufficiently dry – from the corpses of sheep found on or about the shore. That wool he sold by the pound to a local scrap merchant.

Scrap metal was also obtainable, mainly aluminium floats which had broken from the nets of trawlers and floated in. Technology has abolished that occasional source of income – net-floats are now uniformly of plastic. Two or three shillings would be paid for each float, though, as Teddy emphasised, 'Naw so much the money it wiz . . . Jeest the idea ye got it fae the shore'. Three floats of the largest size were reckoned to be sufficient to carry. 'They wirna heavy,' Teddy remarked, 'but they wir clumsy.'[50] His habit of carrying back with him from the shore several of these floats, strung on a rope and dangling over his shoulder, put fright into his mother and a female companion one night on the Kilkerran road. The story has an element of farce to it. Bella Lafferty and her friend were accustomed to visiting a woman who then lived in a cottage close to the Rocky Burn. They were proceeding there on a dark, still winter's night when they became aware of the approach of a horse, as they thought. The clicking of its hooves on the road they could hear faintly, and they stopped and listened. Closer came the sound. Alarmed that Andy McMillan's horse had broken out of its field in Kilkerran Farm – as it not infrequently did – they turned and hurried back to the farm road-end, where they huddled tremulously. Nearer and nearer through the darkness approached the unnerving click-click-click, until at last there appeared in sight not a horse, but Bella Lafferty's son Teddy with his string of metal floats jangling.[51]

Another source of cash – and perhaps the most lucrative of all, though, in honesty, I must declare an utter distaste for the practice and all that it entailed – was raised at the expense of the 'hoodie crow' population. A half-crown (12½p) was paid out at a local bank for each hooded crow head delivered there. An egg was valued at merely sixpence (2½p), so the disparity induced the hunters to mark the nesting places of the crows, allow the eggs to hatch, wait until the young birds had developed almost to the stage of flight, and then strike.

Winkle-picking was – and remains – a reliable, if hard, source of income, and many a poor family was raised on the proceeds of toilsome scourings of the Kintyre shores. The entire Coast abounded in shellfish and, moreover, was fairly accessible from the town. 'Wilkers' have for long frequented these shores, and yet the coaster and the wilker, though shoresmen alike, were essentially distinct types. The coaster, though he might, if pressed for money, gather a bag or two of winkles, was basically intent on leisure and the blessings of peace. The wilker – and this is a generalisation, because cross-over cases there undoubtedly were – put his feet upon the Coast in pursuit of money alone. To simplify, or over-simplify: the distinction was between the material compulsion, and the immaterial.

In his thirty years of going to the Coast, Teddy Lafferty has marked the appearance and disappearance of many who were, in their times, his friends and companions. Absent now are those of the old and obdurate order of coasters with whom his earliest experiences are inextricably twined. And yet, like poignant faces in a fading photograph, their images endure in his faithful memory. In the persistence of his passion for 'the Coast' is embodied, perhaps, the supreme tribute to the ways and values of his vanished friends:

> See, if I get a good deh on the shore, jeest sit ower fae the fire lookin intae the sea or across the shore, wi' a cup o' tea in me han', sippin aweh at ma leisure. Jeest laik that, naw botherin emdy. On top o' a herrin-box . . . shirt-sleeves, gettin the sun aboot me. The sun that bright ye could hardly see the flames o' the fire. Eh?[52]

The Corphin Mermaid

There is, I must immediately admit, no evidence that the Corphin 'mermaid' actually was female. The main witness could not say 'whether its bosom was formed like a woman's or not'. I have let romantic appeal settle the doubt. The obvious approach to the subject of mermaids would be one of scepticism, at the least, but such an approach in this case will not quite do. The matter belongs to neither tradition nor legend. It is to be found in the sworn testimonies of two witnesses, heard before Duncan Campbell, Sheriff-substitute of Kintyre, the Rev. Dr. George Robertson and the Rev. Norman MacLeod, ministers in Campbeltown, and James Maxwell, Chamberlain of Mull. None of these presumably well-adjusted and practical men was disposed to question the truth of the main witness's account and agreed that 'from the manner in which he delivered his evidence, we are satisfied that he was impressed with a perfect belief'.

On the afternoon of Sunday, 18 October, 1811, the tenant of Corphin, John MacIsaac – probably a brother of 'the Dummy', Donald – took a walk by the shore. From the edge of a cliff he noticed 'the appearance of something white' on an offshore rock. Curious and excited, he crawled through a corn field until he reached the shore. By dodging from rock to rock, he got within fifteen yards of the creature, and 'upon looking at the object with attention, he was impressed with great surprise and astonishment at its uncommon appearance'. It was lying flat on the rock, on its belly, with its head towards the sea:

> The upper half of it was white, and of the shape of a human body, and the other half, towards the tail, of a brindled or reddish-grey colour, apparently covered with scales, but the extremity of the tail itself was of a greenish-red shining colour. The head of this animal was covered with long hair, and as the wind blew off the land it sometimes raised the hair over the creature's head, and every time the gust of wind would do this, the animal would lean towards one side, and taking up the opposite hand, would stroke the hair backwards, and then, leaning upon the other side, would adjust the hair on the opposite side of its head in the same manner . . . It would also spread or extend its tail like a fan, to a considerable breadth, and, while so extended, the tail continued in tremulous motion, and when drawn together again it remained motionless, and appeared to be about twelve or fourteen inches broad, lying flat upon the rock.

She was four or five feet long, had disproportionately short arms, and her hair was light brown. He could not say, when asked, whether or not the fingers were webbed. He watched her, from his hiding-place behind a rock, for almost two hours – hoping, he said, that the ebb tide would completely expose the rock and allow him to capture her – but that rapacious scheme was pre-empted when she drew herself to the edge of the rock and tumbled clumsily into the sea.

MacIsaac immediately rose to his feet. He saw her surface, and saw, for the first time, her face, which 'had all the appearance of the face of a human being, with very hollow eyes'. With both hands she was stroking and splashing her breasts, which were half immersed (hence his uncertainty of their sexual characteristics). A few minutes later she disappeared.

An eight-year-old girl also claimed to have seen the mermaid that afternoon. She was Catherine Loynachan, daughter of Lachlan Loynachan in Ballinatunie, a farm about a mile north of Corphin. With a younger brother she had been herding her father's cattle along the shore, and saw the mermaid slide off a rock and into the sea. Her description of form and characteristics corresponds remarkably with John MacIsaac's. This is the final part of her statement:

> After sliding from the rock, it disappeared under water, but immediately thereafter it came above water again, about six yards further out, and turned about, with the face of it towards the shore, where she was standing, and having laid one hand, which was like a boy's hand, upon another rock, it came in nearer to the shore. She saw the face of it distinctly, which had all the appearance of the face of a child, and as white, and at this time the animal was constantly rubbing or washing its breast with one hand, the fingers being close together. After this, the animal continued to look towards her for about half a minute. It [then] swam about and disappeared, but in a very short time thereafter she saw the head and face of this animal appearing above water again, and swimming away south towards the farm of Corphine.

She assumed that she had seen 'a boy that had fallen out of a vessel passing by', and hurried home to tell her mother. Mother, father, and child went down to the shore, but there was nothing – or no one – there.[53]

So, the accounts of the two witnesses, a man and a child, both of them illiterate.[54] An adult might, conceivably, be capable of memorising a mass of peculiar detail, and might also be capable of relating it convincingly under examination; but that such a complex narrative, if invented, could have been sustained and, in the end, have convinced a panel of hard-headed professional men, is improbable in the extreme. And to what end would an ordinary farmer, in 1811, have subjected himself to an ordeal of interrogation in a public building in Campbeltown? An eight-year-old girl simply could not have carried off such an elaborate deception. Collaboration between the two may be ruled out. All that may confidently be stated is that a man and a girl, on different parts of a lonely shore, witnessed a mysterious presence.

The Island

The island of Davaar, which huddles like some stranded leviathan at the mouth of Campbeltown Loch, is both beautifying and protective – the loch's excellence as a natural harbour is attributable to the great bulk of the island, which almost seals its entrance. From the mainland, a tidal bar reaches out to it, like a crooked arm. That link is called the Doirlinn (Gaelic: a tidal isthmus), and across its reach have crunched the boots of generations of coasters, and multitudinous others, both casual picnickers and those intent on viewing the celebrated 'cave painting'.

That depiction of Christ crucified was painted on a wall of the cave in 1887 by Archibald MacKinnon, who later claimed to have been inspired by a dream in which he 'beheld the body of our blessed Saviour on the cross shortly after His Passion'.[55] The entire work was done in secrecy, and the finished painting, when discovered in August of 1887,[56] excited national controversy. Some observers divined in it a supernatural origin, and the then sheriff of Campbeltown, Russell Bell, even suggested that it might be proclaimed a 'miracle' by the Catholic Church, and the island itself venerated as a 'Sacred Lourdes'.[57]

When MacKinnon finally declared his responsibility – substantiated by a signed testimony and a set of photographs showing him in the creative act – a storm of anger and cynicism, which was fiercest in his native town, burst over him.

'Art is Truth' opened the attack, with a letter to the local newspaper: 'The mystery regarding the picture is now solved! The identity of the artist is established, and by what means has it come about? – in as mysterious a manner as was the picture painted. Lest the public should be incredulous as to its authorship, the aid of the photographer was employed; and there stands the artist red-handed, a moment of egotism and vanity strangely illustrated.'[58]

'Proteus' followed with a lengthy denunciation, remarkable for its viciousness: 'So Mr Archibald MacKinnon is the author of the picture on Island Davaar. He has at last gratified the insane cravings of a morbid appetite – he has achieved notoriety ... The picture is the veriest burlesque of the Crucifixion. It does not possess a single redeeming feature; it is defective alike in conception and execution. The face is the face of a ruffian, and vulgarity is writ large in every tone and tint and line of the production ... He cannot paint any higher than his own level – and Mr MacKinnon's level is a pretty low one.'[59]

MacKinnon spent the greater part of his life as an engineer in England. In 1934, when 84 years of age, he returned to Campbeltown to restore his most celebrated work, and was accorded a civic welcome.[60] He died a year later.[61] The painting has since been thrice restored and continues to attract and fascinate visitors and locals alike. Whatever MacKinnon's motives – noble or ignoble, inspired or simply selfish – the prediction of one of his critics has, a century on, a decidedly hollow echo: 'The enthusiasm will die out; the picture will be forgotten. Moss and lichen and mildew and the kindly influence of the elements will give it a hasty oblivion.'[62]

The majority of the Learside coasters were intimately acquainted with 'the Island'. From the Coast, its rearing, cliffy southern aspect is seldom out of view. The choice between crossing to the Island and continuing to the Coast would usually be governed by the state of the tide. If the Doirlinn was ebbing, then as often as not the Island would be their choice; but if the Doirlinn was covered, or almost covered by an incoming tide, then the choice would be to carry on. In their later years, however, such coasting stalwarts as Jock Smith and Donald MacCorkindale were content to pass the Island by. Their gravitation then was to the Coast alone.

The Island too had its devotees, none more faithful than the ageing companions George Stewart and Duncan MacIntyre. Together they would cycle to the Doirlinn, to complete the journey on foot, but pushing their bicycles as they went. For George, in his final frail years, the bicycle served to support him on the plodding way across the shingle bar, and it was his custom, too, when on the Island, to prop up his bicycle, with a blanket spread upon it, as a windbreak.

He had for many years worked his way about the Australian outback, his accounts of which enlivened many an hour, both on the shore and in his little house, now demolished, which stood at the western end of Askomil Walk. That experience had imbued him with a passion, undiminished to the last, for sunlight and the open life. Teddy Lafferty met him frequently at the Sheep'oose (Sheephouse), his invariable Island resort, and remembered an evening there:

> It wiz late summer; it wiz back o' ten o' clock; it wiz dark. We sat at the ould Sheep'oose and we'd a fire gan aa' the time. Ould George wid seh: 'This reminds me of when we used tae be in Australia. It wiz that waarm, ye jeest sat roon a fire aa' night, oot in the north . . .'[63]

For the majority of Island-goers, the roofless Sheep'oose was the traditional halting place. The name is reckoned by some to have originated with the wilkers, and to refer to the ruin's usefulness as a shelter for the Island sheep. Of the history of the house and its successive occupants virtually nothing is known.[64] The nearby well, which no doubt served these unremembered people, contributed to the appeal of the place, because fresh water is scarce on the Island, and there is no more convenient or satisfying source.

Old George, on his return, brought with him from Australia a few ideas which he attempted, by personal example, to introduce among the coasting regulars. One such novelty was the billy-can suspended on a forked stick. The coasters were sceptical. As one remarked, 'It looks aa' right in a film, maybe.' The water would boil in the billy-can satisfactorily enough – of its effectiveness at that stage of the business there was no dispute – but the resultant brew was liable to lose heat rapidly. This failing the coasters magnanimously ascribed to climatic conditions in the northern hemisphere, and in the end George got himself a teapot.[65]

With old George, in a philosophic role, this account will close. The narrator, once again – and finally – is Teddy Lafferty:

> As ould George said tae me long ago on the Island . . . We wir sittin on a nice sunny deh, oh, the waater lik' gless, an ye could feel the heat comin off the rocks an the grevvel, thon kinna shimmerin heat comin up. An I said: 'Oh, this is grett, George. I could sit here for the rest o' ma life.' – 'Aye,' e' sez, 'take the good o' it when ye've got the chance o' it. Good things never last forever – nothin in oor life lasts forever.'[66]

The Stackie

As the Campbeltown coasters followed, in the main, the shore south from the Loch, so the coasters of Dalintober turned their faces north. Coasters essentially these men were, yet their habit did not quite attain the degree of organisation which characterised their town counterparts, nor did there develop anything like the density of tradition of which the 'south coasters' were conscious heirs. The limitation was basically one of geography. The Dalintober coasting groups concentrated on 'the Stackie', that short reach of shore immediately south of Peninver, and dominated by the unmistakable Stackie Rock, which rises between shore and sea. The place was much frequented by wilkers and rabbit hunters, and these – and coasters with them – were accustomed to sheltering in Stackie Cove, which, even until the present century, was a resort of destitutes (p. 126).

A banjo was secreted at the back of the cave for the entertainment of the Stackie coasters. Jock Smith – a namesake of 'Smeesh's', but unrelated to him – first saw that 'lovely instrument' during a poaching foray to the Stackie with his father, Duncan Smith, and Willie Moorhead, an Irishman. He was then a boy of fourteen years, and was warned not to disclose the banjo's hiding-place to anyone, because 'it belangt tae the men on the Coast'. The party had entered the cave to await the rising of the moon, and the case was brought out from its cranny, unwrapped from its protective bag, and Willie Moorhead commenced to 'pleh aal the ould come-aal-yachs'.[67] 'It wiz grett – what a night! Jeest the flickerin o' the fire on the rocks, ye know, an the "Woodbine" lights, an the big mug o' tea.' As they sat there, contentedly, a big moon rose slowly beyond the cave mouth.[68]

At the Stackie the coasters maintained, in the early years of the present century, a little 'tin hut', and there they would spend nights. The motive, for some, was to 'keep aweh fae the drink'. A band of these coasters, numbering perhaps ten or twelve, would set off on the road north, marching in slow step, with the piper 'China' (John Galbraith) leading on.[69]

Vanished now are those who formed that cheerful company; all have gone down the final road which leads – it may be – to a shining Coast where sticks abound, and tea is plentiful, and where 'China', marching as of old between hill and sea, awakens them at morning with a smart jig. May not the cynic, even, hammer out his fantasy at that bright forge between known night and night unknown?

REFERENCES AND NOTES

1. E. Lafferty, 28 Jan. 1981.
2. *CC*, 12 Oct. 1912.
3. E. Lafferty, *op. cit.*
4. So/d4/p9.
5. *Ib.*
6. C 51 So.
7. Min Bk PB So, 25 Nov. 1865.
8. *Ib.*, 6 Feb. 1869.
9. *RD* So, 11 Nov. 1871.
10. E. Lafferty, 1 Feb. 1981; D. MacLachlan, 6 Feb. 1981.
11. E. Lafferty, *ib.*
12. E. Lafferty and D. MacLachlan, 6 Feb. 1981.
13. E. Lafferty, 28 Jan. 1981.
14. *Ib.*, noted 28 Jan. 1982.
15. *Ib.*, noted 14 Jan. 1982.
16. Archibald Smith, his son, noted 16 Jan. 1982.
17. E. Lafferty, 28 Jan. 1981.
18. *Ib.*
19. *CC*, 10 Jan. 1952.
20. Charlie McMillan, noted 19 Feb. 1983.
21. E. Lafferty, 28 Jan. and 2 Feb. 1981, and 19 Jan. 1982 (noted). Contemporaneous with that 'caravan' was another, set up at the north end of the bay at the Second Waters. It was a converted 'Co-op' grocery van, owned by Joseph Morrans, and frequented by him and his brothers, Daniel, Michael, and Archibald, and others (A. Morrans, noted 14 Dec. 1983). Three teen-aged schoolboys – Alasdair Thompson, Derek McKinven, and Robert Davison – almost completed the erection of a wooden hut at the First Waters in the mid-1960s, but the project collapsed, and the unfinished hut with it.
22. E. Lafferty, 18 Feb. 1981.
23. *Ib.*
24. *Ib.*, 28 Jan. 1981.
25. *Ib.*, per James Morran.
26. D. MacLachlan, *op. cit.*
27. E. Lafferty, 28 Jan. 1981.
28. *Ib.*, 1 Feb. 1981.
29. *Ib.*, 2 Feb. 1981.
30. D. MacLachlan, *op. cit.*
31. 26 Aug. 1939.
32. E. Lafferty, 2 Feb. 1981.
33. *Ib.*
34. *Ib.*
35. *Ib.*, noted 23 Jan. 1982.

36. *Ib.*, noted 18 Aug. 1982.

37. *Ib.*, 18 Feb. 1981.

38. *Ib.*, 2 Feb. 1981.

39. D. MacLachlan, *op. cit.*

40. E. Lafferty, 28 Jan. 1981.

41. *Ib.*, 28 Jan. and 1 Feb. 1981; D. MacLachlan and R. Armour, 6 Feb. 1981.

42. P. M. Ellis, investigations officer (Scotland), RSPB, letter to author, 5 Nov. 1981.

43. E. Lafferty, 28 Jan. 1981.

44. *Ib.*

45. *Ib.*

46. *Op. cit.*

47. E. Lafferty and D. MacLachlan, 6 Feb. 1981.

48. D. MacLachlan, *op. cit.*

49. E. Lafferty, 1 Feb. 1981.

50. *Ib.*, 18 Feb. 1981.

51. *Ib.*, 12 June 1981.

52. *Ib.*, 18 Feb. 1981.

53. 'Evidence respecting the Existence of a Mermaid on the Coast of Argyle', *Scots Magazine*, Dec. 1811, 910-13.

54. 'Cannot write' noted at the end of each testimony, *ib.*, 912, 913.

55. *CC*, 3 Sept. 1887, from MacKinnon's testimony, headed 33 Woodbine Street, Liverpool, and dated 29 August 1887.

56. *Ib.*, 20 Aug. 1887. 'Visitors to Island Davaar recently have been surprised to find on the rocky walls of one of the caves on the south-west side of the island a painting supposed to be a reproduction of Munkacsky's famous picture of "Christ on Calvary", recently on view in Glasgow.'

57. *Ib.*, letter of 3 Sept. 1887.

58. *Ib.*

59. *Ib.*, 10 Sept. 1887.

60. *Ib.*, 19 May 1934.

61. On 15 May 1935, at Nantwich – *ib.*, 8 June 1935.

62. 'Proteus', letter to *CC*, 10 Sept. 1887.

63. E. Lafferty, 1 Feb. 1981.

64. In 1909, A. McKellar – Kilkerran Farm, Rokewood, Victoria, Australia – wrote to the head teacher of 'Brumbrae School'. That school no longer existed, and the letter was passed on to Mr Donald Fisher, headmaster of Dalintober School. It read: 'I am a stranger to you . . . I was a little boy going to your school in the year 1852. My father's name was John McKellar. He kept a small butcher's shop . . . I am told I saw the light of day first on Island Davaar. My mother's name was McArthur. Her father was a miller and worked the Calliburn Mill a hundred years ago . . . Please, sir, to enquire if any of my old neighbours mind anything of me.' The appeal – published in *CC*, 20 March 1909 – elicited a few responses, including a letter from one John Robertson, manager of the slaughter-house in Campbeltown, who had 'a distinct recollection of the family, having slept a night in their house on Island Davaar' – *CC*, 3 April 1909.

65. E. Lafferty, 1 Feb. 1981.

66. *Ib.*

67. 'Come-all-youse' – communal songs.

68. J. Smith, 14 Feb. 1983.

69. J. Campbell, 10 Nov. 1980.

ABBREVIATIONS OF WRITTEN SOURCES USED IN APPENDICES

Abbreviations and incomplete references used only in Appendices I-III (general abbreviations will be found on p. xi).

AF — Agriculture and Fisheries, Scottish Record Office (West Register House), Edinburgh.

Black — See TSOS.

FP — Fishermen's Petition, subscribed to in Campbeltown and Carradale in December, 1852, and attached to a complaint against 'trawling' for herring. Ref. AF 37/7.

HMR — Hearth Money Rolls, for the parishes of Ramoan and Culfeightrin, F. Connolly, in *The Glynns* Vol. 1, pp. 10-15, the introduction to which provides an historical background to that tax.

HTL — Hearth Tax List, being a record of hearths in Kintyre in Feb. 1694. Scottish Record Office (ref. E69/3).

ILRI — *The Irish Language in Rathlin Island*, N. M. Holmer, Dublin 1942.

KSC — *Kintyre in the Seventeenth Century*, A. McKerral, Edinburgh 1948.

LMMSWH — *Late Medieval Monumental Sculpture in the West Highlands*, K. A. Steer and J. W. M. Bannerman, HMSO 1977.

MacI — Latimer MacInnes, *Dialect of South Kintyre*, Campbeltown 1934.

MacLysaght — See TSOI.

MacVicar — Rev. A. J., *Surnames Common throughout Kintyre, Islay and Arran in the 17th century*, Campbeltown c. 1935 (pamphlet).

Matheson — Rev. William, from his critical annotations of the penultimate draft of App. II, Nov. 1983.

Ó Baoill — Dr Colm, as above.

ORM — Old Register of Marriages in the Parish of Campbeltown (1820-1854).

RFB — Register of Fishing Boats, I and II, commencing 1869 (MS indicates Modern Series, which is the set of later registers), in the fishery office, Campbeltown.

RTOKG — *A Ramble Through the Old Kilkerran Graveyard*, C. Mactaggart, Campbeltown 1926.

SB — 'Still Books' of the firm of Robert Armour, plumber and coppersmith in Campbeltown, from transcribed extracts in Kintyre Antiquarian Society library, Campbeltown (ref. no. 347).

SBR — Southend Baptismal Records.

TGOK — *The Gaelic of Kintyre*, N. M. Holmer, Dublin 1962.

TRNF — *The Ring-Net Fishermen*, A. Martin, Edinburgh 1981.

TSOI — *The Surnames of Ireland*, E. MacLysaght, Shannon 1969.

TSOS — *The Surnames of Scotland*, G. F. Black, New York 1946.

Irish Immigrant Fishing Families in Campbeltown

The following appendix is as full as possible a representation of the Irish presence in the fishing community of Campbeltown. None of the obvious families − i.e. those whose Irish origin is manifest in both name and religious custom − has been omitted. For the rest, I trust that no offence will be taken by any members of those families whose nominal and religious identities had been abandoned. At its narrowest value, the material provides a gratis genealogical record which could scarcely have been compiled from conventional sources − the availability of the registers of poor for Campbeltown both initiated the project and assured its feasibility. But the purpose of the material is fundamentally sociological, and on that ground I am prepared to justify its inclusion in this work.

Factually, the material is not completely reliable. The various records consulted often failed to agree in the matter of − particularly − age at death. Years of birth could, therefore, only be estimated. The discrepancies were sometimes wide − ten years and more, from one record to another − in which cases I either settled on the source most likely to be correct, or calculated the mean. In all such cases *circa* ('about', abbreviated c.) indicates the uncertainty.

Initially, it had been my intention to provide the Irish Gaelic forms and meanings of native Irish names, but increasing dissatisfaction with the reliability of available sources − not excepting MacLysaght's *The Surnames of Ireland* − dictated the abandonment of that intention.

Capitalisation of surnames in the text denotes a cross-reference. Too great an economic significance ought not to be attached to the occupational description 'farmer' repeatedly found in this appendix. In most, if not all, cases it probably signifies a smallholder.

The supplement to this appendix was compiled entirely from the Censuses 1851-81 (the initial figures in the bracketed references provide the Census year). That supplement consists of Irish-born fishermen in Campbeltown, about whose descendants too little data had materialised to allow further examination.

BLACK. The emergence of the Blacks in the fishing community may be traced to Daniel B, born at Ballycastle c. 1833. (C51/d8/p22; RB 8/10/1855 − RP 1592 gives Rathlin Island) His parents were Archibald B, labourer, born c. 1787 (son of John B, crofter, and Mary McCurdie) and Jane McKinlay, born c. 1798, both on Rathlin. All three names were recorded on the island in 1669: Brian and Allex McCurdy in Kinramer; Pat Black in Ballygill; Malcum McKinly and Arc Black in Kilpatrick. (HMR, 15) There were said to have been three branches of Blacks on Rathlin, one of Scottish descent and the other two of native descent. (ILRI, 5) Daniel B had two known brothers − Duncan, who went to Glasgow as a carpenter, (RP 418) and James, born c. 1837 in Ballycastle, who became a seaman and in 1859 married Ann Sharp in Campbeltown. (RM 18/10/59) He drowned c. 1866. (Min Bk PB Cam, 8/1/67) The Blacks settled in Campbeltown c. 1838. Daniel's first wife was Margaret Morrison, who died 29.4.1874 in Campbeltown, aged 39. Her parents were John M, labourer, born Rathlin, and Mary McCurdie, born Campbeltown. The Morrisons and Blacks were neighbours in the Wide Close in 1851. His second wife was Sarah NEWLANDS, widow of Michael DURNAN. She died 8.2.1898 in the Kirk Close. (RD) Daniel B's first skiff, of which there is record, was the *Maggie* in 1869. She was owned by his father. (RFB I, p57) Daniel B's first marriage produced five fishermen sons − Archibald (8.10.55), Duncan (28.7.58), Daniel (6.10.60), John (28.4.64), and James (27.1.68).

BRANNAN. This name was of brief duration in Kintyre, but merits notice if only to illustrate the vicissitudes by which some families were broken and scattered, while others consolidated and remained. In 1851, James B was living in Burnside Street, Campbeltown, with his wife Elizabeth McCoag – also Irish – and three children, Jane (10), John (8), and Elizabeth (6 months). He was working as a mason's labourer. (C/d3/p25) In December, 1852, he put his name to FP. In February, 1853, his wife died and he deserted his children, saying that he 'would run off to his friends in Rothesay and let the Parish look after his children'. (Let Bk PB Cam, 11/2/53) By July of that year they were in the care of his sister-in-law at Rothesay, and the inspector of poor in Campbeltown was advising his counterpart there to 'take them under your notice as if they were your own paupers and if possible prosecute their cruel and profligate father'. (Ib., 27/7/53) Of James Brannan and his children nothing more is known.

BRODIE. The original form of this name in Campbeltown was Broadley, in common pronunciation 'Broddelty', though the written form 'Brodie' appeared as early as 1863 – Catherine B. (RB 27/12/63) John Broadley, fisherman, a native of Rathlin, (RP 1601) in 1866 deserted his wife, Margaret Kiargan (later McKerral*), born in Ballymena, Co. Antrim, the daughter of John K, farmer, and Martha Lavarty. (C71/d8/p5; RD 23/1/1901) She was left with four young children. Four others – two daughters and two sons – had already left home. The sons, Neil and Michael, then 16 and 14 years old, became fishermen, (RP 390) and before long very successful fishermen. The Brodies were involved, between 1872 and 1900, with 16 fishing boats. Neil skippered three vessels before, in 1877, going into part-ownership of the *Jessie*, which he also skippered. (RFB I, p116) His surname exhibits, in the registers of fishing boats, an unfailing inconsistency – from Bradley (1872), to Brodley (1873), to Braddley (1875) – before it finally settles in the form Brodie. (Ib., pp 72,18,22) His brothers Michael and John – the younger, born in 1857 – also became boat-owners. John and Margaret B's settlement in Kintyre predates 1845. He died about 1881 in Greenock, and she remarried at Oban, in 1882, to a Perthshire 'dealer' Francis Martin. (RP 1601) See BRODIE, Appendix II.

*For Kiargan-McKerral shift see Appendix II under MACKERRAL.

DAVIDSON. William D was born c. 1834 in Co. Tyrone, the son of William D, farmer, and Jane McDonald. He married Janet or Jeannie McMillan of Campbeltown at Rothesay in 1857. Neither of their two sons, John and William John, went to sea. (RP 1590) In 1861 William D was jailed for 30 days, with Duncan O'Hara and two others, for illegal herring fishing (see O'HARA). He appears as a boat-owner in 1879 with the skiff *Emerald* (RFB I, p61) and again in 1883 as part-owner and skipper of the *Annasona*, which was sold six years later. (Ib., II, p93) He died at Campbeltown poor-house in January 1911. (RP 1590) The family name has entirely disappeared from Campbeltown.

DURNAN/DURNIN. MacLysaght (TSOI, 80) gives the anglicised spellings Durnin and Durnian, which latter was the old spoken form in south Kintyre, though never so written. Two families of the name settled in Campbeltown, both of Co. Fermanagh origin, and very probably related.

1. Michael D, military pensioner, born c. 1786, the son of Michael D and Nancy McLennan. (RD 5/5/1875) His wife was Catherine Ward, daughter of Frank W, gardener. (Ib., 29/12/1874) They settled in Campbeltown c. 1836. In 1851, their family, living with them in Bolgam Street, was Mary (24), John (23), labourer, Michael (16), fisherman – all born in Co. Fermanagh – and Francis (13) and Charles (9), both born in Campbeltown. (C/d7/p5) In 1863 Michael applied for poor relief. His wife was then bedridden and he was receiving an army pension of 6d daily. (Min Bk PB Cam, 26/6/63)

2. John D, day labourer, born c. 1791 in the parish of 'Macheramonagh', son of Patrick D, soldier, and Catherine McGuire. He was married twice. His first wife, Bridget Stephen, was Irish-born and died c. 1854 in Campbeltown. His second wife was Eliza Bonnar or Bonner,

born 25.1.1823 at Pans, (RP 844) daughter of James B, glazier. (RM 26/4/1861) Three of his family are known: John – born 1839, Co. Fermanagh, by the first marriage – Charles (14.8.62) and Janet (2.5.65), both by the second marriage and in Campbeltown.

The first boat-owner of the name was Michael, son of Michael. In 1869 he had the smack *Sarah*, which he replaced in 1875 with the *Janet*. (RFB I, pp 32, 104) He evidently turned from fishing to fish-buying in his final years, and died 1.1.1880 aged 48. His widow, Sarah NEWLANDS, in the following year – 9.10.81 – married Daniel BLACK, in whose family the son of her first marriage, Michael – born 22.11.62 – was raised. He fished in partnership with Black in the *Roselea* and the *Ardenlea*, acquired in 1884. (Ib., pp 149, 150)

The -in terminal appears to have developed within the family of John D, though an earlier -ing ending was applied to both families.

FINN. Colloquially in Campbeltown this was MacFinn, a form which has disappeared from speech, though still remembered. There is one published confirmation: 'Fishing Intelligence . . . J. McPhin . . . 200 boxes of herring . . .' (CC 17/9/1887) The family – in 1851, John F (44), gardener, his wife Mary McAulay (38), daughter 'Alley' (12), Mary (8), John (6), and Thomas (4), living in Shore Street (C/d11/p22) – arrived in Campbeltown c. 1849. John F's parents are untraceable, but his wife's were John McA, blacksmith, and Mary Blaney. The sons were born at Larne, Co. Antrim. (RP 1472) A third son, James, was born in Campbeltown in 1858. All three brothers became fishermen, and in 1884 John and Thomas went into partnership at ring-net fishing with the nostalgically named skiffs *Dear Isle* and *Dear Home*, built at Campbeltown in that year. (RFB I, pp 40, 41) The family's fishing tradition is maintained by Cecil F – one of the most successful of the post-war Campbeltown skippers – and his son Thomas.

GRAHAM. In 1851: 1. Samuel (44), fisherman in Bolgam Street, with his wife Rebecca (40), son John (18), fisherman, and daughter Rebecca (2). John's birth in Campbeltown indicates settlement some time before 1833. (C/d7/p11) 2. William (46), fisherman in Shore Street, with his wife Mary McCorkindale (40), daughter Maria (7), and son Andrew (5). The entire family was born in Donegal (Ib. p25) and so could not have arrived in Kintyre earlier than 1846. An older daughter Mary Ann – who in 1854 married a Campbeltown fisherman, Duncan Mathieson, and bore eight children (RP 823) – was born in Greencastle, Inishowen, (C61/d7/p20) which may well be the family's specific origin. William and Samuel, who was also from Donegal, were most likely brothers. Another G fishing family in Campbeltown was of Gigha origin.

HOLLY. This family settled in Campbeltown some time between 1843 and 1851, in which year three members – representing three generations – were living in High Street: Sarah McEachney or Holly (63), widow, born Co. Derry; Samuel H (42), her son, a labourer, born Co. Louth; Samuel H (8), her grandson, born Co. Antrim. (C/d1/p7) Samuel Jr married Margaret Matchard in Campbeltown on 3.7.1867. (RM) They had four children. (RP 1430) In 1888 he was part-owner of, and skipper of the skiff *Bella*, which was sold in the subsequent year. (RFB II, p46) In 1901 his son Archibald (born 23.12.80) owned the skiff *Mary*. (Ib., p154) The name is unremembered in Campbeltown.

LAFFERTY. This family, in Campbeltown, is of relatively recent origin, but has nonetheless extended remarkably. It stems from the marriage, on 9.6.1887, of Edward L, son of Neil L, farmer, and Mary McQue (?MacHugh) in west Donegal, and Mary McKAY, daughter of Denis McK and Margaret McKendrick. (RM) He was then a labourer, but the greater part of his working life was spent as a carter. He had married into a prominent fishing family, and two of his sons – Denis and Archibald – became fishermen. In 1928 he bought John Wylie's *Elizabeth* – a 20-year-old Campbeltown-built skiff – and renamed her the *Iris*. His son Denis took charge of her, and she remained in the family until sold in 1936. (RFB MS I, p53) The last representative in the fishing community was Edward, son of Archibald, who was skipper-owner of the *Kirsteen Anne* until 1977. The pronunciation of the name in Campbeltown is generally 'Lavery'.

H

Kintyre

LAVERY. This family is distinct from the later LAFFERTY line, though, by the early written forms of Lavery – 'Laferty' and 'Laverty' – the names may be cognate. In 1851 the family was living in Shore Street, Campbeltown. Jane Laferty – her own name Morron – was described as a 'mariner's wife', and with her were a daughter Matilda (22) and a son William (13). All were born in Larne, Co. Antrim. (C/d7/p27) Her husband William – born c. 1807, son of John L (RD 12/5/1872) – was absent from that census, as was his elder son James (born in 1831 at Larne). Both, presumably, were at sea.

James was a lifetime sailing, and had experience of the East India trade before, in 1857, he took command of his father's schooner, the *Favourite*. In 1892, after a succession of commands, he acquired the schooner *William and Leigh*, which he worked until his retirement in 1903. (Obit. CC 16/10/1915) His wife, a native of Co. Leitrim, (C91/d22/p1) was Catherine Moore, daughter of Thomas M, land steward, and Mary McDonnagh. (RM 1/6/1858) He died on 9.10.1915.

His son James served an apprenticeship as a joiner, but soon after went to sea and qualified as a master mariner. He took over the *William and Leigh* and worked her about the Western Isles and the Irish coast. (Obit CC 29/8/1936) He died 23.8.1936. His wife, Catherine Campbell, died 23.1.1943.

Only one of the family – William, son of William – appears to have fished. In 1871 he was skipper-owner of the skiff *Mary*, which he gave up less than a year later for the smack *Twilight*. By 1873 he had sold her. (RFB I, pp 64, 81)

McKAY (probably of Scottish Gaelic origin, *MacAoidh*). One of the oldest of the Kintyre clans, many of its members retreated to Antrim following the eclipse of Clan Donald (p. 93). The Irish McKays in Kintyre were evidently all of Antrim origin. The fishing families of that name were:

1. William McK, fisherman and labourer, born c. 1858 in Ballymena, son of William McK, crofter, and Isabella McIntyre (RP 2260) or Betsy McMullan. (RM 21/12/1879) His wife, Isabella Smith, was Campbeltown-born, and his son, also William – born 9.2.88 in Campbeltown – became a fisherman. (RP, op. cit.)

2. Patrick McK, born c. 1849, on 2.3.1877 at Cushendun married Mary Ann Murphy, daughter of John M, farmer, and Mary McKay. His parents were John McK, farmer, and Alice McNeill. McK and his wife, with son John, born 10.1.79 in Ireland, settled in Campbeltown shortly after that birth, for a second son was born in Campbeltown on 25.10.80. Five children followed. In 1900 Patrick McK 'disappeared', and no more is known of him. (RP 1644)

3. John McK, born c. 1858, probably at Cushendun, son of Daniel McK and Mary Scally. (RD 21/8/1931) He did not go directly from Antrim to Campbeltown, but as a young man worked about Greenock and later fished on the Scottish east coast. He lived for some years at Cellardyke, Fife, and was a survivor of the great storm of October, 1881, which devastated the Eyemouth fishing community. (Obit. CC 29/8/1931) An impressive man physically, he was popularly known as 'Big Switchum' or 'Big John'. He died at sea, aged 73, on board his skiff the *Maris Stella*. The year of his settlement is not known. His wife was Ann McKinley.

4. The brothers Archibald, John, and Denis McK. Their parents were Denis McK, distillery workman and labourer, and Margaret McKendrick (also registered as McKendry, McHendry, Kenrick, and even – quite erroneously – McKenzie). Denis McK's parents were Duncan McK, farmer, and Sarah McKay (being also her own surname). Margaret McKendrick's parents were John McK, farmer, and Ann Darroch. (RD 4/3/1894, 8/12/1905) The settlement of that branch of the McKays may be dated to the mid-1870s. John and Denis married, respectively, the sisters Ann and Sibena Murphy, born in Girvan, Ayrshire, of Irish parents – James M, drainer, and Elizabeth Govern. A third M sister, Catherine, married Duncan McMaster, fisherman. (RP 1835, verified in RM) The brothers McK, with the ring-net skiffs the *Noel* and the *Annunciata* (acquired in 1901) and the *Ascension* and the *Angelus* (1904), were unrivalled in the consistency of their success as herring fishermen.

MacMILLAN (*Mac Maoláin* in Irish, *Mac Mhaolain* in Scottish Gaelic, but also, in Ulster, synonymous with MacMullan, TSOI, 162, 169). The abundance of native MacMillans in Kintyre as a whole has made the separation of the two strains, native and immigrant, too difficult to pursue. There seems, however, little doubt that the name MacMillan in Campbeltown is preponderantly of Irish origin. The Irish MacMillans, in local tradition, were reckoned to have been MacMullans and to have adopted the native form for reasons of social advantage, but of that there is no proof. Worth mentioning, however, is the registration of the skiff *Marie* in 1894 by her owner Alex *McMullin*. (RFB II, p10) Who he was remains doubtful, but there is a possibility that he was a son of William McMillan, an Antrim-born fisherman who, in 1851, was living in High Street with his wife Mary and nine children – Archibald (19), Mary (18), William (16), Hugh (13), Alexander (12), John (9), Peter (5), Robert (3), and James, a baby. (C/d1/p26) These children were all born in Campbeltown, which dates William McM's settlement to before 1832. Two other Irish-born fishermen of the name may be added. 1. Peter, born c. 1815, with his Campbeltown-born wife Jane and 10 children in Bolgam Street, 1861. 2. George, born c. 1825, with his Irish wife Rose and three daughters, also in Bolgam Street, 1861. (C/d7/pp 1,7) The former's settlement preceded 1839.

MacVEY. This family appeared in Campbeltown via Sanda Island, where, on 3.5.1891, John McV, fisherman, died at the age of 72. He was the son of Neil McV, labourer. (RD) He settled on Sanda, off Southend, about 1860 and by 1869 had acquired no fewer than four small skiffs, one of which he patriotically named the *Irishman*. (RFB I, p48) The island held, for the greater part of the nineteenth century, a small community of inshore fishermen and their families, whose ruined houses remain. His wife was Catherine Murphy, daughter of Bernard M, soldier, and Isabella McGrier. She died on 26.10.1904 in Campbeltown at the age of 78. (RD) They were married on 15.8.1843 in 'Dicmacreanan' – Tickmacrevan, presumably – Co. Antrim (RB So Par, 16.9.1861)

Their son John was born in Carnlough, Co. Antrim, c. 1847. He married, on 6.2.1871, Catherine, daughter of Peter McMILLAN, fisherman, and Janet (or Jane) McKay, and they had seven known children. (RP 1413) John McV's first recorded charge was the smack *Sir Henry Hancock* in 1873. (RFB I, p16) He skippered two other vessels before, in 1877, going into partnership with William McLellan and others in the ring-net skiffs the *John* and the *Maggie*. (Ib., p117)

John's brother Francis was likewise a fisherman in Campbeltown. He was born c. 1851, also in Ireland, and on 27.10.1879 married Mary, daughter of Daniel BLACK and Margaret Morrison. (RM) The sequel to that marriage remains a mystery, but little more than three years later – on 11.12.1882 – he was able to remarry. His second wife was Jane WHITEFORD, daughter of John W and Agnes McMillan, but the marriage lasted just seven months. (RP 1627)

There were four other children of whom there is record, Thomas, James, Catherine, and Isabella.

MARTIN. This family's sole representative in the fishing community was James, born c. 1833 in Co. Tyrone, son of John M, labourer, and Alice Mulholland, a hawker, both of whom died in Campbeltown. (RP 922) His wife, also Irish-born, was Jane Hamilton, daughter of John H, grocer. (RM 27/12/1860) They evidently had no children, and, he being an only son, with his death in 1898 the family name disappeared from Campbeltown. Both of his sisters married in Campbeltown. The eldest, Susan or Susannah, in 1856 married John O'HARA. (RM 25/11/56) They had eight known children who survived to adulthood. Of their six sons, five – James, Duncan, John, Henry, and Patrick – became fishermen, (RP 1804) and one of their daughters, Mary, married a Howth-born fisherman, Joseph Russell, by whom she was subsequently deserted. (Ib. 1278)

James M and his brother-in-law, John O'H, were fishing together in 1862 with the skiff *Stork*. In March of that year, a fishery officer, visiting Campbeltown to check that the herring close season was being observed by fishermen there, noticed the *Stork* moored at the New Quay and 'carefully covered over with a sail'. He examined the boat and found her speckled with herring scales. Her nets were confiscated and the boat herself hauled ashore. (AF 22/3) James M and John O'H were subsequently charged with a breach of the close season law. Both were admonished, but their boat was forfeited. (Ib. 37/159)

After 1869, M does not appear on record as a boat-owner, but in 1880 he was still working as a fisherman, because in February of that year he broke a leg at Girvan and had to be sent home. (RP 922)

MEENAN. The M line in Campbeltown begins with Thomas, a fish merchant, who settled in Kintyre some time before 1839. His place of origin is unknown, but his parents were Francis M, farmer, and Bridget Connoway. He died 13.4.1893, aged 77. (RD) His wife, Ellen McArthur, belonged to Glenlussa and was the daughter of Donald McA, farm servant, and Kate Bell. (RP 1658; RD 15/5/1902) The ascent of the M family in the fishing community was primarily a feature of the present century, but a son, Daniel, is on record earlier as a boat-owner: the *Ann and Betsy*, with John BRODIE, in 1884; the *Red Ribbon*, with John B and others, in 1888; the *Vampire*, as sole owner, in 1895. (RFB I, p 20; ib. II, pp 39, 112) Daniel married, on 18.4.1876, Ann Campbell, daughter of Alexander C, carter, and Agnes McMillan. (RM) His brother James was also a fisherman – he married Agnes McMillan on 27.4.1891 (RM) – and from him the M fishing family in Campbeltown today descends.

MORRANS/MORANS. The names 'Thomas Moarns' and 'Daniel Morns' appear on FP (1852). In 1850, Thomas Morrans – the recorded spelling and one and the same with the Thomas 'Moarns' above – applied to the Parochial Board of Campbeltown for assistance to repair his fishing boat. He was authorised to have the repairs costed 'and to assign her to the Board', upon their advancing the necessary sum, till he was able to refund the Board'. (Min Bk PB Cam, 26/11/50) These two were, in 1851, living together in Main Street. They were father and son. Thomas was described as a widower and fisherman, aged 73, born in Ireland, and Daniel (see below) as a fisher boy, aged 15. The form of their name there is 'Morrns'. (C/d8/p11) The wife of Thomas M was Rose Robertson, about whom nothing is known. She, too, was almost certainly Irish. Two others of their family – a son and a daughter – are known.

Edward was born c. 1830, but whether in Ireland or in Campbeltown remains doubtful. His marriage registration states Campbeltown, but when in 1897 he applied for admission to the poor-house, suffering from sciatica, he claimed Irish birth – 'Can't say part; has been here from infancy.' (RP 1552) On 20.2.1855 he married Mary Cook, born 5.2.39 at Dalintober, the daughter of James C, fisherman, and Elizabeth Galbraith. The form of his name on that registration is 'Mornes', (RM) yet another variant (to which may be added Morans, Morrens, and Morrins). Of his family of seven, two sons – Archibald and James, both born at Tonadippen, Carradale – became fishermen. The form of the name which the former adopted was 'Morans', and the branch of the family in Campbeltown today which perpetuates that form is descended from his son, Robert Crawford M, who was born on 7.2.1891 and died on 1.4.1976.

Mary, born c. 1827 in Ireland, married Andrew Cuthbertson, born 2.2.29 at Campbeltown, son of Andrew C, seaman, and Agnes McKerral. Their eldest daughter Agnes, born 3.9.54, married Michael BRODIE, fisherman, and their only son, Andrew C, born 8.2.61, followed his father as a fisherman. (RP 1674) The name Cuthbertson – alternatively, Culbertson – has disappeared from Campbeltown.

Daniel, born c. 1834, married Mary McAllister on 5.9.54. She was born 1.7.37 in Campbeltown, the daughter of Alexander McA, weaver, and Margaret Mathieson. (Ib. 1668) Two of their family survived into adulthood. Daniel, born 20.12.61 in Shore Street, on 27.11.83 married Ellen Wareham, daughter of James W, fisherman, and Mary Morrison.

(RM) Catherine, born 28.2.66, also in Shore Street, on 2.9.87 married Dugald Mathieson, fisherman, son of Dugald M, fisherman, and Helen McDougall, (RM) whose sister Mary was the mother of Robert ROBERTSON.

Edward M seems not to have aspired to boat-ownership, but he skippered three boats in which the Cook family – one of the main boat-owning groups in Campbeltown – had interests. His son Archibald, however, owned, or had shares in, a series of five boats, including the *Annie Lee* (1883) and the *Genesta* (1885). (RFB I, p154; II, p103) From 1885-91, Daniel M Jr owned and skippered the skiff *Sweet Home*. (Ib. II, p81) The name is no longer represented in the fishing community.

NEWLANDS. The form in which Nolan has settled. At least ten written forms, more or less interchangeable, are known: Nolan, Noland, Nollan, Knowlan, Nowlan, Nowland, Nouland, Newland, Newlands, and Newlans. The traditional spoken form, though non-existent now, would best be represented by 'Nowlan', 'now' pronounced as the adverb above. George N (see final paragraph) when a young man aboard the Roman Catholic-crewed *Busy Bee* was never referred to other than as 'Nowlan'. (Noted, 20/11/1982)

In 1851, there were six distinct family groups of the name Newlands, or variants, living in Campbeltown. Whether some of these were interrelated is uncertain. Undoubtedly, however, all could not have been of identical origin. Several migratory arrivals are therefore indicated. The merchant James N was born in Co. Derry, (C/d7/p9) but nothing is known of the others.

The first fisherman of the name of whom there is record was George N, born c. 1834 in Glasgow, son of George N, tailor or weaver, and Sarah O'Neill, and a brother of Sarah N (see BLACK, DURNAN). He married Jean McMillan, daughter of Malcolm McM, carter, and Jean Ryburn. (RP 632) In 1869 he was skipper of the skiff *Diver*, and in 1871 of the smack *Kate*. (RFB I, pp 36, 79)

The last fisherman of the name in Campbeltown was also George. Born in 1904, a younger brother of Duncan N, late coxswain of the Campbeltown lifeboat, he is traceable only to his grandfather. He was John N, seaman, born c. 1818 in either Campbeltown or Ireland. On 13.11.60 he married a native of Antrim, Agnes Lynn, born c. 1820, daughter of Hugh L and Helen McCormick. (RP 698; C81/d22/p21; RD 22/4/1901)

O'HARA. The pre-eminent fishing family of Irish origin during the final half of the nineteenth century, its progenitor was Duncan O'H, born c. 1806 at Cushendun, Co. Antrim, the son of Henry O'H, labourer, and Nancy Scally. (RD 10/9/1891; RP 1303) He settled in Campbeltown, during the 1840s, with his first wife, Mary McNeill (who died there), and their three sons John, James, and Duncan, all of whom were Irish-born. His second wife, Margaret Haggerty, whom he married on 25.11.1850, was born in Campbeltown, but of Irish parentage – Charles H, carter, and Mary Docherty. (RD 23/9/1879) They had five daughters, of whom three married local fishermen of Irish extraction – Margaret and Catherine to the FINN brothers, John and James, respectively, and Anne to Archie McKAY.

Duncan O'H and all three of his sons were fishermen. He appears on record in 1852 when, with his eldest son John, he signed FP. During the succeeding decade he evidently had a change of mind on the 'trawling' issue, for in 1861 he was jailed, with three of his crew, for 30 days on a charge of having fished illegally with a 'trawl'. Each had been fined £20, but none could pay. His son James absconded to the West Indies before the case was heard, (AF 37/157) but had returned by 1867, for in that year he married Ann MEENAN – daughter of Thomas M – in Campbeltown. (RM 9/10/67) His brother John later escaped a prison sentence for illegal fishing (see MARTIN).

Between 1869 and 1900, the O'H family – Duncan, his sons, and grandsons, individually or in combinations – owned no fewer than 22 boats, including six smacks, a superior class of craft, signifying advancement and prosperity in the fishing industry of the time. The family's presence in Kintyre has diminished markedly, and there are no longer any fishermen of the name. The O'Haras' ancestral and adopted countries were linked symbolically in the names of a pair of ring-net skiffs built for John O'H in 1883 – the *Shamrock* and the *Thistle*. (RFB I, pp 123, 117)

ROBERTSON. This family's progenitor in Campbeltown was Robert R, hawker, the son of a soldier, James R, and Judea (?Judy) Devine. He was born at sea between Britain and Gibraltar in 1816, but considered himself Irish. (C71/d21/p20) His wife, Catherine McCann, was however of Irish birth. Her parents were Michael McC, hawker, and Mary Kane. They had a family of four – Mary Ann, Hugh, Susan, and Patrick. (RP 969) On 27.10.79 Hugh married Mary Mathieson, born 6.12.59, the daughter of Dugald M, fisherman, and Helen McDougall. Hugh and Mary R had three children, Robert (born 12.5.80), Mary (11.3.82), and Hughina (24.2.84), born one month and a day after her father went down with the Campbeltown schooner *Moy* in the storm of 23 January 1884. His widow on 19.8.87 remarried, to John McIntyre. (RP 1061) Her son, Robert R, became a fisherman and achieved singular distinction as the pioneer of modern ring-netting. (See TRNF, 205-19) This family, which is no longer represented in Campbeltown through a male line, is distinct from the extensive Robertson family which remains prominent in the fishing community, and which descends from James R, fisherman, born 11.12. 1835 – the son of the Dalintober ferryman (p. 132) – and Margaret McNaughton.

SCALLY. This family poses difficulty. The name is probably Irish, and the family tradition attests to an Irish origin, yet there is no conclusive evidence of that. The obvious assumption would be that the name represents an early immigrant arrival, but the possibility – however remote – that it is a form of some 'native' name must be considered. The crucial question here is, for how many generations must a name be established in a particular place before it may be accepted as 'native'? The name S appears on 31.5.1803 with the birth registration of Neil, son of James S and Mary Campbell. Five more children – two of them males – were registered between then and 1819, (ORB I) but the Scallys in Campbeltown evidently descend in the main from Neil and his Kintyre-born wife, Catherine McCormick, daughter of William McC, farmer, and Barbara Thomson. (RD 11/7/1882) In 1851 Neil S was a stonemason, living at Witchburn, Campbeltown, with his wife and four children. (C/d5/p43) A son Archibald, born c. 1855, was a fisherman in 1877 when he married Flora McIlchere, daughter of Donald McI, shoemaker, and Mary McFarlane. (RM 1/3/77) The only instance of boat-ownership in that family was the *Matchless,* which Archibald had from 1884 until 1899. (RFB II, p48) The name is found in the O'HARA and McKAY families from Culfeightrin Parish in the Glens of Antrim, where, in 1669, seven probable forms of the name were recorded. (HMR, 13-14)

SHORT. The progenitor of the Shorts in Campbeltown, James – an Irishman – evidently never settled there, but his wife Agnes McCoag or McCaig, born in 1840, was native. Her parents were John McC, shoemaker, and Agnes McQuilkan, whose origin was probably Rathlin, for their son Neil, also a shoemaker, was born there on 12.11.1823. (RP 1551) In 1866 Agnes S returned to Campbeltown with her three children, Mary, Ann, and Neil. (Ib. 412) Neil, who was born on 12.11.64 in Glasgow, became a fisherman and married Helen McIntyre, born 16.9.65, daughter of John McI, fisherman, and Janet McLean. (Ib. 1422) In July, 1893, he was rowing on Campbeltown Loch with two companions and the boat capsized. Neil S alone drowned. (CC 15/7/93) His two sons, John (born 10.8.90) and Archibald (22.9.92) became fishermen. John was a well-known and very successful skipper, whose partnership with Robert ROBERTSON and company began in1927 with the *Crimson Arrow* and ended in 1949, when S withdrew, retaining the *King Bird.* (See TRNF, 205-19)

WHITEFORD (A Scottish name, from the lands of Whitefoord near Paisley, TSOS, 811). There were, in 1851, four households in Campbeltown bearing the name. All were probably related. An examination of one will suffice. Alexander W, carter, 44, in High Street with his Campbeltown-born wife, Mary Scally, (RD John W, 5/8/1900) and four children, the eldest of whom, John (22), was described as a fisherman. All of these children were born in Campbeltown, which dates his settlement in advance of 1828. (C/d1/p16) Alexander W was elsewhere described as a fisherman. (RD, op. cit.) The family, although identified with fishing into the twentieth century, evidently produced no boat-owners. The origin of Alexander W alone is known. He was a native of Co. Antrim, (C51, op cit.) and the assumption that the entire group of the name W originated there may not be untenable.

SUPPLEMENT

BOYLE, Daniel, 39 (51/d2/p11)
COX, James, 26 (81/d16/p25)
DRUMMOND, Charles, 43 (51/d7/p20)
DUNSMORE, John, 39 (81/d19/p19)
McALISTER, Alexander, 40, Antrim (51/d7/p27)
McAULAY, John, 32 (61/d11/p2)
McISAAC, John, 64 (51/d6/p18)
McKIERGAN, John, 32, Antrim (51/d1/p3)
McLEAN, John, 41 (51/d10/p9)
MAINS, Edward, 17 (51/d7/p19)
SHERRY, Peter, 22 (51/d4/p13)
SINCLAIR, William, 76 (61/d1/p8)
STEEL, James, 36 (51/d11/p12)
STEWART, Campbell, 46, Down (81/d11/p8)
WILKISON, Charles, 57, Antrim (51/d1/p26)

Appendix II

Surname Changes in Kintyre

The following appendix probably does not represent a quarter part of the surnames which underwent conspicuous change in Kintyre during the past 300 years and more. It would be true to say that virtually all Gaelic names suffered mutilation, to a greater or lesser degree, in their conversion into English. Many remain recognisably Gaelic in origin – particularly those which have retained the *mac* ('son of') prefix – but others of demonstrably Gaelic origin have ceased to be recognisably so. Cook, Downie, Martin, Smith, and Taylor are just a few which were originally Gaelic names in Kintyre, though I would stress that all of these are also, in particular Kintyre families, demonstrably non-Gaelic, or at least non-native. The distinction hinges on specific geographical origin.

I have concentrated this study largely on those names for which documentary evidence of change exists, with a few exceptions, attested elsewhere, as *Mac a Bhreatnaich*→Galbraith. Andrew McKerral, in *Kintyre in the Seventeenth Century*, devoted an appendix to 'Highland Personal Names'. Historically and genealogically, the material is both interesting and fairly reliable, but etymologically it is generally quite unsound. He completely fails to demonstrate the evolutionary processes which he presents. For example, he records 'McIlvrennenich'→ 'O'Brennan'→'Arnot', but does not attempt to establish the links. I have, however, denoted with an asterisk those names which McKerral treats as having undergone transformation.

In the selection of examples of name-bearers I have, when confronted with a profusion of documented instances, made my selection on principles of: 1. distributional relevance (i.e. a density of occurrences in a particular area dictated a corresponding representation); 2. locative interest (i.e. preserving place-names which have gone out of currency); 3. occupational interest (i.e. referring to occupations which have become uncommon or which have disappeared).

The only comparatively modern source-book available for this study was G. F. Black's enormous *The Surnames of Scotland*, published in 1946. I referred repeatedly to it, but with increasing reservations, particularly in the matter of etymology. The etymology of personal names is, however, an exceedingly difficult – indeed perilous – matter, and I do not pretend to have resolved the inherent difficulties of the subject, notwithstanding the quality of the advice I was able to procure.

BLUE. From *Mac Gille Ghuirm*, which Black (p. 496) anglicises 'son of the blue lad'. Matheson, however, remarks that *gorm* also means 'raven-haired'. *Gorm* may, alternatively, have been a personal name, but of that there is no obvious evidence. On the available evidence, a north Kintyre surname, distributed through Largieside and into Kilcalmonell Parish, with a fishing family – now represented by one elderly woman – in Carradale. An early anglicised form, McIlgorm, survives in Co. Antrim (p. 94). Duncan McIlgurim in Amod, Barr Glen, 1694 (HTL, 49); Donald and Dugald Blew in Nether Achluskin, K & K Par, 1797 (WHT, 5); Malcom Blue, miller at Clachaig, K & K Par, aged 40 in 1830 (AD14 30/106, 20); Charles Blue, fisherman in Carradale, 1852 (FP); the brothers Dugald (52), John (48), and Donald Blue (30), fishermen at Beallachroy, Kilcal Par, 1861 (C/d2/p12); Neil Blue, shoemaker and fisherman at Airds, Carradale, son of William B, shoemaker, and Ann McKinlay, died 1.9.1894, aged 77 (RD).

BRODIE.* From *Ó Brolcháin* (earlier *Ó Brolchán*), the name of an Irish family of ecclesiastics and stone-masons which first appears on record in the West Highlands in the 14th century. (LMMSWH, 106-7) The standard anglicised forms in the 17th century were O Brol(l)achan and O Brol(l)ochan, as Jon Obrollachan in Clongart, Evir Ob in Craig, Donald

Ob in Balvilling utrach, c. 1630 (SLK), and Donald Obrolochan in Putachan, Archibald Ob in Skerablinrad, and John Ob in Glenramskill moir, 1694 (HTL, 50,54). In the WHT list of 1797-8, the prefix has gone: Donald Brolichan in Drummore (Cam Par), Lachlan B in Achinchork (Oatfield), and Archibald B in Kilchattan (So Par). (pp. 8, 12) The form Brol(l)achan persisted until the close of the 19th century, though occasionally co-existent with Brodie, e.g. Catherine Broll or B, Campbeltown, in 1882, and William B or Brol, tailor, Campbeltown, in 1898, born Calliburn 18.10.28. (RP 984, 1580) O Brallachan — as William O Brallachan (ORB I, 19/4/1796) — Brolachan, Brodelty, and Brodley are all cited in ORBL as antecedents of Brodie. That order may be accepted as the approximate evolutionary sequence ending with Brodie. I have, however, found no evidence of the last two names in Kintyre prior to their appearance from Ireland, c. 1840. The great majority — if not actually all — Brodies now in Kintyre are traceable to an Irish immigrant fisherman, John Broadley or Brodie (see Appendix I, BRODIE). Brodie itself, as a native form, occurs relatively rarely, which suggests limited adoption. Duncan B in Dalaruan, Campbeltown, aged 46 in 1854 — 'I had the farm of Killean until October . . . and lately I came to reside at Campbeltown, where I now work as a labourer' (AD14 54/216, 21); John B, farmer, son of Donald B, farmer, and Janet Smith, died 13.1.1861 at Lagalgarve, K & K Par, aged 49 (RD); Neil B, labourer, born at Corputechan, K & K Par, son of Peter B and Catherine McConechy, died at Campbeltown on 22.9.1871, aged 80 (Ib., RP 486).

COCHRANE. From *Mac Eacharna*, 'son of Eacharna' (which may represent *Each-thighearna*, 'horse-lord'), more usually anglicised 'MacEachran'. Not all MacEachrans took the name Cochrane — indeed, the relative preponderance of MacE over C suggests a very limited adoption. The name C, as a native legacy, has disappeared from Kintyre — the family of painters of that name in Campbeltown originate from the settlement there of Thomas C, master painter, born at Neilston, Renfrewshire, c. 1838. (C71/d6/p12) Alexander Cochrane or McEachran, Culfuar, 20 years old in 1818, witness to a serious assault on John Galbreath, tacksman of Tayinloan, during the Old New Year's Day shinty match on Dalchennan park, Tayinloan (AD14 18/113); Gilbert Cocheran, Lochkearan (Kilcal Par), in 1822, appears as McEacheran and McCocheran in 1823 (SB No 5); Archibald Cochrane or McEachrane, muslin printer, Campbeltown, born 19.5.1819, son of Donald McE, labourer, and Margaret McMillan (RP 1029).

COOK. Derivation difficult. Holmer gives *Mac Cùca* in his transcript of the tradition, taken down from Angus Cook in Crossaig, of 'How the Cooks came to Kintyre'. (TGOK, 137-9) That story attests to an Arran origin, which is not dismissible, for the name has long been associated with that island. A widower and his son, Cook by name, lived at Pirnmill on Arran. They were expert marksmen with bow and arrow and were killing deer. The king of Arran, *Glas nan Cailleach* (literally, 'Grey One of the Old Women'), heard of this and hanged Cook's son. He summoned the father and would have hanged him too, but old Cook tricked the king into removing his helmet, and, when he had done so, clove his skull with a concealed axe. He escaped in a waiting boat and landed in Kintyre at the bay which was afterwards named Port MacCùca. He was granted the protection of Clan Donald and afterwards prospered. Many of the name C in Campbeltown are of recent English extraction. Rob MacCook in Carnmore, Kilcal Par, 1797 (WHT, 4); Archibald McCook, coachman in Tayinloane, aged 27 in 1861 — with his wife Margaret Stewart and children John (10) and George (1); (C K & K/d2/p13) George Cook, labourer in Campbeltown, aged 66 in 1927 — born Tayinloan, son of Archibald C, coachman, and Margaret Stewart (RP 2512).

DOWNIE. Black (p. 511) advances *Mac Gille Domhnaich*, 'son of the Lord's gillie', while MacLysaght (p. 81), examining MacEldowney and variants in Ulster, agrees in the Irish *Mac Giolla Domhnaigh*, 'son of the devotee of the church'. Having considered the evidence of the name in Kintyre, Matheson doubted if *gille* would have been reduced to one syllable in unstressed position, and suggested that both -ol- and -il- (below) represent Gaelic *mhaol*, with which evaluation Ó Baoill inclines to agree. (*Maol* and *gille* – Irish *giolla* – equate in these contexts: 'servant'.) Matheson further questions the assumption that these 17th century examples represent surnames rather than patronymics, *Maol-domhnaich* then being current as a personal name (e.g. Moldonych Mcillicheir in Achaleik or Kilmichell, c. 1630 – SLK). The likeliest form is, therefore, *Mac Mhaol Domhnaich*, which may – or may not – represent 'son of the servant of the Lord'. Gilpatrick McOldonych in Gartgrellane and Gilnave McOldonych in Egill (Uigle) or Ochterane, c. 1630 (SLK); Malcolme McIldonie in Moy, c. 1653 (ib.); John Downie, 'woolweaver' at Achapharick, K & K Par, aged 69 in 1861 (C/d2/p4); Neil D, shoemaker at Tigh na Maole cottage, K & K Par, 75 in 1861 (ib., d4/p1). The skipper of the lugger *Pass-by* of Campbeltown, which was storm-wrecked in the Pentland Firth in September, 1885, was Duncan D of Lochend. He and his crew of seven perished. (CC 26/9/85)

DUNCAN. Represents *Mac Dhonnchaidh* (MacConnochie), 'son of Duncan', whence also the rarer Duncanson. As MacConnochie, was fairly generally distributed in the 17th century, but the shift to D appears to have occured most conspicuously in the Skipness area. As D, was introduced to Kintyre by 19th century Irish immigration – e.g. Robert Duncan, weaver, with sons Daniel and Robert, in Campbeltown, 1851. (C/d4/p26) Archibald Duncan or McConachy, fisherman at Clonaig, charged with committing an assault at Tarbert in 1832 (AD14 32/163); John D (71), retired fisherman in Skipness Village, 1861 (C/d1/p7); Alexander (82), Walter (55), and Grace D (60), at Portagaban, Skip Par, in 1861 (C/d3/p3); Flora McConachy or Duncanson, 1853 (Let Bk PB Cam, 11/2/53).

GALBRAITH. From *Mac a Bhreatnaich*, 'son of the Briton', i.e. of Strathclyde. (TSOS, 285) The name was once common in Gigha, whence, in the 19th century – and presumably earlier – many of the Kintyre G families came. Neill McBretnych in Kilchevan, c. 1630 (SLK); James Galbreth in Kilkeden or Ardnacross, 1694 (HTL, 53); John Galbreath in Killigruer, Peter G in Laggan, Samuel G in Penniver, and James and Donald G in Ardnacross, 1797 (WHT, 6,9); Christina Galbraith, Back Street, Campbeltown, aged 30 in 1861, 'bates (sic) fishing lines' (C/d8/p18); John G, fisherman at Point House, Carradale, aged 40 in 1861 – born Cam Par (C/d3/p1); Donald G, ferryman at Portamacook (Port na Cuthaig), Saddell, aged 34 in 1881 – born Gigha (C/d1/p1). Mactaggart (RTOKG, 24) records the appearance in Kintyre, between 1640 and 1660, of Lowland Galbraiths. John G, farmer in Drumavuling, Southend, in 1881, was born in Dalrymple, Ayrshire c. 1824. (C/d2/p2)

HATTAN.* From *Mac Gille Chatáin* (TSOS, 498 – accent presumed erroneous), Irish *Mac Giolla Chatáin* (TSOI, 128), translated in these sources 'son of the servant/devotee of St. Catan'. A less presumptuous translation would be 'son of Gille Chatain'. McKerral (KSC, 163) considered the name 'very rare' in Kintyre, but that judgement is disputable. It was chiefly of Largieside provenance, but is no longer found anywhere in Kintyre. William McIllechattan in Gartgunnel (near Tangy), 1694 (HTL, 50); Lauchlan McIlchattan, Mains of Saddell, 1694 (ib., 51); Margaret, at Beachmore, appears as 'Chattan' in 1854, and as 'Hattan' and 'Cattan' in 1861. (Min Bk PB K & K Par, 22/8/54, 12/2/61) James and Duncan, sons of Robert MacIlchattan in Auchnacloich, a pendicle of Muasdale, were interviewed as witnesses during a criminal investigation in 1830. Their names appear as MacIlchattan, but each signed himself Hattan. (AD14 30/106, 53, 56)

HAWTHORN.* Probably from Irish *Ó Dreáin* – a family first in Co. Roscommon, but later, by enforced migration, found in Ulster, with the anglicised forms Adrain, O Drean, and Drean. (TSOI, 19, 78) Hawthorn appears to have been a Kintyre pseudo-translation, *droigheann* in Gaelic being 'hawthorn'. Neither (O)Drain nor Hawthorn survives in Kintyre. John Odrain in Knockmurran (Southend) in 1797 (WHT, 10); John, son of Duncan O'Drain and Mary McConochy, born 12.2.1799 (ORB I); Flora Drain, widow (80), at New Orleans in 1851, with her son Duncan (43), a farmer of 15 acres, and a 12-year-old servant, Marion McCallum (C51 Cam Par/d6); Catherine Drain or Hawthorn, mother of poor relief applicant Isabella McKeich, who was born 10.12.1833 in Campbeltown (RP 941); Neil H, rope-maker, Campbeltown, son of Donald H, sailor, and Catherine McEachran, died 28.9.1856, aged 74 (RD).

HENDERSON. From *Mac Eanruig* ('son of Henry'), cf. MacKendrick. Gillecreist McKenrick in Bar; Donald, Connochir, and Gilpadrick McK in Egill (Uigle) or Ochterane (Octoran, a pendicle of Knocknaha); Jon and Donald McK in Kilbryde, c. 1630 (SLK); John Henderson in Killacraw, 1797 (WHT, 6); Archibald H or McKendrick, aged 20 in 1836, son of William McK, farmer at Lailt (AD14 36/113, 83).

KELLY. A problematic name, of which no writer on Kintyre has ventured an explanation. The early form appears to have been O Kelly, which must align it with Irish *Ó Ceallaigh*. The form 'O Kaldie' – Donald in Kilchevan, Hew and Evir in Maichrihanis, and Neil in Knokcantimoir, all c. 1630 (SLK) – probably represents O Kelly. These individuals certainly are appositely located, i.e. in the Machrihanish district. In c. 1653 the evidence is unquestionable: Donald O Kellie in Gartluscan (So Par), Donald O K in Knockhantiebeg, and Donald O K in Beachmoir. (SLK) By the end of the 18th century, the prefix is gone: Chas and Malcom Kellie in Machrihanish; Donald K in Upper Bar; Hugh Kelly in Achaluskin (K & K Par). (WHT, 13,6,5) In 1812 Donald K, Craigach (Craigaig), was operating a whisky-still. (SB I, 11/12/12) In 1816, John K, farmer at Darlochan, and his sons Hector, Peter, John, Archibald, and Robert were examined in connection with the plundering of timbers cast ashore in Machrihanish Bay with the breaking up of the brigantine *Saltcoats*, stranded on the shore below Balivain. (AD14 16/62)

LANG.* From Loynachan, earlier O Loynachan, O Lynachan, O Linachan (derivation doubtful). A numerous Learside/Southend name, a few examples of which will suffice. As 'Olynachan': John in Altnaboduie and Donald in Glenahervy, 1772; Archibald in Faochag, 1773; Archibald in Elerig, 1791; Neil in Machrioch, 1800. As 'Olinachan': Lauchlan in Corfine and Neil in Eden, 1806; Neil in Glenahervie, 1814. David Loynachan in Eden, 1834. (SBR) As Loynachan, was very common in south Kintyre until the late 19th century. In the registers of poor for Campbeltown occur no fewer than 24 individual registrations, in only one of which is Lang quoted alternatively: Neil Lang, 'formerly Loynachan', fisherman, living in Glebe Street, 1899, and then aged 82. (RP 1464) The persistence of the old form, so demonstrated, renders its total disappearance by the turn of the century the more remarkable. Two persons now in Campbeltown do, however, own Loynachan as a middle name.

LITTLESON. *Mac Figeinn*, for *Mac Bhigein, beag*, 'little', being the root (TSOS, 494) – thus, a direct translation. A rare Kintyre surname, of Largieside origin. The sole remaining family of the name in Kintyre is in possession of the farm of Killegruer, Glenbarr. Duncan MacFiggan in Achapharick, K & K Par, 1797 (WHT, 5); Duncan Littleson, farmer at Killegruer, son of John L, farmer, and Catherine Wallace, and husband of Mary Watson, died 5.4.1889 at the age of 79 (RD); Neil L, distillery workman, Parliament Square, Campbeltown, aged 46 in 1861 – born Campbeltown (C/d4/p7).

LOVE. From *Mac Ionmhuinn* (MacKinven), by translating *ionmhuinn*, 'beloved', but see MacKINNON/MacKINVEN. Black (p. 531) asserts that *Mac Ionmhuinn* is 'really a Gaelic rendering of the well-known Ayrshire family name Love, introduced into Kintyre by persecuted Covenanters, to whom the peninsula was a haven of refuge'. He offers not a scrap of evidence, and the statement is best ignored. In a petition, dated 3.9.1852, in favour of 'trawling', and signed by 16 fishermen in the Grogport/Crossaig area, the name Donald Love appears. Pencilled in the margin beside – presumably by a fishery officer – is the remark: 'Son of McKinvin (Donald, who heads the petition – author), Love and McKinvin being the same name.' (AF37/5) That interchangeability – within the same family – can be demonstrated from the registers of birth for Skipness Parish. Colin, b. 27.12.1856, and Archibald, b. 20.3.61, at Crossaig, are both registered as Love, but Christina, b. 21.3.67, and John and Duncan, b. 21.10.68, are McKinven, and their father, Donald, a fisherman, signs himself so. Charles L, weaver at Dunultach, Kilcal Par, son of Archibald L, shoemaker, and Mary Stalker, died 3.6.1857, aged 65 (RD); Dugald L, blacksmith at Dippen in 1861 – born Skip Par (C Sad/d2/p5). The pen-name 'A. K. Love' was purposely adopted by a Campbeltown poet Angus Keith MacKinven, who died at Rouen in 1916 of wounds received during the Battle of the Somme. His verse was later collected, along with that of his younger brother, Donald, who had died of typhoid in Manitoba, Canada, in 1907, at the age of 19. (*A Few Original Poems,* Campbeltown undated)

MacKERRAL.* McKerral (p. 166) derives this from MacKiergan, but his case is not an altogether convincing one – he leaves the transformation undemonstrated. Phonetically, the name could represent either Irish *Mac Cearbhaill* or *Mac Fhearghail,* but no certainty is possible. ORBL, however, it must be admitted, records the same shift: 'Kiergan to McKerral.' In the 17th and 18th centuries, MacKerral, on the available evidence, was a stable form. In SLK (c. 1630) five 'McKerroulls' appear – Gillaspic, Gillicallim reoche, and Donald in Muastill, Jon in Lossat or Glenhantie, and Malcolme in Killewnan – but there is no instance of MacKiergan or any name resembling it. The same applies to all subsequent lists which I have examined within that period, with one exception. In the list of the missionary Patrick Hegarty's converts in Kintyre in the early 17th century (p. 102) appears the name Aphrica Kyaragan. In ORB I – Campbeltown Parish – McKiargan and variants begin to appear in the early 19th century: Mary McKerrall (1794); Janet McKerrall (1795); Malcom McKerrell (1798); John McKiargan (1803); Catherine McKiargan (1806); Peter McKiargan (1807); John McKiargan (1812); Janet Keergan (1819). MacVicar (p. 4) remarked: 'The MacKerrals are locally called Kerigans, but I could never understand the connection. The only explanation I find is that Kerigan is the Irish form.' The explanation could be, I suggest, that early 19th century immigrant MacKiergans – also MacKiargan, MacKeargan, Kiargan, Kergan, Kerigan, and Kerrigan – adopted the native MacKerral, but I am not at all convinced that these instances of McKiargan in ORB I (above) belong entirely, if at all, to Irish stock. As much as may confidently be said is that MacKerral predominated until the early 19th century, and that there followed a century of confusion before, in the 20th century, MacKerral gained exclusive currency. In a poaching case reported as late as 1894, Peter McKeirgan or McKerral, baker, at Cowdenknowes, Campbeltown (CC 3/2/94); Agnes Kerral or Kergan (Let Bk PB Cam, 28/1/1853); Duncan McKerral or Kiargan, sailmaker, Campbeltown (ib., 1/7/1865); Annabella Loynachan or Kerrigan, born 28.7.1811, widow in Campbeltown, 1875 – husband named as Peter McKiargan (RP 811); Marion McKiargan in 1906 becomes Mary McKerral in 1908 (RP 1850, 1924).

MacKINNON/MacKINVEN (*Mac Fhionghuin/Mac Ionmhuinn*) – interchangeable. Black (p. 531) rejects outright the suggestion of a link between the two, but Matheson accepts that *Mac Ionmhuinn* derives from *Mac Fhionghuin.* Matheson: 'There was no such surname as *Mac Ionmhuinn,* except in the minds of those who spelt it that way or accepted the spelling. In pronunciation, the difference is so slight as to make the folk etymology plausible.' John Campbell (recorded 21/10/1980) has the tradition that MacKinnons/MacKinvens – he alternates the forms – came to Kintyre from Skye as 'swordsmen' in a dowry. In the speech of the older people the two names are interchangeable, or perhaps merely inseparable. Thus, in two versions of a story – reproduced in TRNF, 142 – the protagonist, a native of Grogport, is first MacKinven and then MacKinnon. In the precognition of John McCallum, herd at Lagloskin, during the investigation of a complaint of sheep-stealing in 1820, Neil McKinven, ferryman at Tayinloan, appears also as Neil McKinnon – '. . . and proceeded to the house of Neil McKinnon . . .' (AD14 20/112, 3) John McKinnon or McKinven, seaman and fisherman, at Shore Street, Campbeltown, in 1880; born 11.11.1820 at Big Kiln, son of Neil McKinnon or McKinven, rope-spinner, and Margaret Weir. (RP 923) On 28.4.1893 the birth of Christina McKinnon at Grogport was registered. (RB Sad Par) When her father, Archibald, a fisherman, married on 14.6.1887 at Campbeltown, he was registered as McKinven. (RM) To increase the complication, his father, Donald, was also known as LOVE.

MacMURCHY/MacMURPHY – interchangeable, representing Gaelic *Mac Mhurchaidh* or *Mac Mhuirich*, or both. In 1858 Duncan McMurphy, farmer in Monebacach, Skip Par, was registered as dead at the age of 77. The death was reported by a son, Angus McMurphy. (RD 3/4/58) In 1865, another son, Archibald, died at Monebacach. He appears as McMurchy, and Angus, above, who again reported the death, is likewise McMurchy. (Ib., 12/3/65) Angus's son, Gilbert, who died at six days of age in 1869, is also McMurchy. (Ib., 9/2/69) Also in Skip Par, Duncan McMurphy, born 27.3.1858, son of Duncan McMurphy, labourer, and Margaret Wilkison, at Escart. (RB.) Murchy McMurphy, mariner, and Elizabeth Blue married in Campbeltown on 4.12.1820. (ORM) The poet James McMurchy (p. 10) appears as McMurphy in RM (Cam Par 16/6/1859); his sister Isabella is also McMurphy when married, and James himself witnesses as Murphy (RM Cam Par 8/6/58); another sister, Margaret, born in 1818, was registered Murphy (ORB I); his brother Alexander is Murphy in RD (Cam Par 16/7/70).

MATHIESON.* Black (p. 541) gives *Mac Mhatha*, 'son of Matthew', but Matheson considers that the English forms in Kintyre indicate *Mac Math(a)*, retaining the older usage by which there was no lenition after the masculine noun. Tenant farmers of the name 'MacMath' (pronounced 'MacMaa') were abundant in Glenbreackerie and adjacent districts of Southend throughout the 18th and into the 19th century, as the following selection will demonstrate: Archibald in Culinlongart (1768); Neil and John in Glenehanty; John in Ballenamull; Archibald in Cariskey; Archibald in Auchnaslishag (1769); Archibald in Inuncochallich (1774); John in High Remuel (1780); Malcom in Lergybane; Dugald in Gartnacopaig (1781); John in Glenadle; Dugald in Glenedardacrock (1784); Dugald in Dalsmiran; Donald in Ceramenach (1786); John, herd in Lergybawn (1807); Angus in Gartincorach (1810); Dugald in Machribeg (1830). (SBR) The forename *Amhla*, which recurs in 18th century records – e.g. Amhla McMath, Remuil, in 1790 (SBR, 27/1/90) – was evidently, in Kintyre, peculiar to that family. MacMaths farmed Glenahanty in unbroken succession from the 17th century until 1906, when the farm reverted to Lossit Estate. The last tenant-farmer there, Archibald Mathieson, died three years later, at the age of 90. In the notice of his death which appeared in the *Campbeltown Courier,* the form of his name is McMath, which was probably its last appearance in Kintyre. It was said of him that he 'always favoured the old rendering of the name', (Obit. CC, 6/11/09) and it may be considered a fitting tribute to a venerable man of the old stock in Kintyre that, even in death, his traditional preference was respected. Donald Mathieson was a famous Glenbreackerie strongman in the 19th century. He met and fought his great rival, Donald Ban, at the bridge of *Clachan Ùr*, on the road south of Lochorodale. It was said that 'the marks wiz on the ground for long after wherr the two men had been wrastlin'. In the end, 'Donal Maa' broke one of his rival's legs, and the defeated man was carted to Dalsmeran and had his leg set on the kitchen table there. (C. Bannatyne, 17/3/1977; D. McCallum, 28/6/77) Flora Mathieson or McMath, mother of Duncan Drain, mason, Auchinhoan, who married Agness Loran, Saltpans, on 26.11.1857 (RM Cam Par); Mary Mathieson, New Quay Head, Campbeltown, daughter of Neil McMath, farmer, and Mary Greenlees, died 6.5.1904, aged 77 (RD). (*This ought to represent '(the) new village' or something similar, but there is no evidence of settlement nearby. The folk tradition is 'the new stone', which, however, would be *A' chlach ùr.*)

MILLOY. Black (p. 601) maintains that 'the Milloys of Argyll and Bute are descended from the Macloys of Glendaruel', and postulates a Mac-Mil change. He fails, however, to substantiate that statement. Maclysaght (p. 164) remarks that Maloy in Co. Derry was used for MacCloy. MacVicar (p. 5) declares that McIlmaluag became, in Kintyre, Milloy. In the nature of his brief paper, he offers no evidence — but the evidence is available. The Gaelic form was probably *Mac Gille Mo-luaig*. Matheson, however, cautions: 'Though some individual "McIlmaluags" may have adopted "Milloy" as their English surname, this does not prove that all the Milloys are *Mac Gille Mo-luaig*. There can be no connection with *Mac Gille Mo-luaig* etymologically.' In a petition to the Duke of Argyll's chamberlain in Kintyre, dated 21 March 1782, the name 'Hugh Molloy' appears as one of three tenants on the farm of Brunerigan, Southend. Merely a week later, on 30 March, the three submitted another petition, again complaining of damage to arable land by the overflowing of Conieglen Water and by wind-driven sand — but 'Molloy' has become 'McIlmaluig'. (AP, Bundle 1942) Gilnave McIlmaluag in Bar, c. 1653 (SLK); Duncan McIlmaluag in Corputachan and Donald in Killeru, 1694 (HTL, 49,50); Malcom Milloy in Killacraw, 1797 (WHT, 6); Malcom Milloy, cottar at Gaigan, K & K Par, aged 60 in 1830, father of Malcom M, whisky smuggler who had 'left the country' (AD14 30/106, 51); Archibald M, parish beadle, at Clete Glebe, K & K Par, aged 42 in 1861 (C/d2/p16).

PURSELL.* From *Mac an Sporain* (MacSporran), 'son of the purse', by translation (TSOS, 565); cf. MacSparran from *Mac an Sparáin* in Ulster (TSOI, 201). The displacement was limited, and while MacS retains a firm hold in Kintyre, P is about to disappear. The name MacS, beyond its native Kintyre, tends to provoke reactions of disbelief or amusement. The London *Evening News* in 1937 published an article, headed 'A MacSpoof, Perhaps', reporting that 'among unclaimed deposits lying in the Commonwealth Bank of Australia is the item: "Samuel McSporran . . . £1 12s 10d."' This was dismissed in a few lines: 'It doesn't ring true. There never was a Scotsman called McSporran, and if there had been the bank wouldn't be owing him £1 12s 10d. It would be his bank.' (CC, 8/1/1938) Jane McS or P, 25 in 1877, daughter of James P and Euphemia Gilchrist, Campbeltown. (RP 840)

STALKER. From *Mac an Stocair*, 'son of the trumpeter', in Ulster anglicised MacStocker and Stafford. (TSOI, 203) Black (p. 565) suggests, less probably, a derivation from *Mac an Stalcair*, 'son of the (deer-) stalker'. Of north Kintyre provenance, and once very common. Hew and Jon McStokkir in Kilmalouag (Barr Glen), c. 1630 (SLK); Robert McStocker in Clenegart, 1694 (HTL, 49); John McStocar, 'Reighn Taggart above Clachan, now in Auchivraude', 1815 (SB 4); Archibald Stalker, innkeeper at Skipness, aged 39 in 1881 (C/d1/p1). One of the 'characters' in the Largieside towards the close of the 19th century was a little man at Rhunahaorine, who daily would stand 'gazing at the coach as it passes in the afternoon'. Neil Stalker was his name. In July of 1881, when 91 years of age, he cut his peats at a distance of a mile from his home. In October of that year he was among the first in the district to dig and pit his potatoes. He also acted as Estate 'herald', and twice yearly walked the lands of Largie announcing the approach of rent day. Once, when asked his age, he replied with a kind of wonder: '*Tha mi dìreach mu cheud; tha mise faotainn aois mhòr*' – 'I'm just about a hundred; I'm getting a great age.' (CC 5/11/81) He died 1.9.88, aged 98. (RD) In 1924, a collection of verse – titled simply *Poems* – was published by Archibald Stalker, born at Campbeltown on 22.6.1882, the son of Donald S in Drumbeg. (CC 12/4/1924, 3/5/24)

TAYLOR. An occupational name, from *Mac an Tàilleir*, 'son of the tailor'. Mainly, on the available evidence, a south Kintyre name, but also found in Largieside. Eight bearers of the name are recorded in SLK, c. 1630, all in south Kintyre and sharing the form McIntailzor, was one exception – Jon rioche McTailzor in Glenramskil moir. In 1694: Allexr McIntyllour in Remuilichtrach; John McIntylloor in Kilblaan; Angus McIntylloor in Killeru. (HTL, 43,44,50) In 1797: Archibald Tayler in Acharua; Malcom Taylor in Dalmore

(Southend); John T in laigh Smerby; Rob T in Muasdil; John and Archibald T in Dunskeg. (WHT, 11,12,9,5,4) The T fishing family, which was well-known in Dalintober, evidently originated from the settlement, c. 1850, of an Ayrshire fisherman, George T. (C61/d1/p9)

THOMSON. From *Mac Thòmais* (MacComish) and *Mac Thamhais* (MacTavish), both 'son of Thomas'. The name, during the 19th century, was particularly associated with the Muasdale/Glenbarr and Skipness districts. It frequently co-existed with its older forms. When Archibald T, fisherman, died at Scotmill, Kilcal Par, on 18.11.1857 (significantly, he was buried at Skipness), his parents were registered as Donald T, fisherman, and Mary MacTav (being her maiden name). (RD Kilcal) Widow Peter T or Mactav was in K & K Par − location unspecified − in 1855. (Min Bk PB K & K Par, 30/10/55) Dougall McCavis with Jon roy, his son, in Beache, by Muasdale; Donald more, Hector, and Evir McC in Crubistill; Gillicallim McTavis in Kilchevan, c. 1630 (SLK); Donald McCavish in Culinlongart; Duncan McC in Margmonigach; Donald McComas in Corputachan; Malcom Thomson in Achadaduy, 1694 (HTL, 43, 49); John T in Beachmore and Archibald MacTavish in Stramollach, 1797 (WHT, 5,7). When the emigrant ship, *Costpatrick,* bound from London to Auckland, caught fire at sea in November 1874, among the passengers who perished were John and Barbara T and their four children, from Glenbarr. (CC, 2/1/75).

WILKIE. As an indigenous surname has disappeared from Kintyre, but was present (only) in the Grogport-Skipness area in the 19th century, and perhaps earlier. A very uncommon name, probably borne by as few as a couple of families. It is an anglicisation of *Mac Cuilcein* (see also WILKINSON), which was a common name in the area. In the petition of 1852 (see LOVE), the name Donald Wilkie appears above those of Hugh and Donald McQuilkan, all of Crosack (Crossaig). A boat and net belonging to that same Donald W was confiscated in 1853 by a crew of HMS *Porcupine* patrolling the Kilbrannan Sound south of Sunadale, in search of illegal fishermen. Her name was the *Swallow* of Grogport. (AF 37/9) Murdoch McQuilkan or W, in Skipness Village, son of Archibald McQ and Catherine McKinlay, 68 years old in 1864 (RP Sad & Skip Par, p57); Mary W, in Skipness Village, parents as above (but mother's surname recorded as McAuley), 64 years in 1873 (Ib., p96); Donald W, above, was the son of Duncan W, fisherman, and Mary Wilson, and died 10.2.1890, aged 80, at Grogport (RD).

WILKINSON/WILKISON. From *Mac Cuilcein* (MacQuilkan), which in phonetic English is MacCuilken, recorded by MacVicar (p. 3), and in that form still occasionally heard in local speech. According to Black (p. 560), the Gaelic represents 'son of Wilkin' (= Scots Wilkie), diminutive or pet forms of William. Both MacQ and W survive, and seem to be of north Kintyre origin, but W was also introduced from Co. Antrim in the early 19th century (See Supplement to Appendix I). Allan McCulkyn in Crossage and Donald bane and Gillaspic McCulkyne in Sperrassaig, c. 1630 (SLK); Angus and Duncan McQuilken in Margmonigach, 1694 (HTL, 49); Archibald McQuilkan in Runaherin and Finlay McQ in Margmonach, 1797 (WHT, 5,6); John Wilkinson or McQuilkan, mason in Campbeltown in 1881, then aged 48 − son of Angus McQ, born Killean Par (RP 966, 900).

Appendix III

Gaelic-derived Words in the Dialect of Campbeltown

This appendix is not comprehensive in its survey of persisting Gaelic elements in the dialect of Campbeltown. It could have been expanded had I included Gaelic-derived words recorded in isolation. John Campbell, particularly, contributed almost as many words again which could have been accommodated in this list, but for a suspicion that most of them originated with his Gaelic-speaking father (p. 77) and other members of that family. Admittedly, a number of these words were recorded by Latimer MacInnes in *Dialect of South Kintyre* and, so, may have entered John's vocabulary from the wider stream of local dialect; but the principle – that if a recorded word was not substantiated at least once by some other person – has, with one exception (foorach), been adhered to.

The list could also have been curtailed had I restricted it to words which survive functionally in local speech. Those fundamentally obsolete words which I nonetheless admitted to the list are as follows: cam, clooker, dravag, foorach, gadrach, glibe, greeach, kanejach, mayrach/merrach, sleeshach/sleeshag, smoorach, spootcher, and stooie. (I would recall, however, MacInnes's cautionary remarks on the uncertainty of deciding when, in a particular dialect, a word may be considered obsolete (p. 20), and cite the recovery of two of the words discussed in this appendix, viz. crechan and sarach.) The other listed words remain, to varying degrees, both understood and used.

There are, undoubtedly, additional words of limited currency which escaped my attention. No collector, in whatever field, can attain absolute success. The list below contains 13 words unpublished – and presumably uncollected – by MacInnes sixty years and more ago. That the great majority belonged in the fishing community perhaps explains the oversight. Having made a particular study of the Kintyre fishing communities, I was able to tap the technical vocabulary of a traditional industry which should, sixty years back, have yielded MacInnes a dialectal mass, had he but had the particular knowledge to penetrate it. I should say, also, that not a few words – including some which MacInnes considered Gaelic-rooted – have been excluded from this list owing to uncertainty of derivation.

Excepting Calum Brodie, Edward Lafferty, Chrissie McGregor, Archie McMillan, Duncan McSporran, Jean Paterson, Charlie Stewart, and Archie Wilson, informants quoted in this appendix were recorded specifically for the *Historical Dictionary of Scottish Gaelic* project (p. 15).

The abbreviation GCH indicates George Campbell Hay, who read and annotated the penultimate draft of this appendix in October, 1983, and some of whose Tarbert-derived material I have incorporated for its comparative value.

Those words which did not appear in MacInnes's *Dialect* are marked by an asterisk. Standard Gaelic spellings and definitions appended to individual items in the list come from Edward Dwelly's *Illustrated Gaelic-English Dictionary,* to which source concluding page numbers refer.

BOCKAN – a bogle or, more commonly, a vague malevolent spirit, often invoked to pacify troublesome children. At fishing, an unlucky person, usually a passenger, but in Tarbert a lucky person. Also in Tarbert, a repulsive person: 'No one's coming to this house. I think it's me that's the b———.' (GCH) *Bòcan:* hobgoblin, spectre, etc., 103.

BOONYACH* – diarrhoea, but now seldom so understood. Survives in the formulistic expression, '. . . wid gie ye the b———', and variants of that, suggesting an affliction or scunner caused by subjection to silly talk or antics. *Buinneach:* diarrhoea, dysentery, etc., 140.

BOOSE – 1. A surly expression, as in 'What a b——— she had on 'er!'. (A. Wilson, 14/3/83) 2. The mouth or nose – unspecifiable, because surviving only in the expression, 'tae the b———', i.e. drunk. Cf. 'to the beak/nose/gills', etc., all in local currency. BOOSACH – contemptuously, of a person of surly demeanour, as in 'Ask b——— ower there hoot's wrang wae 'im.' *Bus:* mouth, lip, snout, etc.; *busach:* pouting, sullen, 143.

CAITACH – left-handed. The adjectival suffix -er, as in 'A dinna know 'e wiz caitacher till 'e started tae work wi' the chisel', was not recorded by MacI, but now preponderates. In the Gaelic of Tarbert *ciutach*. (GCH) *Ciotach.*

CAM* – a bend, particularly in the bowsprit, mast, yard, etc. of a skiff, and thus primarily a word among – or formerly among – fishermen. The pronunciation 'kyam' was as common, or commoner. In Tarbert 'cem'. (GCH) *Cam:* crooked, curved, bent, etc. 157.

CLOOKER – a net worker. In Campbeltown formerly an occupation common to women. The dwarfish John McEachran when admitted to the poor roll in June, 1878, disabled by bronchitis, was described as a 'cleuker – i.e. net mender'. (RP 861) Also CLOOK, to mend, as in: 'If they seen ye mendin a net, they wid seh – "Ye're at the clookin".' (H. Martin, 21/2/78) *Cliùcair:* mender of shoes or nets, 210.

COLLIGLEEAN – earwig. May still be heard occasionally, even from young people, as C. Brodie, who spoke of seeing 'a c——— in a spider's web'. (18/7/82) Also 'collangleean'. *Collag-lìn*, 234.

CRECHAN – the queen-scallop (*Chlamys opercularis*). MacI, 10, under 'cracken', refers only to scallop-shell (*slige-chreachainn*), a sense which has been entirely lost. The appearance of 'crechan' in the local vocabulary, and on a massive scale, is explicable only by the fishery for these shellfish – also 'queenies' – which developed in the 1960s. Shore-based processing industries in Campbeltown brought the word into general use. It was probably reintroduced from Carradale or Tarbert. *Creachann:* scallop-shell and large ribbed cockle only, 267.

CROOBAN – MacI, 11, defines as 'any kind of crab', but the universal application is now to the edible or 'red' crab (*Cancer pagurus*). 'The crooban' was an imitative children's game in which the participants arched their bodies backwards on to the support of their hands, so that they could move slowly about, crab-like. (Jean Paterson, 18/3/78) *Partan* – any other kind of crab – is now virtually redundant. *Crùban:* crab, 281.

CROOP* – to shrink or contract. In its application to the technique of fastening netting to ropes in the assembling of a herring net, fully explained in TRNF, 116-21. Additional, non-technical uses recorded from J. Campbell, particularly applying to the ageing process. 'Well, I remember this ould man . . . a grett big tall man, he'd be abut six fut two A heard me fether sehin. But 'e wiz croopin in that wee bittie, ye know.' (5/11/80) *Crup.*

CUDDIE/CUDDIN – the fry of the saithe (*Gadus virens*), up to about 5 ins. in length, and before entering its second stage, GLESHAN. *Cudainn*, 287.

DOORIE – pig. Still occasionally heard. Probably from *durraidh*, 'sow', 375. Also DOORKIE*, which just might owe something to *uircean*, 'pig, piglet', 994.

DRAVAG* – a 'scatter' of fish, either sighted in the sea-phosphorescence – 'burning' – or taken in a net. Whichever, a worthless quantity – 'It's only a d——— o' herrin.' (G. Newlands, 21/2/78) *Dràbhag:* scattered multitude, etc., 356.

FALLACHAN – a hoard. MacI, 11, limits his definition so, but the word may now be connoted with a sudden receipt of wealth, a 'windfall'. 'A wish there's a f——— wid faa' on the table ee noo.' (M. McAulay, 7/2/78) *Falachan:* hidden treasure, etc. 408.

FOORACH* – meal and water mixed for refreshment aboard fishing skiffs. From D. McSporran only (17/1/81). Cf. the standard MAIRACH. Presumably connected with *fuarag:* meal and water, etc., 460.

GADRACH* – miscellaneous rubbish. The word's survival was confined to the vocabulary of fishermen, more or less, in a specific application to a catch consisting overwhelmingly of small worthless fish and other creatures. 'Ye took a haul an ye got a mixture o' wee useless stuff.' (D. MacLean, 21/2/78) The form in Carradale is 'gattarach', which has a more general sense. Problematic, but may be from 'gather' – of which 'gadder' is a Scots variant – with Gael. *-ach* suffix.

GALACHPLOCKACH – mumps. Also G-PLOCK, and carrying a meaning identical with BOONYACH – 'Don't gie me yer g———.' The primary sense is not now generally recognised. MacI, 11, renders this 'galarplocach', which is uncorrupted Gael. Piglets were sometimes known as 'galachplockachs', which can scarcely be explained other than as a curious reference to their chubby-jowled appearance. *Galar* (disease) and *plocach* (having large or swollen cheeks), 473, 727.

GLESHAN – a saithe which exceeds about 5 ins., and before entering its third stage, PEUCHTY. *Glasan.*

GLIBE – a glutton, as in 'A proper g———; he wid eat nappit stones'. (C. Stewart, 9/1/78) This deviates from MacI's definition (p. 11), 'a sickly or spawned cod'. He postulates a derivation from *clibein* – any flabby thing, etc., 209 – which must be considered doubtful.

GREEACH – brazier, as carried at sea in the open fishing boats of the nineteenth century, by which tradition the word was well known among the generation of fishermen which died out in the 1970s. *Grìosach:* burning embers, etc., 527.

HECH-HOW – water hemlock (*Oenantha crocata*), MacI, 8. Still occasionally heard. From CC (1/5/1920), reporting the death by poisoning of one Dugald Robertson: 'It appears that he ate a quantity of the roots of a poisonous plant known as hemlock, or, more familiar locally, as "hech how".' *Iteodha*, the corruption of which was persuasively analysed in CC (23/8/1919) by Angus Campbell, who remarked: 'As a dialectic curio hech-how would be hard to beat.' Campbell, a son of Angus C in Glenadale, Southend, died in Glasgow in 1927. (Ib., 14/5/27)

KANEJACH – All comprehension of this word has fragmented and there is no common agreement on meaning. As an example of a particular term which has been irreversibly corrupted, these diverse interpretations are worth ennumerating – 1) a fairy; 2) a ghost; 3) a lover of the fireside; 4) a gigantic sea-dwelling spectre which haunted Davaar Island. The original sense – of wailing, or of a wailer (p. 55) – was, however, perpetuated in parental intimidation of children with warnings of the immediacy of the k——— – in reality cats' yowlings. (D. MacLean, 21/2/78) *Caointeach.*

KYAWED – drunk, which MacI, 11, renders clumsily as 'keeawed' and defines euphemistically as 'gone in liquor'. Now invariably compounded with 'half-', as in 'They wir aa' half-kyawed comin doon', (J. Campbell, 9/11/80) which may or may not indicate an increasing tendency to moderation in local drinking habits! Probably from *ceò*, 'mist', as in Tarbert, 'He's in the kyaw yet', of some one the morning after. (GCH) Cf. the Tarbert 'smocked' and 'half-smocked' (smoked), having an identical meaning.

LOOGIE – having a maimed limb or some such deformity. Current, if but seldom heard. Probably from *liùgach*, 593.

MAYRACH/MERRACH – shellfish in general, which agrees with the standard meaning. For some fishermen, however, the word described cooked shellfish, and in particular winkles. (H. Martin, G. Newlands, 21/2/78) *Maorach*, 630. MAYRACH★ was also used for meal and water mixed as a refreshing drink aboard the skiffs. Refer to TRNF, 105-6. Derivation doubtful.

MOOGER – to go about in a secretive or brooding manner. A malicious sense sometimes implicit, as in 'Goin round on the quiet, gettin aa' information aboot somebody'. (A. Martin, 22/2/78) Adjectivally, MOOGERRY – dour, distrustful. From *mùig:* gloominess, surliness, etc., 676.

MOORLACH – 1) the lesser spotted dogfish (*Scyliorhinus canicula*). Still current among fishermen. 2) A fly, furtive person, as in 'He's a proper m——— that yin'. The latter meaning is problematic. *Mùrlach:* dogfish, and other meanings unconnected with 2), 681.

NYONACH – that form, which accurately preserves the Gael. pronunciation, has increasingly yielded to 'yonach', by loss of the initial 'n'. The meaning likewise has suffered corruption, from 'backward, odd', etc. – unsurpassably expressed in the Scots *gleckit* (C. McCallum, 7/2/78) – to a connotation with 'country folk' or 'Highland folk'. In that relation the word has slipped its adjectival moorings and gone adrift as a noun, as in: 'On the feein deh, they used tae seh, "Oh, the yonachs are aa' in the deh". That wiz them waantin a fee.' (M. McAulay, 7/2/78) *Neònach:* curious, droll, eccentric, strange, etc., 694.

OWDAN – the gurnard, either grey or red (*Trigula gurnardus* and *T. cuculus*). Never a particularly common fish in Kintyre waters, the o——— was, by some fishermen, preferred to haddock. *Cnòdan, cnùdan.*

PEESHRACHS – enchantment or spells (MacI, 12). *Pisreag,* 'sorcery, superstition', with Scots plural.

PEUCHTY – a half-grown saithe. In Tarbert Gaelic *piucaigh.* (GCH) *Piocach.*

PLOOK – a pimple, in which form also common in Scots. *Pluc:* lump, knot, pimple, etc., 728.

SARACH – great trouble or tribulation. General in the fishing community. Curiously, however, though unquestionably a traditional local usage, none of the four elderly retired fishermen I visited in Campbeltown in 1978 could recognise it. It may therefore be considered – with CRECHAN – a revival word, and its restoration is no doubt in great part attributable to exposure to radio conversation between Carradale fishermen, to whom the word remains indispensable. The word was adopted by a Campbeltown-based fisherman of Yorkshire origin, whose use of it in such expressions as 'a wile s———' was ever a source of delight to me. Also current in Tarbert, in such expressions as 'Haven't I the s——— wi' ye!', i.e. 'Haven't I a trial with you'. (GCH) *Sàrach.*

SCALLACH/SCALLYACH – wild mustard, and by extension the seed of that plant. As a waste product in corn-threshing that seed was formerly used as food for caged birds. (E. Lafferty, 1/2/81) *Sgeallag,* 818.

SCROBBAN – the crop of a bird and (jocularly in the main) the human throat. The latter sense preponderates, and J. Campbell alone (19/8/80) was able to explain its primary meaning. There was a family in Campbeltown to which the nickname 'the Scrobbans' was given. *Sgròban:* crop of a bird, etc., 834.

SILE – fry, especially that of herring. *Sìol:* seed. SIL DOO – a plankton organism, the euphausiid *Meganyctiphanes Norvegica. Sìol dubh,* black seed – refer to TRNF, 170-1.

SKATTAN* – the herring (*Clupea harengus*). *Sgadan.*

SKLOORACH – a sloven (MacI, 12). That was evidently a simplification, because even in the late 1970s an additional sense prevailed – i.e. of a useless, awkward person. Hugh MacFarlane in Tarbert advanced an identical explanation: 'That wiz an expression for a fella that wiz in the rodd – "Oot the rodd, ye skloorach."' *Sgliùrach:* slut, slattern, clumsy person, young sea-gull, etc., 827.

SKROOSH* – a crowd of people or animals. John Campbell emphasised the sense of movement – 'They've got tae be in motion some wey or another . . .' (2/2/82) – but in neither Tarbert nor Carradale, in both of which communities the word is widely understood, was any such qualification advanced. It does, however, seem to be onomatopoeic – perhaps based on, or influenced by, Eng. rush. Of very limited currency – noted only from J. Campbell, above, Archie McMillan, and Chrissie McGregor, from whom: 'There was a big s——— o' them' (17/12/83). *Sgruis* (unrecorded in any dictionary).

SLEESHACH/SLEESHAG* – 1) a wood paring, used for kindling fire; 2) a spill, of wood or twisted paper (by transference), for lighting tobacco pipes from fire. The commoner form was -*ag*, but -*ach* was the habitual form with some informants. The two forms were occasionally interchangeable in individual vocabulary. *Sliseag:* spill or shaving of wood, 855.

SMOORACH – dross (MacI, 12), but now more generally applied to drizzle, which is also the case in Carradale and Tarbert. In Tarbert, however, the standard sense survives. *Smùrach:* dross, dust, etc., 861.

SOOGAN* – Has been extended, from its primary meaning, almost to obscurity. 1) a short rope (becket) used for lashing bag of ring-net to boat's side before discharging a catch; 2) . . . and for binding netting or rope in a temporary repair of a damaged net; 3) a useless net – i.e. held together by such repairs – by extension of preceding; 4) a useless person, presumably by further extension. *Sùgan:* rope of twisted straw or heath, etc., 912.

SPOOTCHER – MacI, 13, gives 'a baler', but the name also applied to a small long-handled discharging net used at ring-net fishing, and, later, by transference, to the capacious winch-hoisted brailer (TRNF, 232-3). During a fight between Revenue cuttersmen and smugglers near Skipness in 1815, one of the cuttersmen 'received a blow from Donald McMillan, fisherman and residenter in Dalintober, with a spoutcher, an instrument with a long handle, having a ladle or bucket attached to it for emptying the boat of water'. (AD14 15/95, 15) *Spùidsear,* baling-dish for a boat, 889, but also Scots, *spootcher* and *spoucher.*

STCHYALL/SKYALL* – The liquid essence of this word is but tenuously preserved in its most common application, to a mass of netted fish. Less frequently, to a drop of liquid, e.g. whisky when being dispensed – 'Have a s——— o' this.' Common also in Tarbert and Carradale, where, however, the *sk-* corruption seems not to have set in. *Steall:* gush, plash, considerable quantity of any liquid, torrent, etc., 900.

STOOIE* – end buoy on drift-nets or long-lines. *Stuthaidh,* 909.

Appendix IV

The Thatchers of Glenrea

The first time I came to the shire of Argyle
I went to Dalmore, where I wrought a good while.
My job being finished, Big Jamie did say:
'Will ye gang an theek rashes twa days tae Glenrea?'

Now when I crossed over that mountain so high,
I met an ould man with a patch on his eye,
Who took me for a stranger, sayin, 'What brought you this way?' –
'I was sent by Big Jamie to thatch at Glenrea.'

The farmer spoke shyly, sayin, 'I've little to do.'
Thinks I, 'Perhaps you'd rather have Jamie or Hugh';
And either to frighten me or scare me away –
'Can you theek wi' ould rashes?' says MacNeill o' Glenrea.

'I can theek wi' ould rashes, wi' heather or ling,
Bent, bracken, or dockens, or any wan thing.' –
'Oh, you're just the man'll get plenty tae dae,
And I'll get you a ladder,' says MacNeill o' Glenrea.

Then he brought out a ladder, 'twas like a slide car,
And an ould flail to mend it, all covered with tar.
While the ladder was mendin we went in for our tay;
Troth, it's not a bad offer for to get at Glenrea.

I waited on there till I finished my job,
Then it's oe'r yon wild mountains I had for to jog;
Should I stay in this country till my hair it turns grey,
Oh! I'll never go back for to thatch in Glenrea.

My wife's name's Ann Connell, she lives at the mill,
In a nice little cot at the foot of the hill.
Och! and she does think long when I am away,
But I'll fetch her the money I earned at Glenrea.

As for Big Hughie's wife, she's built up like a hut;
She takes a part from us both for to keep her well up.
She's as fond of the gillstoup as she's of the tay,
And she leaves us onable the rint for to pay.

So I took a notion it's home for to go;
I went to Ballycastle, the wages was low.
I went up unto Hughie, and thus I did say:
'I'll go back to Kintyre, but not to Glenrea.'

So, Hecky and Hughie and Felix and Dan,
With Ezekiel and Jamie and one other man,
All packed up our bundles and set out for the say,
And the first place of landing was Cariskey Bay.

Then down came MacMillan, he gave a loud roar:
'The big Irish thatchers have arrived on our shore.
My master he wants you without any delay
For to go an theek rashes, but not to Glenrea.'

(From the *Campbeltown Courier*, 17 Sept. 1927.)

Index

Aberdeenshire, 75
Achapharick, 34, 35
Achnamara (Arran), 112
airigh, 158
Allt Beithe, 3, 59, 112
Allt Dubh, 143
Amod (Barr Glen), 34
Amod (Glenbreackerie), 157
Anatomy Act (1832), 135
Anderson, James in Taychroman, 35
Annunciata, the fishing skiff, 96
Antrim Coast Road, 87, 107n
Antrim, County, 1, 5, 11, 12, 13, 86, 87, 93-99, 199-203, 205-7, 215
Antrim, Glens of, 12, 13, 87, 93, 94, 96, 206
Ardclinis, 12, 87, 96
Ardglass, 78-9, 99
Ardlamont (poem), 62
Ardnacross, 126
Ardtole, 79
Argyll, the steamship, 97
Argyll, Dukes of, 98, 99, 117, 131, 156, 214
Argyll Estates, 152, 156, 159
Argyllshire Herald, 18
Arinarach, 177
Ark, the (Campbeltown), 84
Ark, the (Tangy), 128
Armagh, County, 86
Armour, Gaelic speakers of the name, 34, 45n
Armour, Alexander in Bealach a' Chaochain, 34
Armour, Robert of Campbeltown, 179
Armoy, 87
Arnicle, 75
Arran, 112, 126, 209
'Art is Truth' (pseudonym), 193
Auchabriad, 136
Auchenhoan, 125, 172, 177, 186, 187
Auchenhoan Head, 177, 183, 184
Auchenlochan, 52, 65
Australia, 37, 194
Ayr, 83, 99
Ayrshire, 2, 34, 47n, 49, 75, 112, 177, 202, 211, 215

bagpipes, 3, 4, 65
Baile mhic Mharcuis, 11
Baile na Maoile, 157
Balfron, 126
balgam − see *bolgam*
Ballinatunie, 192
Ballochantee, 13, 29-30, 135, 136
Ballycastle, 12, 89, 95, 97, 99, 199
Ballygroggan, 89, 141, 144, 151, 158, 159, 164, 169, 171, 172
Ballymacvicar, 157
Ballymena, 200, 202

Ballymenach, 183
Ballywilline, 7
'Ban', Donald (strongman), 213
Bannatyne, Calum, 101, 156, 158, 213
bards, 4-8, 10-12
Barlea, 34
Barnacles, 50
Barr Glen, 75
Barr Mains, 135
Barrel Brig, the, 183
Bastards, the, 171
Bealach a' Chaochain, 7, 34, 76
beggars, 3, 77, 82, 83, 100
Beinn na Faire, 141, 144
Belfast, 15, 83, 97
Bell, Archibald of Tarbert, 37
Bell, Mary in Taychroman, 35
Bell, Sheriff Russell of Campbeltown, 193
Belloch (Balloch), 89
Bellochantuy − see Ballochantee
Bellochochuchan − see Bealach a' Chaochain
Birch Burn − see Allt Beithe
Black, Irish immigrant fishing family in Campbeltown, 199
Black, Rev. Duncan MacLean of Tarbert, 53
Black, G. F. − see *Surnames of Scotland, The*
Blackstock, Gaelic speakers of the name, 34, 45-46n
Bloody Bay, the, 178, 183, 184, 186
Blue, family name, 94, 208
Blue, Rev. Dr. A. Wylie of Campbeltown, 130
boat-dwellers, 127
Bodach nan Gabhar, 157
body-snatching − see grave-robbing
bolgam, 78
Book of the Dean of Lismore, 11, 43
Bowman, Hannah, 123
Bowmore, 30
Brady, Patrick, Irish priest, 102
Brannan, Irish immigrant fishing family in Campbeltown, 200
Brecklate, 7
Britannia, the steamship, 97
Broadley − see Brodie
Brodie, Irish immigrant fishing family in Campbeltown, 200, 209
Brodie, for O'Brollachan, etc., 42, 208-9
Brodie, Rev. Neil − see Brolachan
Brolachan, Neil or Niel of Campbeltown, 42
Brown, Duncan of Drumlemble, 161
Brown, George Douglas, 51
Brown, James of Lochend, 113
Brown, Neil of Campbeltown, 145-6
Brown, Stephen of Campbeltown, 146
Brown, Willie of Drumlemble, 145
Bruce, Gaelic speakers of the name, 34, 46n

Bruford, Alan, 77
bubonic plague, 112, 113
Bute, Island of, 30
Byset, Marjorie, 93

cailleach (harvest home), 35, 46n
'Cailleach na h-Uamh' – see MacCallum, Janet
Cairns, Elizabeth Kiargan or, Irish immigrant, 89
Campbells of Auchinbreck, 22n
Campbells of Kildalloig, 22n
Campbell, Alexander 'Rocky', 129-131
Campbell, Archibald, father of Rev. Duncan (below), 52
Campbell, Archibald, Earl of Argyll, 1
Campbell, Catherine of Tighnabruaich, 51-3, 65
Campbell, Lord Colin, M.P., 40
Campbell, Colin 'Grogport', 74
Campbell, Colin, grandfather of above, 74
Campbell, Rev. Donald of Southend, 26
Campbell, Dugal of Auchrossan, 82
Campbell, Duncan, Sheriff-substitute of Kintyre, 191
Campbell, Rev. Duncan of Tighnabruaich, 52
Campbell, Iain of Campbeltown, 147
Campbell, James of Stonefield, 51
Campbell, John, tradition-bearer, 72-80, 114, 124, 145, 146, 150-1, 212, 216-19
Campbell, John, in 1769, 156
Campbell, Rev. John of Tarbert, 52
Campbell, John Lorne, 12
Campbell, Sheriff John Macmaster of Campbeltown, 32, 36
Campbell, Marion of Kilberry, 170
Campbell, Neil, fisherman of Campbeltown, 104
Campbell, Robert 'Ruch Rob' of Grogport, 74, 75
Campbell, Robert, father of above, 74
Campbeltown, 1, 7, 8, 15-18, 20, 26, 28, 33-42, 56, 72, 75, 78, 79, 82-86, 89-92, 96, 97, 99-105, 110-120, 124-28, 130, 134-37, 139, 145, 152, 156, 175, 177-80, 185, 192, 193, 195, 199-207, 209-15, 216-20
Campbeltown Courier, 10, 17, 39, 50, 64, 65, 110, 116, 117, 118, 120, 121, 123, 125, 128, 154, 179, 180, 185, 213
Campbeltown Town Council, 28, 97-98, 100, 101, 113, 114, 116, 117, 118, 157
camping, 146-8, 164, 177, 180-1, 183, 184, 186, 188-9
'cantering', 76
caointeach – see *céinteach*
Cape 124
Cara Island, 163
caravans at Second Waters, 181-82, 186, 196n
Carmichael, Alasdair, 1, 19, 20
Carmichael, John, fisherman of Ballochantee, 136-37
Carnlough, 203
Carnmore, 7

Carradale, 13, 15, 16, 33, 56, 76, 99, 123, 124, 171, 204, 208, 210, 218, 219, 220
Carradale Point, goats of, 171
Carskey, 94, 99, 101
Catacol, 112
Catholic emancipation, 100-1, 108n
Catholicism – see Roman Catholicism
Cats' Cove, the, 179
Cattadale, 7, 157
cattle, 116, 117, 128, 158, 169
cave-dwelling, 122-27
cave-painting, Davaar – see Davaar cave-painting
Céadach, 77
Ceann Loch – see Campbeltown
céinteach, 55, 60, 218
censuses of population, 36, 86, 87, 89, 92, 122, 126, 178
censuses, Gaelic, 33-34, 39-41, 46n
Ceudach – see Céadach
'China' – see Galbraith, John
cholera, 111-14, 115, 116, 119
Church of Scotland, 26, 27
Cill Aindreis, 54
Cìrean, An, 143
Ciùran Ceòban Ceò, An (poem), 48, 59
Clachaig, 35
Clachan, 14, 29, 31, 137
Clachan Ùr, 213
Clanranald, 7
Clark, Agnes Currie or, of Campbeltown, 139
Clark, Peter of Campbeltown, 137-39
Clement, R. D., 14
Cnoc Maighe (Moy), 9, 141, 147, 162
Cnoc nan Gabhar, 157
Cnocan Leum nan Gabhar, 157
Coast, the – see coasters
coasters, 175-190, 194
Cochrane, family name representing MacEachran, 209
cochull, 5
coindeag, 56
Coleraine, 96
Colville, Gaelic speaker of the name, 34, 45n
Colville, Provost David of Campbeltown, 104
Colville, Duncan, 156, 171
Colville, John, evangelist, 10
Colville, John in Barlea, 34
Colville, John of Campbeltown, 118
Colville, Robert in Crossibeg, 11
Colville, William in Barlea, 34
Comann Gaidhealach, An, 17, 48
Còmhradh nan Rudha (poem), 59
commanach, 56
Conley, John, fisherman of Campbeltown, 112
Conley, W. M., 7, 23n
Constabulary Committee of Argyll, 100
Contributions to a comparative study of Ulster Irish and Scottish Gaelic, 15
Cook, family name, 209
Cook, Angus of Crossaig, 209

Cook, James in Corphin, 178
Corbet, Andrew, Irish pauper, 83
Corphin, 175, 177, 178, 180, 181, 191-92
Corpus Christi College, Oxford, 53, 65
Costpatrick, the emigrant ship, 215
Cove Glen, the, 164
'Covie', tramp, 127
Cowal, 52, 62
crab-fishing, 151
Craigaig, 152-53, 159, 162, 163, 164, 167, 169, 211
Craighill, Lord, 37
Craigs, 41
Creag nan Cuilean, 159
Crockett, R. S., 65
croich, 56
Crossibeg, 11
crows, hooded, 167, 190
crùisle, 56
Cuimhneachan do Ealasaid agus Anna NicMhaoilein (poem), 54
Culfeightrin, 87, 206
Culfuar, 139
Currie/Curry, as a derivative of Mac Mhuirich, 7, 23n
Curry, Archibald in Carnmore, 7
Curry, Archibald in Ballywilline, 7
Curry, Donald in Ranachan, 7
Curry, Donald in Ballywilline, 7
Curry, John in Ranachan, 7
Curry, John in Muasdale, 7
Cushendall, 96, 97, 99
Cushendun, 94, 96, 98, 99, 202, 205

Dál Riada, 1, 6
Dalaruan, 41, 116, 117, 138
Dalintober, 72, 74, 76, 85, 91, 103, 104, 115, 117, 118, 120, 136, 179, 195, 204, 215, 220
Dalsmeran, 213
Darling, Frank Fraser, 159-60
Darroch, Mary of Campbeltown, 84
Davaar Island, 8, 171, 192-95, 197n
Davaar cave-painting, 193
Davidson, Irish immigrant fishing family in Campbeltown, 200
Davidson, Martha, Irish pauper, 85
Defence of the Realm Act (1915), 125
Delargy, John Hamilton, 77
Delary, Hugh, Mary, and Nancy, Irish paupers, 83-4
Derry, County, 5, 22n, 83, 86, 201, 205, 214
destitution, 120, 122, 130
Devil's Kitchen, the, 152
Dialect of South Kintyre, 17
Dictionariolum Trilingue, 12
diet, 89, 148-51, 177, 187
Dillon, Peter, Irish pauper, 85
Dingwall, 37
diphtheria, 129
disease, epidemic, 84, 100, 110-14, 116
Docherty, Barbara, 185

Docherty, Donald, 161-62
Doirlinn, the, 193, 194
Donald, Clan, 1, 7, 93, 209
Donegal, County, 12, 85, 86, 179, 201
Donnelly, Arthur, grave-robber, 137-39
doories, 114
doorkies — see above
Down, County, 86, 207
Downie, family name, 209-10
Downpatrick Recorder, 78
drooglan, 78
drùdhag — see above
Drumlemble, 9, 10, 30, 103, 129, 141, 145, 152, 161, 169
Drumnamucklach, 89
Dublin, 12
Duke of Lancaster, the steamship, 139
Dukes of Argyll — see Argyll, Dukes of
Dummy's (Port), the, 178, 186
Dùn Ach' na h-Àtha, 76
Dùn Bhàn (Ballyggrogan), 151, 152
Dunaverty, siege of, 94
Duncan, family name, 210
Duncan, Irish immigrant family in Campbeltown, 210
Duncanson, family name, 210
dung-heaps, 114, 117
Dunglas, 178
Dunian, Rose, Irish pauper, 83
Dunsmore, Thomas, cave-dweller, 125
Dunsmuir, Martin, 152
Dunure, 49
Durnan, Irish immigrant fishing family in Campbeltown, 200-1
Durnin — see above

Eaglesham, 126
Earadal, 149, 159, 166
Earrann Ghoineach, 55
Easton, Gaelic speakers of the name, 34
Eccles, 53
Edinburgh, 37, 53, 65, 68
Edinburgh, University of, 14
Education Corps, 68
Edward Lhuyd in the Scottish Highlands, 12-13
Eenans, the, 141-153, 159, 160, 161, 164, 166, 167, 168, 175, 187, 188
Eilean nan Gobhar — see Goat Island
Elderslie, 50, 51
Elm, the smack of Dalintober, 79
English School of Campbeltown — see Grammar School
Esplanade, the, 117
eviction of tenants, 121-122
Eyemouth disaster, 202

Falcon Cliff, the — see Dùn Bhàn
Farr, Sutherland, 11
feejag, 78
Feochaig, 89, 99, 178, 179, 182, 188
Fermanagh, County, 86, 200

ferries, Southend to Antrim, 12, 97-99
ferries, Dalintober to Campbeltown, 118, 132n
Fettes College, 53, 64, 65
Fettesian, The, 65-67
fideag – see *feejag*
Finn, Irish immigrant fishing family in
    Campbeltown, 92, 201, 205
Fion Mac Cumhaill, 76
fire, 146, 147, 163, 181, 182, 184-85
First Waters, the, 177, 178, 186
Fisherman, The (poem), 61
Fisherman Speaks, The (poem), 60
fishing and fishermen, 15, 34, 49, 55, 56, 60-63,
    78-9, 90, 91-2, 111-12, 124, 126-27, 136, 138,
    145, 178, 199-207, 216-20
fishing, illegal, 111, 204, 205, 215
fishing from rocks, 148, 151
Fleming, Gaelic speakers of the name, 34
Fleming or Fleeming, Archibald in
    Achapharick, 34
Fletcher, Jane, 52
Flory Loynachan (song) – see *Loynachan, Flory*
Flotsam and Jetsam, 17
Fort William, 126
Four Points of a Saltire, 48
Foyle, the steamship, 97-98
Franciscan order, 101-2
Free Church of Scotland, 52, 53
Fuaran Sléibh, 48

Gaelic bilingualism, 33-37, 40, 77
Gaelic censuses – see censuses, Gaelic
Gaelic, failure to transmit the language to
    children, 32, 41, 75
Gaelic-derived words in the dialect of
    Campbeltown, 216-20
Gaelic dialects of Kintyre, 13-15
Gaelic and education, 28-32, 38
Gaelic language, 1, 2, 4-6, 8, 9, 11-21, 26-44,
    48-50, 52-54, 56, 59, 64, 65, 73-78, 102, 137,
    143
Gaelic and the legal system, 36-37
Gaelic monolingualism, 27, 34-38, 40
Gaelic Folk-tales and Mediaeval Romances, 77
Gaelic, Historical Dictionary of Scottish, 15,
    25n, 216
Gaelic of Kintyre, The, 13, 14, 209
galach-plockachs, 115
Galacher, Widow Samuel, Irish pauper, 83
Galbraith, family name, 210
Galbraith, Calum of Drumlemble, 152
Galbraith, John 'China' of Campbeltown, 195
Galbraith, Lachlan of Saddell, 114
Galdrans, the, 159
gallóglaigh, 95
Galloway, 163
gallowglasses – see *gallóglaigh*
Gartgreillan, 7
Gartloskan, 7, 89
Gartvain, 7
Garvie, John, cave-dweller, 125

Giant's Causeway, 97
Gibson, J. A., 172
Gibson, Dr William of Campbeltown, 118-21
Gigha, 15, 22n, 36, 210
Gille Cochull nan Craiceann, 76-77
Gillespie, 49-51, 111
Girvan, 202, 204
Glas nan Cailleach, 209
Glasgow, 12, 30, 84, 97, 134, 137, 138, 139
Glasgow Evening News, 51
Glasgow, University of, 14, 42, 48, 50, 52, 64
Glasgow and Londonderry Steam Packet
    Company, 97-98
Gleann Eadar da Chnoc, 146
Glen Hoose, the, 146
Glens of Antrim – see Antrim, Glens of
Glenahanty, 146, 159, 213
Glenahervie, 99, 171, 189
Glenbarr, 41, 135, 215
Glenbreackerie, 8, 41, 96, 129, 157, 213
Glenlussa, 10, 204
Glenramskill, 128, 182-3
Glenrea, 95-6
gleshans, 148, 151
Goat Island, 171
goats, wild, 156-172; breeding, 163-66;
    characteristics, 158; culling of, 159, 172;
    desertion of kids, 167-68; diet of, 170-71;
    distribution of, 159; dogs, reaction to, 168-69;
    extermination of, 171; lairs of, 162-63;
    at Mingary, 169, 172; mortality, 160-62;
    in place-names, 157; predations on, 167;
    stocks, minor Kintyre, 171-72; uses of, 158
Graham, Irish immigrant fishing family in
    Campbeltown, 201
Graham, Colin in Campbeltown, 138
Grammar School of Campbeltown, 28
grave-robbing, 134-140
Greece, 49, 68
Greencastle, Inishowen, 201
Greenlees family in Taychroman, 36
Greenock, 83, 97, 202
Grier, William, 85
Grogport, 73, 74, 114
Gruinard, 52, 159
Gulls Den, the, 149-50

Hamilton, Ian, 152
Hamilton, Malcolm, 147, 153
Hamilton, Stewart, 147, 152
Hanley, J. E., 95
Hathway, John, 164-65
Hattan, family name, 210
hawkers, 82, 90, 123, 137
Hawthorn, family name, 210-11
Hay family in Tarbert, 49-50, 52
Hay, Gaelic speakers of the name, 34, 46n
Hay, Catherine – see Campbell, Catherine
Hay, George Campbell, 24, 48-68, 112, 216-19
Hay, George of Tarbert, grandfather of above,
    50

Hay, John MacDougall, 49-51, 65, 111-12
Hay, Sheena, 51, 53
Hay, William of Tarbert, 49
Hegarty, Patrick, Irish priest, 102, 212
Helm, Sandy of Auchenhoan, 187
Henderson, family name, 211
Henderson, Hamish, 96
Henry, Sam of Coleraine, 96
Highland or Gaelic church in Campbeltown,
   26, 37, 38
Highland Society of Scotland, 8
Hill, Gaelic speakers of the name, 34
History of Kintyre, 2
Holly, Irish immigrant fishing family in
   Campbeltown, 201
Holmer, Nils M., 13-14, 15, 34, 209
Holy Island (Arran), 171
Homer (poem), 66-67
Horseshoe Bay, 144, 165
hospitality, 2-3
House with the Green Shutters, The, 51
housing, 89, 110, 118-22, 128-29
Houston, Gaelic speaker of the name, 33, 45n
Houston, Esther, 122-23, 179
Hughes, William of Campbeltown, 177
Hunter, James of Campbeltown, 177
Hunter, Peter of Campbeltown, inspector of
   poor, 37-39
huts, 148, 152-53, 195

Inishowen, 201
innean, 141
Innean Beag, 141
Innean Gaothach, 157
Innean Mór, 141
Inveraray, 50, 139
Inverness-shire, 13, 32
Ireland, 1, 2, 5, 6, 11-13, 17, 78, 83-87, 93-95,
   97-103, 130 (see also under specific counties)
Irish, deportations of, 83-85
Irish, employment of, 89-92, 95
Irish famines, 82, 95
Irish immigrant fishing families in
   Campbeltown, 199-207
Irish Folklore Commission, 77
Irish Franciscan mission to Kintyre, 101-2
Irish kinship contacts, 96-97
Irish in Kintyre, 82-105, 122, 123, 125, 179,
   210, 211, 212
Irish language, 13-15, 40, 102
Irish, origins of in Kintyre, 86-87
Irish paupers, 82-84
Irvine, 75
Islay, 15, 30, 39, 52, 93, 141, 159
Isle of Man, 113

Jackson, Gaelic speakers of the name, 34
Jackson, Duncan, shepherd, 159, 162, 163,
   167-69
Jacob's Well, 55
James IV, King, 11
jerrag, 78

Johnson's Bay, 178, 181, 186
Johnson, Calum of Tarbert, 54-56, 61
Johnson, John of Tarbert, 55
Johnson, Malcolm of Tarbert, 55
Johnson, Ronald of Tarbert and Lochgilphead,
   55
Johnstone, Janet of Tarbert, 51
Justice Court of Argyll, 98

Keil Cave, 122
Keith, family name – see MacKeich
Kelly, family name, 211
Kelly, Rev. Daniel, 26
Kelly, John of Machrihanish, 145
Kennacraig, 51
Keprigan, 7
Kerr, Margaret, 85
Kerranmore, 10, 11
Kerry, County, 77
Kerry Shore, The (poem), 62
Kiargan and variants – see MacKerral
Kilcalmonell Parish, 34
Kilcalmonell and Kilberry Parish, 31, 32
Kilchenzie, 12
Kilchenzie Parish, 36
Kilchousland, 72
Kildalloig, 8, 22n, 124, 175
Kilfinan, 52
Kilkerran, 117, 125, 127-28, 135, 145, 189, 190
Killean and Kilchenzie Parish, 34, 40-41, 89,
   100
Killellen Quarry, 153
Killocraw, 136, 137
killogie, 130
Killough, 99
Killypole (Calliburn), 11
Killypole Loch, 153
Kilmory, 34
Kinloch Park, 116-18
Kintail, 65
Kintyre (poem), 58
Kintyre (book), 19
Kintyre Antiquarian Society, 17
Kintyre, Mull of, 12, 41, 100, 101, 156, 158,
   159, 167, 172
Kintyre in the Seventeenth Century, 2, 111, 208
'Kipples', 104
Knapdale, 6, 52, 125
Knockhanty, 153

Lafferty, Irish immigrant fishing family in
   Campbeltown, 201
Lafferty, Bella of Campbeltown, 189-90
Lafferty, Edward 'Teddy', 146-48, 150-1, 160,
   175, 179, 180-190, 194-95
Lagan Ròaig, 59, 67
Laggan (Glenlussa), 10, 11
Laggan (Machrihanish), 141
Laggan (Tarbert) – see Lagan Ròaig
Lailt, 7
Lake, the – see Leac Bhuidhe
Lamb family in Campbeltown, 134

Lamlash, 126
Lamont, Archibald, ferryman in Southend, 98
Lang, family name, 211
Largie, 31, 137, 214
Largieside, 4, 8, 13, 14, 33, 34, 36, 40-1
Largybaan, 24n, 153-54, 159-63, 168
Largybaan Caves, 154, 163
Larne, 94, 99, 201, 202
Lavery, Irish immigrant family in Campbeltown, 202
Law, Gaelic speakers of the name, 34, 46n
Law, James and Catherine of Tarbert, 41
Layd, 87
Leac Bhuidhe, 151-52
Learside, 124, 184, 194, 211
Leitch, Dougie of Tarbert, 55-56
Leitrim, County, 202
Lephenstrath, 7
Leth-pheighinn Gabhar, 157
Lewis, 1, 50
Lhuyd, Edward, 12-13, 97
Liberator, the skiff of Tarbert, 56
lichen, in diet of goats, 171
Linguistic Atlas and Survey of Irish Dialects, 14-15
Linguistic Survey of Scotland, 14, 15
Lionel (Lewis), 50
Lismore, Dean of, 43
Little Flower, the skiff of Campbeltown, 97
Littleson, family name, 211
Lizzie, the smack of Carradale, 81n
Loaden, the, 183
lobster-fishing, 151
Local Government (Scotland) Act, 1894, 82
Loch Fyne Fisherman, To a (poem), 61
Lochaber, 1, 11, 64
Lochend, 113, 118, 121, 139
Lochend Burn, 117
Lochgelly, 17
Lochgilphead, 55, 123, 125, 130
Lochhead − see Campbeltown
Lochranza, 112
Londonderry, 85, 97, 137
Londonderry, the steamship, 97-98
Loup, 94
Louth, County, 86, 201
Love, family name, 211, 213
Love, A. K. − see MacKinven, Angus Keith
Lowland Church of Campbeltown, 26, 27
Lowland plantations of Kintyre, 1, 2, 26, 82
Lowlanders, Gaelicising of, 33-34
Lowlanders in Kintyre, 26-27, 33-34, 41, 42-43, 45-47n, 50-1, 82, 86, 210
Loynachan, family name − see Lang
Loynachan, Catherine in Ballinatunie, 192
Loynachan, Flory (song), 9, 42
Loynachan, Isabella of Campbeltown, 80
Loynachan, Lachlan in Ballinatunie, 197
Luing, 39
Luinneag (poem), 57, 58-59
lythe, 148, 151

MacAllister, family name, 94
McAllister, Charles, ferryman of Cushendun, 99
McArthur, Archibald of Campbeltown, 177
MacArthur, Colin of Campbeltown, 179
McArthur, James of Campbeltown, 175
MacArthur, Rev. John, 32
McArthur, Willie, 148-50
Mac Bhigein − see Littleson
Mac a Bhreatnaich − see Galbraith
McBride family in Carradale, 75, 80n
McBride, Margaret, 75
MacCaffer, Donald of Campbeltown, 103-4
MacCaig, Archibald of Tarbert, 56
MacCaig, Margaret of Campbeltown, 40
MacCaig, Mary of Campbeltown, 40
MacCaig, Robert in Kildalloig, 175-77
MacCallum, Agnes 'Nanny' − see MacKeich, Agnes
MacCallum, Alexander, tinker, 122
MacCallum, Edward of Campbeltown, 75
MacCallum, Gilbert of Tayinloan, 14
MacCallum, Janet of Sunadale, cave-dweller, 122-24
MacCallum, John of Campbeltown, baker, 79
MacCallum, Malcolm, cave-dweller, 124
MacCambridge, family name, 93-94
MacCamrois, Flora, 93
MacCann, Edmund, Irish priest, 102
McCawish, Lachlan, 102
McCaye (for McKay), 'ffennell' in Ballytearim, 94
MacConachy, Archibald in Achapharick, 35
MacConachy, Duncan in Achapharick, 35
MacConachy, Hugh of Campbeltown, 113
MacConnochie, family name, 210
MacCorkindale, Donald of Campbeltown, 185, 188, 194
McCosenach, Gallicallum in Lephenstrath and Lailt, 7
MacCuaig, Robert of Clachan, 14
McCualsky, Barbara of Southend, 130
Mac Cuilcein − see Wilkie, Wilkinson/Wilkison
MacDonald − see Donald, Clan
MacDonalds of Largie, 6, 8
MacDonald, Angus of Campbeltown, 120-1
MacDonald, Archibald of Macharioch, 94
MacDonald, Donald of Gigha, 78
MacDonald, Donald of Tayinloan, 35
MacDonald, Donald of Campbeltown, policeman, 104
MacDonald, Eoin Mor of Dunnyveg, 93
MacDonald, James in Taychroman, 35
MacDonald, J. R. Mereton of Largie, 31
MacDonald, John, policeman in Machrihanish, 145
MacDonald, John, author's companion, 162, 164-65, 168
MacDonald, William of Ballyshear, 100-1
MacDougall, Alexander of Tarbert, 50
MacDougall, Charles in Auchabraid, 136

MacDougall, Duncan of Southend, 109n
MacDougall, Mary of Tarbert, 50
MacDougall, Neil of Carradale, 15
MacDougall, Peter of Campbeltown, 145
Mac Eacharna – see MacEachran
MacEachen, Alexander, 136
MacEachran, family name, 209
McEachran, Archibald in Kilblaan, 96
McEachran, Archibald of Campbeltown, 177
MacEachran, Colin in Glenahervie, 99
MacEachran, Neil in Glenahervie, 99
Mac Eanruig – see Henderson
Mac Eirc, Fergus Mór, 1
MacFadyen, Agnes Keith of Campbeltown, 74
MacFadyen, Alexander of Campbeltown, 78-79
McFadyen, John of Campbeltown, 168
MacFadyen, Margaret of Campbeltown, 79
MacFarlane, sorcerer of Tarbert, 3
MacFarlane, Hugh of Tarbert, 15, 55, 219
MacFarlane, Margaret of Tarbert, 49
MacFee, John, tinker, 122
Mac Fhionghuin – see MacKinnon
Mac Figeinn – see Littleson
MacGill or MacMillan, Jean in Taychroman, 35
Mac Gille Chatain – see Hattan
Mac Gille Ghuirm – see Blue
Mac Gille mo-luaig – see Milloy
MacGowan, Nancy, 104
McGown, Peter of Dalaruan, 116
McGuire, Bernard, 137
McIlfatrick, Hector of Ballycastle, 95
McIlgorm – see Blue
McIlreavi, John, ferryman in Southend, 98
MacInnes, Duncan, father of below, 17
MacInnes, Latimer, 15-21, 33, 216-20
McIntosh, Catherine of Tarbert, 51
MacIntosh, Peter, 2-6, 8, 29, 112
Macintyre, Dugald, 163
MacIntyre, Duncan of Campbeltown, 194
McIntyre, John of Campbeltown, 177
Mac Ionmhuinn – see MacKinven
MacIsaac family of Corphin, 178
MacIsaac, Donald 'the Dummy', 178, 191
MacIsaac, John in Corphin, 191-92
McKail, Hugh, 52
MacKay, family name, 94
McKay, Irish immigrant fishing families in
    Campbeltown, 92, 96, 202, 205
McKay, Denis, Campbeltown fisherman, 92,
    96, 202
McKay, John, Campbeltown fisherman, 92, 97,
    202
McKay, John, Campbeltown fisherman,
    drowned in 1868, 79-80
MacKay, Margaret in Taychroman, 35
MacKeich, family name, 75
MacKeich, Agnes, 75
MacKeich, Archibald in Arnicle, 75
MacKeith, family name – see MacKeich
MacKeith, Duncan of Saddell, 14
MacKeith, John of Campbeltown, 177

MacKendrick, family name – see Henderson
MacKendrick, George, 146
Mackenzie, David, 163
MacKerral, family name, 212
McKerral, Andrew, 2, 7, 111, 208, 210, 212
MacKiargan and variants – see MacKerral
MacKinlay, Mary of Tarbert, 50
MacKinnon, family name, 212-13
MacKinnon, Archibald, artist, 193
MacKinnon, James of Muasdale, 14
MacKinnon, Maggie of Muasdale, 14
Mackintosh, Donald, 8
MacKinven, family name, 211, 212-13
MacKinven of Strath, 5-6
MacKinven, Angus Keith, 212
MacKinven, Donald, 212
MacKinven, Margaret of Grogport, 74
McKinven, Mary McMillan or, Campbeltown,
    115
MacLachlan, Bob of Campbeltown, 179, 185, 187
MacLachlan, Duncan of Campbeltown, 145,
    151, 179, 187, 188
MacLarty, Catherine, 74
Maclean, Calum Iain, 77
McLean, Donald of Machrihanish, 161
MacLean, Rev. George of Campbeltown, 37-39
McLean, Hector in Taychroman, 35
MacLean, Hugh of Kilchenzie, 12, 13
MacLean, John, grave-robber, 137-40
MacLean, John, cholera victim, 112
MacLean, Ruari of Campbeltown, 161, 166, 168
Maclean, Sorley, 54
MacLellan, Archibald, Dalintober ferryman, 132
MacLellan, Farquhar of Dalaruan, 138
MacLellan, Neil of Campbeltown, 138
McLeod, A., 116
Macleod, Rev. Norman of Campbeltown, 191
MacLysaght, Edward – see *Surnames of
    Ireland, The*
McMarcus/McMarkische, in Kerranmore and
    Laggan, 11
McMarcus, John in Laggan, 11
McMarke, Jo in Tickmacrevan, 12
McMarkee, Don in Ardclinis, 12
McMarkisch, John in Kerranmore and Laggan,
    10
McMarqueis, Neil in Killypole, 11
McMarques, Jon, translator, 11
MacMath(a) – see Mathieson
MacMaths in Machrihanish, 6
McMath, John in Gartavaigh, 102
McMenemy, John, Irish immigrant, 104
Mac Mhaol Domhnaich – see Downie
Mac Mharcuis bardic family, 10-12
MacMharcuis, Ainnrias (Henry) in County
    Antrim, 11
MacMharcuis, Domhnall, 11
MacMharcuis, Giolla na Naemh, 11
MacMhuirich bardic family, 6-8
Mac Mhurchada – see Murphy
Mac Mhurchaidh – see MacMurchy

MacMillan, Irish immigrant fishing family in Campbeltown, 203
McMillan, Andy in Kilkerran, 190
MacMillan, Angus of Tarbert, 51
MacMillan, Anne of Tarbert, 53-54, 112
MacMillan, Archibald in Taychroman, 35
McMillan, Charlie of Campbeltown, 181
MacMillan, Donald in Taychroman, 35
MacMillan, Duncan in Clachaig, 35
McMillan, Duncan in Culinlongart, 109n
MacMillan, Elizabeth of Tarbert, 53-54, 112
MacMillan, Hugh of Tarbert, 51
MacMillan, Jessie of Tarbert, 51, 52
MacMillan, John in Clachaig, 35
McMillan, John in Mingary, 169
MacMullan, variant of MacMillan, 203
MacMurachy, Archibald in Rhunahaorine, 7
MacMurachy, John in Bealach a' Chaochain, 7
MacMurachy, Nicol in Gartgreillan, 7
MacMurchy, family name, 7-8, 10, 213
McMurchy or McMurchie, Donaldus in Kildalloig, 8
MacMurchy, Donald in Ban, 8
MacMurchy, James, Paisley manufacturer, 8
McMurchy, James, poet, 9-10, 213
McMurchy, John, father of above, 10
MacMurchy, William, poet, 4, 8-9, 12
MacMurchy, William in Mey (Moy), 7
McMuirich, Johannes, 7
MacMurphy, family name – see MacMurchy
McMurrich, Gillecallum in Lephenstrath and Lailt, 7
McMurthe or McMurchie, Johannes in Kildallog, 8
McNaghtan, Dugall of Campbeltown, 113
MacNeals of Tirfergus, 5
MacNeill, family name, 94
MacNeills of Antrim, 5
McNeill, Rev. H., 126
MacNeill, Hector of Campbeltown, policeman, 35
MacNeill, Hector of Carskey, 102
MacNeill, James of Southend, 123
MacNeill, Neil 'Buidhe', 5
MacNeill, Torquil, schoolmaster, 6
MacPhail, Sarah in Acha'n Bhealaidh, 29
MacQuilkan – see Wilkinson/Wilkison
McQuorkadell, Lachlan of Campbeltown, 113
MacRae, Christopher of Kintail, 65
MacRae, Rev. John of Southend, 17
MacShannons, 7
McShannon, Donnie of Drumlemble, 152
McShenog, John, ferryman in Southend, 98
Mac an Sporan – see below
MacSporran, family name, 214
McSporran, Samuel, 214
Mac an Stocair – see Stalker
Mactaggart, Col. Charles, 115, 134-35, 210
MacTaggart, Charlie of Campbeltown, 184
MacTaggart, Dan of Campbeltown, 184, 189
MacTaggart, Margaret in Killocraw, 135

MacTaggart, William in Killocraw, 136
Mac an Tàilleir – see Taylor
MacTavish – see Thomson
MacTavish, Hugh in Stewartfield, 82
Mac Thamhais – see Thomson
Mac Thòmais – see Thomson
McVarchis, Donald in Kerranmore, 11
MacVey, Irish immigrant fishing family in Campbeltown, 203
MacVicar, Rev. A. J., 212, 214, 215
MacVoorich's/Voorie's Rock, 8
Macharioch, 94, 123, 179
Machrihanish, 3, 5, 6, 10, 13, 16, 89, 99, 101, 129, 135, 139, 141, 145, 146, 149, 152, 153, 156, 161, 167, 211
Machrimore, 89, 98-99
Mackmarkie, Donald in Laggan, 11
Maidens Planting, 125
Margmonagach, 135, 136, 137
Marquis and variants, family names, 12
Marquis fishing family of Tarbert, 12, 24n
Marseilles, 113
Martin, Irish immigrant fishing family in Campbeltown, 203
Martin, John of Dalintober, 78-79
Mathieson, family name, 213
Mathieson, Archibald in Glenahanty, 213
Mathieson, Donald, Glenbreackerie strongman, 213
Matheson, Rev. William, 208-10, 212-14
Mauchline, Bobby in Mingary, 169
Maxwell, J. Harrison, 122
Maxwell, James, chamberlain of Mull, 191
measles, 111
Mecky's (Cove), 124
medicine, traditional, 124
Meenan, Irish immigrant fishing family in Campbeltown, 92, 204
Memories of Kintyre, 10
mercenaries, 6, 93
mermaid of Corphin, 191-92
Mid-Argyll, 13, 15
Milloy, family name, 214
Minard, 62
Mingary, 169, 172
Mitchell, Gaelic speakers of the name, 33-34, 45-46n
Mitchell, Willie, folk singer, 15
Mitchell, Willie of Campbeltown, 145
Mitchison, Naomi, 171
Mochtàr is Dùghall, 48-49
Muneroy, 98-99
Moorhead, Willie, 195
Morran, James 'Loafs' of Campbeltown, 180, 181, 186
Morrans/Morans, Irish immigrant fishing family in Campbeltown, 92, 204-5
Morrans, Sandy of Campbeltown, 179
Morrison, Kenneth, ferryman in Southend, 99
Moy, foundering of the schooner, 206
Muasdale, 7, 14, 15, 33, 41, 76

Muir, Gaelic speaker of the name, 34, 46n
Muir, Captain Samuel of Dalintober, 132n
Muireadhach Albanach, 6
Mull of Kintyre – see Kintyre, Mull of
Munro, Donald in Margmonagach, 136
Munro, Ian of Drumlemble, 152
Munro, Mary MacKinven or, 135, 136, 138, 139
Munro, Neil, 50
Munro, Robert of Machrihanish, 135
Murphy – see MacMurchy
Mussell Ebb, 115; reclamation of, 116-18

Narachan, 114
National Library of Scotland, 8, 12
Needle Rock, 144
Neilston, 209
New Orleans, 124, 125, 175, 178, 188, 211
New Year's Day, Old, 104, 209
Newland, Archibald, James, Maria Grier, and Maria, paupers, 83-85
Newlands and variants, Irish fishing families of the name, 205
Newton, Norman, 143, 146
NcDonald, Anna, 'papist', 103
NcNeill, More, 102
Norwegian Linguistic Survey, 13
Nua-Bhàrdachd Ghaidhlig, 48

Ó Baoill (O'Boyle), Colm, 11, 15, 210
Ó Brolcháin, Ó Brolchán, 208
O'Brollachan and variants – see Brodie
Ó Ceallaigh – see Kelly
Ó Dalaigh bardic family, 6
Ó Dreáin – see Hawthorn
O'Hampsey or Hempson, Denis, Irish harper, 22n
O'Hara, Irish immigrant fishing family in Campbeltown, 92, 205
O'Hara, Margaret Haggerty or, 90
O'Kelly – see Kelly
O'Loynachan and variants – see Lang
O na Ceithir Àirdean, 48, 54, 64
Oban Times, 39
Old Fisherman, The (poem), 61
Old New Year's Day – see New Year's Day, Old
Ould Rodd, the – 182-83
Oxford Book of Scottish Verse, The, 49
Oxford, University of, 31, 53, 65
oyster-catchers and their eggs as food – 187-88

Paiste Beag, Am, 59
Paitean (Cladh nam), 135, 136, 138, 139
Parochial Board of Campbeltown, 37-38, 79, 83-85, 113-114, 200, 204
Pass-by, the lugger of Campbeltown, 81n, 210
paupers, Irish – see Irish paupers
Peninver, 38, 195
Pennant, Thomas, 125
pigs and pig-keeping, 100, 114-16, 128

Pioneer, the smack of Campbeltown, 104
Pirnmill, 209
place-names, 16, 143-44; in poetry of George Campbell Hay, 57-60
plague, 111-14, 116
poems, 4-6, 9-10, 54, 58-63, 66-67, 131
Pollywilline, 123, 179
Poor Law Amendment Act (1845), 82-84
poor rolls – see registers of poor
Porcupine, HMS, 215
Portavadie, 65
Port na Cuthaig, 114, 210
Port Glasgow, 97
pot-ale, 115
'pottle' – see above
Price, Thomas, tramp, 125
priests, Irish, 101-2
Protection of Birds Act (1954), 188
Protestantism, 21, 101, 103
'Proteus' (pseudonym), 193
Public Health (Scotland) Act (1867), 129
Pursell, family name, 214

Quay Head Tryst, The, 130
'Quebec' (nick-name), 111
'Queen Esther' – see Houston, Esther
Queen Eester's Bey, 178, 183, 185

rabbits, 143, 167, 172; as food, 149, 187
Rae, Nellie of Machrihanish, 145
Rae, Robert of Machrihanish, 145
Ramalina siliquosa, 171
Ramble Through the Old Kilkerran Graveyard, A, 134
Ramoan, 87
Ramsay, Gilbert in Tornalein, 34
Ramsay, Professor William, 42
Ramsey, Ted, 134
Ranachan, 7
Rankin, Professor Robert A., 64-66
Rathlin Island, 13, 40, 87, 141, 199, 200, 206
Rattlesnake, the ferry-boat of Cushendun, 99
Ray, John, 12-13
Red Bay, 94
Red Ribbon, the skiff of Campbeltown, 127
Reformation, the, 21, 102
registers of poor, 86, 90, 124, 211
Reid, Charles, parish priest in Campbeltown, 103
religion, 26-27, 52, 85, 100-105, 126
religious riot in Campbeltown, 103-4
Renfrewshire, 2, 50, 126, 209
Rescue, the skiff of Smerby, 127
resurrectionists – see grave-robbing
Rhum, Island of, 170
Rhunahaorine, 7, 13, 30, 41
ring-net fishing, 56, 59, 63, 91, 206
Rob Roy, the steamship, 97
Robertson, Irish immigrant fishing family in Campbeltown, 206
Robertson, Rev. Dr. George of Campbeltown, 191

Robertson, James, ferryman in Dalintober, 132n, 206
Robison (Robertson), James of Campbeltown, 113
'Rocky' – see Campbell, Alexander
Rocky Burn, the, 190
Roman Catholicism, 85, 89, 97, 101-5
Ross, Roderick Mackenzie, 181
Rothesay, 97, 200
Rover, the steamship, 98
Rowan, Neil of Tayinloan, 14
Ru Stafnish, 181
Rudha Dùin Bhàin
Russell, Billy of Campbeltown, 181

St Ciaran, 125
St Ciaran's Cave, 125
St Columb, the steamship, 98
St Kieran's Church, 105
Saddell, 14, 114, 126, 210
Saddell Parish, 34
Sailor's Grave, the (Arran), 112
Sailor's Grave, the (Kintyre), 144-46
Salonika, 68
Saltcoats, the brigantine, 211
Sanda Island, 102, 113, 203
sanitation, 118-20, 128-29
Scally family in Campbeltown, 206
scarlet fever, 110-11
Scarts Den, the, 149
School of Scottish Studies, 14, 96
schools, 18, 28-32, 38
Scots language, 1, 15-21, 33, 48, 77-78
Scott, Francis George, 61
Scottish Education Department, 32
Scottish Gaelic Studies, 8
Scottish National Dictionary, 17
Scottish Wildlife Trust, 171
'scran', 189-90
sea-pyets – see oyster-catchers
seagull eggs gathered as a food, 149-51
seaweed, in diet of goats, 170
Second Waters, the, 177, 178, 180-83, 185, 187, 188
Seeker, Reaper (poem), 62-63
Seònaid, the skiff of Tarbert, 56
Sgeir nan Gall, 146
sheep, 117, 156-57, 158, 159, 161, 163, 166, 167, 169, 170, 171, 189, 194
Sheep'oose, the, 194
Sheep Island, 113
sheep-stealing, 212-13
shielings, 158
shinty, 104, 109n, 209
Short, Irish immigrant fishing family in Campbeltown, 206
Sillars, Donald in Culfuar, 139
Sinclair, Annie in Ballygroggan, 145
Sinclair, Donald in Ballygroggan, 159, 160, 162-64, 167-70, 172
Sinclair, Duncan in Ballygroggan, 144-45, 159

Sinclair, Jenny in Ballygroggan, 159
Sinclair, Margaret of Tarbert, 55
Singing Rock, the, 144
Sireadh, the skiff of Minard, 62
Skipness, 3, 14, 58, 73, 210, 214, 215
Skipness Parish, 34
Skye, Isle of, 212
Smerby, 127
Smerby Cove – see Stackie Cove
Smith, Duncan of Campbeltown, 195
Smith, Iain Crichton, 48, 54
Smith, Jock of Campbeltown, 195
Smith, Rev. Dr. John, 26-27
Smith, John 'Smeesh' of Campbeltown, 180, 181, 186, 194
Smith, William, 114-15
snares, 149, 151
'snig', 151
Snobs's Well, 179, 185
sorcery, 3
Southend, 3, 7, 12, 13, 17, 26, 34, 41, 89, 93, 95-104, 122, 123, 130, 178, 182, 210, 213
Southed, Relief Church of, 17, 26
Speirs, Hugh of Campbeltown, 115
Sròn Gharbh, 152
Stackie, the, 195
Stackie Cove, 125-27, 195
Stacks, the, 149
Stalker, family name, 214
Stalker, Archibald, writer, 214
Stewart, Andrew in Calliburn, 82
Stewart, Caroline of Southend, 96
Stewart, Charles, 31
Stewart, George of Campbeltown, 194-95
Stewart, John of Campbeltown, 82
Stiallaig, 52
Stirlingshire, 120
Strath, 5-6
Strath Mor, 104
Strone, 13
Summerhill, 169
Sunadale, 123-24
superstition, 55, 89
surnames, transformation of, 41-44, 208-15
Surnames of Ireland, The, 209, 210, 214
Surnames of Scotland, The, 208-15
Synod of Argyll, 11, 101-3

tait, 78
tales, traditional, 2, 4-6, 72-74, 76-78, 80, 101, 112, 124
Tarbert, 3, 12, 14-16, 33, 34, 36, 41, 49-53, 55-58, 62, 67, 68, 91, 111-13, 128, 210, 216, 217, 219, 220
Taychroman, 35-36
Tayinloan, 14, 35
Taylor, family name, 214-15
Taylor, John, ferryman in Dalintober, 132n
Taynamaol, 137, 139
tea, 184, 186-87
thatched houses, 75, 89, 95, 110, 128

Thatchers of Glenrea, The (song), 95-96, 221
Thomond, 12
Thomson, family name, 215
Thomson, Professor Derick S., 11, 14, 63
Thomson, Dugald, schoolmaster in
  Ballochantee, 30
Thomson, George of Muasdale, 14
Thomson, James of Drumlemble, 152-53
Thomson, Neil 'P.O.' of Muasdale, 14, 15, 33
Three Brothers, The (poem), 60
Tickmacrevan, 12, 87, 203
Tighnabruaich, 52
Times, The, 31
tinkers, 122, 126
Tirfergus (Glen), 5, 6, 153
Tirfergus, weaver of, 5-6
Tobar an Tighearna, 55
Todd, George, Jessie, and Katie, 13, 24n
Torchoillean, 129
Tornalein, 34
Town Council of Campbeltown –
  see Campbeltown Town Council
Tunisia, 49
Two Brothers, The (poem), 49
Tyrone, County, 86, 200, 203
typhus fever, 100, 111

Uamh Ròpa – see Scarts Den, the
Uist, 7, 39
Ulster, 1, 87, 102, 209, 210, 214

vagrancy – see beggars

Wagner, Professor Heinrich, 15
Wallace, Gaelic speakers of the name, 34,
  45-46n
Wallace, Rob in Kilmory, 34
Ward, Cornelius, Irish priest, 101-2
water, 125, 129, 152, 179, 185-86, 194
Watson, Gaelic speakers of the name, 33,
  45n
Watson, Archibald of Campbeltown, 33
Watson, Jean, 10
Watson, John in Amod (Barr Glen), 34
Watson, John in Bealach a' Chaochain, 34
Wee Man's (Cove), the, 124
whisky, illicit, 73, 139, 214
Whiteford, Irish immigrant fishing families in
  Campbeltown, 206-7
Whitehouse, 31
whooping cough, 111
'wilk brae', 187
Wilkie, family name, 215
Wilkinson/Wilkison, family names, 207,
  215
Wind on Loch Fyne, 48, 60, 66
winkle-picking, 80, 123, 126, 131, 190,
  195
Witch's Cove, the, 123

yachting, 96